PRINCIPLES OF BIOMETRY

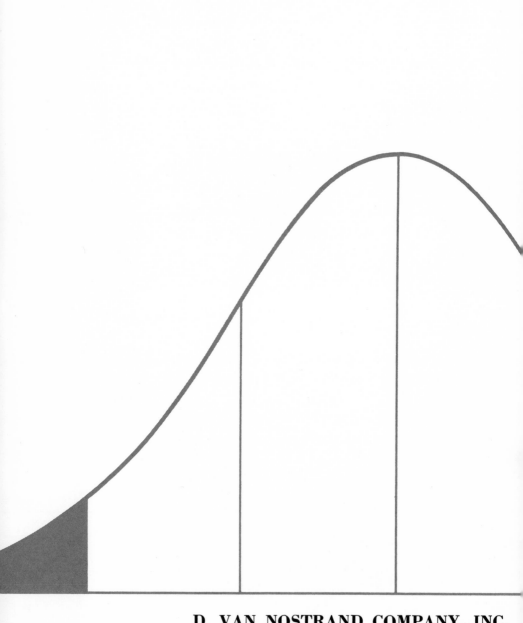

D. VAN NOSTRAND COMPANY, INC.

STATISTICS FOR BIOLOGISTS

PRINCIPLES OF
BIOMETRY

CHARLES M. WOOLF

Professor of Zoology, Arizona State University

Princeton, New Jersey   Toronto   London   Melbourne

Van Nostrand Regional Offices: *New York, Chicago, San Francisco*

D. Van Nostrand Company, Ltd., *London*

D. Van Nostrand Company (Canada), Ltd., *Toronto*

D. Van Nostrand Australia Pty. Ltd., *Melbourne*

Library of Congress Catalog Card No. 68-29921

PRINTED IN THE UNITED STATES OF AMERICA

Dedicated to the memory of
Dr. James A. Jenkins (1904–1965) Professor of Genetics
at the University of California (Berkeley)
who introduced me to the principles of biometry.

Preface

This textbook evolved from a mimeographed syllabus which was used in a one-term course for seniors and graduate students in the biological sciences at Arizona State University and the University of Utah, and in a course for residents and staff of the College of Medicine at the latter institution.

A knowledge of the principles of biometry is a necessity for anyone contemplating quantitative research in the biological sciences. Yet, many students and research workers, because of other responsibilities and busy schedules, encounter difficulty in finding the necessary time to become properly schooled, since adequate training usually requires a sequence of two or three courses. A further hindrance is the fact that many biologists are limited in mathematical background; hence, they shy away, unfortunately, from courses in mathematical statistics. Consequently, in departments of biological and medical sciences, there is a need for a one-term course that surveys biometrical techniques commonly used in research, but at the same time presents as much theory as elementary algebra and logic will allow. This textbook was written for such a course. It was written for biologists by a person trained in biology.

Experience has demonstrated that the principles of biometry are not learned from listening to a series of lectures or by the intent reading of a textbook. Considerable practice is required to develop the ability to analyze data, to employ effectively the automatic calculator, and to appreciate the derivation of formulae and the meaning of statistical concepts. The problems at the end of each chapter may be used for this purpose. Additional material should be sought elsewhere. The most valuable part of a biometry course is a well-designed laboratory.

The data found in this textbook are all ficticious. However, many of the experimental situations and illustrative measurements were suggested by my colleagues and students at Arizona State University and the University of Utah, on the basis of their research, experiences, or inquiries.

I am indebted to the Literary Executor of the late Sir Ronald A. Fisher, F. R. S., Cambridge; to Dr. Frank Yates, F. R. S., Rothamsted; and to Messrs. Oliver & Boyd Ltd., Edinburgh, for permission to abridge Tables III, IV, and V from their book *Statistical Tables for Biological, Agricultural, and Medical Research.*

CHARLES M. WOOLF

Contents

H Test, 307   **20.4** Chi-Square Test for Related Samples, 311
20.5 Wilcoxon Signed Rank Test, 312   **20.6** Friedman χ_r^2 Test, 314
20.7 The Spearman Rank-Correlation Coefficient, 316   **20.8** Other
Non-Parametric Tests, 318.

CHAPTER ONE

Introduction

The word *statistics* has multiple meanings. In the common usage of the word, *statistics is synonymous with numerical facts or data*. In the statement, "I wish to obtain statistics on the number of cases of smallpox reported in the United States during the year 1966," the word statistics could be replaced by the word data, and the interpretation of the statement would remain the same. Another meaning elevates it to the status of a science. *Statistics is the science dealing with the designing of experiments leading to the collection of numerical facts and the method of analyzing, interpreting, and presenting these numerical facts.* A third meaning is as follows: *Statistics are measurements which characterize samples.* This third meaning of the word becomes clear after more insight is obtained into the science of statistics.

Biometry, or its equivalent *biostatistics,* may be defined as the application of statistics as a science to biology.

A question often raised by a novice research worker is, "Should I learn statistical methods?" What he is asking is whether or not he should learn about the science of statistics. The answer to this question is strongly in the affirmative. Even though some types of research data are best presented in simple charts or graphs or by simple statements summarizing the results, other types need detailed analysis before an objective interpretation is possible. The science of statistics has a definite place in research work. Much may be lost by ignoring its potentialities. A survey of current biological and medical literature will impress any reader with the need for research workers to become familiar with statistical methods. Letters such as P, t, and F, appear with regularity. Terms such as *mean square, regression coefficient,* and *standard error* occur usually with no explanation. Authors thus make certain assumptions about the background of today's readers and since they do so, an understanding of statistical methods is essential for a research worker: *A knowledge of statistical methods enables a research worker to make intelligent use of the current literature.* A second reason why a mastery of the fundamentals of this science is important concerns the subject of designing experiments: *A knowledge of statistical methods opens up new paths of experimental procedures.* The importance of statistical methods as a guide in planning research studies cannot be overstressed. A knowledge of the methods of designing experiments will enable a research worker to plan a study in such a way that the maximum amount of information can be obtained for a given expenditure of time, money, and effort. A third reason for acquiring statistical skills is apparent: *A knowledge of statistical methods enables a research worker to collect, analyze, and present his own data in the most meaningful and expeditious manner.* It must be emphasized, however, that the method of collecting, analyzing, or presenting data is a logical consequence of the design of the experiment. Therefore, the time to consider what techniques will be employed is before the study is begun, not after the data have been collected. A disregard of this principle can result in accumulated data that are partially or completely devoid of meaning. It is not the purpose of statistical methods to disentangle poorly collected data. A statistician is not one who salvages experiments, no matter how poorly they are designed.

Basic concepts in the science of statistics are: populations, samples, and arrays of measurements.

1.1   Populations

A taxonomist may be interested in the wing length of a given species of mosquito. A physiologist may be interested in the systolic blood pressure of children with rheumatic fever. Other investigators may be interested in heights, weights, lengths, and widths. These are examples of quantitative measurements. Each measurement may be represented by X. For example, if the height of each adult male in the city of San Francisco were determined in inches, the resultant would be an array of measurements. If the number of adult males in the city is N, the individual measurements might be $X_1 = 72.5$ inches, $X_2 = 69.1$ inches, $X_3 = 72.5$ inches, etc., up to and including $X_N = 70.6$ inches. Some of the measurements would occur more commonly than others. The ith measurement is symbolized by X_i (read X sub i) where i can be replaced by 1, 2, 3, 4, . . . or N. This array of measurements would constitute a population.

Although a population often refers to all the individuals of a particular kind living in a geographical area, in statistical methods a population can be defined as an array of measurements. A population may be finite or indefinitely large. It may actually exist or may be completely imaginary.

The height measurements from San Francisco would constitute a population that is large and finite. A physiologist may be interested in the systolic blood pressure of all rheumatic children between the ages of 10 and 16 presently living in a given geographical area. The population in this case consists of an array of systolic blood-pressure measurements, each corresponding to an individual child of the specified age group from the geographic area. The size of the geographical area, the population density, and the percentage of affected children would determine whether the population of measurements is large or small. A taxonomist interested in making a study of wing length of a given subspecies of mosquito from a given area would likely be dealing with a very large population. It would consist of all the measurements of wing length of all the mosquitoes from that area.

1.2 Samples

Even though the concept of a population is fundamental in statistical thinking, it is apparent that populations are usually impracticable or impossible to deal with due to their size and inaccessibility, or as will be demonstrated by subsequent examples, their imaginary character. Information is obtained about populations with the use of *samples*. A sample is defined as a subgroup of a population. The important type of sample, in statistics, is a *random sample*. A random sample is one taken in such a manner that each measurement in the population has an equal and independent chance of being included. In actual practice, the size of the sample will vary depending on the expense, convenience, and time involved in carrying out the sampling. The size of a sample is symbolized by n. The measurements in the sample are symbolized by X_1, X_2, X_3, etc., up to and including X_n. It is important to distinguish between N and n, where N is the population size and n is the sample size. An array of measurements may constitute a sample or a population.

Randomness is a feature that should be striven for, but whether it is actually achieved in practical work may be questionable. For the adult males in San Francisco or the rheumatic children referred to previously, a random sample of measurements might be achieved by the use of a city directory and school health records. Individuals could be selected for study by some chance method such as the use of random numbers. Such a method could not be used in the mosquito study. The investigator can only hope that whatever method he decides upon to select his mosquitoes, or whatever method he is forced to use or is convenient to use, will give an array of measurements comparable to what he might have gotten if his sampling method had been random.

A unique relationship exists in some cases between populations and samples.

In experimental work, the sampling technique employed often creates an imaginary population. Assume that 10 mice were fed an experimental diet and the increase in growth over two months was measured in grams. The population in this case is completely imaginary and consists of all growth measurements that might have occurred if an indefinitely large number of mice of similar genetic background had been treated in the same manner and raised under the same environmental conditions. The sample would consist of the 10 measurements actually obtained, and is assumed to be a random sample of the measurements that might possibly have occurred. Similarly, if a plant geneticist crossed two strains of corn and measured the height of 100 first-generation plants, the sample would consist of the 100 measurements. The population is imaginary and consists of all the height measurements that might be obtained from first-generation plants raised under similar environmental conditions.

1.3   Rules of Summation

In statistics, the Greek letter Σ is used as the symbol for summation. For example, if it is necessary to designate that all the measurements in a population are to be summed, the symbol is

$$\sum_{i=1}^{N} X_i$$

which reads, "sum of the measurements (X values) from i equals 1 up to and including i equals N." The symbol for summation is often abbreviated as $\Sigma_1^N X_i$, or simply ΣX_i. In this book the symbol $\Sigma_1^N X_i$ will be used.

RULE 1. $\displaystyle\sum_{1}^{N} X_i = X_1 + X_2 + X_3 + \cdots + X_N$

The sum of a series of measurements each multiplied by a constant is equal to the constant times the summation of the measurements.

RULE 2. $\displaystyle\sum_{1}^{N} aX_i = a \sum_{1}^{N} X_i$

This is shown as follows:

$$\sum_{1}^{N} aX_i = aX_1 + aX_2 + aX_3 + \cdots + aX_N$$
$$= a(X_1 + X_2 + X_3 + \cdots + X_N)$$
$$= a \sum_{1}^{N} X_i$$

The sum of an array of constants is equal to N times the value of the constant.

RULE 3. $\displaystyle\sum_1^N a = Na$

Other rules of summation are derived below:

RULE 4. $\displaystyle\sum_1^N aX_iY_i = aX_1Y_1 + aX_2Y_2 + aX_3Y_3 + \cdots + aX_NY_N$

$$= a(X_1Y_1 + X_2Y_2 + X_3Y_3 + \cdots + X_NY_N)$$

$$= a\sum_1^N X_iY_i$$

RULE 5. $\displaystyle\sum_1^N (X_i + Y_i) = (X_1 + Y_1) + (X_2 + Y_2) + (X_3 + Y_3)$

$$+ \cdots + (X_N + Y_N)$$

$$= (X_1 + X_2 + X_3 + \cdots + X_N)$$
$$+ (Y_1 + Y_2 + Y_3 + \cdots + Y_N)$$

$$= \sum_1^N X_i + \sum_1^N Y_i$$

RULE 6. $\displaystyle\sum_1^N (X_i + Y_i)^2 = \sum_1^N (X_i^2 + 2X_iY_i + Y_i^2)$

$$= (X_1^2 + 2X_1Y_1 + Y_1^2) + (X_2^2 + 2X_2Y_2 + Y_2^2)$$
$$+ (X_3^2 + 2X_3Y_3 + Y_3^2) + \cdots$$
$$+ (X_N^2 + 2X_NY_N + Y_N^2)$$

$$= (X_1^2 + X_2^2 + X_3^2 + \cdots + X_N^2)$$
$$+ (2X_1Y_1 + 2X_2Y_2$$
$$+ 2X_3Y_3 + \cdots + 2X_NY_N) + (Y_1^2 + Y_2^2$$
$$+ Y_3^2 + \cdots + Y_N^2)$$

$$= \sum_1^N X_i^2 + 2\sum_1^N X_iY_i + \sum_1^N Y_i^2$$

1.4 Parameters

A population consists of an array of measurements. In addition, a population may be characterized by measurements. For example, an array of measurements will have an average value known as the *mean*. The mean characterizes a population of measurements as to central tendency. An array of measurements can be characterized as to variability by a measurement known as variance, a measurement whose square root is known as standard deviation. An array of measurements can be characterized as to skewness by a measurement known as *gamma-one*, and as to kurtosis by a measurement known as *gamma-two*.

The mean, variance, gamma-one, and gamma-two are known as parameters. Parameters are defined as measurements which characterize populations.

1.5   System of Moments

The above-mentioned parameters come from the system of moments. Their origin can be illustrated by considering a lever and fulcrum (g) with forces (f_i) distributed along the lever at positions X_i.

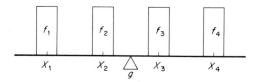

Figure 1.1 Lever and fulcrum (g) with forces (f_i) at X_i position on the lever.

A single moment is defined as *force* $\times$ *distance*, or $f_i(X_i - g)$. The total moment is the sum of the single moments. If there are forces at N positions along the lever, the total moment is expressed as:

$$\text{Total moment} = f_1(X_1 - g) + f_2(X_2 - g) + f_3(X_3 - g)$$

$$+ \cdots + f_N(X_N - g) = \sum_1^N f_i(X_i - g)$$

The system is in equilibrium if the total moment is equal to zero, or

$$\sum_1^N f_i(X_i - g) = 0$$

If each force is set equal to one unit, this expression becomes:

$$\sum_1^N 1(X_i - g) = \sum_1^N (X_i - g) = 0$$

The position of the fulcrum is of primary concern. The total moment is equal to zero when the fulcrum is placed at a position along the lever so that the summation of the $(X_i - g)$ values is equal to zero. This can be shown by the following example:

$X_1 = 30$ $X_2 = 40$ $g = 50$ $X_3 = 60$ $X_4 = 70$

The sum of the deviations is:

$$\sum_{1}^{N} (X_i - g) = (30 - 50) + (40 - 50) + (60 - 50) + (70 - 50)$$
$$= (-20) + (-10) + (+10) + (+20) = 0$$

For the given values of X, the total moment would not equal zero if the fulcrum were at any point other than 50.

1.6 The Mean as a Measure of Central Tendency

The mean of a population of measurements corresponds to the position of the fulcrum along a lever when the system is in equilibrium. Assume there is a population of N measurements. These measurements vary from a low value to a high value (i.e., they form a distribution). *The mean is formally defined as that point on the distribution where the sum of all the deviations between that point and each measurement is equal to zero.* The mean of a population is symbolized by μ. Deviations can be symbolized by $X_i - \mu$. The sum of the negative deviations equals the sum of the positive deviations.

The definition of the mean is expressed as:

$$(X_1 - \mu) + (X_2 - \mu) + (X_3 - \mu) + \cdots + (X_N - \mu) = 0$$

or $\sum_{1}^{N} (X_i - \mu) = 0$.

The mean corresponds to the position of the fulcrum. Measurements correspond to positions along the lever, and since each measurement has equal importance, $f_i = 1$.

Solving for μ gives the formula for the mean:

$$\sum_{1}^{N} (X_i - \mu) = 0$$
$$\sum_{1}^{N} X_i - N\mu = 0, \text{ therefore } \sum_{1}^{N} X_i = N\mu$$

and consequently,

$$\mu = \frac{\sum_{1}^{N} X_i}{N}$$

This formula indicates that the mean of a population is equal to the sum of all the measurements divided by the total number.

1.7   The *r*th Total Moment About the Mean

The expression for the *r*th total moment about the mean may be written:

$$\sum_{1}^{N} (X_i - \mu)^r$$

When $r = 1$, the expression is known as the first total moment about the mean. Substituting 2, 3, and 4 in place of r leads to measures of variability,

Table 1.1   The *r*th Total Moment About the Mean.

$$\sum_{1}^{N}(X_i - \mu)^r$$	*r*th total moment about the mean.
$$\sum_{1}^{N}(X_i - \mu)^1$$	First total moment about the mean. The value is zero from definition of the mean.
$$\sum_{1}^{N}(X_i - \mu)^2$$	Second total moment about the mean. The value can vary theoretically from zero to + infinity. This moment can be used as a measure of variability.
$$\sum_{1}^{N}(X_i - \mu)^3$$	Third total moment about the mean. The value can vary theoretically from zero to ± infinity. This moment is a measure of skewness.
$$\sum_{1}^{N}(X_i - \mu)^4$$	Fourth total moment about the mean. The value can vary theoretically from zero to + infinity. This moment is a measure of kurtosis.

skewness, and kurtosis, respectively. These are summarized in Table 1.1. Total moments about the mean higher than the fourth are of no interest in statistical methods.

1.8 The Variance as a Measure of Variability

Even though the sum of all the deviations about the mean is equal to zero, the *sum of the squares of the deviations* will equal zero only if all the measurements in the population have the same value as the mean. In all other cases, the sum will have a positive value other than zero. Theoretically, the term $\Sigma_1^N (X_i - \mu)^2$, known as the second total moment about the mean, can vary from zero to plus infinity. It can be used as a comparative measure of variability when the populations which are to be compared have the same number of measurements. Assume there are two populations, A and B, which have the same mean, but in population A the measurements are grouped around the mean, while in population B the measurements show more variability. If the frequency with which each measurement occurs is plotted, the population of measurements might be represented as shown in Figure 1.2. The calculation of the second total moment for each population would show clearly that population B is more variable than population A. The second total moment would be larger for population B than population A. For example, the second total moment about the mean for the measurements 48 and 52 is 8, while for the measurements 40 and 60, it is 200.

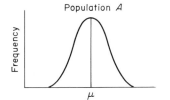
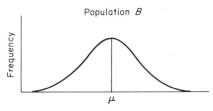

Figure 1.2 Populations with the same mean but showing different degrees of variability.

The second total moment about the mean has one serious limitation which makes it impractical to use as a comparative measure. Its value is dependent not only upon the size of the deviations, but also upon the number of deviations as well. Therefore, it can only be used as a comparative measure when divided by N. This results in a measurement that is known as the second unit moment about the mean, or briefly, the second moment about the mean. This measure of variability is commonly known as variance, and symbolized by

σ^2 or V_2. The variance of a population can be defined formally as the second moment about the mean.

$$\sigma^2 = V_2 = \frac{\sum\limits_{1}^{N} (X_i - \mu)^2}{N}$$

The square root of the variance is known as the *standard deviation*.

$$\sigma = \sqrt{\frac{\sum\limits_{1}^{N} (X_i - \mu)^2}{N}}$$

The standard deviation, in addition to being used as a measure of variation, has some special properties with reference to a normal or Gaussian population. The properties of a normal population will be presented in more detail in another section, but it will be instructive to introduce some of its characteristics here (see Figure 1.3).

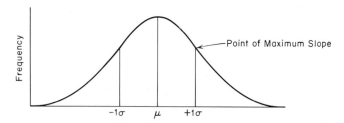

Figure 1.3 Normal distribution with mean and standard deviation.

The curve representing a normal population is symmetrical (bell-shaped) about a vertical line marking the position of the mean on the base line. The symmetry of the curve is such that equidistant on both sides of the vertical line marking off the position of the mean there is a point of maximum slope or inflection. The distance along the base line between the vertical line indicating the position of the mean and a similar line marking the point of maximum slope is equal to one standard deviation. The area under the curve included between the two vertical lines at plus and minus one standard deviation from the mean is 0.683 of the total area. This indicates that 68.3% of all the measurements in a normal population lie between plus and minus one standard deviation.

1.9   Gamma-One as a Measure of Skewness

Many populations may have similar values for the mean and the variance, yet if the distributions of measurements making up the populations were to be represented by curves, it would be observed that some are vastly different than others. Some of the curves could be non-symmetrical. When a population has a preponderance of measurements on one side of the mean, it is said to be skewed. If there are fewer measurements on the left side of the mean than on the right side, it is said to be negatively skewed. A positively skewed population is one with fewer measurements on the right side of the mean than on the left (see Figure 1.4).

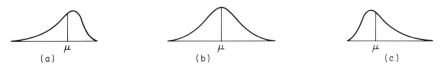

Figures 1.4 Examples of symmetrical and non-symmetrical populations. (a) Negatively skewed curve; (b) symmetrical curve; (c) positively skewed curve.

Cubing the deviations about the mean and summing, results in the third total moment about the mean, which indicates whether skewness is present, and if so, whether it is positive or negative. However, different populations can only be compared as to the degree of skewness by the third total moment about the mean when they have the same number of measurements. This is corrected by dividing by N. The resulting measurement is called the third moment about the mean, and is symbolized by V_3.

$$V_3 = \frac{\sum_{1}^{N} (X_i - \mu)^3}{N}$$

Cubing the deviations between each measurement and the mean gives increased importance to the measurements far away from the mean as compared with those close to the mean. This can be shown by a simple model. Assume that four items were selected from a population that deviate from the mean by $+2$, $+3$, $+4$, and -9 units. Cubing these deviations gives $+8$, $+27$, $+64$, and -729. Summing results in a total of -630. The negative deviation (-9), when cubed, gives a larger value than the sum of the cubes of the three numerically smaller positive deviations. Therefore, the third moment about the mean of a skewed population will take on the sign of the long tail. If the long tail is to the left of the mean, the third moment about the mean will have a negative value; if it is to the right of the mean, the third moment about the mean will have a positive value. In a symmetrical curve the third moment about the mean will be zero. The more pronounced the degree of skewness, the larger will be the value (either positive or negative) of the third moment about the mean.

The third moment about the mean is dependent upon the cube of the original units. Therefore, comparisons as to the amount of skewness present in different populations would only be legitimate if the same units were used in each case. For example, the third moment about the mean could not be used to compare the degree of skewness of a population of weights (in grams) with a population of heights (in centimeters). For this reason the third moment about the mean is not often used directly as a measure of skewness. Another measurement has been derived that is divorced from units, and is consequently more useful from a comparative standpoint. This measurement is called gamma-one, and is symbolized by g_1. It is obtained by dividing the third moment by the second moment raised to the "three-halves" power.

$$g_1 = \frac{V_3}{(V_2)^{3/2}}$$

If gamma-one is positive, the population is positively skewed; if it is negative, then negative skewness is present; and if gamma-one is equal to zero, the population is symmetrical.

1.10   Gamma-Two as a Measure of Kurtosis

A population may be symmetrical but still be different in structure from a normal population. For example, a curve drawn to represent a population may show more peakedness or less peakedness than a normal population. This is known as *kurtosis*. A peaked curve is referred to as a *leptokurtic curve*, and a flattop curve as a *platykurtic curve*. The fourth moment about the mean, using a normal population as a standard, will indicate whether kurtosis is present, and if so, will classify it as to type.

$$V_4 = \frac{\sum_1^N (X_i - \mu)^4}{N}$$

As higher moments are dealt with, the measurements in the extreme tails of a curve become increasingly important. When plus and minus deviations are raised to the fourth power, they all become positive.

The method by which the fourth moment about the mean serves as a measure of kurtosis is best understood by referring to a normal population. Suppose several measurements in the vicinity of plus and minus one standard deviation from the mean were shifted, some going away from the mean (toward the tails) and others going in the direction of the mean. A curve drawn to represent the population would be a leptokurtic curve with a peaked center and long tails. Since there are more extreme measurements in a leptokurtic population than found in a normal population, its fourth moment is larger than that for a normal population.

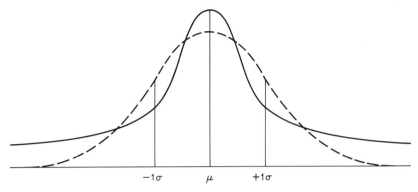

Figure 1.5 Comparison of leptokurtic (————) and normal curve (– – – – –).

Now suppose that several measurements in the vicinity of the mean and several measurements far removed from the mean (in the tails) were shifted in the direction of plus and minus one standard deviation. A curve drawn to represent this population would be platykurtic with short tails and a flat top (high shoulders). This population would have less extreme deviations than a normal population, and consequently, it would have a smaller fourth moment.

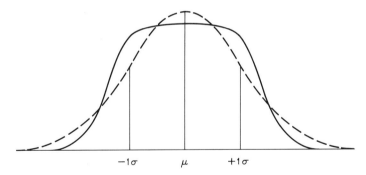

Figure 1.6 Comparison of platykurtic (————) and normal curve (– – – – –).

The fourth moment, by itself, is not a completely suitable measure of kurtosis, since it is dependent upon the fourth power of the original units. This difficulty can be removed by dividing the fourth moment by the square of the second moment. This results in a measure that is divorced from units. Its value computed for a normal distribution is equal to 3. Incorporating 3 into the formula results in a parameter that is a useful measure of kurtosis. It is called gamma-two and is symbolized by g_2.

$$g_2 = \frac{V_4}{(V_2)^2} - 3$$

For a normal population, gamma-two is equal to zero. For a leptokurtic population it will have a positive value, and for a platykurtic population it will have a negative value. The degree of kurtosis is indicated by the numerical value of this parameter.

As a summary, suppose that two populations were characterized by the parameters given in Table 1.2.

Table 1.2 Parameters of Two Theoretical Populations.

Parameter		Population 1	Population 2
Mean	(μ)	110.0	95.0
Variance	(σ^2)	39.4	144.0
Gamma-one	(g_1)	0.0	0.0
Gamma-two	(g_2)	−1.6	0.0

A comparison of the parameters shows that the mean of population 1 is larger than that of population 2 by 15 units. Population 2 is more variable than population 1. Both are symmetrical. Population 1 is platykurtic, while population 2 is normal.

1.11   Other Parameters

In addition to the parameters originating from the system of moments, other parameters can be devised which characterize populations.

The *median* of a population is defined as the middle measurement. One half the measurements are less than the value and one half are greater. The *mode* of a population is the measurement that occurs most frequently. A population may have more than one mode. The median and mode, along with the mean, are measures of central tendency. In a normal population, the mean, median, and mode are identical. In a skewed population, this is not the case.

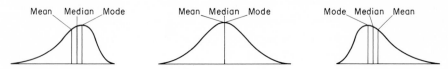

Figure 1.7 Comparison of the values of the mean, median, and mode, in normal and skewed populations.

In addition to the variance, the *range* is a parameter that aids in characterizing a population as to variability. The range is simply the difference between extreme measurements. If the measurements in a population vary from 45.2 inches to 75.9 inches, the range is $75.9 - 45.2 = 30.7$.

Other parameters may be encountered that characterize a population. However, those derived from the system of moments are the most functional.

Problems

1. Define or identify the following terms:
(a) Statistics; (b) populations; (c) random sample; (d) single moment; (e) total moment; (f) parameter; (g) first, second, third, and fourth total moments about the mean; (h) mean of a population; (i) variance of a population; (j) standard deviation of a population; (k) gamma-one; (l) gamma-two; (m) leptokurtosis; (n) platykurtosis; (o) median of population; (p) mode of a population; (q) range of a population.

2. Distinguish between a real and an imaginary population. Give examples of both types.

3. By using the rules of summation, prove the following equivalent:

$$\sum_1^N (X_i - X_j)^2 = \sum_1^N X_i^2 - 2\sum_1^N X_iX_j + \sum_1^N X_j^2$$

4. From the first total moment about the mean, derive the equation for the mean of a population.

5. Discuss why the second unit moment about the mean is a more useful measure of variability than the second total moment.

6. Discuss why gamma-one is a more useful measure of skewness than the third unit moment.

7. For a given population, $\mu = 75$, $\sigma^2 = 64$, $g_1 = 0.0$ and $g_2 = 0.0$. Give the limits that include 68.3% of the measurements in this population.

8. A cardiologist studied cholesterol levels (mg./100 ml. serum) of 200 males of age 50. Distinguish between the sample and population.

9. A mammalogist was interested in the weight of adult male wolves presently living in a given geographic area. He trapped 10 and determined the weight of each (lbs.). Distinguish between the sample and population.

10. Fifty newly weaned male mink were placed on a special diet. The increase in weight (lbs.) was determined for a 6-month period. Distinguish between the sample and population.

11. A herpetologist collected 29 frogs (*Hyla versicolor*) in a forested area. He measured the snout-vent length (mm.). Distinguish between the sample and population.

12. Distinguish between:
(a) population of measurements and population of individuals; (b) sample of measurements and sample of individuals.

CHAPTER TWO

Statistics: Estimates of Parameters

Four measurements (mean, variance, gamma-one, gamma-two) which can be used to characterize populations were discussed in the previous chapter. In biological work, these parameters are seldom known but can be estimated. Estimates of parameters are called statistics or estimators.

2.1 Rules of Expectation

Before the subject of estimation can be fully appreciated, it is necessary to consider the subject of *mathematical expectation*. Suppose that a single measurement is taken at random from a population. This measurement is a random variable and could correspond to X_1, X_2, X_3, or X_N. The question can be proposed, "What is the mean of all the values that this particular X value might have been?" This is symbolized using the letter E, and is given as $E(X_i)$. It is formally read as "the expectation of X sub i" or "the expected value of X sub i." The answer to the above question is the mean of the population from which the X value was taken.

RULE 1. $E(X_i) = \mu$

The operative interpretation of E is to sum all the possible random variables and divide by the total number. In this case the total number is N.

The expectation of a constant, by the above interpretation, must be the constant.

RULE 2. $E(a) = a$

Likewise, the expectation of all possible X values, each multiplied by a constant, is equal to the constant times the expectation of the X values.

RULE 3. $E(aX_i) = aE(X_i)$

Another rule deals with the expectation of the sum of paired measurements.

RULE 4. $E(X_i + X_j) = E(X_i) + E(X_j)$

An important rule deals with the expectation of the product of paired measurements that are independent of each other.

RULE 5. $E(X_iX_j) = E(X_i)E(X_j)$

If the measurements are not independent, Rule 5 does not hold. The measurements are independent if an X_i value is paired randomly with any X_j measurement. This would not be true if a small X_i value tended to be paired with a small X_j value, and if a large X_i value tended to be paired with a large X_j value.

Table 2.1 Demonstration of rules 4 and 5 of mathematical expectation when measurements are independent.

Column 1	Column 2	Column 3	Column 4
X_i	X_j	$X_i + X_j$	X_iX_j
2	2	4	4
2	3	5	6
2	4	6	8
3	2	5	6
3	3	6	9
3	4	7	12
4	2	6	8
4	3	7	12
4	4	8	16
$E(X_i) = 3$	$E(X_j) = 3$	$E(X_i + X_j) = 6$	$E(X_iX_j) = 9$

A demonstration of Rules 4 and 5 occurs in Table 2.1. It is assumed that populations 1 and 2 are both small and finite, each consisting of the measurements 2, 3, and 4. If an X_i measurement is picked at random from population 1 and at the same time an X_j measurement is picked at random from population 2, then a 2 could be paired with a 2, 3, or 4; a 3 with a 2, 3, or 4; and a 4 with a 2, 3, or 4. This arrangement is illustrated in columns 1 and 2 of Table 2.1. The mean of column 1 plus the mean of column 2 equals the mean of column 3 (Rule 4). The mean of column 1 times the mean of column 2 equals the mean of column 4 (Rule 5).

Table 2.2 Demonstration of mathematical expectations when the measurements are not independent.

Column 1	Column 2	Column 3	Column 4
X_i	X_j	$X_i + X_j$	$X_i X_j$
2	2	4	4
3	3	6	9
4	4	8	16
$E(X_i) = 3$	$E(X_j) = 3$	$E(X_i + X_j) = 6$	$E(X_i X_j) = 9.67$

If independence is not present, one possible arrangement is shown in Table 2.2. In this situation an X_i value is not paired randomly with an X_j value. Positive correlation is present, since a small X_i value is paired with a small value, and a large X_i value is paired with a large X_j value. In Table 2.2, the mean of column 1 plus the mean of column 2 equals the mean of column 3. This demonstrates that Rule 4 holds for independently or positively correlated measurements. The mean of column 1 times the mean of column 2 does not equal the mean of column 4, which demonstrates that rule 5 is only true when independence is present.

Now assume that a random sample of n measurements is taken from a population and the measurements are summed. The sum of the measurements is also a random variable. This could be shown by taking repeated random samples of size n, and determining the sum of the measurements for each. Variability would certainly occur among the sums. What is the mean of all these possible summation values? The expectation of the sum of the measurements is symbolized by:

$$E\left(\sum_1^n X_i\right)$$

This is equivalent to $E(X_1 + X_2 + X_3 + \cdots + X_n)$, which becomes $E(X_1) + E(X_2) + E(X_3) + \cdots + E(X_n)$ by Rule 4. In this case, X_1 represents the first measurement in each sample (or the top measurement in a column of figures which is to be added), X_2 the second, X_3 the third, and X_n the nth. If an indefinitely large number of samples is taken, then the first measurement (X_1) *of each sample* could have any X_i value. The same is true for X_2, X_3, and X_n. Consequently, $E(X_1)$ can be read: "the mean of all the measurements that X_1 could have been." With this interpretation, $E(X_1) = E(X_2) = E(X_3) = E(X_n) = E(X_i) = \mu$.

RULE 6. $\displaystyle E\left(\sum_1^n X_i\right) = E(X_1 + X_2 + X_3 + \cdots + X_n)$

$$= E(X_1) + E(X_2) + E(X_3) + \cdots + E(X_n)$$

$$= nE(X_i)$$

Another rule follows directly:

RULE 7. $\displaystyle E\left(\sum_1^n X_i^2\right) = nE(X_i^2)$

The last rule to be presented deals with the expectation of the square of the sum of a sample of measurements. Before proceeding with this rule, it is necessary to consider the method for obtaining the number of combinations of n items taken 2 at a time. The number of different combinations of 4 letters taken 2 at a time is 6. These are: ab, ac, ad, bc, bd, and cd. The number of different combinations of 3 letters taken 2 at a time is 3: ab, ac, and bc. The formula is: $n(n-1)/2$, where n is the total number of items.

RULE 8. $\displaystyle E\left(\sum_1^n X_i\right)^2 = E(X_1 + X_2 + X_3 + \cdots + X_n)^2$

The expansion of this multinomial gives n terms of the type X_i^2 and $n(n-1)/2$ terms of the type $2 X_i X_j$. Therefore

$E(X_1 + X_2 + X_3 + \cdots + X_n)^2$

$= E(X_1^2 + X_2^2 + \cdots + X_n^2 + 2X_1X_2 + 2X_1X_3 + \cdots + 2X_{n-1}X_n)$

$= E(X_1^2) + E(X_2^2) + E(X_3^2) + \cdots + E(X_n^2) + 2E(X_1X_2)$
$\quad + 2E(X_1X_3) + \cdots + 2E(X_{n-1}X_n)$

$$[Note:\ 2E(X_iX_j) = 2E(X_i)E(X_j) = 2\mu^2]$$

$= nE(X_i^2) + \dfrac{n(n-1)}{2}\, 2\mu^2 = nE(X_i^2) + n(n-1)\mu^2$

2.2   Estimate of the Population Mean

The mean (μ) of a population may be estimated by the mean of a random sample. The latter is symbolized by $\bar{x}$.

$$\text{Sample mean} = \bar{x} = \frac{\sum\limits_{1}^{n} X_i}{n}$$

The mean ($\bar{x}$) of a random sample is an unbiased estimate of the population mean (μ). An unbiased statistic is defined as one that has the parameter as its mean expectation. This is symbolized as $E(\bar{x}) = \mu$. The proof is as follows:

$$E(\bar{x}) = E\left(\frac{\sum\limits_{1}^{n} X_i}{n}\right)$$

$$= \frac{1}{n}E\left(\sum\limits_{1}^{n} X_i\right)$$

$$= \frac{1}{n}nE(X_i)$$

$$= E(X_i) = \mu$$

The median and mode of a sample are also unbiased estimates of the mean of a normal population. The median is defined as the middle value of a group of measurements if there is one; otherwise, it is an interpolated middle value. For a sample with the measurements 4, 6, 8, 9, and 10, the median is 8. When there is an even number of measurements, such as 4, 6, 8, and 9, the median is the average of the two middle values: $\frac{6 + 8}{2} = 7$. The median is central in the sense that half the measurements are larger and half are smaller.

The sample mode is defined as the measurement with the maximum frequency, if there is one. The measurements 3, 4, 5, 5, 6, 6, 7, 7, 7, 8, 8, and 9, have a mode of 7. The measurements 3, 4, 5, 6, 8, and 9 have no mode. A sample may have more than one mode.

Even though the mean, median, and mode of a sample are all unbiased estimates of the mean of a normal population, the mean is the preferred statistic because it is more *reliable*. A *reliable* statistic is one that will give estimates showing limited variability. It is best defined in the relative sense. The most reliable statistic is one that on the average, for a given sample size, will come the closest to the value of the parameter. The mean is more reliable than the median, and the median is more reliable than the mode. A reliable statistic is often referred to as a precise or an efficient statistic.

2.3   Estimate of the Population Variance

The variance of a population is represented by the equation

$$\sigma^2 = \frac{\sum_{1}^{N} (X_i - \mu)^2}{N}$$

This equation reveals that the variance is equal to the mean of all the $(X_i - \mu)^2$ values. Hence, the variance of a population can also be represented by the equation

$$\sigma^2 = E(X_i - \mu)^2$$

By using the first four rules of mathematical expectation, the formula for variance can be expressed in another useful form:

$$\sigma^2 = E(X_i - \mu)^2$$
$$= E(X_i^2 - 2X_i\mu + \mu^2)$$
$$= E(X_i^2) - 2\mu E(X_i) + \mu^2$$
$$= E(X_i^2) - 2\mu^2 + \mu^2$$
$$= E(X_i^2) - \mu^2$$

This expression for variance will be used repeatedly in derivations in the present and succeeding chapters of this text. This equation also reveals that $E(X_i^2) = \sigma^2 + \mu^2$, which is another useful rule of mathematical expectation.

The variance of a population is best estimated by the variance of a sample:

$$\text{Sample variance} = s^2 = \frac{\sum_{1}^{n} (X_i - \bar{x})^2}{n - 1}$$

$$\text{(GENERAL FORMULA)}$$

where $\bar{x}$ is the sample mean and n is the sample size. If a calculator or a table of squares is available, the calculation of a sample variance is expedited by using another formula:

$$s^2 = \frac{\sum_{1}^{n} (X_i - \bar{x})^2}{n - 1}$$

$$= \frac{\sum_{1}^{n} (X_i^2 - 2\bar{x}X_i + \bar{x}^2)}{n - 1}$$

$$= \frac{\sum_1^n X_i^2 - 2\bar{x}\sum_1^n X_i + n\bar{x}^2}{n-1}$$

$$= \frac{\sum_1^n X_i^2 - 2\dfrac{\left(\sum_1^n X_i\right)^2}{n} + n\dfrac{\left(\sum_1^n X_i\right)^2}{n^2}}{n-1}$$

$$= \frac{\sum_1^n X_i^2 - 2\dfrac{\left(\sum_1^n X_i\right)^2}{n} + \dfrac{\left(\sum_1^n X_i\right)^2}{n}}{n-1}$$

$$= \frac{\sum_1^n X_i^2 - \dfrac{\left(\sum_1^n X_i\right)^2}{n}}{n-1} \qquad \text{(WORKING FORMULA)}$$

The denominator of $(n-1)$ for the variance of a sample presents a problem which is solved by a consideration of the subject of expectation. Since the formula for population variance contains N in the denominator, it might appear appropriate to use n in the denominator in calculating sample variance. Yet, if this is done, the resulting statistic underestimates the population variance. Dividing by $n-1$ results in an unbiased statistic. The proof is shown as follows:

$$E\left[\frac{\sum_1^n (X_i - \bar{x})^2}{n-1}\right] = \frac{1}{n-1}E\left[\sum_1^n (X_i - \bar{x})^2\right]$$

$$= \frac{1}{n-1}E\left[\sum_1^n X_i^2 - \frac{\left(\sum_1^n X_i\right)^2}{n}\right]$$

$$= \frac{1}{n-1}\left[E\left(\sum_1^n X_i^2\right) - \frac{1}{n}E\left(\sum_1^n X_i\right)^2\right]$$

$$\qquad \text{(See Rules 7 and 8)}$$

$$= \frac{1}{n-1}\left\{nE(X_i^2) - \frac{1}{n}[nE(X_i^2) + n(n-1)\mu^2]\right\}$$

$$= \frac{1}{n-1}[nE(X_i^2) - E(X_i^2) - (n-1)\mu^2]$$

$$= \frac{1}{n-1}[E(X_i^2)(n-1) - (n-1)\mu^2]$$

$$= \frac{n-1}{n-1}[E(X_i^2) - \mu^2]$$

$$= E(X_i^2) - \mu^2$$

$$= \sigma^2$$

If n is used in the denominator, the expectation becomes $\dfrac{n-1}{n}\sigma^2$. This can be determined by following through the above proof, substituting n in place of $n-1$

$$E\left[\frac{\sum_{1}^{n}(X_i - \bar{x})^2}{n}\right] = \frac{n-1}{n}\sigma^2$$

When n becomes very large, $\dfrac{n-1}{n}$ approaches 1. For this reason, some authors state that the denominator should be $n-1$ for small samples, but if the sample is large, it is justifiable to divide by n. However, it is always a good habit to use $n-1$ in the denominator, regardless of the size of the sample.

A sample variance, in addition to being an unbiased estimate, is also the most reliable estimate of the population variance that is available.

The numerator of the formula for sample variance is commonly called sum of squares, which is an abbreviation of sum of the squared deviations. The denominator is referred to as degrees of freedom.

$$s^2 = \frac{\text{Sum of Squares}}{\text{Degrees of Freedom}}$$

The term degrees of freedom refers to the number of independent measurements that are available for the estimation of σ^2. If a sample were taken of n measurements, the estimate of σ^2 would be based on n independent measurements only if deviations were obtained from the population mean instead of the sample mean. In this case the formula would be:

$$\frac{\sum_{1}^{n}(X_i - \mu)^2}{n}$$

This is an unbiased statistic which is more reliable than the sample variance (s^2), but of course it is unrealistic since it assumes μ is known. Substituting $\bar{x}$ in its place results in an estimate of σ^2 based on $n-1$ independent measurements. This is best visualized from an example.

Assume that a random sample of four measurements was taken from a population where $\mu = 10$. The sum of squares would come from the formula:

$$\sum_{1}^{n}(X_i - \mu)^2$$

The X_1, X_2, X_3, and X_4 measurements could take any X_i measurement, i.e., they have *freedom to vary*. If the measurements were $X_1 = 12$, $X_2 = 7$, $X_3 = 10$, $X_4 = 15$, then the squared deviations become: $(12-10)^2$, $(7-10)^2$,

$(10 - 10)^2$, $(15 - 10)^2$. Using this method, the estimate of σ^2 would be based on n (or 4) independent measurements.

However, if μ is not known, and $\bar{x}$ is used in its place, the sum of squares would come from the formula:

$$\sum_1^n (X_i - \bar{x})^2$$

where $\bar{x} = 11$. Now X_1, X_2, and X_3 have freedom to vary, i.e., they are independent, but if they are assigned the values $X_1 = 12$, $X_2 = 7$, $X_3 = 10$, then X_4 is not independent. It is a fixed value because the mean ($\bar{x}$) of the four measurements is known. That is,

$$\bar{x} = \frac{X_1 + X_2 + X_3 + X_4}{4}$$

If $\bar{x} = 11$, $X_1 = 12$, $X_2 = 7$, and $X_3 = 10$, then X_4 can only be 15, since

$$\frac{12 + 7 + 10 + 15}{4} = 11.$$

The squared deviations become $(12 - 11)^2$, $(7 - 11)^2$, $(10 - 11)^2$, $(15 - 11)^2$. Three of the measurements are independent, but because $\bar{x}$ is used in place of μ, the nth measurement is fixed.

The general rule is that in order to have an unbiased estimate of a population variance, the sum of squares calculated from the sample data must be divided by the number of independent measurements. Since $\bar{x}$ is used in place of μ in the formula for sample variance, the number of independent measurements becomes $n - 1$. It also follows that in computing an unbiased estimate of a population variance, one degree of freedom is lost each time a parameter in the formula is replaced by a statistic. Replacing μ by $\bar{x}$ in the numerator changes the denominator from n to $n - 1$.

2.4   Sample Standard Deviation

The square root of the sample variance is known as the sample standard deviation:

$$s = \sqrt{\frac{\sum_1^n (X_i - \bar{x})^2}{n - 1}} = \sqrt{\frac{\sum_1^n X_i^2 - \frac{\left(\sum_1^n X_i\right)^2}{n}}{n - 1}}$$

Curiously, even though the sample variance (s^2) is an unbiased estimate of the population variance (σ^2), the sample standard deviation (s) is not an unbiased estimate of the population standard deviation.

$$E(s^2) = \sigma^2 \qquad E(s) \neq \sigma$$

A bias is introduced by taking the square root. This can be demonstrated by a simple model. The mean of the numbers 4, 9, and 16 equals 9.67. The square roots of the numbers are 2, 3, and 4, respectively. The mean of the square roots is 3, which is not the square root of 9.67.

2.5 Calculation of a Sample Mean, Variance, and Standard Deviation.

Six rats were fed a special diet and the increase in growth over a given length of time was measured in grams. It is usually convenient to arrange the data in magnitude array.

Table 2.3

Increase in Growth (grams) X	$X - \bar{x}$	$(X - \bar{x})^2$	X^2
2.7	−0.55	0.3025	7.29
2.9	−0.35	0.1225	8.41
3.2	−0.05	0.0025	10.24
3.3	0.05	0.0025	10.89
3.6	0.35	0.1225	12.96
3.8	0.55	0.3025	14.44
Total 19.5	Total 0.00	Total 0.8550	Total 64.23

Calculation of the sample mean:

$$\bar{x} = \frac{\sum_{1}^{n} X_i}{n} = \frac{19.5}{6} = 3.25$$

Calculation of the variance by use of the general formula:

$$s^2 = \frac{\sum_{1}^{n} (X_i - \bar{x})^2}{n - 1} = \frac{0.8550}{5} = 0.171$$

Calculation of the variance by use of the working formula:

$$s^2 = \frac{\sum\limits_1^n X_i^2 - \dfrac{\left(\sum\limits_1^n X_i\right)^2}{n}}{n-1} = \frac{64.23 - \dfrac{(19.5)^2}{6}}{5} = \frac{0.8550}{5} = 0.171$$

Calculation of the standard deviation:

$$s = \sqrt{s^2} = \sqrt{0.171} = 0.414$$

2.6   Estimates of Gamma-One and Gamma-Two

Occasions may arise when it is desirable to determine if a population is skewed or has kurtosis, and if so, to estimate the degree of departure from normality. A common procedure for testing whether a population is normally distributed is by testing the "goodness of fit" of a large sample with a normal distribution by a chi-square method. This procedure will be discussed in a later chapter. However, estimates of gamma-one and gamma-two can be calculated. The estimates are known as k statistics. Since k statistics are seldom calculated in actual practice, they will not be discussed here. Snedecor (1956) has presented an excellent review of the use of k statistics.*

2.7   Use of Statistics Other Than The Mean, Variance, and Standard Deviation

Since the median is less reliable than the mean, it is less commonly used. However, occasions often arise when it may be accurate enough to answer a particular question. For example, assume that an experiment is being carried out to obtain an estimate of the average time required for seeds of a given variety to germinate. If 25 seeds were to be tested, the procedure would be to use the time required for the 13th seed to germinate as the estimate of central tendency. Similarly, if 14 patients were given a drug on the same day, determining the number of days required for the 7th and 8th patients to show relief of symptoms, and dividing by 2, would give the sample median. The other patients would not have to be as closely followed.

A commonly used measure of variability is the range of a sample. The range is defined as the difference between the largest and smallest measurement in the distribution. Insight as to the variability of a population can be ob-

---

*See the list of references at the back of the book for this and other references cited throughout the text.

tained rapidly by determining the value of this statistic. Comparisons can then be made with ranges computed on other samples of similar size.

Many of the concepts discussed in this chapter can be demonstrated by a simple model. Assume that a population consists of three Leprechauns who weigh 3, 4, and 5 pounds. The mean of this small finite population consisting of $N = 3$ measurements is 4 pounds:

$$\mu = \frac{\sum\limits_{1}^{N} X_i}{N} = \frac{3 + 4 + 5}{3} = \frac{12}{3} = 4$$

The variance, or second moment about the mean, is 0.667:

$$\sigma^2 = \frac{\sum\limits_{1}^{N} (X_i - \mu)^2}{N} = \frac{(3 - 4)^2 + (4 - 4)^2 + (5 - 4)^2}{3} = \frac{2}{3} = 0.667$$

Suppose that all possible samples of size 2 $(n = 2)$ are taken from this population. As each Leprechaun is sampled and weighed he is returned to the population; hence it is possible for the same Leprechaun to be represented twice in the same sample. Using this procedure the total number of different possible samples is nine. The sampling procedure is represented as follows:

	3	4	5
3	Sample 1	Sample 2	Sample 3
4	Sample 4	Sample 5	Sample 6
5	Sample 7	Sample 8	Sample 9

For each sample, various statistics can be calculated. The formula for each statistic is given at the headings of the columns in Table 2.4. Each column represents a *sampling distribution* of nine statistics.

The mean of all the statistics in column 1 is 4, demonstrating that the mean of all the possible sample means equals the population mean, or as expressed in the language of mathematical expectation, $E(\bar{x}) = \mu$.

Likewise, the mean of the statistics in column 2 is 0.667, which is the value of the population variance. This is expected since the statistic $\dfrac{\sum\limits_{1}^{n} (X_i - \bar{x})^2}{(n - 1)}$ is an unbiased estimate of σ^2. However, if the sum of squares is divided by n instead of the number of independent measurements $(n - 1)$, the mean of all

Table 2.4

	$\dfrac{\sum\limits_{1}^{N'} X_i}{n}$	$\dfrac{\sum\limits_{1}^{N}(X_i - \bar{x})^2}{n-1}$	$\dfrac{\sum\limits_{1}^{N}(X_i - \bar{x})^2}{n}$	$\dfrac{\sum\limits_{1}^{N}(X_i - \mu)^2}{n}$	$\sqrt{\dfrac{\sum\limits_{1}^{N}(X_i - \bar{x})^2}{n}}$
Sample 1	3.0	0.0	0.0	1.0	0.0
Sample 2	3.5	0.5	0.25	0.5	0.7071
Sample 3	4.0	2.0	1.0	1.0	1.4141
Sample 4	3.5	0.5	0.25	0.5	0.7071
Sample 5	4.0	0.0	0.0	0.0	0.0
Sample 6	4.5	0.5	0.25	0.5	0.7071
Sample 7	4.0	2.0	1.0	1.0	1.4141
Sample 8	4.5	0.5	0.25	0.5	0.7071
Sample 9	5.0	0.0	0.0	1.0	0.0
Mean	4.0	0.667	0.333	0.667	0.6285

statistics is 0.333, as shown in column 3. This is a numerical demonstration of

the theorem $E\left[\dfrac{\sum\limits_{1}^{n}(X_i - \bar{x})^2}{n}\right] = \dfrac{n-1}{n}\sigma^2$, since $\dfrac{2-1}{2}(0.667) = 0.333$.

Insight into the concept of reliability can be obtained by comparing the statistics appearing in columns 2 and 4. The means of both columns are 0.667,

as expected from the theorems $E\left[\dfrac{\sum\limits_{1}^{n}X_i - \bar{x})^2}{(n-1)}\right] = \sigma^2$ and $E\left[\dfrac{\sum\limits_{1}^{n}(X_i - \mu)^2}{n}\right]$

$= \sigma^2$. Each statistic is an unbiased estimate of the population variance, yet

it was stated previously in this chapter that $\dfrac{\sum\limits_{1}^{n}(X_i - \mu)^2}{n}$ is a more reliable

statistic. This can be observed by noting the ranges of the two sampling distributions. In column 2 the statistics range from 0 to 2, but in column 4 they range from only 0 to 1. Thus, on the average, for a given sample size

$\dfrac{\sum\limits_{1}^{n}(X_i - \mu)^2}{n}$ comes closer to the value of the parameter $(\sigma^2 = 0.667)$ than

$\dfrac{\sum\limits_{1}^{n}(X_i - \bar{x})^2}{(n-1)}$.

Sample standard deviations are given in column 5. The mean of this sampling distribution of statistics is 0.6285. Note that this value is not $\sqrt{\sigma^2} = \sqrt{0.667} = 0.8167$, which demonstrates again that even though $E(s^2) = \sigma^2$, that $E(s) \neq \sigma$.

In chapter 3 the properties of a sampling distribution of sample means will be discussed in detail; however, it will be instructive to demonstrate numerically one property with the above model. The variance, or second moment about the mean, of the sampling distribution of sample means is symbolized by $\sigma_{\bar{x}}^2$. This variance can be calculated directly from the nine statistics appearing in column 1.

$$\begin{aligned}\sigma_{\bar{x}}^2 &= \tfrac{1}{9}[(3-4)^2 + (3.5-4)^2 + (4-4)^2 + (3.5-4)^2 + (4-4)^2 \\ &\quad + (4.5-4)^2 + (4-4)^2 + (4.5-4)^2 + (5-4)^2] \\ &= \tfrac{1}{9}(1 + 0.25 + 0 + 0.25 + 0 + 0.25 + 0 + 0.25 + 1) \\ &= 3/9 = 0.333\end{aligned}$$

In the next chapter it will be proven that $\sigma_{\bar{x}}^2 = \dfrac{\sigma^2}{n}$, where σ^2 is the variance of the population from which the random sample is taken and n is the size of the sample. For this model, $\sigma_{\bar{x}}^2 = \dfrac{0.667}{2} = 0.333$, as shown above.

Problems

1. An investigator obtained 50 newly born guinea pigs. Half were given Diet A and the other half Diet B. After a specified period of time the gain in weight was determined in grams for each guinea pig.

Treatment with Diet A (data arranged in magnitude array)

69.0	75.3	79.9	84.2	88.1
69.1	76.1	80.1	84.5	88.5
70.5	77.4	80.2	86.1	89.2
72.7	77.5	81.5	87.2	89.3
75.2	79.5	83.1	87.9	90.2

(a) Describe the population from which the above sample was taken. (b) Give the formula for the mean of this population. (c) Give the formula for the variance of this population. (*Note:* In the following calculations round off the final answers to one more decimal than found in the original data.) (d) Calculate the best estimate of the population mean. (e) Calculate the best estimate of the population variance. (f) Calculate the sample standard deviation. (g) Determine the sample median and mode.

2. By using the rules of mathematical expectation, prove the following theorems:

(a) $E\left[\dfrac{\sum_1^n (X_i - \mu)^2}{n}\right] = \sigma^2$ (b) $E\left[\dfrac{\sum_1^n (X_i - \bar{x})^2}{n}\right] = \dfrac{n-1}{n}\sigma^2$

3. Prove that a sample mean ($\bar{x}$) is an unbiased estimate of the population mean (μ).

4. Prove that a sample variance (s^2) is an unbiased estimate of the population variance (σ^2).

5. Fifteen adult male mice of a given species were collected in a meadow. The left ear of each was measured (mm.).

14.2	18.2	17.4
17.9	16.4	17.6
16.5	19.1	16.9
16.0	20.1	18.7
20.0	16.3	15.4

(a) Calculate the mean of the sample. (b) Calculate the variance of the sample using the general formula. (c) Calculate the variance of the sample using the working formula. (d) Calculate the sample standard deviation. (e) Determine the sample median.

6. Define *degrees of freedom*. Demonstrate that when a population variance is estimated, the number of degrees of freedom is $n - 1$ when the sample mean is used in the equation of the estimator.

7. Twelve children with phenylketonuria were tested for the level of serum phenylalanine. The measurements (mg.%) were as follows:

26.71	29.25	24.79	32.97
36.20	20.62	27.70	29.00
25.29	36.72	28.24	32.59

(a) Calculate the sample mean and sample standard deviation. (b) Distinguish between the population and the sample.

8. Measurements of taxonomic interest were made on 15 female turtles (*Trionyx spinifer*.) One measurement was width of carapace as percentage of length.

86.4	87.5	85.8
83.2	82.9	87.4
87.1	84.6	88.3
83.8	85.5	82.4
85.4	83.7	86.0

Calculate the sample mean and sample standard deviation.

CHAPTER THREE

The Normal Curve of Error and Probability

The concept of the normal distribution was introduced in Chapter 1. The curve representing a normal distribution is known as the normal curve of error, or normal curve. The normal curve has the following equation:

$$Y = \frac{1}{\sigma\sqrt{2\pi}}e^{-(X-\mu)^2/2\sigma^2}$$

where π is a constant equal to 3.1416, e is a constant equal to 2.7183, X corresponds to a point on the horizontal axis, and Y is the corresponding point on the vertical axis.

The above equation shows that a normal curve can be specified completely if μ and σ are known. Since σ can take any value, there could be an infinite number of different normal curves with the same mean.

For practical purposes, the curve runs into the baseline slightly past three standard deviations from the mean, even though theoretically it extends infinitely far in both directions. The term standard deviation was first used by Karl Pearson in 1893.

If the curve representing the measurements in a population is a normal curve, the population is defined as a *normal population*.

A table is available (Table I*) whereby proportionate areas under the normal curve can be found between any two points on the horizontal axis. This table deserves special consideration. The standard deviation is set

Note: Roman-numeral tables (Table I, Table II, etc.) are listed in the Appendix for easy reference, while Arabic-numeral tables (Table 2.3, etc.) are near where cited in the text.

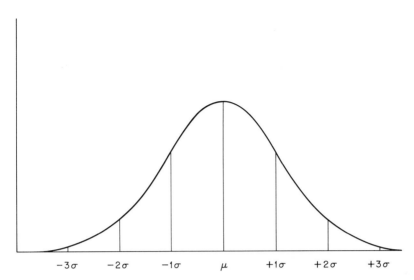

equal to one unit of measure. All values of X on the horizontal axis are measured in regard to how far they deviate from μ in terms of σ. The standard deviation is used as a *standard of measurement*. A value of X, for example, may be twice as far from the mean as the standard deviation, it may be 1.5 times as far, 0.46 times as far, etc.

The measure of how far a given value of X deviates from μ in terms of σ is symbolized by c. Some authors use the symbol z, but z will be reserved in this text for a value that will be encountered in the subject of correlation. The formula for c is:

$$c = \frac{X - \mu}{\sigma}$$

PROBLEM 1. The mean of a normal curve is equal to 50 with a standard deviation of 5. What is the value of c for X equal to 40? Interpret the meaning.

$$c = \frac{40 - 50}{5} = \frac{-10}{5} = -2$$

Answer: The value of X is twice as far from μ as 1σ. Furthermore, X is left of the mean as signified by the negative sign.

PROBLEM 2. In the same curve, what is the value of c for X equal to 52? Interpret the meaning.

$$c = \frac{52 - 50}{5} = \frac{2}{5} = 0.4$$

Answer: The value of X is 0.4 of the distance form μ as 1σ. It is to the right of μ. Entering the table for the areas under a normal curve (Table I) with a value of c gives the proportionate area under the curve to the left of any point X.

PROBLEM 3. A normal curve has a mean of 50 and a standard deviation of 5. What proportion of the total area under the curve is left of 40?

Answer: Calculate the value of c and obtain the proportionate area from the table.

$$c = \frac{40 - 50}{5} = -2$$

The table shows that the proportionate area left of 40 equals 0.0227.

PROBLEM 4. In the same curve, what proportion of the area under the curve is right of 62.5?

Answer: Obtain the proportionate area left of 62.5. Subtract this from 1 in order to obtain the proportionate area under the curve right of 62.5.

$$c = \frac{62.5 - 50}{5} = \frac{12.5}{5} = 2.5$$

The proportionate area left of 62.5 is equal to 0.9938; consequently $1 - 0.9938 = 0.0062$ is the proportionate area under the curve right of 62.5.

PROBLEM 5. A normal population has a mean of 50 and a standard deviation of 5. What proportion of the measurements in the population have values between 45 and 55 (or $\mu \pm 1\sigma$)?

Answer: From the table it is noted that the proportionate area left of 45 is 0.1587. Likewise, the proportionate area right of 55 is 0.1587. The proportionate area left of 45 and right of 55 is $0.1587 + 0.1587 = 0.3174$. Therefore, the proportionate area between 45 and 55 is $1 - 0.3174 = 0.6826$. *This states that 68.26% of all the measurements in a normal population are included within the limits $\mu \pm 1\sigma$.* (If the values in Table I had 5 or more decimal places, this proportionate area would have been 0.6827. In this text, the proportionate areas under the normal curve will be based on the 4 decimal values given in Table I).

3.1   Elementary Probability

It is common knowledge that if a coin is tossed, the probability that a head will occur is one-half. Also, the probability is one-sixth that a four will occur if a die is tossed. For our purposes, probability can be defined as follows.

When dealing with equally likely events, the probability of a success is the ratio of the number of ways in which the event can succeed to the total number of ways involved. Using an honest die, for example, the probability that a four will occur is expressed as:

$$P(4) = \frac{n_1}{n_1 + n_2} = \frac{1}{1 + 5} = \frac{1}{6}$$

where $P(4)$ is the probability of the event 4, n_1 is the number of ways in which the event can happen, n_2 is the number of ways the event can fail, and consequently $n_1 + n_2$ is the total number of ways involved.

The definition of probability has two corollaries. (1) If event A is certain to happen, its probability is equal to 1. If event A is certain to fail, its probability is zero. In every other case it is a value between 0 and 1. (2) If event A has a probability of success of P, the probability of failure is $1 - P$.

PROBLEM 6. A card is drawn at random from a deck of cards. What is the probability that it is the queen of spades?

Answer: The total number of cards in a deck is 52. There is only 1 way of succeeding, and 51 ways of failing on a single draw. The probability of success is $1/52 = 0.01923$. This means that in 1.923% of the trials, a success will occur.

PROBLEM 7. Cards numbered from 1 up to and including 100 are placed in a hat. What is the probability that a card pulled at random will have a number less than 60?

Answer: The number of cards is 100. There are 59 ways of succeeding and 41 ways of failing. The probability of success is $59/100 = 0.59$. In 59% of such trials, a number less than 60 will be drawn.

PROBLEM 8. For the same cards discussed in the preceding problem, what is the probability that a number less than 40 or greater than 60 will be drawn?

Answer: There are 39 ways (1 through 39) of getting a number less than 40, and 40 ways (61 through 100) of getting a number greater than 60. Therefore,

$$P = \frac{39 + 40}{100} = \frac{79}{100} = 0.79$$

PROBLEM 9. A normal population has a mean of 50 and a standard deviation of 5. What is the probability that a single X value taken at random will have a value of 40 or smaller?

Answer: The proportionate area left of 40 under a normal curve is 0.0227. Therefore,

$$P = \frac{\text{Proportionate area under the curve left of 40}}{\text{Total area under the curve}}$$

$$= \frac{0.0227}{1.0000} = 0.0227$$

PROBLEM 10. A normal population has a mean of 50 and a standard deviation of 5. What is the probability that a single X value taken at random will have a value of 40 or smaller, or 60 or greater?

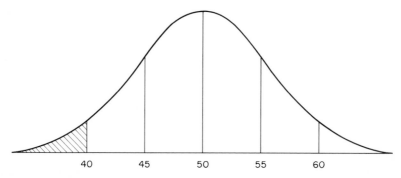

Answer: The proportionate area left of 40 is 0.0227. The proportionate area right of 60 is 0.0227. Therefore,

$$P = \frac{\text{Proportionate area left of 40 and right of 60}}{\text{Total Area}}$$

$$= \frac{0.0227 + 0.0227}{1.0000} = 0.04554$$

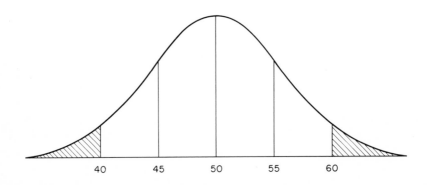

3.2   Sampling Distribution of Sample Means

The concept of a sampling distribution is an important one in statistical methods. Assume that the mean ($\bar{x}$) of a random sample of 20 measurements was calculated. Assume further that the sample was taken from a normal population. This sample mean would have a specific value, say 26.021 grams. If another random sample of 20 measurements were taken from this same population, the mean of this second sample would likely have a different value, say 27.637 grams.

The question may now be asked, "What are all the possible values of the sample means that might occur under the specified sampling procedure, and what would be the frequency of each?" This imaginary array of sample means constitutes a sampling distribution of means, and importantly, the sampling distribution follows a normal distribution.

The mean of the sampling distribution of sample means is equal to the population mean.

$$E(\bar{x}) = \mu$$

The variance (second moment about the mean) of the sampling distribution of means can be expressed as the mean of all the $(\bar{x}_i - \mu)^2$ values:

$$\sigma_{\bar{x}}^2 = E(\bar{x}_i - \mu)^2$$

By the rules of mathematical expectation, another formula for this variance can be derived.

$$\sigma_{\bar{x}}^2 = E(\bar{x} - \mu)^2 = E(\bar{x}^2 - 2\bar{x}\mu + \mu^2)$$

$$= E\left[\frac{\left(\sum_1^n X_i\right)^2}{n^2} - 2\frac{\sum_1^n X_i}{n}\mu + \mu^2\right]$$

$$= \frac{1}{n^2}[nE(X_i^2) + n(n-1)\mu^2] - \frac{2\mu}{n}E\left(\sum_1^n X_i\right) + \mu^2$$

$$= \frac{nE(X_i^2)}{n^2} + \frac{n(n-1)\mu^2}{n^2} - \frac{2\mu n\ E(X_i)}{n} + \mu^2$$

$$= \frac{E(X_i^2)}{n} + \frac{n\mu^2 - \mu^2}{n} - 2\mu^2 + \mu^2$$

$$= \frac{E(X_i^2)}{n} + \frac{n\mu^2}{n} - \frac{\mu^2}{n} - \mu^2 = \frac{E(X_i^2)}{n} - \frac{\mu^2}{n}$$

$$= \frac{E(X_i^2) - \mu^2}{n} = \frac{\sigma^2}{n}$$

The square root of this term is the standard deviation of the sampling distribution of means.

$$\sigma_{\bar{x}} = \sqrt{\frac{\sigma^2}{n}} = \frac{\sigma}{\sqrt{n}}$$

This standard deviation is commonly known as the standard error of the mean. By definition, a standard error is a standard deviation of a sampling distribution.

If the mean (μ) and the variance (σ^2) of a normal population are known, the properties of the sampling distribution can be completely specified. For example, if $\mu = 27.0$, $\sigma^2 = 9$, and $n = 9$, the sampling distribution has a mean of 27.0 and a standard deviation of 1. This indicates that 68.26% of all the sample means will lie between 26 and 28.

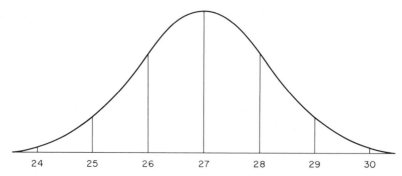

Figure 3.1 Sampling distribution of sample means where

$$E(\bar{x}) = \mu = 27.0 \text{ and } \sigma_{\bar{x}} = \frac{\sigma}{\sqrt{n}} = \frac{3}{\sqrt{9}} = 1$$

Table 3.1   Effect of sample size on the standard deviation $(\sigma_{\bar{x}})$ of the sampling distribution of sample means when the population mean (μ) is 27.00 and the population variance (σ^2) is 9.00.

Sample Size (n)	Standard Deviation of Sampling Distribution $\sigma_{\bar{x}} = \frac{\sigma}{\sqrt{n}} = \frac{3}{\sqrt{n}}$	Limits including 68.26% of all sample means
4	1.50	25.50 – 28.50
9	1.00	26.00 – 28.00
16	0.75	26.25 – 27.75
36	0.50	26.50 – 27.50
100	0.30	26.70 – 27.30
400	0.15	26.85 – 27.15

The data in Table 3.1 demonstrate that the reliability of a sample mean ($\bar{x}$) increases with sample size, i.e., if an investigator wishes to estimate the mean of a normal population, the probability of approaching the value of the parameter increases with the sample size.

A consideration of sampling distributions leads to a precise definition of a reliable statistic. The most reliable statistic can be defined as one whose sampling distribution has the smallest variance for a given sample size. A sample mean is more reliable than a sample median or sample mode.

PROBLEM 11. A normal population has a mean (μ) of 27.00 and a variance (σ^2) of 9.00. What is the probability that the mean ($\bar{x}$) of a random sample of size 9 taken from that population will have a value of 24.5 or less?

Answer: The sampling distribution has a mean of 27.00 and a standard deviation of 1.00. The sample mean ($\bar{x}$) is $2\frac{1}{2}$ times as far from the mean of the sampling distribution as one standard deviation. The equation for c becomes:

$$c = \frac{\bar{x} - \mu}{\sigma_{\bar{x}}} = \frac{x - \mu}{\sqrt{\dfrac{\sigma^2}{n}}} = \frac{24.5 - 27.0}{\sqrt{\dfrac{9}{9}}} = \frac{-2.5}{1} = -2.5$$

From Table I, it is determined that the proportionate area left of 24.5 is 0.0062. The P value becomes:

$$P = \frac{\text{Proportionate area left of 24.5}}{\text{Total area}} = \frac{0.0062}{1.0000} = 0.0062$$

PROBLEM 12. A normal population has a mean (μ) of 120.00 and a variance (σ^2) of 64. What is the probability that a sample mean ($\bar{x}$) computed from a random sample of size 16 will have a value 114.0 or less, or 120.0 or greater?

Answer: The sampling distribution has a mean of 120.0 and a standard deviation of:

$$\sigma_{\bar{x}} = \sqrt{\frac{\sigma^2}{n}} = \frac{\sigma}{\sqrt{n}} = \frac{8}{\sqrt{16}} = \frac{8}{4} = 2.0$$

The c value used to determine the proportionate area left of 114 is equal to:

$$c = \frac{\bar{x} - \mu}{\sigma_{\bar{x}}} = \frac{114 - 120}{2} = \frac{-6}{2} = -3.0$$

From Table I this area is determined to be 0.0013.

The proportionate area left of 120.00 is 0.5000, which comes from:

$$c = \frac{\bar{x} - \mu}{\sigma_{\bar{x}}} = \frac{120 - 120}{2} = 0.0$$

Since the proportionate area right of 120.0 is $1 - 0.5000 = 0.5000$, the proportionate area left of 114 and right of 120 becomes $0.0013 + 0.5000 = 0.5013$. The probability value is the same.

$$P = \frac{\text{Area in both tails}}{\text{Total area}} = \frac{0.0013 + 0.5000}{1} = 0.5013$$

These examples demonstrate the usefulness of the sampling distribution of means in the solution of probability problems concerning sample means. There are two major assumptions included in these probability problems. The first is that the sample is random. The second is that the sample is taken from a normal population. There is a certain amount of leeway in the second assumption, but not in the first. If the population is normal in form, then the sampling distribution of means will always be normal. Even if the population has slight or moderate skewness or kurtosis, as long as the sample size is reasonably large, the sampling distribution will approach normality so closely that for practical purposes it can be assumed to be normal. Therefore, under these conditions the probability values will be valid. However, if the population deviates markedly from normality, i.e., has extreme skewness or kurtosis, and the sample size is relatively small, the sampling distribution will not be normal in form. Table I cannot be used for a non-normal sampling distribution. This suggests that an investigator should have some knowledge of the structure of the population from which his samples are taken; however, since slight or even moderate skewness or kurtosis can be tolerated, the assumption of normality can often be made without serious error.

Problems

1. A negatively skewed population has a mean of 150 and a variance of 100. (a) If samples of size 1 ($n = 1$) were taken at random from this population, what would be the appearance of the sampling distribution of sample means? Give the mean and standard deviation of the sampling distribution. (b) If samples of size 25 were taken at random from this population, what would be the appearance of the sampling distribution of sample means? Give the mean and standard deviation of the sampling distribution.

2. A normal population has a mean of 52.5 and a variance of 16. What is the probability that a measurement selected at random has a value of 50.1 or less?

3. A normal population has a mean of 100.0 and a variance of 100.0 What is the probability that a measurement selected at random will have a value of 95.0 or less, or 105 or greater?

4. A normal population has a mean of 172.5 and a variance of 144. Assume that an infinitely large number of random samples of size 9 were taken from this population and the mean ($\bar{x}$) computed on each.
(a) Give the values of the mean and standard deviation of this sampling distribution.
(b) Draw the curve representing this sampling distribution. Along the horizontal axis, give the values of the mean, ± 1 standard deviation, ± 2 standard deviations, ± 3 standard deviations. (*Note*: remember that ± 1 standard deviation is at the point of inflection and the curve approaches the base line slightly past ± 3 standard deviations.) (c) What two limits will include 68.26% of all the sample means? (d) Which is more variable, the sampling distribution of means or the population of measurements? Explain. (e) Derive the formula for the standard deviation of the sampling distribution. (f) Give the definition of a "standard error."

5. A normal population has a mean of 180 and a variance of 144. Assume that an infinitely large number of samples of size 9 were taken at random from this population and the mean ($\bar{x}$) computed on each.
(a) Give the values of the mean and standard deviation of this sampling distribution.
(b) Draw the curve representing this sampling distribution. (c) What proportion of the sample means will have values between 178 and 182? (d) What proportion of the sample means will have values between 174 and 186? (e) What is the probability that the mean of a single random sample will lie between 176 and 184? (f) If a single sample

mean picked at random is decreased in value by 4 units ($\bar{x} - a = L_1$) and increased in value by 4 units ($\bar{x} + a = L_2$), what is the probability that the limits L_1 and L_2 will include the value of 180? What is the probability that these limits *will not* include the value of 180?

6. A normal population has a mean of 38.50 and a standard deviation of 1.75. What proportion of the measurements in the population have values between 35.00 and 38.50? If the population consists of 129,640 measurements, how many lie between 35.00 and 38.50?

7. Assume that a population has a variance of 64. Discuss why a sample of $n = 64$ will yield a more reliable estimate of the population mean than a sample of $n = 16$.

8. A normal population has a mean of 50 and a variance of 64. (a) What is the probability that a sample mean based on a random sample of $n = 64$ will have a value of 48 or less, or 52 or greater? (b) What is the probability that a sample mean based on a random sample of $n = 64$ will have a value between 49 and 51? (c) If the mean of a random sample ($n = 64$) is decreased in value by 1 unit ($\bar{x} - a = L_1$) and increased in value by 1 unit ($\bar{x} + a = L_2$), what is the probability that the limits L_1 and L_2 will include the value 50?

9. Assume that the mean performance on a standard I.Q. test is 100 and the standard deviation is 15. Assume further that the measurements are distributed normally. (a) What proportion of the general population has an I.Q. below 85? (b) What proportion of the general population has an I.Q. below 70? (c) What proportion of the general population has an I.Q. above 115? (d) What proportion of the general population has an I.Q. above 137.5?

10. Assume that in a given age group, the mean systolic blood pressure is 85 and the variance is 100. If the population is normal, what is the probability that the mean of a random sample will be greater than 87: (a) if $n = 25$? (b) if $n = 100$?

CHAPTER FOUR

Test of Significance

A test of significance is a statistical tool that aids an investigator in deciding whether an observed result deviates from some expected value because of chance alone, or whether some factor or factors other than chance are interacting. A test of significance follows a specific pattern:

1. State the null hypothesis to be tested.
2. State the significance level.
3. Calculate a probability value (P value) associated with the null hypothesis.
4. Reject or accept the null hypothesis.

Before proceeding with the subject of a test of significance, it is appropriate to consider the effect on a population mean (μ) and variance (σ^2) of a uniform change in each measurement. The following rule can be stated:

Adding (subtracting) a constant to (from) each measurement in a population increases (decreases) the mean by a value equal to the constant, but does not change the variance.

$$\text{New mean} = \frac{\sum_{1}^{N} (X_i + a)}{N}$$

$$= \frac{\sum_{1}^{N} X_i + Na}{N}$$

$$= \mu + a$$

$$\text{New variance} = \frac{\sum_{1}^{N}[(X_i + a) - (\mu + a)]^2}{N}$$

$$= \frac{\sum_{1}^{N}[X_i + a - \mu - a]^2}{N}$$

$$= \frac{\sum_{1}^{N}(X_i - \mu)^2}{N}$$

$$= \sigma^2$$

A common procedure in experimental work is to give individuals "treatments" such as subjecting them to new diets, drugs, different environments, etc. Assume that 25 mice from strain A were fed a standard diet and 25 mice from the same strain were given a special diet. Population 1 would consist of an indefinitely large number of growth measurements obtained from mice fed the standard diet. Population 2 would consist of an indefinitely large number of growth measurements obtained from mice fed the special diet. Both populations are imaginary. If the special diet does not influence growth any differently than the standard diet, then $\mu_1 = \mu_2$, and $\sigma_1^2 = \sigma_2^2$. However, if the special diet tends to increase or decrease the growth of each mouse, then $\mu_1 \neq \mu_2$, but $\sigma_1^2 = \sigma_2^2$. The conclusion is, therefore, that treatments acting in an additive way affect means but not variances.

4.1   Sampling From a Single Population When the Variance Is Known

A test of significance will be introduced by using a fictitious example. A normal population has a mean (μ) of 24.5 and a variance (σ^2) of 16.0. This is obviously an unrealistic situation, since parameters are seldom known. The investigator wishes to test the effect of a new treatment. He proposes to take a random sample of individuals from the population and give each the treatment. If the treatment is effective, the mean ($\bar{x}$) of this sample will not be an unbiased estimate of $\mu = 24.5$. The procedure, then, is to compare the sample mean ($\bar{x}$) with the population mean (μ). If the sample mean is nearly equal to the population mean, he will assume that the treatment is ineffective, but if it is much smaller or greater than the population mean, he will conclude otherwise.

1. Null hypothesis: H_0: The treatment is ineffective.

The null hypothesis, symbolized by H_0, may be written: $H_0: \mu = 24.5$, where μ is the mean of the treated population. This implies that the mean of the treated population equals the mean of the untreated population.

A null hypothesis specifies (1) a population or populations, (2) an alternative hypothesis, and (3) a sampling distribution. A single population is specified for this test, which is the treated population. It has a mean of 24.5 and a variance of 16.0. If the null hypothesis is rejected, an alternative hypothesis (H_1) will be accepted. The alternative hypothesis states that the treatment will increase or decrease performance. It is written H_1: $\mu \neq 24.5$. The investigator selects 25 individuals at random and gives each the treatment. This results in a random sample of 25 measurements from the population of measurements. The sampling distribution specified by the null hypothesis consists of the means ($\bar{x}$) of all possible samples of size 25 taken at random from a population with a mean of 24.5 and a variance of 16.0 The mean of this sampling distribution is equal to $\mu = 24.5$ since $E(\bar{x}_i) = \mu$. The variance of the sampling distribution is σ^2/n, where $\sigma^2 = 16$ and $n = 25$.

2. Significance level: 0.05

The investigator states that he will accept the null hypothesis if his calculated P value (to be discussed later) is greater than 0.05 and reject the null hypothesis if it is less than 0.05.

3. Calculation of the P value.

Assume that the mean of the sample of 25 measurements is $\dfrac{\sum\limits_{1}^{n} X_i}{n} = 26.9$.

The probability value of interest in this test of significance is the probability of obtaining the observed deviation (plus or minus), or greater deviation (plus or minus), on the basis of the null hypothesis. The observed deviation is the difference between the mean of the sample and the mean of the sampling distribution of means.

$$\text{Observed deviation} = \bar{x} - \mu = 26.9 - 24.5 = +2.4$$

Since the interest is in plus and minus deviations, the problem could be rephrased: "The probability value of interest in this test of significance is the probability of obtaining a sample mean of 26.9 or larger, or 22.1 or smaller, on the basis of the null hypothesis." The value 22.1 is -2.4 deviations from the mean of the sampling distribution. The method for determining the probability value was given in Chapter 3. Two c values can be calculated.

$$c = \frac{\bar{x} - \mu}{\sigma_{\bar{x}}} = \frac{\bar{x} - \mu}{\sqrt{\dfrac{\sigma^2}{n}}} = \frac{26.9 - 24.5}{\sqrt{\dfrac{16}{25}}} = \frac{+2.4}{0.8} = +3.0$$

$$c = \frac{\bar{x} - \mu}{\sigma_{\bar{x}}} = \frac{\bar{x} - \mu}{\sqrt{\dfrac{\sigma^2}{n}}} = \frac{22.1 - 24.5}{\sqrt{\dfrac{16}{25}}} = \frac{-2.4}{0.8} = -3.0$$

Entering Table I with $c = +3.0$ yields a proportionate area under the normal curve left of 26.9 of 0.9987, and therefore, a proportionate area right of 26.9 of $1 - 0.9987 = 0.0013$. Similarly, entering the table with $c = -3.0$ yields a proportionate area left of 22.1 of 0.0013. The probability value of interest becomes:

$$P = \frac{\text{Proportionate area left of 22.1} + \text{Proportionate area right of 26.9}}{\text{Total area}}$$

$$= \frac{0.0013 + 0.0013}{1} = 0.0026$$

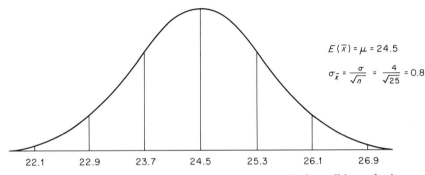

$$E(\bar{x}) = \mu = 24.5$$

$$\sigma_{\bar{x}} = \frac{\sigma}{\sqrt{n}} = \frac{4}{\sqrt{25}} = 0.8$$

| 22.1 | 22.9 | 23.7 | 24.5 | 25.3 | 26.1 | 26.9 |

Figure 4.1 Sampling distribution of means associated with the null hypothesis.

Since the P value is obtained by doubling the area in one tail of the curve, it can be obtained directly from Table II, known as the Table of c. Only one c value needs to be calculated and the sign is ignored. Entering Table II with $c = 3.0$ will yield a P value less than 0.01 and greater than 0.001 ($0.01 > P > 0.001$). These limits include the value ($P = 0.0026$) obtained from Table I. Since accurate values are seldom needed, the use of Table II in obtaining P values is the preferred method.

4. Reject or accept the null hypothesis.

A significance level of 0.05 was decided upon in the design of the experiment. The observed P value (0.0026) is less then 0.05, and therefore the null hypothesis is rejected. The investigator concludes that the difference between the sample mean ($\bar{x}$) and sampling distribution mean (μ) is not solely due to chance. He therefore accepts the alternative hypothesis (H_1). Since $\bar{x}$ is larger than μ, he has evidence that the treatment increases performance.

The deviation between $\bar{x}$ and μ is termed a *significant deviation* if the observed P value is less than 0.05, and a *highly significant deviation* if the P value is less than 0.01. The deviation is not significant if the P value is greater than 0.05. From Table II, it is observed that a c value between 1.96 and 2.58 is indicative of a significant deviation, while a c value greater than 2.58 is indicative of a highly significant deviation.

4.2   Error of the First Kind (Type I Error)

The investigator rejected the null hypothesis. He may have rejected a true hypothesis. This is known as an error of the first kind, or Type I error. How is this possible? The observed P value states that if the hypothesis is true, and therefore the mean of the sampling distribution is 24.5, the observed deviation (plus or minus), or greater deviation (plus or minus) will occur because of chance alone, in 0.26% of similar trials. If an event is expected to occur once in about 385 trials, *this may be that time.* If so, an error of the first kind has been made by rejecting the hypothesis, which means that the deviation was caused by chance and not by treatment.

If during the design of an experiment, the investigator sets the significance level at 0.05, then he accepts the fact that he is running a 5% risk of rejecting a true null hypothesis. If he considers this risk too high, he may wish to use some other signficance level, such as 0.02, 0.01, or even 0.001.

4.3   Error of the Second Kind (Type II Error)

If an investigator accepts the null hypothesis when it is false, he has made an error of the second kind, or Type II error. How is this possible? The treatment may be effective, but *because of random sampling,* the sample mean $(\bar{x})$ does not deviate significantly from the mean of the sampling distribution specified by the null hypothesis. An example is shown in Figure 4.2. Assume that a sampling distribution specified by a null hypothesis has a mean (μ) of 50 and a standard deviation $(\sigma_{\bar{x}})$ of 2.0. A sample mean greater than 53.92

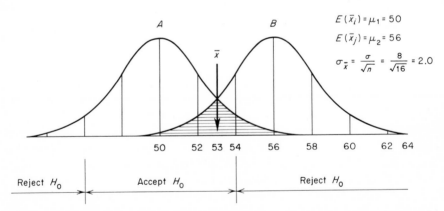

Figure 4.2 Two different sampling distributions of sample means. Distribution A is specified by the null hypothesis. The sample mean of $\bar{x} = 53$ is a member of distribution B, but does not deviate significantly from $\mu = 50$.

(rounded off to 54), or less than 46.08 (rounded off to 46) would lead to the rejection of the null hypothesis (using the 0.05 level of significance). The values 46.08 and 53.92 are derived from the expression $\mu \pm 1.96\ \sigma_{\bar{x}}$. If the treatment were to increase the performance of each individual by 6 units, the sample mean ($\bar{x}$) would be an unbiased estimate of 56, *not* 50. If $\bar{x} = 53.0$, the P value associated with the null hypothesis is between 0.20 and 0.10 (Table II).

$$c = \frac{\bar{x} - \mu}{\sigma_{\bar{x}}} = \frac{53 - 50}{2} = \frac{3}{2} = 1.5$$

$$0.20 > P > 0.10$$

The null hypothesis would be accepted since P is greater than 0.05. The sample mean does not deviate significantly from $\mu = 50$, and likewise it does not deviate significantly from $\mu = 56$.

$$c = \frac{\bar{x} - \mu}{\sigma_{\bar{x}}} = \frac{53 - 56}{2} = \frac{-3}{2} = -1.5$$

$$0.20 > P > 0.10$$

Since the treatment is actually effective, an error of the second kind is made by accepting the null hypothesis.

A Type II error is made whenever a sample mean is an unbiased estimate of a mean other than the mean of the population specified by the null hypothesis, and the null hypothesis is accepted. Hypotheses are never completely proven or disproven by a test of significance. Hypotheses are only rejected or accepted, with one of four consequences being possible:

1. A true hypothesis will be accepted.
2. A false hypothesis will be rejected.
3. A true hypothesis will be rejected (Type I error).
4. A false hypothesis will be accepted (Type II error).

4.4 Choice of Significance Level

When an investigator designs an experiment, what level of significance should he choose? If he chooses the 0.05 level, he will reject true hypotheses 5% of the time. If he chooses the 0.01 level, this type of error will only be made 1% of the time. However, decreasing the probability of a Type I error increases the probability of a Type II error. The problem then becomes, which is worse; an error of the first kind or an error of the second kind? The decision is left to the investigator. The 0.05 level of significance is usually employed as a compromise by the majority of investigators.

4.5   Efficiency of a Test of Significance

An efficient test is one that enables an investigator to make few Type II errors. Efficiency can be expressed numerically:

$$\text{Efficiency} = 1 - \text{Probability of a Type II error.}$$

The efficiency is 0.80, for example, if the probability of accepting a false hypothesis is 0.20. In a practical situation the probability of a Type II error *is never known*. However, when a sample is taken from a single population, the probability of this type of error occurring is influenced by (1) sample size, and (2) the magnitude of the treatment effect. These relationships can be shown with examples.

Situation 1

The population specified by a null hypothesis has a mean of 50 and a variance of 64. The treatment effect is + 6 units. The mean of the population from which the sample is taken is 56. A sample size of 64 is decided upon.

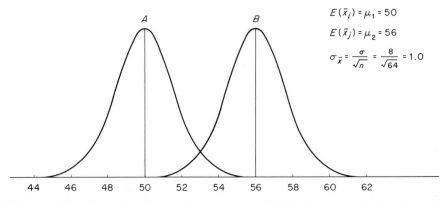

$$E(\bar{x}_i) = \mu_1 = 50$$
$$E(\bar{x}_j) = \mu_2 = 56$$
$$\sigma_{\bar{x}} = \frac{\sigma}{\sqrt{n}} = \frac{8}{\sqrt{64}} = 1.0$$

Figure 4.3 Sampling distribution of means. Distribution A is specified by the null hypothesis. The sample mean $(\bar{x})$ is a member of distribution B.

Figure 4.3 illustrates the two sampling distributions: Distribution A is the one specified by the null hypothesis. The sample mean belongs to Distribution B. Since the curves barely overlap, the chance of a Type II error is near zero. When n is 16, as illustrated in Figure 4.2., the curves overlap. This shows that for a given treatment effect, efficiency increases with an increased sample size.

Situation 2

The same situation prevails here as in Situation 1, except that the treatment effect is +12 units, and the sample size is 16. The sampling distributions are represented in Figure 4.4. The sampling distribution specified by the null hypothesis and the true sampling distribution barely overlap. The probability is low that a Type II error would be committed. Comparing Figure 4.4 with Figure 4.2 shows that for a given sample size, efficiency increases with an increased treatment effect.

A large sample is needed to reject the hypothesis when the treatment effect is small.

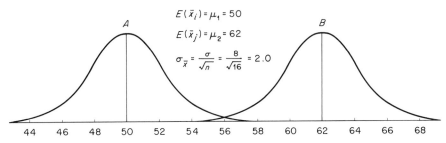

Figure 4.4 Sampling distribution of means. Distribution A is specified by the null hypothesis. The sample mean $(\bar{x})$ is a member of distribution B.

4.6 Confidence Limits for a Population Mean

When a sample mean is shown to deviate significantly from the mean of a population specified by the null hypothesis, the question becomes: "What is the numerical value of the population mean that the sample mean is an unbiased estimate of?" Even though this population mean cannot be specified accurately, can certain limits be set up that are likely to include it? The setting of such limits, known as confidence limits, is an important part of statistical methods. The estimation of parameters and the setting of confidence limits, along with tests of significance, constitute that part of statistical methods known as *statistical inference*.

If a sampling distribution of means has a mean (μ) of 50 and a standard deviation $(\sigma_{\bar{x}})$ of 2.0, 68.26% of all sample means will have values between 48 and 52, or $\mu \pm 1\sigma_{\bar{x}}$. The probability that a given sample mean will have a value between 48 and 52 is 0.6826. The probability that it will not is 0.3174. Now, if a sample mean has a value between 48 and 52, and it is decreased and increased by 2 (i.e., $1\sigma_{\bar{x}}$), the range set apart by the lower limit (L_1) and upper limit (L_2) will include 50. For example, if $\bar{x} = 49$, the limits become:

$$L_1 = \bar{x} - 1\sigma_{\bar{x}} = 49 - 2 = 47$$

$$L_2 = \bar{x} + 1\sigma_{\bar{x}} = 49 + 2 = 51$$

If $\bar{x}$ does not have a value between 48 and 52, the limits will not include μ. The decision as to whether or not the limits will include μ depends, then, on whether or not $\bar{x}$ lies between $\mu \pm 1\sigma_{\bar{x}}$. The following probability statement can be made: The probability that L_1 and L_2 will include μ is 0.6826. These limits are known as the 68.26% confidence limits.

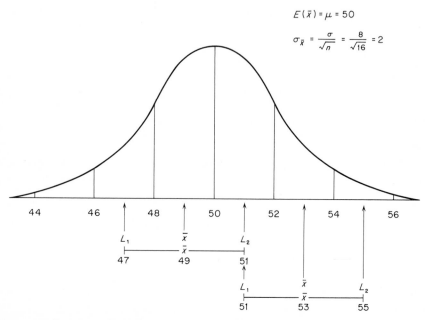

Figure 4.5 Sampling distribution of means. The limits set apart by $\bar{x} \pm 1\sigma_{\bar{x}}$ will include μ if $\bar{x}$ lies between $\mu \pm 1\sigma_{\bar{x}}$.

From Table II (table of c) it can be determined that 95% of all sample means will lie between $\mu \pm 1.96\ \sigma_{\bar{x}}$, and 99% will lie between $\mu \pm 2.58\ \sigma_{\bar{x}}$. Following the same reasoning as above, the 95% confidence limits are given by $\bar{x} \pm 1.96\ \sigma_{\bar{x}}$, and the 99% confidence limits by $\bar{x} \pm 2.58\ \sigma_{\bar{x}}$.

The concept of confidence limits can now be utilized in the solution of a practical problem. It was determined in the above example of a test of significance that the sample mean, $\bar{x} = 26.9$, deviates significantly from the population mean, $\mu = 24.5$. "What population mean is the observed sample mean an unbiased estimate of?" Since the variance of the population is known to be 16, and the sample size is 25, the standard error is 0.8, i.e.,

$$\sigma_{\bar{x}} = \sqrt{\frac{\sigma^2}{n}} = \sqrt{\frac{16}{25}} = 0.8$$

68.26% Confidence Limits

$$L_1 = \bar{x} - 1\sigma_{\bar{x}} = 26.9 - 0.8 = 26.1$$
$$L_2 = \bar{x} + 1\sigma_{\bar{x}} = 26.9 + 0.8 = 27.7$$

The probability is 0.6826 that 26.1 and 27.7 include the population mean.

95% Confidence Limits

$$L_1 = \bar{x} - 1.96\sigma_{\bar{x}} = 26.9 - (1.96)(0.8) = 25.33$$

$$L_2 = \bar{x} + 1.96\sigma_{\bar{x}} = 26.9 + (1.96)(0.8) = 28.47$$

The probability is 0.95 that 25.33 and 28.47 include the population mean.

99% Confidence Limits

$$L_1 = \bar{x} - 2.58\sigma_{\bar{x}} = 26.9 - (2.58)(0.8) = 24.84$$

$$L_2 = \bar{x} + 2.58\sigma_{\bar{x}} = 26.9 + (2.58)(0.8) = 28.96$$

The probability is 0.99 that 24.84 and 28.96 include the population mean.

The confidence limits probability statement can be given in another form. An investigator might say, "I am 95% confident that L_1 and L_2 will include the population mean."

Confidence limits serve as a comparative measure of reliability; the smaller the range, the more reliable the statistic is as an estimate of the parameter. For example, if the 95% confidence limits from one study range from 46 to 54, while from another study they extend from 48.5 to 49.1, the statistic from the latter study would be a more reliable estimate of the parameter. Confidence limits serve as a test of reliability, for they show how reliable the statistic is as an estimate of the parameter,

A test of reliability and a test of significance are the reverse of each other. In a test of significance, an investigator begins with a population mean (μ) and makes implications about a sample mean ($\bar{x}$). That is, a sample mean deviates non-significantly, significantly, or highly significantly from μ. In a test of reliability, an investigator begins with a sample mean and makes implications about μ. That is, the probability is 0.95, for example, that the limits $\bar{x} \pm 1.96\sigma_{\bar{x}}$ will include μ.

The relationship between a test of reliability and a test of significance can be shown algebraically. A c test is given by:

$$\pm c = \frac{\bar{x} - \mu}{\sigma_{\bar{x}}}$$

Solving for μ gives:

$$\mu = \bar{x} \pm c\sigma_{\bar{x}}$$

Setting c equal to 1, 1.96, and 2.58 gives the 68.26%, 95%, and 99% confidence limits, respectively. For a given population variance, the range of the confidence limits will decrease with an increase in sample size.

4.7 One-Tailed Test of Significance

The above example of a test of significance was a two-tailed test. The null hypothesis was $H_0: \mu = 24.5$. The alternative hypothesis stated that the treatment will increase *or* decrease performance ($H_1: \mu \neq 24.5$). What if the alternative hypothesis had been made more specific and stated that (1) the treatment increases performance, or (2) that it decreases performance? This implies that the investigator knows something about the treatment. For example, he may consider adding additional vitamins to a diet. The amount added may or may not improve the diet, *but he knows that it will not harm it*. Many such situations arise in research. The test of significance for this situation is known as a one-tailed test. For the vitamin example, the hypotheses would become:

H_0: treatment is ineffective

H_1: treatment increases performance

A one-tailed test may be illustrated with the data used in the two-tailed test. The hypotheses are expressed as:

$$H_0: \mu = 24.5$$
$$H_1: \mu > 24.5$$

The c value will be the same as before:

$$c = \frac{\bar{x} - \mu}{\sigma_{\bar{x}}} = \frac{26.9 - 24.5}{0.8} = \frac{2.4}{0.8} = 3.0$$

The P value of interest for a given c value is different in the two-tailed and one-tailed tests. Since μ cannot be less than the mean of the population specified by the null hypothesis, the interest centers only on plus deviations. The sample mean ($\bar{x}$) may be smaller than $\mu = 24.5$, but this is because of chance variation and not because of the effect of the treatment. If the null hypothesis is true, 50% of the sample means would be smaller than 24.5. The P value of interest in this one-tailed test is the probability of obtaining the observed plus deviation or larger plus deviation, on the basis of the null hypothesis.

The proportionate area under the normal curve right of 26.9 is 0.0013 (see Table I).

$$P = \frac{\text{Proportionate area right of sample mean}}{\text{Total area}} = \frac{0.0013}{1} = 0.0013$$

The null hypothesis is rejected on the basis of the 0.05 significance level. For the two-tailed test, the P value was 0.0026. This shows that a one-tailed test is more efficient than a two-tailed test because it leads to a smaller probability value.

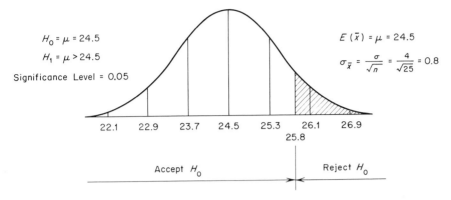

$H_0 = \mu = 24.5$

$H_1 = \mu > 24.5$

Significance Level = 0.05

$E(\bar{x}) = \mu = 24.5$

$\sigma_{\bar{x}} = \dfrac{\sigma}{\sqrt{n}} = \dfrac{4}{\sqrt{25}} = 0.8$

22.1   22.9   23.7   24.5   25.3   26.1   26.9

25.8

Accept H_0 Reject H_0

Figure 4.6 One-tailed significance test. The hypothesis is rejected when a sample mean is at least 1.64 standard deviations right of 24.5. Rejection region is right of $24.5 + 1.64(0.8) = 25.8$.

When Table II (table of c) is used in a one-tailed test, the 0.10 level in the table becomes the 0.05 level, and the 0.02 level is the 0.01 level. For a significance level of 0.05, a sample mean 1.64 or more standard deviations away from the sampling distribution mean will cause the hypothesis to be rejected. This is illustrated in Figure 4.6. For a two-tailed test, c has to be at least 1.96 before the hypothesis is rejected. If a calculated c value were 1.75, the rejection or acceptance of the null hypothesis would depend on the nature of the alternative hypothesis. The choice as to whether a two-tailed or one-tailed test should be carried out depends on the nature of the alternative hypothesis, as outlined in Table 4.1. In general, a two-tailed test should be used unless an obvious reason exists justifying a one-tailed test.

If an alternative hypothesis states that the treatment is effective in in-

Table 4.1 Two-tailed and one-tailed test when the mean (μ) of the population specified the null hypothesis is 24.5.

Hypotheses	Type of Test
1. $H_0 : \mu = 24.5$ $H_1 : \mu \neq 24.5$	Two-tailed
2. $H_0 : \mu = 24.5$ $H_1 : \mu > 24.5$	One-tailed
3. $H_0 : \mu = 24.5$ $H_1 : \mu < 24.5$	One-tailed

creasing performance, but the sample mean is actually smaller than μ, the null hypothesis is immediately accepted and *no c value should be calculated*. An occasion may arise, however, when the acceptance of the null hypothesis is not satisfactory. For example, what if the mean of the sampling distribution specified by the null hypothesis is 50, H_1: $\mu > 50$, the standard error ($\sigma_{\bar{x}}$) is 2.0, and $\bar{x}$ is 30? Something is likely wrong with the design of the experiment or the alternative hypothesis.

4.8 Test of Significance When the Variance is Unknown

The variance of a population is seldom, if ever, known. Because of this, the methods of conducting a test of significance and setting confidence limits discussed above are unrealistic. A reasonable solution is to estimate the population variance. This leads to the concept of a true and estimated standard deviation of the sampling distribution of means.

$$\text{True Standard Error of the Mean} = \sigma_{\bar{x}} = \sqrt{\frac{\sigma^2}{n}} = \frac{\sigma}{\sqrt{n}}$$

$$\text{Estimated Standard Error of the Mean} = s_{\bar{x}} = \sqrt{\frac{s^2}{n}} = \frac{s}{\sqrt{n}}$$

As n becomes large, s^2 approaches the value of σ^2, and therefore the estimated standard error approaches the value of the true standard error. Consequently, when n is very large, the estimated standard error may be used justifiably in place of the true standard error in a test of significance or in the setting of confidence limits. But the basic problem becomes, "What inference can be made if the sample size is small?" Under this situation, $s_{\bar{x}}$ may differ widely from $\sigma_{\bar{x}}$. It would not be suitable to evaluate the significance of an observed deviation when the measurement used as a standard (i.e., the standard deviation of the sampling distribution) may be in error. This was an insurmountable problem at the beginning of the present century. It was finally solved in 1908 by W.S. Gosset (1876–1937), a research chemist employed by the Guinness Brewery in Ireland. Gosset received statistical training in England and pursued the small-sample problem. He derived the important equation for the "sampling distribution of t." Gosset wrote under the pen name of "Student."

The t distribution is best appreciated by considering first the c distribution. From a normal population with a known mean and variance, a sampling distribution of sample means may be imagined. If one sample mean were placed in the formula,

$$c = \frac{\bar{x} - \mu}{\sigma_{\bar{x}}}$$

a c value would be obtained. If this were repeated for each of the means making up the sampling distribution, the resultant would be a sampling distribution of c values. The sign of each c value would depend on whether $\bar{x}$ is larger or smaller than μ.

The sampling distribution of c values is normal with a mean of zero and a standard deviation of 1.

$$\text{Mean of } c \text{ values} = E(c) = E\left[\frac{\bar{x} - \mu}{\sigma_{\bar{x}}}\right] = \frac{1}{\sigma_{\bar{x}}}E(\bar{x} - \mu) = 0$$

$$\text{Variance of } c \text{ values} = \sigma_c^2 = E(c - 0)^2 = E(c)^2$$

$$= E\left[\frac{\bar{x}_i - \mu}{\sigma_{\bar{x}}}\right]^2 = \frac{1}{\sigma_{\bar{x}}^2}E(\bar{x}_i - \mu)^2$$

$$= \frac{1}{\sigma_{\bar{x}}^2} \cdot \sigma_{\bar{x}}^2 = 1$$

$$\text{Standard deviation of } c \text{ values} = \sqrt{1} = 1$$

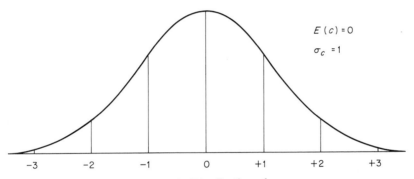

Figure 4.7 Distribution of c.

The properties of the distribution of c (see Figure 4.7) are given in Tables I and II, i.e., 68.26% of all c values lie between -1 and $+1$; 95% lie between -1.96 and $+1.96$; and 99% lie between -2.58 and $+2.58$.

An investigator may state that the sampling distribution specified by the null hypothesis, when the population variance is known, is the distribution of c values instead of the sampling distribution of means. If so, the probability value of interest is the probability of obtaining the observed c value, or greater c value, on the basis of the null hypothesis. For a two-tailed test, plus and minus c values are of interest, but for a one-tailed test only plus or minus values are considered.

Instead of a c value, a t value may be computed:

$$t = \frac{\bar{x} - \mu}{\sqrt{\dfrac{s^2}{n}}} = \frac{\bar{x} - \mu}{s_{\bar{x}}}$$

A sampling distribution of t values may be imagined if the mean ($\bar{x}$) and variance (s^2) of a random sample are computed, inserted into the t formula, and the sampling and computational procedures repeated indefinitely. If n is very large, the sampling distribution of t values will approximate the sampling distribution of c values, because s^2 in each case will approach σ^2. As n becomes smaller, a greater divergence occurs between the two types of sampling distributions.

"Student" derived the formula demonstrating that the sampling distribution of t values is based on the number of degrees of freedom available for the estimation of the population variance. A t distribution has more items in the tail of the curve than the c distribution. As the number of degrees of freedom is decreased, the t distribution becomes even more leptokurtic.

For a given number of degrees of freedom, the probability of obtaining an observed plus or minus t value, or greater plus or minus t value, is given in Table III. The table is known as the t table. The number of degrees of freedom in the left column extends from 1 to ∞. For an infinite number of degrees of freedom, t values are equal to c values.

An example of a t test will now be given: A physiologist has a drug that he believes will decrease blood pressure in human beings. He wishes to determine the blood pressure of a sample of individuals before and after injection of the drug, and record the difference.

1. Null hypothesis: H_0: $\mu = 0$; Alternative hypothesis: H_1: $\mu > 0$.

The null hypothesis states that the drug is ineffective. The population specified by the null hypothesis consists of an indefinitely large number of measurements, which are differences. These measurements, which are plus, minus, and zero, have a mean of zero and an unknown variance. The sign is plus if the blood pressure is higher before administration of the drug than after. It is minus if the blood pressure is lower before treatment than after. A measurement of zero occurs if no change occurs in the blood pressure.

The alternative hypothesis states that the drug decreases blood pressure. This calls for a one-tailed test of significance. The sampling distribution specified by the null hypothesis is a t distribution with $n - 1$ degrees of freedom.

2. Significance level: 0.05.

The investigator selects 10 subjects and from each determines the difference X_i. The data are as follows:

$$\text{Sample mean} = \bar{x} = \frac{\sum_{1}^{n} X_i}{n} = \frac{235.9}{10} = 23.59$$

| Difference in blood pressure before and after administration of drug. ||
	X_i
	+22.5
	+17.3
	+26.1
	+20.2
	+19.0
	+29.9
	+30.6
	+21.2
	+26.3
	+22.8
$\sum\limits_{1}^{n} X_i$	235.9
$\sum\limits_{1}^{n} X_i^2$	5747.13

$$\text{Sample variance} = s^2 = \frac{\sum\limits_{1}^{n}(X_i - \bar{x})^2}{n-1} = \frac{\sum\limits_{1}^{n} X_i^2 - \frac{\left(\sum\limits_{1}^{n} X_i\right)^2}{n}}{n-1}$$

$$= \frac{5747.13 - \frac{(235.9)^2}{10}}{9}$$

$$= \frac{182}{9} = 20.25$$

$$\text{Estimated standard error} = s_{\bar{x}} = \sqrt{\frac{s^2}{n}}$$

$$= \sqrt{\frac{20.25}{10}} = 1.423$$

3. Calculate the P value associated with the null hypothesis.

The probability value of interest is the probability of obtaining the observed $+t$ value or greater $+t$ value on the basis of the null hypothesis, for $n - 1 = 10 - 1 = 9$ degrees of freedom.

$$t = \frac{\bar{x} - \mu}{s_{\bar{x}}} = \frac{+23.59}{1.423} = +16.58$$

The t table is entered with 9 degrees of freedom. The proportionate area under the leptokurtic curve right of $+16.58$, for 9 degrees of freedom is not given in the table, but it is less than 0.01. Therefore $P < 0.01$.

4. Reject or accept the null hypothesis.

The null hypothesis is rejected because of the small P value. Since the significance level is 0.05 and a one-tailed test is employed, a calculated t value as large or larger than $+1.83$ (t value at 0.10 level for 9 degrees of freedom) would cause the hypothesis to be rejected. If a two-tailed test had been used, a calculated t value as large or larger than $+2.26$ (t value at 0.05 level for 9 degrees of freedom) would bring about the rejection of the hypothesis.

4.9   Confidence Limits When the Population Variance Is Unknown

Since it was concluded above that the sample of measurements was not taken from the population of measurements specified by the null hypothesis, the next step is to set confidence limits for the mean of the population the sample was taken from. Since

$$\pm t = \frac{\bar{x} - \mu}{s_{\bar{x}}},$$

solving for μ gives: $\mu = \bar{x} \pm t s_{\bar{x}}$.

If the 95% confidence limits are to be calculated, the t value at the 0.05 level for $n - 1$ degrees of freedom is inserted into the formula. For 9 degrees of freedom this value is 2.26. The 95% confidence limits become:

$$L_1 = \bar{x} - t_{0.05}s_{\bar{x}} = 23.59 - 2.26(1.423) = 20.37$$

$$L_2 = \bar{x} + t_{0.05}s_{\bar{x}} = 23.59 + 2.26(1.423) = 26.81$$

The probability is 0.95 that the limits 20.37 and 26.81 will include μ. If the investigator wishes to calculate the 99% confidence limits, a t value of 3.25 is used in the formula, which is the t value at the 0.01 level for 9 degrees of freedom. Note that a P value of exactly 0.3174 is not given in Table III. This indicates that the 68.26% confidence limits cannot be directly calculated. If the investigator presents confidence limits based on $\bar{x} \pm s_{\bar{x}}$, he implies that he is "approximately two-thirds" confident that the limits will include μ.

In a publication, it is important to make clear which confidence limits are being employed. This is appropriately done by a short statement or by the use of symbols such as $\bar{x} \pm s_{\bar{x}}$ for the "two-thirds" confidence limits; $\bar{x} \pm t_{0.05}s_{\bar{x}}$ for the 95% confidence limits; and $\bar{x} \pm t_{0.01}s_{\bar{x}}$ for the 99% confidence limits.

The concept of confidence limits can be approached in a different manner. Sampling distributions of t are leptokurtic, unless the number of degrees of freedom is infinite. The mean of each sampling distribution of t is zero. From Table III, it can be determined, for example, that for 9 degrees of freedom, the probability is 0.95 that a calculated t value will fall within the limits -2.26 and $+2.26$. This implies that 2.5% of the area under this leptokurtic curve is left of -2.26 and 2.5% is right of $+2.26$.

The statement that the probability is 0.95 that t will be equal to or greater than -2.26 and equal to or less than $+2.26$ can be expressed as follows:

$$P[-2.26 \leq t \leq +2.26] = 0.95$$

For any number of degrees of freedom, the general expression becomes:

$$P[-t_{0.05} \leq t \leq +t_{0.05}] = 0.95$$

Since $t = (\bar{x} - \mu)/s_{\bar{x}}$, the expression can be rewritten

$$P\left[-t_{0.05} \leq \frac{\bar{x} - \mu}{s_{\bar{x}}} \leq +t_{0.05}\right] = 0.95$$

Multiplying through by $s_{\bar{x}}$ changes the inequality to

$$P[-t_{0.05}s_{\bar{x}} \leq \bar{x} - \mu \leq +t_{0.05}s_{\bar{x}}] = 0.95$$

Transposing $\bar{x}$ gives

$$P[-\bar{x} - t_{0.05}s_{\bar{x}} \leq -\mu \leq -\bar{x} + t_{0.05}s_{\bar{x}}] = 0.95$$

Multiplying through by -1 changes the signs and also the direction of the inequality:

$$P[\bar{x} + t_{0.05}s_{\bar{x}} \geq \mu \geq \bar{x} - t_{0.05}s_{\bar{x}}] = 0.95$$

This expression is equivalent to

$$P[L_2 \geq \mu \geq L_1] = 0.95$$

Substituting into this expression the values for L_1 and L_2 determined for the above blood-pressure problem gives

$$P[26.81 \geq \mu \geq 20.37] = 0.95$$

and reads that the probability is 0.95 that μ is equal to some value within the limits 20.37 and 26.81.

Problems

1. Assume that the mean of a normal population is 50 and the variance is 36. An investigator selected 16 individuals at random from this population and subjected each to a treatment. He knew that *if* the treatment had any effect at all it would decrease performance. He decided to use the 0.05 level of significance. The mean of the sample was 41.
(a) State the null hypothesis. What is the alternative hypothesis? (b) What value of c will cause the investigator to reject the null hypothesis? (c) Describe the sampling distribution of means specified by the null hypothesis? Give the mean and standard deviation of this sampling distribution. (d) Calculate the c value. On the basis of the observed c value, should the hypothesis be accepted or rejected? Is there a chance of a Type I or II error? Explain. (e) Give the 95% confidence limits for the mean of the population from which the sample was actually taken.

2. State in words the meaning of the expression: $P[-1.96 \leq c \leq +1.96] = 0.95$. Show how the 95% confidence limits for a population mean can be derived from this expression.

3. An investigator compared the yields of two different varieties of barley at 9 different experimental stations in different parts of the United States. A plot of each variety was grown at each of the stations. The number of bushels per plot was recorded. He wished to determine if there was any difference in yield for the two varieties. He decided to use the 0.05 level of significance. For each station the following measurement was taken: yield (bushels) of variety A minus yield (bushels) of variety B.
(a) State the null hypothesis and alternative hypothesis. What value of t will lead to rejection of the null hypothesis? (b) Describe the population specified by the null hypothesis. What is the mean of this population? Give the formulae for the mean and true standard deviation of the sampling distribution of means specified by the null hypothesis. Why is the true standard deviation of this sampling distribution unknown? Give the formula for the estimated standard deviation of the sampling distribution of means.
The sample consists of the following measurements:

$$+11 \quad +9 \quad +14 \quad +7 \quad -1 \quad +5 \quad +7 \quad +13 \quad +12$$

(c) Calculate $\bar{x}$ and s^2. (d) Calculate the t value. (e) Should the null hypothesis be accepted or rejected? Is there a chance of making a Type I or Type II error? Explain. (f) If you reject the null hypothesis, calculate the 95% confidence limits for the mean of the population from which the sample was taken.

4. Determine the 95% confidence limits for the population means estimated in problems 1, 5, 7, and 8 at the end of Chapter 2.

5. Defend the following statement: Treatment effects acting in an additive manner influence means but not variances.

6. Discuss experimental situations when an investigator might prefer to use a significance level of 0.01 rather than 0.05, and vice versa.

7. A normal population has a mean of 50 and a variance of 64. What is the probability that the mean of a sample based on 16 measurements will fall within the limits $\mu \pm 2.58 \, \sigma_{\bar{x}}$? If the mean of a random sample is decreased in value by $2.58 \, \sigma_{\bar{x}}$ units ($\bar{x} - 2.58 \, \sigma_{\bar{x}} = L_1$) and increased in value by $2.58 \, \sigma_{\bar{x}}$ units ($\bar{x} + 2.58 \, \sigma_{\bar{x}} = L_2$), what is the probability that L_1 and L_2 will include 50?

8. Discuss what factor determines whether a test of significance should be one-tailed or two-tailed. Which type has the higher probability of leading to the rejection of the null hypothesis? Why?

9. An article appearing in a journal stated that the average tail length of a given subspecies of mouse is 73 mm. A graduate student measured 20 museum specimens of this subspecies. The values are as follows:

71 83 76 83 77 79 80 84 78 69 80 77 75 83 79 81 79 78 79 72

(a) Test the hypothesis that the sample was taken from a population with a mean of 73. (Use the 0.05 level of signficance.) (b) Set the 95% confidence limits for the mean of the population the sample was taken from, assuming that the museum specimens constitute a random sample.

10. In a given population, the mean age of females giving birth to a child is 26.6 years. This value is based on a very large number of births and can be assumed to be a parameter. Twelve children were born with a chromosomal abnormality. The ages of the mothers were:

25 34 41 39 42 27 26 39 34 46 36 38

(a) Test the hypothesis that no maternal age effect exists for this disorder. (Use the 0.05 level of significance.) (b) Determine the 95% confidence limits for the mean of the population from which the sample was taken.

CHAPTER FIVE

Group Comparison Test

A common procedure in statistical methods is for an investigator to take a random sample from two different populations and then to compare the sample means, $\bar{x}_1$, and $\bar{x}_2$. If $\mu_1 = \mu_2$, then both statistics are estimates of the same parameter, and any difference between them is due to errors of random sampling. It becomes a question of determining how large a difference will be allowed between $\bar{x}_1$ and $\bar{x}_2$ before it becomes necessary to conclude that they are estimates of different parameters.

If the measurements in one sample are independent of those in the other, the appropriate test is known as a *group comparison test*. There are two major assumptions:

(1) Both populations are distributed normally.

(2) The variances of the populations are equal, i.e., $\sigma_1^2 = \sigma_2^2$.

In a group comparison test, the interest centers on the difference $\bar{x}_1 - \bar{x}_2$. This difference will be zero or will have a plus or minus sign, depending on whether $\bar{x}_1$ is equal to, larger, or smaller than $\bar{x}_2$. Even though an investigator only observes one difference, he may ask himself, "What are the possible differences that might have occurred?" A theoretical sampling distribution can be imagined where each possible difference is plotted against frequency. This sampling distribution is normal in form and is called a sampling distribution of differences between sample means.

Mean of the sampling distribution $= E(\bar{x}_i - \bar{x}_j) = E(\bar{x}_i) - E(\bar{x})_j = \mu_1 - \mu_2$

The variance of the sampling distribution comes directly from the formula for the second moment about the mean: $E(\text{variable} - \text{mean})^2$, where the variable is $(\bar{x}_j - \bar{x}_j)$ and the mean is $(\mu_1 - \mu_2)$.

Variance of the sampling distribution

$$= E[(\bar{x}_i - \bar{x}_j) - (\mu_1 - \mu_2)]^2$$
$$= E[\bar{x}_i - \bar{x}_j - \mu_1 + \mu_2]^2$$
$$= E[(\bar{x}_i - \mu_1) - (\bar{x}_j - \mu_2)]^2$$
$$= E[(\bar{x}_i - \mu_1)^2 + (\bar{x}_j - \mu_2)^2 - 2(\bar{x}_i - \mu_1)(\bar{x}_j - \mu_2)]$$
$$= E(\bar{x}_i - \mu_1)^2 + E(\bar{x}_j - \mu_2)^2$$
$$= \frac{\sigma_1^2}{n_1} + \frac{\sigma_2^2}{n_2}$$

The crossproduct encountered in the above derivation equals zero since $(\bar{x}_i - \mu_1)$ and $(\bar{x}_j - \mu_2)$ are independent variables and therefore

$$2E(\bar{x}_i - \mu_1)(\bar{x}_j - \mu_2) = 2E(\bar{x}_i - \mu_1)E(\bar{x}_j - \mu_2) = 0$$

In the formula, σ_1^2 and σ_2^2 are the variances of populations 1 and 2, respectively, and n_1 and n_2 represent the sizes of the samples taken from the two populations. The sample sizes do not have to be equal.

The square root of the above formula is the standard deviation of the sampling distribution of differences between sample means. It is often referred to as the standard error of the difference, and symbolized by $\sigma_{\bar{x}_i-\bar{x}_j}$ or $\sigma_{\bar{x}_1-\bar{x}_2}$. The latter symbol is read "the standard deviation of the possible differences between $\bar{x}_1$ and $\bar{x}_2$." Note that $\bar{x}_1$ may take any $\bar{x}_i$ value and similarly, $\bar{x}_2$ may take any $\bar{x}_j$ value.

True standard error of the difference $= \sigma_{\bar{x}_1-\bar{x}_2} = \sqrt{\dfrac{\sigma_1^2}{n_1} + \dfrac{\sigma_2^2}{n_2}}$

The sampling distribution can now be defined completely since its mean and standard deviation are known.

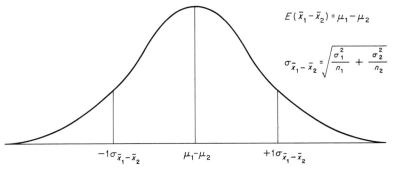

Figure 5.1 Sampling distribution of differences between sample means.

For the null hypothesis $\mu_1 = \mu_2$, a c value could be calculated by use of the formula:

$$c = \frac{\text{(Observation)} - \text{(Mean of the sampling distribution)}}{\text{True standard error}}$$

$$= \frac{(\bar{x}_1 - \bar{x}_2) - (\mu_1 - \mu_2)}{\sqrt{\dfrac{\sigma_1^2}{n_1} + \dfrac{\sigma_2^2}{n_2}}} = \frac{\bar{x}_1 - \bar{x}_2}{\sqrt{\dfrac{\sigma_1^2}{n_1} + \dfrac{\sigma_2^2}{n_2}}}$$

The term $\mu_1 - \mu_2$ cancels out of the numerator, since by the null hypothesis $\mu_1 = \mu_2$; therefore, $\mu_1 - \mu_2 = 0$. Since treatments, acting in an additive way, affect means but not variances, and it is assumed that $\sigma_1^2 = \sigma_2^2$, the formula for c can be changed to:

$$c = \frac{\bar{x}_1 - \bar{x}_2}{\sqrt{\sigma^2 \left(\dfrac{1}{n_1} + \dfrac{1}{n_2} \right)}}$$

The value of σ^2 can be estimated in three different ways:

(1) Variance of sample 1 with $n_1 - 1$ degrees of freedom.
(2) Variance of sample 2 with $n_2 - 1$ degrees of freedom.
(3) Pooled variance with $(n_1 - 1) + (n_2 - 1)$ degrees of freedom.

The third method gives an estimate based on the most degrees of freedom and therefore is the preferred method. The pooled variance is symbolized by s_p^2.

If $n_1 = n_2$, the pooled variance can be calculated as follows:

$$\text{Pooled variance} = s_p^2 = \frac{s_1^2 + s_2^2}{2}$$

If $n_1 \neq n_2$, pooled variance is obtained by adding the sum of squares and dividing by the sum of the degrees of freedom.

$$\text{General formula for pooled variance} = s_p^2 = \frac{\sum_1^n (X_i - \bar{x}_1)^2 + \sum_1^n (X_j - \bar{x}_2)^2}{(n_1 - 1) + (n_2 - 1)}$$

Working formula for pooled variance $= s_p^2$

$$= \frac{\left[\sum_1^n X_i^2 - \dfrac{\left(\sum_1^n X_i \right)^2}{n} \right] + \left[\sum_1^n X_j^2 - \dfrac{\left(\sum_1^n X_j \right)^2}{n} \right]}{(n_1 - 1) + (n_2 - 1)}$$

The estimated standard error of the difference is given by:

$$s_{\bar{x}_1 - \bar{x}_2} = \sqrt{s_p^2 \left(\frac{1}{n_1} + \frac{1}{n_2} \right)}$$

The t test becomes:

$$t = \frac{\bar{x}_1 - \bar{x}_2}{\sqrt{s_p{}^2\left(\dfrac{1}{n_1} + \dfrac{1}{n_2}\right)}}$$

Degrees of freedom $= (n_1 - 1) + (n_2 - 1)$

5.1 Example of a Group Comparison Test

An investigator wishes to compare the effects of two different diets on the growth of rats. The null and alternative hypotheses are:

$$H_0: \mu_1 = \mu_2$$

$$H_1: \mu_1 \neq \mu_2$$

Two different populations are specified by the null hypothesis. It is assumed that $\sigma_1{}^2 = \sigma_2{}^2$. The sampling distribution used in the test of significance is a t distribution for $(n_1 - 1) + (n_2 - 1)$ degrees of freedom. The alternative hypothesis calls for a two-tailed t test. The investigator decided upon the 0.05 significance level, giving him a 5% risk for a Type I error.

The investigator had at his disposal 50 newly weaned rats. He randomly divided the rats into equal groups. One group is fed diet 1 and the other diet 2. During the course of the experiment several rats died in each group, giving sample sizes of:

$$n_1 = 21 \text{ (Diet 1)}$$

$$n_2 = 22 \text{ (Diet 2)}$$

After a specified length of time, the investigator measured the weight of each rat in grams. The data are shown in the table on the following page.

The pooled variance is calculated by the use of the working formula:

$$s_p{}^2 = \frac{\left[68{,}709.88 - \dfrac{(1{,}200.6)^2}{21}\right] + \left[68{,}404.50 - \dfrac{(1{,}216.8)^2}{22}\right]}{(21 - 1) \quad + \quad (22 - 1)}$$

$$= \frac{69.86 + 104.4}{41} = 4.25$$

Now that an estimate of σ^2 is available, a t value can be calculated.

$$t = \frac{\bar{x}_1 - \bar{x}_2}{s_{\bar{x}_1 - \bar{x}_2}} = \frac{\bar{x}_1 - \bar{x}_2}{\sqrt{s_p{}^2\left(\dfrac{1}{n_1} + \dfrac{1}{n_2}\right)}} = \frac{57.17 - 55.31}{\sqrt{4.25\left(\dfrac{1}{21} + \dfrac{1}{22}\right)}} = \frac{+1.86}{0.6289}$$

$$= +2.96$$

$$\text{D.F.} = (n_1 - 1) + (n_2 - 1) = (21 - 1) + (22 - 1) = 41 \quad P < 0.01$$

	Diet 1		Diet 2	
	58.5	56.2	55.4	54.4
	57.2	59.4	57.2	54.3
	58.4	60.1	49.8	53.1
	57.9	58.3	51.5	56.2
	56.4	58.2	53.6	58.5
	59.8	56.8	57.9	57.2
	54.2	57.7	55.6	56.5
	53.7	58.2	56.4	57.9
	58.1	56.5	53.4	56.3
	53.4	56.0	52.7	55.7
	55.6		56.0	57.2
$\sum_1^n X_i$	1,200.6		1,216.8	
$\sum_1^n X_i^2$	68,709.88		67,404.50	
$\bar{x}$	57.17		55.31	

For 41 degrees of freedom, a t value of 2.96 is highly significant. The null hypothesis is rejected. The results indicate that diet 1 is the preferred diet. Because the null hypothesis is rejected, a Type I error is possible.

If the alternative hypothesis had been given as $\mu_1 < \mu_2$ or $\mu_1 > \mu_2$, a one-tailed test would have been the proper test. In this case the 0.10 level in the t table would be used as the 0.05 level; hence the null hypothesis would have been rejected if t were greater than 1.68. This value comes from the t table for 41 degrees of freedom.

5.2   Confidence Limits for the Difference Between Population Means

From this experiment it was concluded that $\mu_1 \neq \mu_2$. It is now of interest to set confidence limits for the true difference existing between μ_1 and μ_2. From the formula:

$$\pm t = \frac{(\bar{x}_1 - \bar{x}_2) - (\mu_1 - \mu_2)}{\sqrt{s_p^2 \left(\frac{1}{n_1} + \frac{1}{n_2}\right)}}$$

solving for $\mu_1 - \mu_2$ gives:

$$\mu_1 - \mu_2 = (\bar{x}_1 - \bar{x}_2) \pm t\sqrt{s_p^2\left(\frac{1}{n_1} + \frac{1}{n_2}\right)}$$

The 95% confidence limits become:

$$L_1 = (\bar{x}_1 - \bar{x}_2) - t_{0.05}s_{\bar{x}_1 - \bar{x}_2} = 1.86 - (2.02)(0.6289) = 0.59$$

$$L_2 = (\bar{x}_1 - \bar{x}_2) + t_{0.05}s_{\bar{x}_1 - \bar{x}_2} = 1.86 + (2.02)(0.6289) = 3.13$$

The t value of 2.02 comes from the t table at the 0.05 level for $(n_1 - 1) + (n_2 - 1) = 41$ degrees of freedom.

The investigator is 95% confident that the true difference between μ_1 and μ_2 lies somewhere between 0.59 and 3.13.

5.3 Confidence Limits for Population Means

Since the pooled variance is a better estimate of the population variance than either of the two sample variances taken alone, it is proper to use the pooled variance in setting confidence limits for the individual population means encountered in a group comparison test. The formula for the 95% confidence limits is:

$$\mu = \bar{x} \pm t_{0.05}\sqrt{\frac{s_p^2}{n_1}}$$

where $t_{0.05}$ is the t value at the 0.05 level for $(n_1 - 1) + (n_2 - 1)$ degrees of freedom.

95% Confidence Limits for μ_1

$$L_1 = 57.17 - 2.02\sqrt{\frac{4.25}{21}} = 56.26$$

$$L_2 = 57.17 + 2.02\sqrt{\frac{4.25}{21}} = 58.08$$

95% Confidence Limits for μ_2

$$L_1 = 55.31 - 2.02\sqrt{\frac{4.25}{22}} = 54.42$$

$$L_2 = 55.31 + 2.02\sqrt{\frac{4.25}{22}} = 56.20$$

Problems

1. (a) Derive the formulae for the mean and true standard deviation of the sampling distribution of differences between sample means encountered in the group comparison

test. State all the assumptions for both of the derivations. (b) If the population variance were known, give the equation for testing the null hypothesis: $\mu_1 = \mu_2$. (c) Since it is assumed that $\sigma_1^2 = \sigma_2^2$, show how the population variance can be estimated. How many degrees of freedom are associated with this estimate? Show how this estimate is utilized in testing the null hypothesis $\mu_1 = \mu_2$.

2. An investigator obtained the means of two samples selected at random from two normally distributed populations. In each case the sample size was $n = 20$. The null and alternative hypotheses were as follows:

$$H_0: \mu_1 = \mu_2$$
$$H_1: \mu_1 > \mu_2$$

He decided to use the 0.01 level of significance. The sample means were:

$$\bar{x}_1 = 20.1$$
$$\bar{x}_2 = 21.5$$

Based on these observations, he accepted the null hypothesis. Why?

3. By using a paper-chromotography technique, a geneticist studied the concentration of sepiapteridines in the eyes of two different strains of *Drosophila melanogaster*. Heads of males were removed and squashed on paper. The concentration was determined quantitatively by a fluorometric method. The results are as follows:

Strain A: 40.1 46.8 48.4 39.6 44.5 46.4 41.0 40.0 41.2 46.2

Strain B: 55.8 59.1 64.2 61.9 60.4 63.2 57.8 59.1 60.0 64.3

The null and alternative hypotheses were $H_0: \mu_1 = \mu_2$ and $H_1: \mu_1 \neq \mu_2$. The geneticist decided to use the 0.05 level of significance.

(a) Calculate the t value. Should the hypothesis be accepted or rejected? Why? (b) Determine the 95% confidence limits for the true difference between μ_1 and μ_2. (c) Determine the 95% confidence limits for μ_1 and μ_2.

4. A mammalogy graduate student compared the weights of adult male wolves from two different geographical locations. The values (lbs.) are as follows:

Sample 1: 93.6 85.6 81.7 85.9 90.3 87.3 82.6 88.3

Sample 2: 83.2 81.4 79.3 81.5 75.2 86.9 81.0 84.2 78.7 82.2

Test the null hypothesis that $\mu_1 = \mu_2$. (Use the 0.05 level of significance.) What would be the most probable alternative hypothesis?

5. The serum urate level (mg./100 ml.) was compared in 10 male gout patients and 10 normal (non-gout) males.

Gout males	Normal males
6.2	4.5
12.0	4.1
8.1	6.2
8.9	4.3
8.3	4.6
9.4	3.8
7.4	2.2
11.1	6.8
7.9	4.6
9.2	4.2

(a) Test the null hypothesis that gout patients and normal males have the same serum urate levels. ($H_0: \mu_1 = \mu_2$; $H_1: \mu_1 > \mu_2$) Use the 0.05 level of significance. (b) Determine the 95% confidence limits for μ_1, μ_2 and $\mu_1 - \mu_2$.

6. Serum enzyme studies were carried out on five patients with progressive muscular dystrophy and five normal controls. The activity levels for phosphohexoisomerase were as follows:

Controls	Patients
5.0	12.9
4.8	10.0
5.9	15.5
6.5	11.4
4.1	12.9

(a) Test the null hypothesis that dystrophic and normal individuals have the same enzyme activity level. ($H_0: \mu_1 = \mu_2$; $H_1: \mu_1 \neq \mu_2$) Use the 0.05 level of significance. (b) Determine the 99% confidence limits for μ_1, μ_2 and $\mu_1 - \mu_2$.

7. Phosphohexoisomerase activity was determined for 10 normal females and 10 normal males.

Females	Males
5.4	5.9
5.1	6.2
6.1	4.8
4.9	6.1
4.8	5.2
5.4	4.6
6.4	4.5
4.2	5.4
5.4	6.1
5.9	4.1

Test the hypothesis that males and females have the same enzyme activity level. ($H_0: \mu_1 = \mu_2$; $H_1: \mu_1 \neq \mu_2$) Use the 0.05 level of significance.

8. Two new types of rations were fed to pigs.
(a) Using the 0.05 level significance, test the hypothesis that no difference exists between the diets in regard to effect on gain in weight. ($H_0: \mu_1 = \mu_2$; $H_1: \mu_i \neq \mu_2$).
(b) Set the 95% confidence limits for μ_1 and μ_2.

Ration 1	Ration 2
34	36
36	31
28	24
24	37
29	24
31	31
36	37

Pairing Design Test

The pairing design test is used to determine the significance of the difference between two sample means when positive correlation exists between paired measurements in the two samples. This is in contrast to the group comparison test which assumes that the measurements are independent. The pairing design test is also known as the individual comparison test.

If the lengths of the right and left arms were determined for a sample of individuals for the purpose of comparing sample means, the data could be compiled as follows:

Individual	Right Arm	Left Arm
1	X_1	X_1
2	X_2	X_2
3	X_3	X_3
.	.	.
.	.	.
n	X_n	X_n
	$\bar{x}_1$	$\bar{x}_2$

The sample means should be compared by use of the pairing design test, since a close similarity exists between the length of the right and left arm of any one individual. In general, if an individual has a long right arm, his left arm is also long. If his right arm is short, his left arm is short. Consequently, large measurements in the first sample tend to be paired with large measurements in the second sample; small measurements in the first sample tend to be paired with small measurements in the second sample. This is known as positive correlation.

When an investigator wishes to test the significance of two sample means and he knows that positive correlation exists between the paired measurements in the two samples, the pairing design test should be used in preference to the group comparison test, since the pairing design test is more efficient. If the paired measurements in the two samples are independent, the group comparison test is more efficient than the pairing design test. The more efficient test has a higher probability of showing that a difference exists between μ_1 and μ_2 when such is actually the case. There is less chance of making a Type II error (i.e., accepting a false hypothesis) if the more efficient test is being employed.

Insight as to whether positive correlation is present can often be obtained by examining the two samples. The method is to observe large and small values in sample 1 and compare them with the paired values in sample 2. If a large value in sample 1 tends to be paired with a large value in sample 2, and a small value in sample 1 tends to be paired with a small value in sample 2, then positive correlation is likely present. The nature of the investigation will, in almost all cases, dictate whether the pairing design or group comparison test should be used. In many investigations, the pairing of measurements is not reasonable and the group comparison test is the more logical test. In the

Table 6.1 Means and Variances of Population 1, Population 2, and the Population of Differences Encountered in the Pairing Design Test.

	Measurements in Population 1	Measurements in Population 2	Population of Differences
	X_1 X_2 X_3 $\cdot$ $\cdot$ $\cdot$ X_N	X_1 X_2 X_3 $\cdot$ $\cdot$ $\cdot$ X_N	d_1 d_2 d_3 $\cdot$ $\cdot$ $\cdot$ d_N
Mean	$\mu_1 = \dfrac{\sum\limits_{1}^{N} X_i}{N}$	$\mu_2 = \dfrac{\sum\limits_{1}^{N} X_j}{N}$	$\mu_d = \dfrac{\sum\limits_{1}^{N} d_i}{N} = \mu_1 - \mu_2$
Variance	$\sigma_1{}^2 = \dfrac{\sum\limits_{1}^{N} (X_i - \mu_1)^2}{N}$	$\sigma_2{}^2 = \dfrac{\sum\limits_{1}^{N} (X_j - \mu_2)^2}{N}$	$\sigma_d{}^2 = \dfrac{\sum\limits_{1}^{N} (d_i - \mu_d)^2}{N}$ $= \sigma_1{}^2 + \sigma_2{}^2 - 2\omega$

pairing design test, n_1 must equal n_2, which is not true for the group comparison test.

The theory behind a pairing design test will now be presented. The initial interest is in two different populations, each with a mean (μ_1 and μ_2) and a variance (σ_1^2 and σ_2^2). In a pairing design test, no assumption is made that $\sigma_1^2 = \sigma_2^2$. Paired measurements are taken from each population. The difference is obtained between these paired measurements. The question then becomes: "What differences might occur if this procedure were repeated for all measurements in the two populations?" The differences between the paired measurements constitute a third population. For example, population 1 could consist of blood-pressure readings "before" injection of a drug, and population 2 could consist of blood-pressure readings "after" injection of a drug. By determining the "before" and "after" readings for N individuals and the differences between these readings, a population of differences is created. It is assumed that this population of differences is distributed normally. This procedure is illustrated in Table 6.1.

6.1　Mean of the Population of Differences

The individual differences in the population of differences are represented by d_i. The mean (μ_d) of the population of differences is given as:

$$\mu_d = E(d_i) = \frac{\sum\limits_{1}^{N} d_i}{N}$$

Since $d_i = X_i - X_j$, the mean can also be expressed in the following way:

$$\mu_d = E(X_i - X_j) = E(X_i) - E(X_j) = \mu_1 - \mu_2$$

6.2　Variance of the Population of Differences

The variance of the population of differences is given by:

$$\sigma_d^2 = E(d_i - \mu_d)^2 = \frac{\sum\limits_{1}^{N} (d_i - \mu_d)^2}{N}$$

Yet, importantly, the variance can also be expressed in another form:

$$\sigma_d^2 = E[(X_i - X_j) - (\mu_1 - \mu_2)]^2 = E[X_i - X_j - \mu_1 + \mu_2]^2$$
$$= E[(X_i - \mu_1) - (X_j - \mu_2)]^2$$
$$= E[(X_i - \mu_1)^2 + (X_j - \mu_2)^2 - 2(X_i - \mu_1)(X_j - \mu_2)]$$
$$= E(X_i - \mu_1)^2 + E(X_j - \mu_2)^2 - 2E(X_i - \mu_1)(X_j - \mu_2)$$
$$= \sigma_1^2 + \sigma_2^2 - 2\omega$$

Since positive correlation exists between the X_i and X_j measurements, the terms $(X_i - \mu_1)$ and $(X_j - \mu_2)$ found in the crossproduct are not independent. Therefore, $E(X_i - \mu_1)(X_j - \mu_2)$ *does not* equal $E(X_i - \mu_1)\ E(X_j - \mu_2)$. Because of this inequality the crossproduct does not drop out. The expression

$$E(X_i - \mu_1)(X_j - \mu_2) = \frac{\sum_{1}^{N} (X_i - \mu_1)(X_j - \mu_2)}{N}$$

is known as covariance and symbolized by ω.

Covariance can be used as a measure of correlation. If ω is 0, the variables in question are independent. If ω has a positive value, positive correlation is present. This can be demonstrated by a simple model. The numbers 2, 3, and 4 have a mean of 3. The numbers 4, 5, and 6 have a mean of 5. In Table 6.2, the numbers are paired, assuming independence. The sum of the crossproducts equals zero. In Table 6.3. positive correlation is present. The sum of the crossproducts has a positive value.

Table 6.2 Example of Zero Covariance.

Series 1	Series 2	$(X_i - \mu_1)(X_j - \mu_2)$
2	4	$(2-3)(4-5) = +1$
2	5	$(2-3)(5-5) = 0$
2	6	$(2-3)(6-5) = -1$
3	4	$(3-3)(4-5) = 0$
3	5	$(3-3)(5-5) = 0$
3	6	$(3-3)(6-5) = 0$
4	4	$(4-3)(4-5) = -1$
4	5	$(4-3)(5-5) = 0$
4	6	$(4-3)(6-5) = +1$
$\mu_1 = 3$	$\mu_2 = 5$	Sum $= 0$

Table 6.3 Example of Positive Covariance.

Series 1	Series 2	$(X_i - \mu_1)(X_j - \mu_2)$
2	4	$(2-3)(4-5) = +1$
3	5	$(3-3)(5-5) = 0$
4	6	$(4-3)(6-5) = +1$
$\mu_1 = 3$	$\mu_2 = 5$	Sum $= +2$

The decision then, as to whether or not the pairing design or group comparison test should be used, depends on the value of the covariance. If ω equals zero, the group comparison test is the more efficient test. If ω has a plus value, the pairing design test is the more efficient test.

6.3   Sampling Procedure in a Pairing Design Test

From a population of differences, a finite sample can be taken of n measurements. The mean ($\bar{x}_d$) of this sample, obtained by:

$$\bar{x}_d = \frac{\sum\limits_{1}^{n} d_i}{n},$$

is an unbiased estimate of the population mean. A sampling distribution of sample means can be imagined, with a mean equal to μ_d and a variance of $\frac{\sigma_d{}^2}{n}$. This sampling distribution is normal in form and is called the *sampling distribution of means of samples of differences*. The standard deviation of this sampling distribution is commonly referred to as the standard error of the mean difference.

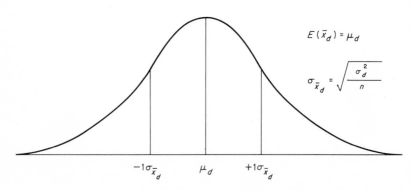

Figure 6.1 Sampling distribution of means of samples of differences.

If the variance of the population of differences were known, a c value could be calculated as follows:

$$c = \frac{\bar{x}_d - \mu_d}{\sigma_{\bar{x}_d}} = \frac{\bar{x}_d - \mu_d}{\sqrt{\dfrac{\sigma_d{}^2}{n}}}$$

However, since σ_d^2 is usually not known, the proper estimate is the variance of the sample of differences.

$$s_d^2 = \frac{\sum_1^n (d_i - \bar{x}_d)^2}{n-1} = \frac{\sum_1^n d_i^2 - \dfrac{\left(\sum_1^n d_i\right)^2}{n}}{n-1}$$

The value of σ_d^2 can also be estimated in a much more involved manner:

$$s_d^2 = \frac{\sum_1^n (X_i - \bar{x}_1)^2}{n-1} + \frac{\sum_1^n (X_j - \bar{x}_2)^2}{n-1} - 2\frac{\sum_1^n (X_i - \bar{x})(X_j - \bar{x}_2)}{n-1}$$

$$= s_1^2 + s_2^2 - 2w$$

A t value becomes:

$$t = \frac{\bar{x}_d - \mu_d}{s_{\bar{x}_d}} = \frac{\bar{x}_d - \mu_d}{\sqrt{\dfrac{s_d^2}{n}}}$$

where $s_{\bar{x}_d}$ is the estimated standard error of the mean difference.

6.4   Example of a Pairing Design Test

In Chapter 4, an example of a test of significance was given dealing with blood-pressure determinations from 10 individuals before and after the injection of a drug. This is clearly a pairing design test, since a high blood pressure before injection will still tend to be high after injection; a low blood pressure before injection will still tend to be low after injection.

The null hypothesis states that the drug is ineffective, i.e., H_0: $\mu_d = 0$. Since $\mu_d = \mu_1 - \mu_2$, the null hypothesis may be phrased as H_0: $\mu_1 - \mu_2 = 0$, or H_0: $\mu_1 = \mu_2$. The population specified by the null hypothesis is the population of differences, with a mean (μ_d) of zero. The alternative hypothesis states that the drug will decrease blood pressure (H_1: $\mu_d > 0$, or H_1: $\mu_1 > \mu_2$). This calls for a one-tailed test. The investigator chooses the 0.05 significance level, and a value of n equal to 10. The data are given on p. 76.

Note that $\quad \bar{x}_d = \dfrac{\sum_1^n d_i}{n} = \dfrac{\sum_1^n (X_i - X_j)}{n} = \dfrac{\sum_1^n X_i}{n} - \dfrac{\sum_1^n X_j}{n} = \bar{x}_1 - \bar{x}_2$

This is demonstrated by the data: $\bar{x}_1 - \bar{x}_2 = 142.71 - 119.12 = +23.59$.

Blood Pressure			
Individual	Before Drug	After Drug	Difference
1	142.0	119.5	+22.5
2	130.3	113.0	+17.3
3	126.7	100.6	+26.1
4	160.5	140.3	+20.2
5	128.9	109.9	+19.0
6	147.8	117.9	+29.9
7	152.0	121.4	+30.6
8	135.6	114.4	+21.2
9	164.2	137.9	+26.3
10	139.1	116.3	+22.8
Sample Mean	$\bar{x}_1 = 142.71$	$\bar{x}_2 = 119.12$	$\bar{x}_d = +23.59$
			$\displaystyle\sum_1^n d_i = 235.9$
			$\displaystyle\sum_1^n d_i^2 = 5{,}747.13$

The variance of the sample of differences is given by:

$$s_d^2 = \frac{5{,}747.13 - \dfrac{(235.9)^2}{10}}{9} = 20.25$$

The estimated standard error of the mean difference equals:

$$s_{\bar{x}_d} = \sqrt{\frac{20.25}{10}} = 1.423$$

A t value can now be calculated:

$$t = \frac{\bar{x}_d}{s_{\bar{x}_d}} = \frac{+23.59}{1.423} = +16.58$$

Since the calculated t is greater than the value 1.83 found in the t table for 9 degrees of freedom, the null hypothesis is rejected.

Confidence limits for the true value of μ_d, or $\mu_1 - \mu_2$, are obtained in the ordinary fashion.

$$\mu_d = \bar{x}_d \pm t\sqrt{\frac{s_d{}^2}{n}}$$

The 95% confidence limits are:

$$L_1 = 23.59 - 2.26(1.423) = 20.37$$

$$L_2 = 23.59 + 2.26(1.423) = 26.81$$

The investigator can be 95% confident that the difference between μ_1 and μ_2 is within the limits 20.37 and 26.81.

6.5 Comparison of the Efficiency of the Group Comparison and Pairing Design Tests

As stated before, the decision whether to use the group comparison or pairing design test depends on whether the paired measurements in the two samples are independent or show positive covariance. The use of a non-efficient test increases the probability that an investigator will make a Type II error.

In a test of significance, there are two situations that will increase the likelihood that the null hypothesis will be rejected. (1) The first is the occurrence of a high t value. For example, at the 0.05 level of significance for 5 degrees of freedom and a two-tailed test, a t value of 2.01 is not significant, but a t value of 2.61 is significant. (2) The second situation is a large number of degrees of freedom. For a two-tailed test, at the 0.05 level of significance, a t value of 2.10 is significant for 26 degrees of freedom, but not for 16 degrees of freedom.

Assume that there are two random samples of similar size ($n_1 = n_2 = n$) taken from two normal populations with known variances.

A group comparison test would be carried out as follows:

$$c = \frac{\bar{x}_1 - \bar{x}_2}{\sqrt{\dfrac{\sigma_1{}^2}{n} + \dfrac{\sigma_2{}^2}{n}}} \tag{1}$$

A pairing design test would be carried out as follows:

$$c = \frac{\bar{x}_d}{\sqrt{\dfrac{\sigma_d{}^2}{n}}}$$

Since $\bar{x}_d = \bar{x}_1 - \bar{x}_2$, the c test for the pairing design would also be:

$$c = \frac{\bar{x}_1 - \bar{x}_2}{\sqrt{\dfrac{\sigma_d^2}{n}}}$$

Now, $\sigma_d^2 = \dfrac{\displaystyle\sum_1^N (d_i - \mu_d)^2}{N}$, but it also is equal to $\sigma_1^2 + \sigma_2^2 - 2\omega$.

Consequently, the c test for the pairing design becomes:

$$c = \frac{\bar{x}_1 - \bar{x}_2}{\sqrt{\dfrac{\sigma_1^2 + \sigma_2^2 - 2\omega}{n}}}$$

or

$$c = \frac{\bar{x}_1 - \bar{x}_2}{\sqrt{\dfrac{\sigma_1^2}{n} + \dfrac{\sigma_2^2}{n} - 2\dfrac{\omega}{n}}} \tag{2}$$

A comparison of the c test for the group comparison and pairing design tests, formulae (1) and (2), shows only one difference. The c test for the pairing design test has the term $-2\,\omega/n$ in the denominator. When the paired measurements are independent, this term is equal to zero. Therefore, the standard errors for the two c tests as well as the c values would be exactly equal. If the paired measurements are not independent and the covariance has a positive value, the standard error for the pairing design would be smaller due to the presence of the term $-2\,\omega/n$, and consequently the c value would be increased.

Now in actual practice the true standard errors in the test are unknown and have to be estimated. When the paired measurements are independent, the estimated standard errors,

$$\sqrt{s_p^2\left(\frac{1}{n} + \frac{1}{n}\right)} \text{ and } \sqrt{\frac{s_d^2}{n}}$$

used in the denominators of the t tests, are both estimates of the same value. Yet the group comparison test is more efficient and is the preferable test because it has twice as many degrees of freedom: $(n - 1) + (n - 1)$ vs. $(n - 1)$.

When the paired measurements are not independent, the denominators of the two tests are not estimates of the same value. Due to the presence of positive covariance, the denominator of the pairing-design t test is an estimate of a smaller value. The larger the value of the true covariance, the smaller the estimate is likely to become. The reduction in the value of the denominator increases the value of t. Therefore, the pairing design test is more efficient when there is positive covariance because of this increase in the value of t. The pairing design test is the preferable test under this condition, even though only half the number of degrees of freedom is available. The larger t value compensates adequately for the reduction in the number of degrees of freedom.

The above principles can be illustrated best with a numerical example. A plant breeder wishes to compare the yields of two different varieties of wheat planted at twelve different experimental stations. A plot of each variety was grown at each station and the number of bushels per plot was recorded. He wished to determine whether the two varieties have different yielding ability. The null hypothesis states that $\mu_1 = \mu_2$. The alternative hypothesis is $\mu_1 \neq \mu_2$. The plant breeder chooses the 0.05 significance level.

The data are as follows:

Station	Variety 1	Variety 2
1	21.4	17.6
2	20.9	15.0
3	23.2	21.7
4	19.8	18.1
5	23.1	21.5
6	18.9	13.6
7	25.6	24.7
8	28.7	27.9
9	26.2	25.2
10	22.7	19.1
11	37.0	33.9
12	31.5	25.3

The analysis by the group comparison test is as follows:

	Variety 1	Variety 2
$\sum_{1}^{n} X_i$	299.0	263.6
$\sum_{1}^{n} X_i^2$	7,757.90	6,158.12
$\bar{x}$	24.92	21.97

The pooled variance becomes:

$$s_p{}^2 = \frac{\left[7{,}757.90 - \dfrac{(299.0)^2}{12}\right] + \left[6{,}158.12 - \dfrac{(263.6)^2}{12}\right]}{(12 - 1) + (12 - 1)} = 30.71$$

The t test is as follows:

$$t = \frac{24.92 - 21.97}{\sqrt{30.71\left(\dfrac{1}{12} + \dfrac{1}{12}\right)}} = 1.30$$

With 22 degrees of freedom, the P value falls between 0.30 and 0.20. On the basis of this P value, the null hypothesis is accepted.

From the design of the study, it might be expected that the pairing design test would be the more efficient test. This is because different stations were used. If environmental conditions were ideal at a specific station, then the yield of both varieties would be increased. Adverse environmental conditions would decrease the yield of both types. This can be noted from the data. The highest yield of variety 1 occurred at station 11. The highest yield of variety 2 occurred at this same station. The lowest yield for both varieties occurred at station 6. The data point out that positive correlation is present. The covariance found in the formula for the variance of the population of differences *does not* equal zero.

The differences between the paired measurements are $+3.8$, $+5.9$, $+1.5$, $+1.7$, $+1.6$, $+5.3$, $+0.9$, $+0.8$, $+1.0$, $+3.6$, $+3.1$, $+6.2$.

Sample of Differences

$\sum\limits_{1}^{n} d_i$	35.4
$\sum\limits_{1}^{n} d_i^2$	148.50
$\overline{x}_d$	2.95

The variance of the sample equals:

$$s_d{}^2 = \frac{148.50 - \dfrac{(35.4)^2}{12}}{11} = 4.01$$

The t test becomes:

$$t = \frac{2.95}{\sqrt{\dfrac{4.01}{12}}} = 5.10$$

With 11 degrees of freedom, the P value is less than 0.01. The null hypothesis is rejected.

A comparison of the conflicting results shows that if the group comparison test had been used to test the sample means, a Type II error would have been made.

Problems

1. An investigator studied the concentration of brine shrimp in different areas of a salt lake by two different methods. He was interested in testing the hypothesis that the two methods would give similar results. It was known that the concentration of brine shrimp varied in different areas of the lake. Ten areas were selected at random. The measurement taken was the number of brine shrimp per container of water.

Area 1	Method 1	Method 2
1	11	6
2	8	7
3	32	19
4	17	14
5	10	10
6	17	12
7	9	7
8	19	16
9	30	20
10	7	6

(a) Test the hypothesis $\mu_1 = \mu_2$ by the pairing design test. Use the 0.05 level of significance. (b) Test the hypothesis $\mu_1 = \mu_2$ by the group comparison test. Use the 0.05 level of significance. (c) Which test is the proper one to use? Why?

2. An investigator had 20 newly weaned mice at his disposal. Half were given diet A and half diet B. After six weeks, the weights were taken. The mice in each sample were numbered 1 through 10. By using the group comparison test, the t value was 2.18. The investigator then ran a pairing design test by comparing mouse 1 from sample 1 with mouse 1 from sample 2, mouse 2 from sample 1 with mouse 2 from sample 2, etc. The t value was 2.19.

(a) Using the 0.05 level of significance, discuss whether the hypothesis $\mu_1 = \mu_2$ would be rejected or accepted by these two tests. (b) Which test is the proper one to use? Why?

3. A botanist studied the number of seeds per capsule in a given plant species. He wished to test the hypothesis that flowers in the upper and lower parts of plants set the same number of seeds ($H_0: \mu_d = \mu_1 - \mu_2 = 0; H_1: \mu_d \neq 0$). Ten plants were selected. The upper and lower parts were arbitrarily determined for each plant. Each measurement is a mean number of seeds per capsule in the upper or lower part of a plant.

Plant	Upper Part	Lower Part
1	4.8	5.6
2	5.1	4.8
3	3.7	3.2
4	5.1	5.4
5	2.9	3.1
6	4.4	5.1
7	4.2	3.9
8	6.4	5.9
9	4.2	3.8
10	2.5	2.8

(a) Does it appear that positive covariance is present? (b) Calculate t. Should the hypothesis be accepted or rejected? Use the 0.05 level of significance.

4. Tomato plants given fertilizer treatments A or B were grown in a greenhouse where environmental conditions (light and heat) were extremely variable. Twelve positions were established on the greenhouse benches. Two plants were placed at each position. Treatment A was applied to one and Treatment B to the other. The yield of each plant was expressed as kilograms of ripe fruit.

Position	Treatment A	Treatment B
1	1.25	1.10
2	1.54	1.32
3	1.27	1.30
4	1.32	1.00
5	1.09	0.90
6	0.98	0.64
7	1.43	1.32
8	0.98	1.08
9	0.95	0.84
10	1.36	1.21
11	1.25	1.12
12	0.84	0.53

(a) Does it appear that positive covariance is present? (b) Test the null hypothesis that the treatments have the same effect. ($H_0: \mu_d = 0$; $H_1: \mu_d \neq 0$). Use the 0.05 level of significance. (c) If you reject the null hypothesis, set the 95% confidence limits for μ_d.

5. Ten patients were given a drug. Blood pressure was determined before and after the administration of the drug.

Patient	Before	After
1	130	134
2	145	146
3	160	179
4	128	120
5	132	139
6	165	162
7	140	140
8	153	150
9	149	146
10	180	184

Test the hypothesis that the drug has no influence on blood pressure ($H_0: \mu_d = 0$; $H_1: \mu_d \neq 0$). Use the 0.05 level of significance.

CHAPTER SEVEN

Introduction to Analysis of Variance
Completely Randomized Design — Model I

It has been shown in the two preceding chapters that the group comparison or pairing design test can be used to test the null hypothesis $\mu_1 = \mu_2$. What procedure should be followed when samples are taken from more than two populations so that more than two sample means are available for comparison? One seemingly logical solution would be to compare the sample means two-by-two by a t test until all comparisons were made. For example, assume that samples were taken from 10 different populations. The number of different combinations of 10 sample means taken two at a time is 45, which indicates that 45 different t values could be calculated. In addition to the inconvenience of calculating all these t values, there is a reason why this procedure is not appropriate. Differences between sample means can occur because they are estimates of different parameters, and also because of random sampling. If a large number of random samples were taken from a single population, the means of these samples would show variability even though they are all unbiased estimates of the same parameter. In theory, the difference between the extreme means of a sampling distribution is large. If means on opposite ends of a sampling distribution were compared by a t test, they would be significantly different from each other at the 0.05 level of significance. In fact, if all means from a sampling distribution were compared by a t test, many would be significantly different from each other even though they are all estimates of the same parameter. This is forcefully brought out by the data in Table 7.1, which show the consequence of testing extreme means from a distribution of means by a t test when each sample mean is an unbiased estimate of the same parameter. As the number of means in the distribution increases, the probability that the extreme means will be significantly different also increases.

Table 7.1   Consequences of Comparing extreme means from a distribution of means by a t test.

Number of Sample Means In Distribution	Frequency at which extreme means will be significantly different when the 0.05 significance level is used.
2	5%
3	about 13%
6	about 40%
10	about 60%
20	about 90%
∞	100%

Thus, a group comparison test or pairing design test is not valid for testing the null hypothesis $\mu_1 = \mu_2$, when the sample means are extreme means from a distribution of sample means, if k is larger than 2. Furthermore, neither test is valid for comparing two sample means selected from a distribution of means because *they appear* to be significant. This is because extreme or near-extreme means tend to be picked. The importance of this cannot be over-emphasized. An investigator is treading on dangerous ground if he carries out a t test on suggestions taken from the data. When t tests are carried out because the sample means appear to be significant, Type I errors occur at a high frequency. There is no question that this accounts for some of the conflicting data found in the scientific literature. For example, assume that a taxonomist took samples from different populations of field mice and measured the skull lengths. He noticed that the sample means could be placed in magnitude array, and that the extreme means were quite different from each other. He compared these means by a t test, and published results stating that the two populations are significantly different from each other for this character. It is likely that he made a Type I error.

The same error could be made by the pharmacologist who tests the effect of six different drugs on rats, and then compares 2 or 3 of the sample means by a t test because they appear to significantly differ from each other.

One solution to the problem of what procedure to follow, when samples are taken from three or more populations, is the *analysis-of-variance* technique, developed by the prominent English statistician and geneticist, R. A. Fisher, in the 1920s. Analysis of Variance is now the cornerstone of statistical inference. Three basic designs will be considered in this and later chapters:

completely randomized design, randomized-block design, and Latin-square design.

7.1 Completely Randomized Design (Model I)

For simplicity, a completely randomized design will be illustrated by considering only 2 samples with 4 measurements per sample.

An investigator wished to study the effects of two different fertilizers (A and B) on the growth of young tomato plants. The null hypothesis states that $\mu_1 = \mu_2$. The alternative hypothesis is $\mu_1 \neq \mu_2$. He decides upon the 0.05 level of significance. As stated above, $n_1 = n_2 = 4$.

The pots were randomized as to location on a greenhouse bench. Randomization is a guard against environmental factors that may or may not invalidate the conclusions of the study. Even when it is known that these factors are non-effective, it is still advisable to randomize. It can be done by drawing numbers from a hat, or tossing a coin. After a specified time, the plant heights were determined in inches. The data are given in Table 7.2. The jth measurement occurring in the ith column is symbolized by X_{ij}.

Table 7.2

A	B
33	29
39	36
29	22
29	28
$\bar{x}_1 = 32.50$	$\bar{x}_2 = 28.75$
Grand mean $(\bar{x})$	
30.62	

The means of the samples are symbolized by $\bar{x}_i$. In addition, there is a grand mean which is symbolized by $\bar{x}$. If $n_1 = n_2$, as in this case, the grand mean is simply the average of the two sample means:

$$\bar{x} = \frac{32.50 + 28.75}{2} = 30.62$$

If $n_1 \neq n_2$, the grand mean is obtained by summing all the measurements in both samples and dividing by the total number:

$$\bar{x} = \frac{245}{8} = 30.62$$

In this experiment the number of measurements in the samples is given as n, while the number of samples is k. From both samples there are nk measurements.

$$\text{Sample Mean} = \bar{x}_i = \frac{\sum\limits_{1}^{n} X_{ij}}{n}$$

$$\text{Grand Mean} = \bar{x} = \frac{\sum\limits_{1}^{nk} X_{ij}}{nk}$$

In addition to each sample variance, there is a total variance known as *total mean square*, which is given as:

$$\text{Total Mean Square} = \frac{\sum\limits_{1}^{nk} (X_{ij} - \bar{x})^2}{nk - 1}$$

It is instructive to deal with the numerator of the total mean square:

$$\sum\limits_{1}^{nk} (X_{ij} - \bar{x})^2$$

It states that to obtain the difference between each measurement and the grand mean, square the difference, repeat for all measurements, and then sum. The difference between the grand mean and the first measurement in the first sample, for example, is given as:

$$33 - 30.62 = 2.38$$

This total deviation can be divided into two parts. The first part is the difference between the measurement and the sample mean. The second part is the difference between the sample mean and the grand mean.

$$(33 - 30.62) = (33 - 32.50) + (32.50 - 30.62)$$

$$2.38 = 0.50 + 1.88$$

Consequently:

$$(X_{ij} - \bar{x}) = (X_{ij} - \bar{x}_i) + (\bar{x}_i - \bar{x})$$

Squaring both sides gives:

$$(X_{ij} - \bar{x})^2 = (X_{ij} - \bar{x}_i)^2 + (\bar{x}_i - \bar{x})^2 + 2(X_{ij} - \bar{x}_i)(\bar{x}_i - \bar{x})$$

Summing the squared deviations from 1 through n gives:

$$\sum_1^n (X_{ij} - \bar{x})^2 = \sum_1^n (X_{ij} - \bar{x}_i)^2 + n(\bar{x}_i - \bar{x})^2 + 2(\bar{x}_i - \bar{x}) \sum_1^n (X_{ij} - \bar{x}_i)$$

The term $(\bar{x}_i - \bar{x})^2$ is constant for any one sample and therefore the summation from 1 through n gives $n(\bar{x}_i - \bar{x})^2$. The last term is equal to zero since the summation of the deviations about the mean for any one sample is zero. The above equation becomes:

$$\sum_1^n (X_{ij} - \bar{x})^2 = \sum_1^n (X_{ij} - \bar{x}_i)^2 + n(\bar{x}_i - \bar{x})^2$$

Summation is now carried out from 1 through k.

$$\sum_1^k \sum_1^n (X_{ij} - \bar{x})^2 = \sum_1^k \left[\sum_1^n (X_{ij} - \bar{x}_i)^2 \right] + n \sum_1^k (\bar{x}_i - \bar{x})^2$$

The sign $\Sigma_1^k \Sigma_1^n$ is equivalent to Σ_1^{nk}. The terms of the equation are designated as follows:

$$\sum_1^{nk} (X_{ij} - \bar{x})^2 = \text{Total Sum of Squares}$$

$$n \sum_1^k (\bar{x}_i - \bar{x})^2 = \text{Treatments Sum of Squares}$$

$$\sum_1^k \left[\sum_1^n (X_{ij} - \bar{x}_i)^2 \right] = \text{Error Sum of Squares}$$

The total sum of squares is equal to the sum of the error sum of squares and the treatments sum of squares.

In the above example the sum of squares can be calculated as follows:

Total Sum of Squares $= (29 - 30.62)^2 + (36 - 30.62)^2 + (22 - 30.62)^2$
$+ (28 - 30.62)^2 + (33 - 30.62)^2 + (39 - 30.62)^2$
$+ (29 - 30.62)^2 + (29 - 30.62)^2 = 193.875$

Treatments Sum of Squares $= 4[(28.75 - 30.62)^2 + (32.50 - 30.62)^2]$
$= 28.125$

Error Sum of Squares $= [(29 - 28.75)^2 + (36 - 28.75)^2 + (22 - 28.75)^2$
$+ (28 - 28.75)^2] + [(33 - 32.50)^2 + (39 - 32.50)^2$
$+ (29 - 32.50)^2 + (29 - 32.50)^2] = 165.750$

In actual practice, these values are usually calculated with the aid of working formulae which are derived as follows:

Derivation of the Working Formula for Total Sums of Squares

$$\sum_1^{nk} (X_{ij} - \bar{x})^2 = \sum_1^{nk} (X_{ij}^2 - 2\bar{x}X_{ij} + \bar{x}^2) = \sum_1^{nk} X_{ij}^2 - 2\bar{x} \sum_1^{nk} X_{ij} + nk\bar{x}^2$$

Substituting $\bar{x} = \dfrac{\sum\limits_{1}^{nk} X_{ij}}{nk}$ into the equation gives:

$$\sum_{1}^{nk} (X_{ij} - \bar{x})^2 = \sum_{1}^{nk} X_{ij}^2 - 2\frac{\left(\sum\limits_{1}^{nk} X_{ij}\right)^2}{nk} + \frac{\left(\sum\limits_{1}^{nk} X_{ij}\right)^2}{nk}$$

$$= \sum_{1}^{nk} X_{ij}^2 - \frac{\left(\sum\limits_{1}^{nk} X_{ij}\right)^2}{nk}$$

Derivation of the Working Formula for Treatments Sum of Squares

$$n\sum_{1}^{k} (\bar{x}_i - \bar{x})^2 = n\sum_{1}^{k} (\bar{x}_i^2 - 2\bar{x}\bar{x}_i + \bar{x}^2)$$

$$= n\left(\sum_{1}^{k} \bar{x}_i^2 - 2\bar{x}\sum_{1}^{k} \bar{x}_i + k\bar{x}^2\right)$$

Substituting $\bar{x}_i = \dfrac{\sum\limits_{1}^{n} X_{ij}}{n}$ and $\bar{x} = \dfrac{\sum\limits_{1}^{nk} X_{ij}}{nk}$ into the equation gives:

$$n\sum_{1}^{k} (\bar{x}_i - \bar{x})^2 = n\sum_{1}^{k} \frac{\left(\sum\limits_{1}^{n} X_{ij}\right)^2}{n^2} - 2n\frac{\sum\limits_{1}^{nk} X_{ij}}{nk} \cdot \sum_{1}^{k} \frac{\left(\sum\limits_{1}^{n} X_{ij}\right)}{n} + nk\frac{\left(\sum\limits_{1}^{nk} X_{ij}\right)^2}{(nk)^2}$$

$$= \sum_{1}^{k} \frac{\left(\sum\limits_{1}^{n} X_{ij}\right)^2}{n} - 2\frac{\left(\sum\limits_{1}^{nk} X_{ij}\right)^2}{nk} + \frac{\left(\sum\limits_{1}^{nk} X_{ij}\right)^2}{nk}$$

$$= \sum_{1}^{k} \frac{\left(\sum\limits_{1}^{n} X_{ij}\right)^2}{n} - \frac{\left(\sum\limits_{1}^{nk} X_{ij}\right)^2}{nk}$$

Derivation of the Working Formula for Error Sum of Squares

$$\sum_{1}^{k}\left[\sum_{1}^{n} (X_{ij} - \bar{x}_i)^2\right] = \sum_{1}^{k}\left[\sum_{1}^{n} X_{ij}^2 - 2\bar{x}_i \sum_{1}^{n} X_{ij} + n\bar{x}_i^2\right]$$

Substituting $\bar{x}_i = \dfrac{\sum\limits_{1}^{n} X_{ij}}{n}$ into the equation gives:

$$\sum_{1}^{k}\left[\sum_{1}^{n} (X_{ij} - \bar{x}_i)^2\right] = \sum_{1}^{k}\left[\sum_{1}^{n} X_{ij}^2 - 2\frac{\left(\sum\limits_{1}^{n} X_{ij}\right)^2}{n} + \frac{\left(\sum\limits_{1}^{n} X_{ij}\right)^2}{n}\right]$$

$$= \sum_{1}^{k}\left[\sum_{1}^{n} X_{ij}^2 - \frac{\left(\sum\limits_{1}^{n} X_{ij}\right)^2}{n}\right]$$

These working formulae can now be used to obtain the sum of squares.

	A	B	
	33	29	
	39	36	
	29	22	
	29	28	
$\sum\limits_{1}^{n} X_{ij}$	130	115	$\sum\limits_{1}^{nk} X_{ij} = 245$
$\sum\limits_{1}^{n} X_{ij}^{2}$	4,292	3,405	$\sum\limits_{1}^{nk} X_{ij}^{2} = 7,697$
$(\sum\limits_{1}^{n} X_{ij})^{2}$	16,900	13,225	
$\dfrac{(\sum\limits_{1}^{n} X_{ij})^{2}}{n}$	4,225	3,306.25	$\sum\limits_{1}^{k} \dfrac{(\sum\limits_{1}^{n} X_{ij})^{2}}{n} = 7,531.25$
$\sum\limits_{1}^{n} X_{ij}^{2} - \dfrac{(\sum\limits_{1}^{n} X_{ij})^{2}}{n}$	67.00	98.75	$\sum\limits_{1}^{k}\left[\sum\limits_{1}^{n} X_{ij}^{2} - \dfrac{(\sum\limits_{1}^{n} X_{ij})^{2}}{n}\right] = 165.75$

$$\text{Total Sum of Squares} = \sum_{1}^{nk} X_{ij}^{2} - \frac{\left(\sum\limits_{1}^{nk} X_{ij}\right)^{2}}{nk} = 7697 - \frac{(245)^{2}}{8}$$
$$= 193.875$$

$$\text{Treatments Sum of Squares} = \sum_{1}^{k} \frac{\left(\sum\limits_{1}^{n} X_{ij}\right)^{2}}{n} - \frac{\left(\sum\limits_{1}^{nk} X_{ij}\right)^{2}}{nk} = 7531.25 - \frac{(245)^{2}}{8}$$
$$= 28.125$$

$$\text{Error Sum of Squares} = \sum_{1}^{k}\left[\sum_{1}^{n} X_{ij}^{2} - \frac{\left(\sum\limits_{1}^{n} X_{ij}\right)^{2}}{n}\right] = 165.75$$

The sum of squares can now be placed in an analysis-of-variance table.

Table 7.3

Source of Variation	Degrees of Freedom	Sum of Squares	Mean Square
Total	7	193.875	
Treatments	1	28.125	28.125
Error	6	165.750	27.625

The degrees of freedom, as well as the sum of squares, are additive. Formulae for obtaining the degrees of freedom are:

$$\text{Total} = nk - 1$$

$$\text{Treatment} = k - 1$$

$$\text{Error} = k(n - 1)$$

A mean square is equal to sum of squares divided by degrees of freedom. Therefore, the values in the last column are self-evident.

The above method of dividing total sum of squares and degrees of freedom into two or more parts is known as partitioning:

$$\text{Total Mean Square} = \frac{\sum_{1}^{nk} (X_{ij} - \bar{x})^2}{nk - 1} = \frac{\sum_{1}^{k}\left[\sum_{1}^{n} (X_{ij} - \bar{x}_i)^2\right] + n\sum_{1}^{k} (\bar{x}_i - \bar{x})^2}{k(n - 1) + (k - 1)}$$

Degrees of freedom can be obtained by the use of the above formulae, or can be determined from the rule that one degree of freedom is lost each time a parameter is estimated, as follows.

7.2   Total Degrees of Freedom

In the formula for total sum of squares, the deviations are based on the grand mean, which is a statistic. There are 8 measurements, so the number of total degrees of freedom is 7. As a general rule, the number of total degrees of freedom is one less than the total number of measurements in all samples.

7.3   Treatments Degrees of Freedom

The grand mean is also the point of reference for treatments sum of squares. Since the number of sample means is 2, the number of degrees of freedom is 1. As a general rule, the number of degrees of freedom for treatments is one less than the number of samples.

7.4　Error Degrees of Freedom

Since sample means are used as the point of reference for error sum of squares, the number of degrees of freedom associated with each sample is $n - 1$. The number of degrees of freedom for error is the sum of the $n - 1$ values, or $3 + 3 = 6$. As a general rule, error degrees of freedom equals total degrees of freedom minus treatments degrees of freedom.

7.5　The F Test

The decision whether to accept or reject the null hypothesis depends on the results of an F test, where F is obtained by dividing Treatments Mean Square by Error Mean Square:

$$F = \frac{\text{Treatments Mean Square}}{\text{Error Mean Square}}$$

The letter F is used as a tribute to the man who introduced the analysis of variance technique: R. A. Fisher.

The rationale for an F test comes from a consideration of the sampling distribution of F values. This can be visualized by considering two populations, each with the same variance. If a random sample were taken from each population and the variance determined for each sample, the ratio of s_1^2/s_2^2 gives an F value. Repeating this process indefinitely would result in a sampling distribution of F values. The range of this distribution is from zero to an indefinitely large number with a positive value.

The sampling distribution of F values is dependent on the number of degrees of freedom that are available for estimating the population variances. A different distribution results each time the number of degrees of freedom in either the numerator or denominator is changed. Figure 7.1 shows two different F distributions. One distribution has 2 degrees of freedom for both the numerator and denominator, while the other has 9 for the numerator and 8 for the denominator. The area under a curve to the right of any point on the X axis can be determined once the distribution is specified. This area divided by the total area under the curve gives a P value.

$$P = \frac{\text{Area under the curve to the right of any point}}{\text{Total area under the curve}}$$

The probability of getting any observed value of F or greater F value can be obtained. For example, with the aid of tables it can be shown that if 12 degrees of freedom are available for estimating σ^2 in both the numerator and denominator of the variance ratio, the probability is 0.05 that an F value of 2.7 or greater will occur, and the probability is 0.01 that an F value of 4.2 or greater will occur.

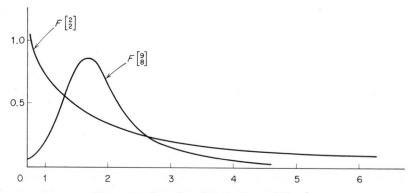

Figure 7.1 Sampling distributions of F values.

As will be shown in a later section, if the population means are equal, error mean square and treatments mean square are both estimates of the same parameter, which is σ^2. Consequently, F = Treatments Mean Square/Error Mean Square will be an estimate of 1.00. If the population means are not equal, then even though error mean square will still estimate σ^2, treatments mean square will estimate some larger value. Therefore, under this situation, F = Treatments Mean Square/Error Mean Square will estimate some value larger than 1.00.

The technique, then, is to determine if a computed F value is significantly larger than 1.00. Tables are available for various levels of significance. Table IV gives F values at the 0.05 and 0.01 levels of significance for varying numbers of degrees of freedom in the numerator and denominator. The top row gives the number of degrees of freedom for the numerator and the left column the number for the denominator. From the table, it can be seen that for 1 degree of freedom for the numerator (Treatments) and 6 for the denominator (Error), an F value of 6.0 or greater will occur 5% of the time under the specifications of the null hypothesis. This can be symbolized by:

$$F\left[\begin{matrix}1\\6\end{matrix}0.05\right] = 6.0$$

For the same number of degrees of freedom, Table IV shows that an F value of 13.7 or greater will occur 1% of the time if Treatments and Error Mean Square are both estimates of the same parameter:

$$F\left[\begin{matrix}0\\6\end{matrix}0.01\right] = 13.7$$

The actual computed F value is:

F = Treatments Mean Square/Error Mean Square = 28.125/27.625 = 1.02

Since 1.02 is less than 6.0, the null hypothesis is accepted. For this study, the null hypothesis would have been rejected if the computed F value had been greater than 6.0. Furthermore, for this study, an F value smaller than 6.0 would have been termed non-significant; an F value greater than 6.0 but smaller than 13.7 would have been termed significant; and an F value greater than 13.7 would have been considered as highly significant.

7.6 Expectations of Treatments and Error Mean Square (Model I)

It was stated that when the means of the populations are not equal, treatments mean square is an estimate of a value which is larger than σ^2. The exact expectation for treatments mean square can be determined when certain assumptions are stated.

Since measurements making up a population are theoretically obtained from individuals exposed to a certain treatment, or from individuals belonging to a given species or variety, etc., it should be clear that populations are defined, or are referred to, in terms of treatments, species, or varieties. In the above example of a completely randomized design, two different fertilizers were tested; therefore, samples were taken from two different populations. The investigator could repeat his experiment using the same fertilizers. The populations are "fixed," i.e., if the experiment were repeated in the future, samples could be taken from the same populations. The investigator carried out the experiment because he wished to compare the effects of two different fertilizers. The interest was in population means. When the interest is in the detection and estimation of constant relations among the means of fixed populations, the investigator assumes an *Anaylsis-of-Variance Model*, known as Model I. Other models will be presented in later chapters.

In Model I experiments, there are k fixed populations. Each population has a mean (μ_i). There is also a grand mean (μ) which is the mean of all the measurements in the k populations. If $N_1 = N_2 = \cdots = N_k$, the grand mean could be represented by:

$$\text{Grand mean} = \mu = \frac{\sum_1^k \mu_i}{k}$$

It is assumed that the measurements in each of the k populations are normally and independently distributed and that the variances of the populations are equal ($\sigma_1^2 = \sigma_2^2 = \sigma_k^2$). For demonstrative purposes, assume that $\mu_1 = 56$, $\mu_2 = 52$, and the grand mean is $\mu = 54$. The effect of treatment 1 is $+2$ units, and the effect of treatment 2 is -2 units. If a treatment effect is symbolized by T, a population mean is given by:

$$\mu_i = \mu + T$$

For population 1, this is:

$$56 = 54 + (+2)$$

and for population 2, it is:

$$\mu_i = \mu + T$$

$$52 = 54 + (-2)$$

A given measurement may differ from the population mean by errors of random sampling, or what is known as an error effect. The jth measurement (random variable) drawn from the ith population is given by:

$$X_{ij} = \mu_i + e$$

where e is the error effect. If the error effect for a random variable from population 1 is -1 units, then the random variable has a value of 55.

$$X_{ij} = \mu_i + e$$

$$55 = 56 + (-1)$$

Considering both the treatment effect and error effect at the same time gives the expression:

$$X_{ij} = \mu + T + e$$

$$55 = 54 + (+2) + (-1)$$

Since $T = (\mu_i - \mu)$ and $e = (X_{ij} - \mu_i)$, the expression can be rewritten as:

$$X_{ij} = \mu + (\mu_i - \mu) + (X_{ij} - \mu_i)$$

where μ and $(\mu_i - \mu)$ are fixed constants, and therefore the sum of squares $\Sigma_1^k (\mu_i - \mu)^2$ is a fixed constant.

Since X_{ij} are random variables that are normally and independently distributed with a mean of μ_i and a variance of σ^2, it follows that $(X_{ij} - \mu_i)$ are also random variables that are normally and independently distributed with a mean of zero and a variance of σ^2.

$$\text{Mean} = E(X_{ij} - \mu_i) = 0$$

$$\text{Variance} = E[(X_{ij} - \mu_i) - 0]^2 = E(X_{ij} - \mu_i)^2 = \sigma^2$$

The assumptions for a completely randomized design (Model I) can now be summarized.

1. Random variables are distributed normally.
2. Samples are random.

3. Populations have homogeneous variances ($\sigma_1^2 = \sigma_2^2 = \sigma_k^2$).
4. Random variables are independently distributed (i.e., no covariance).
5. Relationship between population means and grand mean is constant.
6. Effects are additive.

If these assumptions are true, the expectations for error and treatments mean squares are as follows:

$$E \text{ [Error Mean Square]} = \sigma^2$$

$$E \text{ [Treatments Mean Square]} = \sigma^2 + \frac{n}{k-1} \sum_1^k (\mu_i - \mu)^2$$

These expectations are derived using the rules of mathematical expectation encountered in Chapter 2. Since expectations of mean squares are the basis for specific F tests, as will become even more apparent in later chapters, it will be informative to follow through these derivations for at least this model. It should be noticed that in the lengthy derivations of the expectation of treatments mean square, it is often necessary to add and then subtract certain values, such as $(+\mu - \mu)$ or $(+\bar{x} - \bar{x})$.

$E \text{ [Error Mean Square]}$

$$= E\left\{ \frac{\sum_1^k \left[\sum_1^n (X_{ij} - \bar{x})^2 \right]}{k(n-1)} \right\} = E\left\{ \frac{\sum_1^k \left[\sum_1^n X_{ij}^2 - \frac{\left(\sum_1^n X_{ij}\right)^2}{n} \right]}{k(n-1)} \right\}$$

$$= \frac{1}{k(n-1)} E\left\{ \sum_1^k \left[\sum_1^n X_{ij}^2 - \frac{\left(\sum_1^n X_{ij}\right)^2}{n} \right] \right\} = \frac{k}{k(n-1)} E\left[\sum_1^n X_{ij}^2 - \frac{\left(\sum_1^n X_{ij}\right)^2}{n} \right]$$

$$= \frac{1}{n-1} \left\{ nE(X_{ij}^2) - \frac{1}{n}[nE(X_{ij}^2) + n(n-1)\mu^2] \right\}$$

$$= \frac{1}{n-1} \left[nE(X_{ij}^2) - \frac{nE(X_{ij})^2}{n} - \frac{n(n-1)\mu^2}{n} \right]$$

$$= \frac{1}{n-1} [nE(X_{ij}^2) - E(X_{ij}^2) - (n-1)\mu^2]$$

$$= \frac{1}{n-1} [E(X_{ij}^2)(n-1) - \mu^2(n-1)] = \frac{E(X_{ij}^2)(n-1)}{n-1} - \frac{\mu^2(n-1)}{n-1}$$

$$= E(X_{ij}^2) - \mu^2 = \sigma^2$$

Before determining the expectation of Treatments Mean Square, another formula will be derived for Treatments Mean Square:

Treatments Mean Square

$$= \frac{n\sum_{1}^{k} (\bar{x}_i - \bar{x})^2}{k-1} = \frac{n}{k-1}\sum_{1}^{k} (\bar{x}_i - \bar{x})^2$$

$$= \frac{n}{k-1}\sum_{1}^{k} (\bar{x}_i - \bar{x} + \mu - \mu)^2 = \frac{n}{k-1}\sum_{1}^{k} [(\bar{x}_i - \mu) - (\bar{x} - \mu)]^2$$

$$= \frac{n}{k-1}\sum_{1}^{k} [(\bar{x}_i - \mu)^2 - 2(\bar{x}_i - \mu)(\bar{x} - \mu) + (\bar{x} - \mu)^2]$$

$$= \frac{n}{k-1}\left[\sum_{1}^{k} (\bar{x}_i - \mu)^2 - 2(\bar{x} - \mu) \cdot \sum_{1}^{k} (\bar{x}_i - \mu) + k(\bar{x} - \mu)^2 \right]$$

$$= \frac{n}{k-1}\left\{ \sum_{1}^{k} (\bar{x}_i - \mu)^2 - 2(\bar{x} - \mu) \cdot \sum_{1}^{k} [(\bar{x}_i - \mu) + (\bar{x} - \bar{x})] + k(\bar{x} - \mu)^2 \right\}$$

$$= \frac{n}{k-1}\left\{ \sum_{1}^{k} (\bar{x}_i - \mu)^2 - 2(\bar{x} - \mu) \cdot \sum_{1}^{k} [(\bar{x}_i - \bar{x}) + (\bar{x} - \mu)] + k(\bar{x} - \mu)^2 \right\}$$

$$= \frac{n}{k-1}\left[\sum_{1}^{k} (\bar{x}_i - \mu)^2 - 2(\bar{x} - \mu) \cdot k(\bar{x} - \mu) + k(\bar{x} - \mu)^2 \right]$$

$$= \frac{n}{k-1}\left[\sum_{1}^{k} (\bar{x}_i - \mu)^2 - 2k(\bar{x} - \mu)^2 + k(\bar{x} - \mu)^2 \right]$$

$$= \frac{n}{k-1}\left[\sum_{1}^{k} (\bar{x}_i - \mu)^2 - k(\bar{x} - \mu)^2 \right]$$

$$= \frac{n}{k-1}\left[\sum_{1}^{k} (\bar{x}_i - \mu + \mu_i - \mu_i)^2 - k(\bar{x} - \mu)^2 \right]$$

$$= \frac{n}{k-1}\left\{ \sum_{1}^{k} [(\bar{x}_i - \mu_i) + (\mu_i - \mu)]^2 - k(\bar{x} - \mu)^2 \right\}$$

$$= \frac{n}{k-1}\left\{ \sum_{1}^{k} [(\bar{x}_i - \mu_i)^2 + 2(\bar{x}_i - \mu_i)(\mu_i - \mu) + (\mu_i - \mu)^2] - k(\bar{x} - \mu)^2 \right\}$$

$$= \frac{n}{k-1}\left[\sum_{1}^{k} (\bar{x}_i - \mu_i)^2 + 2\sum_{1}^{k} (\bar{x}_i - \mu_i)(\mu_i - \mu) + \sum_{1}^{k} (\mu_i - \mu)^2 - k(\bar{x} - \mu)^2 \right]$$

The expectation of Treatments Mean Square now becomes:

E [Treatments Mean Square]

$$= E\left\{ \frac{n}{k-1}\left[\sum_{1}^{k} (\bar{x}_i - \mu_i)^2 + 2\sum_{1}^{k} (\bar{x}_i - \mu_i)(\mu_i - \mu) + \sum_{1}^{k} (\mu_i - \mu)^2 \right.\right.$$
$$\left.\left. - k(\bar{x} - \mu)^2 \right] \right\}$$

$$= \frac{n}{k-1}\left\{ E\left[\sum_1^k (\bar{x}_i - \mu_i)^2 + 2\sum_1^k (\bar{x}_i - \mu_i)(\mu_i - \mu) + \sum_1^k (\mu_i - \mu)^2 \right. \right.$$

$$\left. \left. - k(\bar{x} - \mu)^2 \right] \right\}$$

$$= \frac{n}{k-1}\left[kE(\bar{x}_i - \mu_i)^2 + 2kE(\bar{x}_i - \mu_i)E(\mu_i - \mu) + \sum_1^k (\mu_i - \mu)^2 \right.$$

$$\left. - kE(\bar{x} - \mu)^2 \right]$$

$$= \frac{n}{k-1}\left[k\frac{\sigma^2}{n} + \sum_1^k (\mu_i - \mu)^2 - k\frac{\sigma^2}{nk} \right]$$

$$= \frac{n}{k-1}\left[\frac{k\sigma^2}{n} - \frac{\sigma^2}{n} + \sum_1^k (\mu_i - \mu)^2 \right]$$

$$= \frac{n}{k-1}\left[\frac{\sigma^2}{n}(k - 1) + \sum_1^k (\mu_i - \mu)^2 \right]$$

$$= \sigma^2 + \frac{n}{k-1}\sum_1^k (\mu_i - \mu)^2$$

If the population means are equal, the sum of squares, $\Sigma_1^k (\mu_1 - \mu)^2$, found in the expectation of Treatments Mean Squares equals zero, and consequently, error and treatments mean squares both estimate σ^2. If the population means are not equal, the expectation of treatments mean squares exceeds σ^2 by the quantity:

$$\frac{n}{k-1}\sum_1^k (\mu_i - \mu)^2$$

For the fertilizer experiment, where $k = 2$ and $n = 4$, the expectation for treatments mean square is:

$$\sigma^2 + 4\sum_1^2 (\mu_i - \mu)^2$$

The null hypothesis (H_0) for a Model I experiment becomes:

$$\sum_1^k (\mu_i - \mu)^2 = 0$$

The alternative hypothesis (H_1) is given as:

$$\sum_1^k (\mu_i - \mu)^2 \neq 0$$

which may also be expressed as $\Sigma_1^k (\mu_i - \mu)^2 > 0$ for a two-tailed test and $\mu_1 > \mu_2$ or $\mu_1 < \mu_2$, for a one-tailed test when $k = 2$. A one-tailed test is not realistic when $k > 2$.

A consideration of the expectations and the null hypothesis demonstrates the legitimacy of the F test discussed previously. When the null hypothesis is true, F = Treatments Mean Square/Error Mean Square is an estimate of:

$$\frac{\sigma^2 + \dfrac{n}{k-1}\sum_1^k (\mu_i - \mu)^2}{\sigma^2}$$

which equals 1 since $\Sigma_1^k (\mu_i - \mu)^2$ equals zero.

7.7   Confidence Limits for Population Means

Confidence limits for population means in a Model I experiment are determined in the normal fashion by using the formula for the standard error of the mean, $\sqrt{\sigma^2/n}$. The best estimate of σ^2 is error mean square. Using the data from the fertilizer experiment, the estimated standard error is equal to $\sqrt{27.625/4} = 2.628$. The t table is entered with the number of degrees of freedom for error, which in this case is 6. The 95% confidence limits are given below.

Treatment	95% Confidence Limits $\mu_i = \bar{x}_i \pm t_{0.05}\, s_{\bar{x}}$
A	$L_1 = 28.75 - (2.45)(2.628) = 22.31$ $L_2 = 28.75 + (2.45)(2.628) = 35.19$
B	$L_1 = 32.50 - (2.45)(2.628) = 26.06$ $L_2 = 32.50 + (2.45)(2.628) = 38.94$

7.8   A Model I Experiment with Multiple Treatments

A fictitious example will now be given of a completely randomized design (Model I) with four treatments.

Assume that an investigator studies the effects of four different diets on the growth of albino rats. Sixty newly weaned rats from an inbred strain were divided randomly into four equal groups. The rats of each group were placed on a different diet. After a specified length of time, the weight of each rat was determined in grams. The null hypothesis (H_0) is that:

$$\sum_1^k (\mu_i - \mu)^2 = 0$$

Table 7.4

	Diet 1	Diet 2	Diet 3	Diet 4	
	81	71	79	81	
	80	69	76	84	
	67	72	71	83	
	74	79	75	76	
	70	69	79	82	
	70	79	71	86	
	69	83	75	92	
	68	83	77	83	
	69	79	68	80	
	73	71	75	86	
	70	69	79	82	
	77	70	81	83	
	75	68	79	81	
	74	75	68	74	
	73	72	70	85	
$\bar{x}_i$	72.67	73.93	74.87	82.53	
$\sum_1^n X_{ij}$	1,090	1,109	1,123	1,238	$\sum_1^{nk} X_{ij} = 4{,}560$
$\sum_1^n X_{ij}^2$	79,460	82,383	84,335	102,426	$\sum_1^{nk} X_{ij}^2 = 348{,}604$
$\dfrac{(\sum_1^n X_{ij})^2}{n}$	79,206.67	81,992.06	84,075.27	102,176.26	$\sum_1^k \dfrac{(\sum_1^n X_{ij})^2}{n} = 347{,}450.26$
$\sum_1^n X_{ij}^2 - \dfrac{(\sum_1^n X_{ij})^2}{n}$	253.33	390.94	259.73	249.74	$\sum_1^k \left[\sum_1^n X_{ij}^2 - \dfrac{(\sum_1^n X_{ij})^2}{n} \right] = 1{,}153.74$

The alternative hypothesis (H_1) is:

$$\sum_{1}^{k} (\mu_i - \mu)^2 \neq 0$$

As an aid in calculation, it is appropriate to compute first:

$$\frac{\left(\sum\limits_{1}^{nk} X_{ij}\right)^2}{nk} = \frac{(4{,}560)^2}{60} = 346{,}560$$

because it appears in the working formulae for both Total and Treatments Sum of Squares. This term is known as the *correction factor*.

$$\text{Total Sum of Squares} = \sum_{1}^{nk} X_{ij}^2 - \frac{\left(\sum\limits_{1}^{nk} X_{ij}\right)^2}{nk} = 348{,}604 - 346{,}560$$
$$= 2{,}044.00$$

$$\text{Treatments Sum of Squares} = \sum_{1}^{k} \frac{\left(\sum\limits_{1}^{n} X_{ij}\right)^2}{n} - \frac{\left(\sum\limits_{1}^{nk} X_{ij}\right)^2}{nk}$$
$$= 347{,}450.26 - 346{,}560 = 890.26$$

$$\text{Error Sum of Squares} = \sum_{1}^{k}\left[\sum_{1}^{n} X_{ij}^2 - \frac{\left(\sum\limits_{1}^{n} X_{ij}\right)^2}{n}\right] = 1{,}153.74$$

The terms *treatments* and *error* can often be replaced by expressions better describing the situation at hand. For example, in this study the term *diets* would be more descriptive than treatments, and error could be replaced by individuals. Diets Sum of Squares would then express the proportion of the total variability, as measured by sum of squares, which is due to the use of different diets, and Individual Sum of Squares would express that proportion due to individuals, which is considered, in the analysis, to be uncontrollable. The term *error* is often replaced in the scientific literature by *within samples* and *treatments* by *between* or *among samples*.

The F value to test the null hypothesis is $296.75/20.60 = 14.4$. Since this value is larger than the value (between 4.5 and 4.1) found in the F table at

Table 7.5　Analysis of Variance Table.

Source of Variation	Degrees of Freedom	Sum of Squares	Mean Square
Total	59	2,044.00	
Diets	3	890.26	296.75**
Individuals	56	1,153.74	20.60

the 0.01 probability level for 3 degrees of freedom in the numerator, and 56 in the denominator, the calculated F value is highly significant and the null hypothesis should be rejected.

A highly significant F can be represented by placing two asterisks by Diets Mean Square, as above. A single asterisk would indicate that the F value was significant, and no asterisks that it was non-significant.

7.9   Comparison of Individual Means in Analysis of Variance

The alternative hypothesis (H_1) is accepted that differences exist among the four population means. At least two of the population means are different, but there may be as many as four different population means. The above F test does not provide information as to the specific number.

An investigator may not be content with this conclusion, for he usually wants to know which population means are equivalent and which are different. When such an alternative hypothesis is accepted, the next step depends upon the original design of the experiment. For example, (1) all four diets may have been experimental diets, or (2) three may have been experimental diets and one a standard diet used as a control. In the first case, the investigator would be interested in determining if any differences exist among the experimental diets, while in the second, he would be interested in determining whether differences exist among the three experimental diets and if the experimental diets as a group, or individually, are different from the standard diet.

Case 1: Four Experimental Diets.

When the alternative hypothesis (H_1) is accepted that at least two different populations are involved, it is not legitimate to select any two of the sample means and run a t test just because the difference between them appears to be large. Furthermore, if the F value is not significant, further t tests should not be carried out. As discussed previously, extreme sample means are likely to be significant when compared by a t test, when actually they are estimates of the same parameter. If an indefinitely large number of samples of size n were taken from the same population, the extreme and near-extreme sample means would be significant at the 0.05 level of significance on the basis of a t test. Yet F *would not* be significant, showing that the samples were all taken from the same population.

Information as to which populations means are equivalent and which are different can often be obtained with the aid of a multiple-range test. Different multiple-range tests are available which vary in efficiency, such as the Student–Newman–Keuls test, the Duncan test, and the procedures of Scheffe and Tukey. The merits of each of these tests have been reviewed by Scheffe (1959) and Winer (1962). The test that will be presented here is the one initiated by Student and developed further by Newman and Keuls, which accounts for its name: the Student–Newman–Keuls multiple-range test. Occasionally it is referred to in textbooks and scientific literature as the Newman–Keuls, or simply, the Keuls multiple-range test.

Type I errors occur at a high frequency when extreme means are compared by a t test. The probability of a Type I error increases as the number of sample means making up the distribution increases. By knowing the probability of a Type I error for each value of k, a correction can be made. If the investigator wishes to test the hypothesis that the extreme sample means are estimates of the same parameter, the appropriate test is:

$$q = \frac{w}{s_{\bar{x}}}$$

where w is the difference between extreme means and $s_{\bar{x}}$ is the estimated standard error of the mean.

For the above data, $\bar{x}_1 = 72.67$ and $\bar{x}_4 = 82.53$ are the extreme means; therefore, $w = 82.53 - 72.67 = 9.86$. The estimated standard error becomes:

$$s_{\bar{x}} = \sqrt{\frac{s^2}{n}} = \sqrt{\frac{20.60}{15}} = 1.172$$

The value of q is:

$$q = \frac{w}{s_{\bar{x}}} = \frac{9.86}{1.172} = 8.41$$

The calculated value of q is then compared with a tabulated value (Table V) at the 0.05 or 0.01 levels. If the calculated value of q is larger than the tabulated value, the null hypothesis is rejected. For this example, the table is entered for 56 degrees of freedom and $k = 4$. The latter indicates that the extremes of 4 sample means are being compared. The tabulated value is between 3.79 and 3.74 at the 0.05 level, and between 4.70 and 4.59 at the 0.01 level. The difference between the extreme means is therefore highly significant.

This test of significance can be visualized in another way. Since $q = w/s_{\bar{x}}$, then $w = qs_{\bar{x}}$. From the q table for 56 degrees of freedom, when k is 4, the value of 3.74 is obtained. Unless extreme accuracy is required, it is customary to use the closest value in the table. In this case it is the value for 60 degrees of freedom. Substituting $q = 3.74$ and $s_{\bar{x}} = 1.172$ into the equation gives:

$$w = qs_{\bar{x}} = (3.74)(1.172) = 4.38$$

The interpretation can now be as follows: *The extremes of four sample means will be significant at the 0.05 level for the given standard error, if the difference between these means is 4.38 or larger.* Since the observed difference is 9.86, the null hypothesis of no difference should be rejected.

The above technique now leads to a valuable method for comparing sample means. For the data, q values are obtained at the 0.05 level for $k = 2, 3,$

k	2	3	4
q	2.83	3.40	3.74
$q\,s_{\bar{x}}$	3.32	3.98	4.38

and 4. The figures are placed in the first two rows of the above table. In the third row, $q\,s_{\bar{x}}$ values are calculated.

The interpretation of the $q\,s_{\bar{x}}$ values is the same as given above. For the given estimated standard error, the extremes of four means will be significant if the difference is 4.38 or larger. If only two means are present, the difference will be significant if it is 3.32 or larger.

When $k = 2$, a q test is similar to a t test. This is demonstrated as follows:

$$t = \frac{\bar{x}_1 - \bar{x}_2}{\sqrt{s^2\left(\frac{1}{n} + \frac{1}{n}\right)}} = \frac{w}{\sqrt{2\frac{s^2}{n}}} = \frac{w}{\sqrt{2}\sqrt{\frac{s^2}{n}}} = \frac{w}{(1.4142)s_{\bar{x}}}$$

Therefore:

$$w = (t)(1.4142)(s_{\bar{x}})$$

For 56 degrees of freedom, $t = 2.00$ at the 0.05 level.
Substitution gives:

$$w = (2.00)(1.4142)(1.172) = 3.32$$

This is the same value that was obtained by use of the q table. In fact, multiplying each value at the 0.05 level for various degrees of freedom by 1.4142 gives the value of q when $k = 2$.

To initiate a multiple-range test, the sample means should be placed in magnitude array.

A	B	C	D
72.67	73.93	74.87	82.53

Comparing A with B is the same as comparing extremes when $k = 2$. The same is true for any adjacent means, such as B with C, and C with D. Comparing A with C is the same as comparing extreme means when $k = 3$. The same is true comparing B with D. Comparing A with D is the same as comparing extreme means when $k = 4$. Since the difference between extreme measurements is a range, this test is known as a multiple-range test.

The procedure is as follows:
Compare larger means with mean A until a significant difference is found.

(a) $\overline{\underset{73.93}{B}} - \overline{\underset{72.67}{A}} = 1.26 < 3.32$ Accept null hypothesis

Draw line under A and B (see below)

(b) $\overline{\underset{74.87}{C}} - \overline{\underset{72.67}{A}} = 2.20 < 3.98$ Accept null hypothesis

Draw line under A and C

(c) $\overline{\underset{82.53}{D}} - \overline{\underset{72.67}{A}} = 9.87 > 4.38$ Reject null hypothesis

Compare larger means with mean B until a significant difference is found.

(d) $\overline{\underset{74.87}{C}} - \overline{\underset{73.93}{B}} = 0.93 < 3.32$ Accept null hypothesis

Draw line under B and C

(e) $\overline{\underset{82.53}{D}} - \overline{\underset{73.93}{B}} = 8.60 > 3.98$ Reject null hypothesis

Compare larger mean with mean C.

(f) $\overline{\underset{82.53}{D}} - \overline{\underset{74.87}{C}} = 7.66 > 3.32$ Reject null hypothesis

The results can now be summarized. A line under the means indicates these means do not deviate significantly.

$\overline{A}$	$\overline{B}$	$\overline{C}$	$\overline{D}$
72.67	73.93	74.87	82.53

In a graphic way this demonstrates that $\bar{x}_1 = 72.67$, $\bar{x}_2 = 73.93$, and $\bar{x}_3 = 74.87$, are all estimates of the same parameter, while $\bar{x}_4 = 82.53$ is an estimate of a different parameter.

As another example, assume that six sample means are calculated in a completely randomized design, when $n = 5$ and $s_{\bar{x}} = 2.00$. The number of degrees of freedom for error is $k(n - 1) = 24$. The means are $\bar{x}_1 = 22.7$, $\bar{x}_2 = 14.2$, $\bar{x}_3 = 23.1$, $\bar{x}_4 = 33.2$, $\bar{x}_5 = 31.9$, and $\bar{x}_6 = 16.4$. Arranged in magnitude array, the means are:

$\overline{A}$	$\overline{B}$	$\overline{C}$	$\overline{D}$	$\overline{E}$	$\overline{F}$
14.2	16.4	22.7	23.1	31.9	33.2

With the use of appropriate q values for 24 degrees of freedom, the following table can be constructed:

k	2	3	4	5	6
q	2.92	3.53	3.90	4.17	4.38
$q\, s_{\bar{x}}$	5.94	7.06	7.80	8.34	8.76

The means can now be compared:

(a) $\dfrac{B}{16.4} - \dfrac{A}{14.2} = 4.2 < 5.94$ Accept null hypothesis

Draw line under A and B

(b) $\dfrac{C}{22.7} - \dfrac{A}{14.2} = 8.5 > 7.06$ Reject null hypothesis

(c) $\dfrac{C}{22.7} - \dfrac{B}{16.4} = 6.3 > 5.94$ Reject null hypothesis

(d) $\dfrac{D}{23.1} - \dfrac{C}{22.7} = 0.4 < 5.94$ Accept null hypothesis

Draw line under C and D

(e) $\dfrac{E}{31.9} - \dfrac{C}{22.7} = 9.2 > 7.06$ Reject null hypothesis

(f) $\dfrac{E}{31.9} - \dfrac{D}{23.1} = 8.8 > 5.94$ Reject null hypothesis

(g) $\dfrac{F}{33.2} - \dfrac{E}{31.9} = 1.3 < 5.94$ Accept null hypothesis

Draw line under E and F

Graphically, the results are:

A	B	C	D	E	F
14.2	16.4	22.7	23.1	31.9	33.2

It is concluded that $\bar{x}_2 = 14.2$ and $\bar{x}_6 = 16.4$ are estimates of the same parameter; $\bar{x}_1 = 22.7$ and $\bar{x}_3 = 23.1$ estimate the same parameter; and $\bar{x}_5 = 31.9$ and $\bar{x}_4 = 33.2$ estimate the same parameter. This indicates that three different population means are present.

For many experiments, as above, analysis of variance coupled with a multiple-range test present clear results. In some cases the results of a multiple-range test will not be completely satisfactory. For example, assume there are three sample means to be compared when $s_{\bar{x}} = 2.00$, $n = 11$, and error degrees of freedom $= k(n - 1) = 30$.

k	2	3
2	2.89	3.49
$q\, s_{\bar{x}}$	5.78	6.98

The means arranged in magnitude array are:

A	B	C
15.1	18.6	22.8

Comparing the means gives:

(a) $\dfrac{B}{18.6} - \dfrac{A}{15.1} = 3.5 < 5.78$ Accept null hypothesis

Draw line under A and B

(b) $\dfrac{C}{22.8} - \dfrac{A}{15.1} = 7.7 > 6.98$ Reject null hypothesis

(c) $\dfrac{C}{22.8} - \dfrac{B}{18.6} = 4.2 < 5.78$ Accept null hypothesis

Draw line under B and C

The results are as follows:

$$\underline{\underset{15.1}{A} \qquad \underset{\underline{18.6}}{B} \qquad \underset{22.8}{C}}$$

It is concluded that a significant difference exists between $\bar{x} = 15.1$ and $\bar{x} = 22.8$, but not between $\bar{x} = 15.1$ and $\bar{x} = 18.6$, nor between $\bar{x} = 22.8$ and $\bar{x} = 18.6$. This may seem contradictory, such as $a = b$, $b = c$, but $a \neq c$, but it should be stressed that the purpose of a multiple-range test is to suggest where significant differences exist among sample means. It is a valuable aid when used and interpreted properly, if only to point the way towards further experimentation. In these experiments increased efficiency should be sought for by increasing the value of n.

Case II. Three Experimental Diets and One Control Diet.

If the original F test shows that a significant difference exists somewhere among the sample means, *and if* the experiments involved experimental treatments and a control treatment, then it is permissible for an investigator to follow the procedures discussed in this section. By designing an experiment in this way, it is usually implied that the investigator wishes to know if any differences exist among the experimental treatments and if the experimental treatments are different from the control.

Assume that diets 1, 2, and 3 are the experimental diets and diet 4 is the control diet. The procedure is to ignore diet 4 to begin with and to carry out a typical analysis to test the null hypothesis that $\mu_1 = \mu_2 = \mu_3$. Much of the data for this test are already available. The necessary data are summarized in Table 7.6.

Experimental Diets Sum of Squares

$$= \sum_1^k \frac{\left(\sum_1^n X_{ij}\right)^2}{n} - \frac{\left(\sum_1^{nk} X_{ij}\right)^2}{nk}$$

$$= \frac{(1,090)^2}{15} + \frac{(1,109)^2}{15} + \frac{(1,123)^2}{15} - \frac{(3,322)^2}{45}$$

$$= \frac{(1,090)^2 + (1,109)^2 + (1,123)^2}{15} - \frac{(3,322)^2}{45} = 36.58$$

Table 7.6

	Diet 1	Diet 2	Diet 3	Sum
$\sum\limits_{1}^{n} X_{ij}$	1,090	1,109	1,123	$\sum\limits_{1}^{nk} X_{ij} = 3,322$
n	15	15	15	$nk = 45$
$\bar{x}_i$	72.67	73.93	74.87	

Diets 1, 2, and 3 can now be grouped, and the sum of squares computed to compare the mean of this group with the control mean.

Table 7.7

	Group 1 (Diets 1, 2, and 3)	Group 2 (Control Diet 4)	Sum
$\sum\limits_{1}^{n} X_{ij}$	3,322	1,238	4,560
n_i	45	15	60
$\bar{x}_i$	73.82	82.53	

Using the exact procedure as above for calculating Treatments Sum of Squares, the computations are:

$$\text{Groups Sum of Squares} = \frac{(3,322)^2}{45} + \frac{(1,238)^2}{15} - \frac{(4,560)^2}{60}$$

$$= 245,237.42 + 102,176,26 - 346,560$$

$$= 347,413.68 - 346,560.00$$

$$= 853.68$$

Now note that the sum of Experimental Diets and Groups Sum of Squares calculated above is equal to the original Treatments Sum of Squares (36.58 + 853.68 = 890.26). The degrees of freedom follow a similar pattern. Since there are three experimental diets, the number of degrees of freedom for Experimental Diets is two. There are two groups, so there is one degree of freedom for this source of variation. This is a case of *partitioning* the Treatments Sum of Squares and Degrees of Freedom into component parts. In Analysis of Variance this is a common procedure. Partitioning is a method of further analyzing the data. Treatments Sum of Squares can be partitioned into as many components as there are degrees of freedom. However, as stressed above, partitioning is only done when the intent to do so was stated in the original design of the experiment. It is not legitimate to partition from suggestions drawn from the data.

The results are placed in a typical analysis-of-variance table where Experimental Diets and Groups are placed under the category of Diets (Treatments).

Table 7.8   Analysis of Variance Table.

Source of Variation	Degrees of Freedom	Sum of Squares	Mean Square
Total	59		
Experimental Diets (1, 2, 3)	2	36.58	18.29
Groups (1, 2, 3, vs. 4)	1	853.68	853.68**
Individuals	56	1,153.74	20.60

Two F tests can now be carried out. In the calculation of Experimental Diets Sum of Squares, the control diet was ignored. It would have been possible to have continued the analysis and obtained a new Individuals Mean Square. However, this estimation would have been based on only 42 degrees of freedom. An estimate based on 56 degrees of freedom is already available, and consequently should be used in both F tests.

To test the null hypothesis of no differences among the experimental diets, the appropriate test is: $F = 18.29/20.60 = 0.89$. Since this value is less than 1.00, the null hypothesis is automatically accepted.

The mean of group 1 (diets 1, 2, and 3 combined) is 73.82, while the mean of group 2 (control diet) is 82.53. To test the null hypothesis that these two sample means estimate the same parameter, the test becomes: $F = 853.68/20.60 = 41.44$. The F value is highly significant. It is concluded that the experimental diets are similar, and as a group they are inferior to the control diet.

In investigations where several treatments are to be compared with a control, a multiple-range test may be used. The control mean is ranked with the others. Other methods are outlined in Steel and Torrie (1960) and Winer (1962).

7.10 A Completely Randomized Design When the Sample Size Is Not Constant

Equal sample sizes are important in analysis of variance. In fact, the majority of designs have this requirement. An investigator should always strive for equal sample sizes when designing his experiment. Yet, for various types of biological studies, this is not always feasible. The completely randomized design has the advantage over the other designs, to be discussed later, of not requiring equal sample sizes. This quality makes it a useful design.

When the samples vary in size, minor changes must be made in the formulae for computing sum of squares and degrees of freedom. The general formula for Treatments Sum of Squares is changed from:

$$n \sum_{1}^{k} (\bar{x}_i - \bar{x})^2 \text{ to } \sum_{1}^{k} n_i(\bar{x}_i - \bar{x})^2.$$

Otherwise, the method of computing the sum of squares with the general formulae proceeds as outlined above. When using the working formulae, no difficulties are encountered if each of the terms:

$$\left(\sum_{1}^{n} X_{ij} \right)^2$$

used in computing Error Sum of Squares is divided by its own value of n. The expression nk is no longer applicable, but the equivalence of the terms nk and $\Sigma_1^k n_i$; $\Sigma_1^{nk} X_{ij}$ and $\Sigma_1^k \Sigma_1^n X_{ij}$; $\Sigma_1^{nk} X_{ij}^2$ and $\Sigma_1^k \Sigma_1^n X_{ij}^2$ is obvious upon inspection.

A mammalogist made a comparative study of four widely separated populations of pocket gophers. Samples were taken from these populations and measurements of taxonomic interest were made on the specimens. One of these measurements was the length of the nasals in millimeters. The data for adult males are given in Table 7.9.

$$\text{Total Sum of Squares} = \sum_{1}^{k} \sum_{1}^{n_i} (X_{ij} - \bar{x})^2 = \sum_{1}^{k} \sum_{1}^{n_i} X_{ij}^2 - \frac{\left(\sum_{1}^{k} \sum_{1}^{n_i} X_{ij} \right)^2}{\sum_{1}^{k} n_i}$$

$$= 4{,}988.38 - \frac{(345.8)^2}{24} = 5.98$$

Table 7.9

	1	2	3	4	
	14.7	14.5	14.6	13.9	
	14.5	14.9	14.5	14.0	
	14.8	14.4	14.9	14.2	
	14.9	15.0	15.1	13.9	
	14.6	14.6	14.7	13.4	
	14.7			14.0	
				13.9	
				13.1	
$\displaystyle\sum_1^{n_i} X_{ij}$	88.2	73.4	73.9	110.4	$\displaystyle\sum_1^{k}\sum_1^{n_i} X_{ij} = 345.8$
$\displaystyle\sum_1^{n_i} X_{ij}^2$	1,296.64	1,077.78	1,089.52	1,524.44	$\displaystyle\sum_1^{k}\sum_1^{n_i} X_{ij}^2 = 4,988.38$
n_i	6	5	5	8	$\displaystyle\sum_1^{k} n_i = 24$
$\displaystyle \bar{x}_i = \frac{\sum_1^{n_i} X_{ij}}{n_i}$	14.70	14.68	14.76	13.80	
$\displaystyle \frac{(\sum_1^{n_i} X_{ij})^2}{n_i}$	1,296.540	1,077.512	1,089.288	1,523.52	$\displaystyle\sum_1^{k}\frac{(\sum_1^{n_i} X_{ij})^2}{n_i} = 4,986.86$
$\displaystyle \sum_1^{n_i} X_{ij}^2 - \frac{(\sum_1^{n_i} X_{ij})^2}{n_i}$	0.100	0.268	0.232	0.92	$\displaystyle\sum_1^{k}\left[\sum_1^{n} X_{ij}^2 - \frac{(\sum_1^{n_i} X_{ij})^2}{n_i}\right] = 1.52$

$$\text{Treatments Sum of Squares} = \sum_1^k n_i(\bar{x}_i - \bar{x})^2 = \sum_1^k \frac{\left(\sum_1^{n_i} X_{ij}\right)^2}{n_i} - \frac{\left(\sum_1^k \sum_1^{n_i} X_{ij}\right)^2}{\sum_1^k n_i}$$

$$= 4{,}986.86 - \frac{(345.8)^2}{24} = 4.46$$

$$\text{Error Sum of Squares} = \sum_1^k \left[\sum_1^{n_i} (X_{ij} - \bar{x}_i)^2 \right]$$

$$= \sum_1^k \left[\sum_1^{n_i} X_{ij}^2 - \frac{\left(\sum_1^{n_i} X_{ij}\right)^2}{n_i} \right]$$

$$= 1.52$$

$$F = \frac{1.487}{0.076} = 19.6$$

Table 7.10

Source of Variation	Degrees of Freedom	Sum of Squares	Mean Square
Total	23	5.98	
Treatments	3	4.46	1.487**
Error	20	1.52	0.076

From the F table it is found that $F\left[\begin{smallmatrix}3\\20\end{smallmatrix}\, 0.01\right] = 4.9$; therefore, Treatments Mean Square is highly significant. The four sample means do not estimate the same parameter.

Since the intention to partition in a given way was not implied in the design of the experiment, partitioning is not permissible. Since n is not constant, a multiple-range test as shown above cannot be carried out. This latter fact illustrates one major reason why it is so desirable to have equal sample sizes in biological research. If the sample sizes are not too unequal, and *only* approximate results are needed, one solution is to use the multiple-range test where n is set equal to the smallest sample size.

Even though the solution to the problem may require further experimentation, information as to which population means are equivalent and which are different can often be obtained with the aid of confidence limits. The 95% confidence limits for each of the population means are given below using error mean square = 0.076, with 20 degrees of freedom, as the best estimate of the population variance.

Table 7.11

Population Mean	$\mu_i \;=\; \bar{x}_i \;\pm\;(2.09)\sqrt{\dfrac{0.076}{n_i}}$
μ_1	$L_1 = 14.70 - 0.235 = 14.465$ $L_2 = 14.70 + 0.235 = 14.935$
μ_2	$L_1 = 14.68 - 0.258 = 14.422$ $L_2 = 14.68 + 0.258 = 14.938$
μ_3	$L_1 = 14.76 - 0.258 = 14.502$ $L_2 = 14.76 + 0.258 = 15.018$
μ_4	$L_1 = 13.80 - 0.204 = 13.596$ $L_2 = 13.80 + 0.204 = 14.004$

The rule is as follows: If the 95% confidence limits do not overlap, the difference between the two sample means being compared would be significant at the 0.05 level if they were compared by a t test. It seems likely from observing the above confidence limits that $\mu_1 = \mu_2 = \mu_3 \neq \mu_4$.

The use of confidence limits in this manner is not strictly comparable to a test of significance. The t value can be significant at the 0.05 level, but the limits may still overlap slightly. The model below, using a group comparison test, demonstrates this fact.

Population 1	*Population 2*
$\mu_1 = ?$	$\mu_2 = ?$
$\sigma_1{}^2 = 100$	$\sigma_2{}^2 = 100$

Assume that from each population, a sample of 100 measurements was taken, and the sample means were 48 and 51, respectively.

$$t = c = \frac{\bar{x}_1 - \bar{x}_2}{\sqrt{\sigma^2\left(\dfrac{1}{n_1} + \dfrac{1}{n_2}\right)}} = \frac{48 - 51}{\sqrt{100\left(\dfrac{1}{100} + \dfrac{1}{100}\right)}} = 2.12$$

Since the population variances are known, the P value is obtained for an infinite number of degrees of freedom $(0.05 > P > 0.02)$. The difference is significant. The 95% confidence limits are now informative.

Table 7.12

Population Mean	$\mu_i = \bar{x}_i \pm c_{0.05}\sqrt{\dfrac{\sigma^2}{n}}$
μ_1	$L_1 = 48 - 1.96 = 46.04$ $L_2 = 48 + 1.96 = 49.96$
μ_2	$L_1 = 51 - 1.96 = 49.04$ $L_2 = 51 + 1.96 = 52.96$

It is observed that L_1 for μ_2 is less than L_2 for μ_1. The limits overlap, but P from the t test is less than 0.05. Nevertheless, the rule stated above holds, because if the limits do not overlap, then t will be significant.

The use of confidence limits is not too satisfactory for the detection of differences between population means when k is larger than 2, for the same reason that the exclusive use of a t test is not satisfactory. This is due to the problem of extreme and near-extreme means.

7.11 Relationship Between the Completely Randomized Design and the Group Comparison Test

A test of significance can be carried out by either the completely randomized design or group comparison test whenever $k = 2$. When two sample means are to be compared, the pooled variance (s_p^2) of the group comparison test is identical to Error Mean Square of the completely randomized design; and t^2 from the former is equal to F from the latter. In fact, whenever there is one degree of freedom in the numerator of an F test, $\sqrt{F} = t$.

Even though the results of the two tests are similar, many investigators prefer to compute an F value because of a short-cut method that is available. By algebraic derivation, Treatments Mean Square can be expressed as follows:

$$\text{Treatments Mean Square} = \frac{n(\bar{x}_1 - \bar{x}_2)^2}{2} \text{ or } \frac{\left(\sum_1^n X_i - \sum_1^n X_j\right)^2}{2n}$$

The F test becomes:

$$F = \frac{\text{Treatments Mean Square}}{\text{Pooled Variance}} = \frac{\dfrac{\left(\sum_1^n X_i - \sum_1^n X_j\right)^2}{2n}}{s_p^2}$$

Problems

1. Assume that an investigator carried out an experiment using the completely randomized design and obtained the following data in grams.

Treatment 1	Treatment 2	Treatment 3
16.2	18.9	19.2
16.1	22.4	20.3
15.9	19.3	19.1
17.4	20.2	18.4
16.3	19.2	22.4
18.7	18.9	20.4
17.4	22.6	23.1
16.1	23.0	19.2
15.3	19.6	18.7
15.7	19.3	22.3

(a) Assuming Model I, write the mathematical model expressing the assumptions of this model. (b) Fill out an analysis-of-variance table under the headings: Source of Variation; Degrees of Freedom; Sum of Squares; and Mean Square. (c) Give the expected values for Treatments and Error Mean Squares. (d) Test the null hypothesis: $H_0: \Sigma_1^k(\mu_i - \mu)^2 = 0$. (e) Analyze the data further by use of the multiple-range test. What are your conclusions? (f) Determine the 95% confidence limits for the three population means. (g) Assume that Treatment 1 is the control and Treatments 2 and 3 are experimental treatments. Partition Treatments Sum of Squares and Degrees of Freedom in order to test the hypothesis that no difference exists between the experimental treatments, and the experimental treatments as a group are not different from the control. (h) Do the analyses in parts (e), (f), and (g) yield the same or conflicting results?

2. Scorpions were collected in three different geographical areas. The measurement taken was the number of teeth in the right pectine. The measurements for females are as follows:

Area 1	Area 2	Area 3
16	22	20
19	21	17
17	19	19
22	24	19
19	25	21
20	22	18
19	21	16
15	19	15
21	26	19
18	22	20
16	27	14
	23	20
	21	
	24	

(a) By calculating an F value, test the hypothesis that $\mu_1 = \mu_2 = \mu_3$. (b) Set the 95% confidence limits for μ_1, μ_2, and μ_3. (c) What are your overall conclusions?

3. A mammalogist made a study of four widely separated populations of squirrels (*Citellus variegatus*). One measurement of taxonomic interest was the ratio of the height of the foramen magnum divided by its width.

Area 1	Area 2	Area 3	Area 4
0.81	0.74	0.79	0.69
0.82	0.69	0.73	0.74
0.70	0.74	0.73	0.79
0.76	0.78	0.79	0.72
0.72	0.76	0.75	0.79
0.73	0.73	0.74	0.68
0.74	0.80	0.78	0.74
0.80	0.68	0.81	0.72
0.79	0.72	0.69	0.79
0.77	0.71	0.74	0.74
0.74	0.76	0.77	0.70
0.78	0.75	0.64	0.71

(a) Test the hypothesis that $\mu_1 = \mu_2 = \mu_3 = \mu_4$. What is your conclusion? (b) Determine the 95% confidence limits for each population mean.

4. A large field was subdivided into plots. Three strains of corn were grown in the field, with a variety being assigned randomly to each plot. The yields (bushels per plot) were as follows:

Variety 1	Variety 2	Variety 3
7.9	6.1	8.8
5.6	4.5	9.3
7.2	4.9	12.0
6.4	5.3	12.2
7.1	5.7	10.1
6.9	6.1	12.3
6.4	4.8	10.4
7.4	5.9	9.7

(a) Test the hypothesis that $\mu_1 = \mu_2 = \mu_3$. (b) Analyze the data further by use of the multiple-range test. What are your conclusions? (c) Determine the 95% confidence limits for the three population means.

5. Using chromatography and fluorometry, a Drosophila geneticist investigated the concentration of sepiapteridines in the eyes of five different strains of *Drosophila melanogaster*.

Strain 1	Strain 2	Strain 3	Strain 4	Strain 5
60.2	60.4	80.2	62.1	90.4
65.7	62.1	85.7	66.0	94.2
61.8	63.4	81.4	61.4	88.4
64.9	60.2	84.1	64.5	87.3
60.0	65.4	85.9	60.9	86.2

(a) Test the null hypothesis that $\Sigma_1^k(\mu_i - \mu)^2 = 0$, (b) Analyze the data further by the multiple-range test. What are your conclusions? (c) Determine the 95% confidence limits for the population means.

CHAPTER EIGHT

Completely Randomized Design
Components-of-Variance Model (Model II)

In a Model II experiment, it is assumed that the measurements are drawn randomly from a composite population. This population has a mean (μ) which is a fixed constant. The population is capable of being subdivided into subpopulations, each with a mean (μ_i) and a common variance (σ^2). Each subpopulation consists of N measurements. The number (K) of subpopulations is usually assumed to be indefinitely large, but may not be.

The subpopulation means may or may not be equal. The variance of the subpopulation means is expressed as:

$$\sigma_{\mu_i}{}^2 = E(\mu_i - \mu)^2 = \frac{\sum_1^K (\mu_i - \mu)^2}{K}$$

The variance of the measurements within each subpopulation has the formula:

$$\sigma^2 = E(X_{ij} - \mu_i)^2 = \frac{\sum_1^N (X_{ij} - \mu_i)^2}{N}$$

Another parameter of interest is $\sigma_T{}^2 = (X_{ij} - \mu)^2$, which is the total variance, or a measure of the variability of all measurements in the population. It can be demonstrated that $\sigma_T{}^2 = \sigma_{\mu_i}{}^2 + \sigma^2$.

If X_{ij} is the jth item picked at random from the ith subpopulation, it can be represented as:

$$X_{ij} = \mu + (\mu_i - \mu) + (X_{ij} - \mu_i)$$

Transposing gives

$$X_{ij} - \mu = (\mu_i - \mu) + (X_{ij} - \mu_i)$$

Squaring both sides results in

$$(X_{ij} - \mu)^2 = (\mu_i - \mu)^2 + (X_{ij} - \mu_i)^2 + 2(\mu_i - \mu)(X_{ij} - \mu_i)$$

The expectation becomes

$$\sigma_T^2 = E(X_{ij} - \mu)^2 = E(\mu_i - \mu)^2 + E(X_{ij} - \mu_i)^2 + 2E(\mu_i - \mu)E(X_{ij} - \mu_i)$$

$$= E(\mu_i - \mu)^2 + E(X_{ij} - \mu_i)^2 = \sigma_{\mu_i}^2 + \sigma^2$$

This demonstrates that when dealing with a composite population, the variance, denoted by σ_T^2, which is a measure of the variability of measurements (X_{ij}) about the population mean (μ), can be broken down into component parts. One component (σ^2) is a measure of the variation of the measurements (X_{ij}) within each subpopulation. The second component $(\sigma_{\mu_i}^2)$ is a measure of the variation of the subpopulation means (μ_i). The variances σ^2 and $\sigma_{\mu_i}^2$ are independent, and both are components of σ_T^2. This explains why Model II is referred to as the "components-of-variance model."

The sampling procedure in a Model II experiment is as follows: (1) k subpopulations are picked at random. (2) From each subpopulation n measurements are taken. The purpose of this sampling procedure is to obtain an estimate of $\sigma_{\mu_i}^2$ and σ^2.

The distinction between Model I and Model II studies can now be emphasized. In Model I experiments, the interest is in the detection and estimation of fixed relations among *means* of populations. In Model II experiments the interest is in the detection and estimation of the components of *variance*. Thus, if the parameters of interest are means, Model I is assumed. If the parameters of interest are variances, Model II is assumed.

An example of a Model II experiment will now be presented. An ornithologist was interested in the lengths of eggs produced by a given species of bird. He sampled 8 nests at random and measured the length (mm.) of each egg occurring in each nest. If all developing gametes were functional, the number of eggs that could be produced by a female bird would be indefinitely large. Therefore, the number of eggs actually found in a nest is only a sample of the potential number. The measurements made on the potential number occurring in each nest constitute a subpopulation. All these potential measurements from all K subpopulations make up the population.

The ornithologist wished to learn if a correlation exists within a subpopulation. That is, if one egg in a nest is small, the other eggs should tend to be small. Or, if one egg is large, the other eggs should tend to be large. If so, the mean egg length should vary from nest to nest. This would be a case of positive correlation.

The investigator was interested in variances. Since $\sigma_T^2 = \sigma_{\mu_i}^2 + \sigma^2$, it follows that if there is no variability among subpopulation means, then $\sigma_T^2 = \sigma^2$. Thus the total variability is all due to variability within subpopulations. In this case there would be no within-nest correlation. However, if $\sigma_{\mu_i}^2$ does not equal zero, then the total variance consists of two components, and it would be concluded that positive within-nest correlation is present.

The objectives of this Model II experiment are (1) to obtain an estimate of σ^2; (2) to determine whether $\sigma_{\mu_i}^2$ differs from zero; and if so (3) to obtain an estimate of $\sigma_{\mu_i}^2$. The calculations leading to an Analysis-of-Variance table are identical for Model I and Model II experiments (see Tables 8.1 and 8.2).

In a Model II experiment, the difference between each subpopulation mean and the population mean (μ) is symbolized by $T = \mu_i - \mu$, which represents the subpopulation effect. In addition, each measurement (X_{ij}) differs from the subpopulation mean (μ_i) by the error effect, symbolized by $e = X_{ij} - \mu_i$. The jth measurement picked at random from the ith subpopulation is given as

$$X_{ij} = \mu + T + e$$
$$= \mu + (\mu_i - \mu) + (X_{ij} - \mu_i)$$

Since the subpopulations are picked at random, the subpopulation effects ($\mu_i - \mu$) are random variables, *and not fixed as in a Model I* experiment. This is the main distinction between Model I and Model II experiments. (In the egg study, the nests were picked at random, and the interest was not in specific nests. Another investigator in a different area who also carried out a study such as this one would use different nests). Similarly, as in a Model I experiment, the random variables ($X_{ij} - \mu_i$) in a Model II experiment are normally and independently distributed with a mean of zero and a variance of σ^2. In a Model II experiment the random variables ($\mu_i - \mu$) are independently and normally distributed with a mean of zero and a variance of $\sigma_{\mu_i}^2$.

$$\text{Mean} = E(\mu_i - \mu) = 0$$
$$\text{Variance} = E[(\mu_i - \mu) - 0]^2 = E(\mu_i - \mu)^2 = \sigma_{\mu_i}^2$$

The assumptions for a completely randomized design (Model II) can be summarized as follows:

(1) The random variables ($X_{ij} - \mu_i$) and ($\mu_i - \mu$) are distributed normally.
(2) Subpopulations are picked at random.
(3) Samples from each subpopulation are random.
(4) Subpopulations have homogeneous variances ($\sigma_1^2 = \sigma_2^2 = \cdots = \sigma_K^2$).
(5) The random variables ($X_{ij} - \mu_i$) and ($\mu_i - \mu$) are independently distributed (i.e., no covariance).
(6) Effects (subpopulation and error) are additive.

Table 8.1 Nests.

	1	2	3	4	5	6	7	8	
	19.6	18.4	20.4	22.4	18.9	19.7	22.4	22.0	
	19.4	18.9	19.4	23.1	19.2	21.0	23.2	23.4	
	19.7	19.1	21.7	25.2		20.3	20.7	24.1	
	20.1		22.1	19.9		20.9	19.2		
			18.4	22.1			23.9		
			19.6						
$\sum_1^{n_i} X_{ij}$	78.80	56.40	121.60	112.70	38.10	81.90	109.40	69.50	$\sum_1^{k}\sum_1^{n_i} X_{ij} = 668.40$
$\sum_1^{n_i} X_{ij}^2$	1,552.62	1,060.58	2,474.54	2,554.83	725.85	1,677.99	2,408.34	1,612.37	$\sum_1^{k}\sum_1^{n_i} X_{ij}^2 = 14,067.12$
n_i	4	3	6	5	2	4	5	3	$\sum_1^{k} n_i = 32$
$\dfrac{(\sum_1^{n_i} X_{ij})^2}{n_i}$	1,552.36	1,060.32	2,464.43	2,540.26	725.81	1,676.90	2,393.67	1,610.08	$\sum_1^{k}\dfrac{(\sum_1^{n_i} X_{ij})^2}{n_i} = 14,023.83$
$\sum_1^{n_i} X_{ij}^2 - \dfrac{(\sum_1^{n_i} X_{ij})^2}{n_i}$	0.26	0.26	10.11	14.57	0.04	1.09	14.67	2.29	$\sum_1^{k}\left[\sum_1^{n_i} X_{ij}^2 - \dfrac{(\sum_1^{n_i} X_{ij})^2}{n_i}\right] = 43.29$

$$\text{Correction Factor} = \frac{\left(\sum_1^k \sum_1^{n_i} X_{ij}\right)^2}{\sum_1^k n_i} = \frac{(668.40)^2}{32} = 13{,}961.21$$

$$\text{Total Sum of Squares} = \sum_1^k \sum_1^{n_i} X_{ij}{}^2 - \frac{\left(\sum_1^k \sum_1^{n_i} X_{ij}\right)^2}{\sum_1^k n_i}$$

$$= 14{,}067.12 - 13{,}961.21 = 105.91$$

$$\text{Nest Sum of Squares} = \sum_1^k \frac{\left(\sum_1^{n_i} X_{ij}\right)^2}{n_i} - \frac{\left(\sum_1^k \sum_1^{n_i} X_{ij}\right)^2}{\sum_1^k n_i}$$

$$= 14{,}023.83 - 13{,}961.21 = 62.62$$

$$\text{Within-Nest Sum of Squares} = \sum_1^k \left[\sum_1^{n_i} X_{ij}{}^2 - \frac{\left(\sum_1^{n_i} X_{ij}\right)^2}{n_i} \right] = 43.29$$

Table 8.2

Source of Variation	Degrees of Freedom	Sum of Squares	Mean Square
Total	31	105.91	
Nests	7	62.62	8.95**
Within Nests	24	43.29	1.80

When there are k samples of n measurements and Model II is assumed, the following expectations can be derived.

$E[\text{Error (Within Nest) Mean Square}] = \sigma^2$

$$E[\text{Treatments (Nests) Mean Square}] = \frac{\sigma^2(k-1) + n\sigma_{\mu_i}{}^2(k-1)}{k-1} = \sigma^2 + n\sigma_{\mu_i}{}^2$$

When the sample size is not constant, as in the above example, and Model II is assumed, Error Mean Square is still an estimate of σ^2, but the expectation of Treatments Mean Square (Nests Mean Square) is more complex.

$$E[\text{Treatments Mean Square}] = \frac{\sigma^2(k-1) + \left[\sum_1^k n_i - \frac{\sum_1^k n_i{}^2}{\sum_1^k n_i}\right]\sigma_{\mu_i}{}^2}{k-1}$$

This is simplified by

$$E[\text{Treatments Mean Square}] = \sigma^2 + n_0 \sigma_{\mu_i}^2$$

where $n_0 = \dfrac{\sum\limits_{1}^{k} n_i - \dfrac{\sum\limits_{1}^{k} n_i^2}{\sum\limits_{1}^{k} n_i}}{k - 1}$

If the sample sizes are equal, then $n_0 = n$. Otherwise the value of n_0 is always smaller than the mean of the n values.

The null hypothesis for a Model II experiment is $\sigma_{\mu_i}^2 = 0$. The F test for the egg data becomes Nest Mean Square/Within-Nest Mean Square $= 8.95/1.80 = 4.97$. This F value is highly significant and therefore it is concluded that variation exists among subpopulation (nest) means (i.e., $\sigma_{\mu_i}^2 \neq 0$).

The variance (σ^2) within subpopulations is estimated by Within-Nest Mean Square, or 1.80. Since it is concluded that the variance ($\sigma_{\mu_i}^2$) of the subpopulation means is not zero, it is now appropriate to estimate the value of this component of variance. This is done by utilizing Nests and Within-Nests Mean Squares.

Within-Nests Mean Square (s^2) has σ^2 as its expectation, while the expectation of Nests Mean Square ($s^2 + n_0 s_{\mu_i}^2$) is $\sigma^2 + n_0 \sigma_{\mu_i}^2$. Thus, Nests Mean Square $= s^2 + n_0 s_{\mu_i}^2 = 8.95$ where $s^2 = 1.80$ and n_0 is given by:

$$n_0 = \frac{\sum\limits_{1}^{k} n_i - \dfrac{\sum\limits_{1}^{k} n_i^2}{\sum\limits_{1}^{k} n_i}}{k - 1} = \frac{32 - \dfrac{140}{32}}{7} = 3.95$$

(Note that $\Sigma_1^k n_i^2$ is obtained from $4^2 + 3^2 + 6^2 + 5^2 + 2^2 + 4^2 + 5^2 + 3^2 = 140$)

The value of $s_{\mu_i}^2$ can now be obtained from the expression:

$$s_{\mu_i}^2 = \frac{\text{Nest Mean Square} - \text{Within-Nest Mean Square}}{n_0}$$

$$= \frac{8.95 - 1.80}{3.95}$$

$$= 1.81$$

Estimates of the components of variance are now available: $s^2 = 1.80$ is an estimate of σ^2, and $s_{\mu_i}^2 = 1.81$ is an estimate of $\sigma_{\mu_i}^2$. The estimate of the total variance (σ_T^2) is $s_T^2 = s^2 + s_{\mu_i}^2 = 1.80 + 1.81 = 3.61$.

One value of the estimates of the components of variance is in comparing the degree of variability of different composite populations. Another important usage of the estimates is in the calculation of an intraclass correlation coefficient. The subject of intraclass correlation will be presented in a later chapter.

Problems

1. A plant physiologist sampled 5 plants at random. Five leaves were selected at random from each plant. The ascorbic acid concentration was determined for each leaf.

Plant 1	Plant 2	Plant 3	Plant 4	Plant 5
6.0	10.2	10.6	5.4	10.4
5.8	9.4	10.9	5.9	9.6
6.1	10.1	11.1	6.2	10.1
5.4	9.8	10.1	5.7	9.9
5.9	9.6	9.8	5.8	10.1

(a) Which model is being assumed, Model I or Model II? Why? (b) Distinguish among the populations, subpopulations, and samples. (c) Fill out an analysis-of-variance table for the following sources of variation: Total, Plants, and Leaves. (d) Test the hypothesis $\sigma_{\mu_i}^2 = 0$. (e) Estimate the values of σ_T^2, $\sigma_{\mu_i}^2$ and σ^2.

2. Discuss in detail the differences between a Model I and a Model II experiment. Under what conditions would you say a treatment effect is fixed or a random variable?

3. Measurements of taxonomic interest were made on biting lice (Mallophaga) found on hornbill birds. Ten birds (*Bucorvus abyssinicus*) were selected at random. Six male lice of a given species were selected at random from each bird. One measurement was width (mm.) of prothorax.

Bird	Measurements (mm.)					
1	0.44	0.49	0.41	0.42	0.43	0.44
2	0.42	0.43	0.49	0.46	0.42	0.45
3	0.48	0.49	0.41	0.43	0.46	0.41
4	0.50	0.42	0.41	0.45	0.49	0.43
5	0.46	0.42	0.41	0.50	0.42	0.43
6	0.43	0.41	0.45	0.48	0.43	0.42
7	0.42	0.41	0.49	0.41	0.47	0.44
8	0.49	0.40	0.50	0.43	0.44	0.45
9	0.52	0.43	0.40	0.50	0.42	0.43
10	0.45	0.41	0.47	0.44	0.50	0.47

(a) Distinguish among the populations, subpopulations, and samples. (b) Fill out an analysis-of-variance table for the following sources of variation: Total, Host, and Individuals (c) Test the hypothesis: $\sigma_{\mu_i}^2 = 0$. (d) What is your conclusion concerning the variation of measurements for individuals on one host and among hosts?

4. Twelve hybrid plants were randomly selected. Five leaves were randomly selected from each plant. Measurements (mm.) were made of the length of the leaf blade and petiole and the following ratio was determined: leaf blade length/petiole length. The investigator wished to determine if the plants were from the same gene pool, i.e., if any variation exists among subpopulation means.

Plant	Measurements				
1	27	33	28	31	36
2	60	61	53	51	64
3	55	46	49	51	58
4	65	60	60	54	69
5	40	47	41	49	50
6	25	36	32	31	29
7	61	54	59	62	57
8	26	33	39	24	32
9	55	55	49	62	57
10	61	67	59	61	58
11	54	61	52	64	60
12	30	28	29	32	34

(a) Test the hypothesis $\sigma_{\mu_i}^2 = 0$. (b) What are your conclusions?

5. An entomologist used head breadths (mm.) of honey bees (female workers) to determine whether genetic differences exist among hive subpopulations in a given geographic area. He was concerned with variation within subpopulations and among subpopulation means. The analysis-of-variance table was as follows:

Analysis of Variance Table (Head Breadths of Honey Bees).

Source of Variation	Degrees of Freedom	Sum of Squares	Mean Squares
Total	1199	11.1474	
Hives	11	0.4554	0.04140
Workers	1188	10.6920	0.00900

(a) How many hives were selected randomly? (b) How many bees were selected randomly from each hive? (c) Discuss why this is not a Model I experiment? (d) Test the hypothesis $\sigma_{\mu_i}^2 = 0$. (e) What do you conclude about the variation among subpopulation (hive) means? (f) Estimate σ_T^2, $\sigma_{\mu_i}^2$, and σ^2.

Randomized-Block Design

When samples are taken from two populations (i.e., $k = 2$), the sample means can be compared by either the group comparison test or completely randomized design when no covariance exists between the paired measurements. F determined from the completely randomized design will equal t^2 from the group comparison test. When $k > 2$, and the measurements are independent, the completely randomized design is the appropriate method of comparing sample means.

If covariance exists between paired measurements, the sample means can be compared by the pairing design test or by an analysis-of-variance technique known as the randomized-block design. F from the randomized-block design will equal t^2 from the pairing design test. It is logical that the randomized-block design is the appropriate method of comparing sample means when $k > 3$ and the measurements are not independent.

The importance of the randomized-block design in statistical inference becomes even more evident when environmental variability and efficiency are considered. The group comparison test and the completely randomized design are specifically designed to avoid a Type II error when the measurements in each sample vary from each other because of errors of random sampling. The measure of this within-sample variation is the pooled variance. It is instructive to compare the formulae for t and F in the group comparison test and completely randomized design, respectively:

Group Comparison Test

Completely Randomized Design

$$t = \frac{\bar{x}_1 - \bar{x}_2}{\sqrt{s_p^2\left(\frac{1}{n} + \frac{1}{n}\right)}}$$

$$F = \frac{n\sum_{1}^{k}(\bar{x}_i - \bar{x})^2/(k-1)}{s_p^2}$$

Both formulae contain pooled variance $(s_p{}^2)$ in the denominator. Any factor that increases the variation within the samples, such as covariance between paired measurements, decreases the efficiency of the test, since increasing pooled variance decreases the value of t and F, if other factors remain the same. In agricultural experiments the measurements within the samples may vary from each other not only because of chance but also because each variable may represent a measurement made on a plant grown under a different environmental condition. Data collected over a long period of time may also be subject to increased variability. Environmental conditions as well as methods of collecting data change with time. A plant grown in a greenhouse during one season of the year may be subject to different growing conditions than if it had been grown during another season of the year.

The larger the value of the pooled variance, the less likely it is that an investigator will conclude that the population means are different when such is actually the case. Consequently, factors that tend to increase the variability within the samples should be controlled. This problem can be approached experimentally and statistically.

Experimental control of the variability is brought about by designing and conducting the experiment in such a manner that environmental and other extraneous factors are maintained as constant as possible. In field and greenhouse experiments, for example, such factors as soil, heat, light, water, fertilizer, humidity, etc., should be considered.

The influence of a large number of degrees of freedom on the efficiency of an experiment has already been discussed. When n is a large value, the estimate of σ^2 is based on a larger number of degrees of freedom. However, increasing the value of n can have an adverse effect on the estimate of σ^2. Although it is feasible that environmental conditions in a small section of a greenhouse or a field can be made relatively homogeneous, as soon as it is necessary to expand the experiment, as necessitated by a large value of n, the ability to control the variability experimentally is lessened. In many cases, when n is increased, the estimate of σ^2 is increased as well. It is well known that different sections of the same field vary greatly in terms of available water, soil content, etc. Large fields show more heterogeneity than small fields. Conditions within the same greenhouse are also extremely variable. One greenhouse bench may be exposed to different lighting and heating conditions than another. Therefore, for certain types of large experiments, it is a difficult task to experimentally control the variability within the samples.

The simplest design which gives a statistical control of the variability is the randomized-block design. Its advantage over the completely randomized design is that it attempts to remove from the estimate of σ^2 some of the variability which is introduced by extraneous factors. When properly used, the randomized-block design is a very efficient test.

The success of the randomized-block design depends on the ability of the investigator to recognize the presence of factors which might increase the value of the estimate of σ^2. In agricultural field experiments the procedure is to divide the field into a series of blocks. The number of blocks is noted as n. The primary consideration is that the soil and other environmental facters within the blocks are homogeneous. For this reason it is advisable to limit the size of the blocks. Rectangular or square blocks are most often used so that the blocks are as compact as possible.

Each block is divided into the same number of plots of a given size and shape. If there are four treatments, then there are four plots in each block. Each treatment is represented once in each block. The number of plots per block is noted as k. The allocation of the treatments to the plots within each block is done at random.

If there are n blocks, then there are n replications of the treatments. The total number of plots or measurements in the experiment is therefore the number of treatments multiplied by the number of replications, or nk.

In field experiments where there is a soil-fertility gradient running in one direction, the experimental layout might appear as shown in the diagram below. This assumes that the gradient runs in a north-south direction. For example, the most fertile soil might be in the northern part of the field with the least fertile in the southern part. There are six blocks with four treatments $(A, B, C, \text{ and } D)$.

Block 1	B	C	A	D
Block 2	D	C	B	A
Block 3	B	A	D	C
Block 4	D	A	C	B
Block 5	C	B	A	D
Block 6	A	D	B	C

N ↑
W ← → E
↓ S

Arranging the blocks and plots as shown increases the likelihood that the soil fertility within each block is relatively constant. The soil fertility from one block to another, however, would vary. The location of the blocks with reference to each other is immaterial. They may be adjacent to each other, as shown above, or they may be separated by strips of non-experimental land.

In experimental studies with animals, such as nutrition studies, the animals may be placed into blocks according to weight, age, or some other factor that may increase the variability. In laboratory studies, time trends are often important. The effects of time can be removed by running all the combinations of treatments during one specified period. The procedure can then be repeated over and over at later periods. Each period then becomes a replication (block).

9.1 Example of a Randomized-Block Design

A plant physiologist was investigating the salt-tolerance properties of four different subspecies of a salt-desert shrub. In one experiment he was attempting to determine which subspecies would grow better in the presence of a 0.3% salt solution. Seeds were placed in suitable containers and after a given length of time the growth of each plant was determined. Measurements were made in grams (oven-dry weight). The experiment was carried out in a greenhouse where lighting and heating conditions were far from uniform. Because of limited space in the greenhouse, blocks (replications) were set up in different regions in the greenhouse. Ten blocks were used and the sub-species were randomized in each block. Every attempt was made to keep the light and heat variables as uniform per block as possible. The data are given in Table 9.1. In a randomized-block design, a given measurement occurs in a given row and column, and is referred to as the measurement in the ith column and the jth row. The measurements (X_{ij}) and their squares (X_{ij}^2) are summed columnwise and rowwise.

The difference between the grand mean $(\bar{x})$ and measurement in the ith column and jth row can be obtained. For example, the measurement in block 2 for subspecies D has a value of 1.69. The difference between this measurement and the grand mean is $X_{ij} - \bar{x} = 1.69 - 1.469 = 0.221$.

This total deviation can be partitioned as follows: One part is the difference between the mean of block 2 and the grand mean, and another part is the difference between the mean of sample D and the grand mean, or $(\bar{x}_j - \bar{x})$ + $(\bar{x}_i - \bar{x})$.

$$\text{These become: } (\bar{x}_j - \bar{x}) = (1.575 - 1.469) = 0.106$$

$$(\bar{x}_i - \bar{x}) = (1.519 - 1.469) = 0.050$$

$$\text{Sum} = 0.156$$

The sum of these two parts is 0.156, which is not equal to the total deviation of 0.221. There is a remainder which is equal to $0.221 - 0.156 = 0.065$. This remainder can be expressed algebraically as follows:

$$(X_{ij} - \bar{x}) - (\bar{x}_i - \bar{x}) - (\bar{x}_j - \bar{x}) = (X_{ij} - \bar{x}_i - \bar{x}_j + \bar{x})$$

Table 9.1

Block	Sub-species A	Sub-species B	Sub-species C	Sub-species D	$\sum_1^k X_{ij}$	$\sum_1^k X_{ij}^2$	$\bar{x}_j$
1	1.28	1.41	1.40	1.43	5.52	7.6314	1.380
2	1.43	1.62	1.56	1.69	6.30	9.9590	1.575
3	1.29	1.49	1.43	1.42	5.63	7.9455	1.408
4	1.43	1.68	1.59	1.62	6.32	10.0198	1.580
5	1.26	1.40	1.46	1.47	5.59	7.8401	1.397
6	1.39	1.56	1.58	1.56	6.09	9.2957	1.522
7	1.31	1.55	1.47	1.47	5.80	8.4404	1.450
8	1.37	1.60	1.51	1.51	5.99	8.9971	1.498
9	1.38	1.54	1.44	1.58	5.94	8.8460	1.487
10	1.27	1.44	1.42	1.44	5.57	7.7765	1.392
$\sum_1^n X_{ij}$	13.41	15.29	14.86	15.19	$\sum_1^{nk} X_{ij} = 58.75$		
$\sum_1^n X_{ij}^2$	18.0223	23.4563	22.1256	23.1473		$\sum_1^{nk} X_{ij}^2 = 86.7515$	
$\bar{x}_i$	1.341	1.529	1.486	1.519			$\bar{x} = 1.469$

Substituting into this term gives $(1.69 - 1.519 - 1.575 + 1.469) = 0.065$. Consequently, the total deviation can be partitioned into three parts:

$$(X_{ij} - \bar{x}) = (\bar{x}_i - \bar{x}) + (\bar{x}_j - \bar{x}) + (X_{ij} - \bar{x}_i - \bar{x}_j + \bar{x})$$

Squaring each side gives:

$$\begin{aligned}
(X_{ij} - \bar{x})^2 = {} & (\bar{x}_i - \bar{x})^2 + (\bar{x}_j - \bar{x})^2 + (X_{ij} - \bar{x}_i - \bar{x}_j + \bar{x})^2 \\
& + 2(\bar{x}_i - \bar{x})(\bar{x}_j - \bar{x}) + 2(\bar{x}_i - \bar{x})(X_{ij} - \bar{x}_i - \bar{x}_j + \bar{x}) \\
& + 2(\bar{x}_j - \bar{x})(X_{ij} - \bar{x}_i - \bar{x}_j + \bar{x})
\end{aligned}$$

Summing from 1 through n and then 1 through k gives:

$$\sum_1^{nk} (X_{ij} - \bar{x})^2 = n \sum_1^{k} (\bar{x}_i - \bar{x})^2 + k \sum_1^{n} (\bar{x}_j - \bar{x})^2 + \sum_1^{nk} (X_{ij} - \bar{x}_i - \bar{x}_j + \bar{x})^2$$

| Total Sum of Squares | Treatments Sum of Squares | Blocks (Replication) Sum of Squares | Error (Remainder) Sum of Squares |

Working formulae for total, treatments, and blocks sum of squares are easily derived from the general formulae. Error sum of squares is obtained by subtraction.

$$\text{Total Sum of Squares} = \sum_1^{nk} X_{ij}^2 - \frac{\left(\sum_1^{nk} X_{ij} \right)^2}{nk}$$

$$\text{Treatments Sum of Squares} = \sum_1^{k} \frac{\left(\sum_1^{n} X_{ij} \right)^2}{n} - \frac{\left(\sum_1^{nk} X_{ij} \right)^2}{nk}$$

$$\text{Blocks Sum of Squares} = \sum_1^{n} \frac{\left(\sum_1^{k} X_{ij} \right)^2}{k} - \frac{\left(\sum_1^{nk} X_{ij} \right)^2}{nk}$$

Error Sum of Squares = Total Sum of Squares minus Treatments Sum of Squares minus Blocks Sum of Squares

Note that the working formulae of total, treatments, and blocks sum of squares each contain the correction factor: $(\sum_1^{nk} X_{ij})^2 / nk$.

$$\text{Correction Factor} = \frac{\left(\sum_1^{nk} X_{ij} \right)^2}{nk} = \frac{(58.75)^2}{40} = 86.28906$$

The correction factor should be calculated first and then used in the ap-

propriate place in the determination of total, treatments, and blocks sum
of squares.

$$\text{Total Sum of Squares} = \sum_1^{nk} X_{ij}^2 - \frac{\left(\sum_1^{nk} X_{ij}\right)^2}{nk}$$

$$= 86.7515 - 86.28906 = 0.46244$$

$$\text{Treatments Sum of Squares} = \sum_1^k \frac{\left(\sum_1^n X_{ij}\right)^2}{n} - \frac{\left(\sum_1^{nk} X_{ij}\right)^2}{nk}$$

$$= \frac{(13.41)^2 + (15.29)^2 + (14.86)^2 + (15.19)^2}{10}$$

$$- 86.28906$$

$$= 86.51679 - 86.28906 = 0.22773$$

$$\text{Blocks Sum of Squares} = \sum_1^n \frac{\left(\sum_1^k X_{ij}\right)^2}{k} - \frac{\left(\sum_1^{nk} X_{ij}\right)^2}{nk}$$

$$= \frac{(5.52)^2 + (6.30)^2 + (5.63)^2 + \cdots + (5.57)^2}{4}$$

$$- 86.28906$$

$$= 86.49112 - 86.28906 = 0.20206$$

Error Sum of Squares $= 0.46244 - 0.22773 - 0.20206 = 0.03265$
An analysis-of-variance table may now be completed.

Table 9.2

Source of Variation	Degrees of Freedom	Sum of Squares	Mean Square
Total	39	0.46244	
Subspecies	3	0.22773	0.07591
Blocks	9	0.20206	0.02245
Error	27	0.03265	0.00121

The number of degrees of freedom for each source of variation can be
obtained by deduction or from the following formulae:

$$\text{Total} = nk - 1$$

$$\text{Treatments} = k - 1$$

$$\text{Blocks} = n - 1$$

$$\text{Error} = (k - 1)(n - 1)$$

9.2   The Assumptions Underlying a Randomized-Block Design (Model I)

The measurements (X_{ij}) obtained in an experiment carried out as a randomized-block design are placed in a table with n rows and k columns. The n measurements in the ith column are those made on individuals given the same treatment or belonging to the same subspecies, species, variety, etc. The k measurements occurring in the jth row are those made on individuals occurring in the same block.

The division of the table into n rows and k columns results in nk cells. A single measurement (X_{ij}) occurs in each cell. What value might this measurement have? If the experiment were repeated indefinitely, the measurements in the ith cell of the jth row would vary about an average value called the cell mean, symbolized by μ_{ij}, and would form a normal distribution with a variance symbolized by σ^2. The one measurement actually occuring in each cell is a sample from a population of measurements. Thus, in this randomized-block design the sample size is one.

The means of the cell means columnwise are symbolized by μ_i, while the means of the cell means rowwise are symbolized by μ_j. In addition, there is a general mean (μ) which is the mean of all the cell means.

$$\mu_i = \frac{\sum_1^n \mu_{ij}}{n}, \; \mu_j = \frac{\sum_1^k \mu_{ij}}{k}, \; \mu = \frac{\sum_1^n \mu_j}{n} = \frac{\sum_1^k \mu_i}{k} = \frac{\sum_1^{nk} \mu_{ij}}{nk}$$

The cell means (μ_{ij}), row means (μ_j), column means (μ_i), and general mean (μ) can be represented in the table given below. Hypothetical values are given for these means when $k = 2$ and $n = 3$.

	A	B	μ_j
	49	53	51
	48	52	50
	47	51	49
μ_i	48	52	$\mu = 50$

The cell means are related to the row means, column means, and general mean in an additive fashion, i.e.,

$$\mu_{ij} = \mu + T + B$$

where μ is the general mean, T is the treatment (column) effect, and B is the block (row) effect. The cell mean in the first row and first column differs from the general mean because of a $+1$ block effect and a -2 treatment effect. Thus

$$\mu_{ij} = \mu + T + B$$
$$= 50 + (-2) + (+1)$$
$$= 49$$

If environmental conditions were constant from block to block, the block effect (B) would be zero.

A given measurement (X_{ij}) occurring in the ith column and jth row differs from the cell mean (μ_{ij}) by an error effect (e). The value of this random variable is given by

$$X_{ij} = \mu + T + B + e$$

where $T = (\mu_i - \mu)$, $B = (\mu_j - \mu)$, and $e = (X_{ij} - \mu_{ij})$. The general mean, treatment effects, and block effects are fixed constants so that

$$\sum_1^k (\mu_i - \mu) = \sum_1^n (\mu_j - \mu) = 0$$

and the random variables $(X_{ij} - \mu_{ij})$ are normally and independently distributed with a mean of zero and a common variance σ^2.

When the above assumptions are true, the mean squares in a randomized-block design have the following expectations:

(1) Expectation for Treatments Mean Square

$$E\left[\frac{n \sum_1^k (\bar{x}_i - \bar{x})^2}{k - 1}\right] = \sigma^2 + \frac{n}{k - 1} \sum_1^k (\mu_i - \mu)^2$$

(2) Expectation for Blocks Mean Square

$$E\left[\frac{k \sum_1^n (\bar{x}_j - \bar{x})^2}{n - 1}\right] = \sigma^2 + \frac{k}{n - 1} \sum_1^n (\mu_j - \mu)^2$$

(3) Expectation for Error Mean Square

$$E\left[\frac{\sum_1^{nk} (X_{ij} - \bar{x}_i - \bar{x}_j + \bar{x})^2}{(n - 1)(k - 1)}\right] = \sigma^2$$

The null hypothesis in a randomized-block design (Model I) is that the treatment (column) means are equal, i.e., $\mu_1 = \mu_2 = \mu_3 = \cdots = \mu_k$. This is also expressed by

$$\sum_1^k (\mu_i - \mu)^2 = 0$$

The F test is now apparent.

For the above experiment of different subspecies grown in a 0.3% salt solution, the F ratio is: species mean square/error mean square.

$$F = \frac{0.07591}{0.00121} = 62.7$$

From the F table it is observed that $F\left[\begin{matrix} 3 \\ 27 \end{matrix} 0.01\right] = 4.6$. The F value is highly significant so the null hypothesis should be rejected.

The 95% confidence limits for the population means can be obtained in the ordinary way from the formulae:

$$\mu_i = \bar{x}_i \pm t_{0.05}\sqrt{s^2/n}$$

where s^2 is error mean square. The t table is entered with the number of degrees of freedom associated with the estimate of σ^2, i.e., error degrees of freedom.

$$s_{\bar{x}} = \sqrt{\frac{s^2}{n}} = \sqrt{\frac{0.00121}{10}} = 0.0110$$

Error degrees of freedom $= 27$

$$t_{0.05} = 2.05$$

Table 9.3 95% Confidence Limits for Population Means.

Subspecies	Sample Mean $(\bar{x}_i)$	$\mu_i = \bar{x}_i \pm (2.05)(0.0110)$	
A	1.341	$L_1 = 1.318$	$L_2 = 1.364$
B	1.529	$L_1 = 1.506$	$L_2 = 1.552$
C	1.486	$L_1 = 1.463$	$L_2 = 1.509$
D	1.519	$L_1 = 1.496$	$L_2 = 1.542$

The sample means and 95% confidence limits can be expressed graphically. The vertical lines represent sample means and the horizontal bars represent the confidence intervals (see page 134).

Using overlapping or non-overlapping of the 95% confidence limits as the criterion, it may be concluded that $\mu_A \neq \mu_B = \mu_C = \mu_D$. Yet, the 95% confidence limits for μ_B and μ_C only overlap slightly, and slight overlapping will occur when the sample means are barely significant at the 0.05 level. A more efficient test is needed.

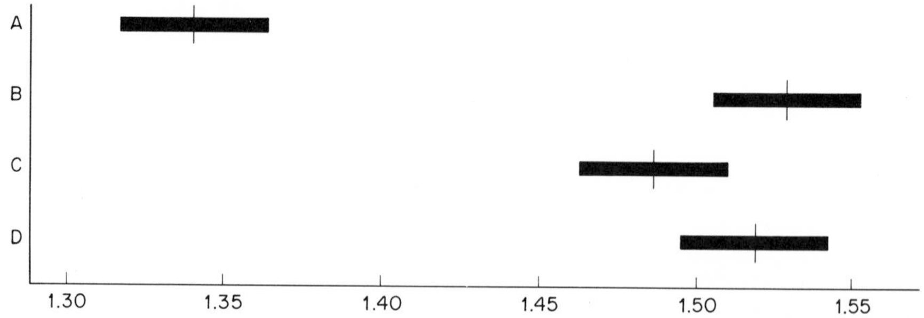

The sample means obtained in a randomized-block design can be analyzed further by (1) a multiple-range test, and (2) partitioning of treatments sum of squares and degrees of freedom if the intent to do so were implied in the design of the experiment *and* if treatments mean square is significant. A multiple-range test is appropriate here, but partitioning is not since no intent to do so was implied in the beginning.

By use of the q table (0.05 level), the necessary values for a multiple-range test can be calculated, using $s_{\bar{x}} = 0.0110$ and degrees of freedom equal to 27.

k	2	3	4
q	2.89	3.49	3.85
$qs_{\bar{x}}$	0.0318	0.0384	0.0424

The means can now be compared:

(a) $\underset{1.486}{\underline{C}} - \underset{1.341}{\underline{A}} = 0.145 > 0.0318$ Reject null hypothesis

(b) $\underset{1.519}{\underline{D}} - \underset{1.486}{\underline{C}} = 0.033 > 0.0318$ Reject null hypothesis

(c) $\underset{1.529}{\underline{B}} - \underset{1.519}{\underline{D}} = 0.010 < 0.0318$ Accept null hypothesis
Draw a line under D and B

(d) $\underset{1.529}{\underline{B}} - \underset{1.486}{\underline{C}} = 0.043 > 0.0382$ Reject null hypothesis

The results are given below:

A	C	D	B
1.341	1.486	1.519	1.529
		――――	――――

9.3 Comparison of Efficiency of the Randomized-Block and Completely Randomized Designs

The purpose of the randomized-block design is to remove from the estimate of σ^2 the variability due to environmental or other factors. This is done with the use of blocks.

It is instructive to compare the mathematical models for the randomized-block and completely randomized designs. The only difference is the presence of the block effect ($B = \mu_j - \mu$) in the model for the randomized-block design.

Mathematical Model for the Completely Randomized Design

$$X_{ij} = \mu + T + e$$

Mathematical Model for the Randomized-Block Design

$$X_{ij} = \mu + T + B + e$$

The model for the randomized-block design takes into consideration the possibility of a true environmental effect, and with the use of blocks, separates it from the estimate of σ^2 used in the F test. The model for the completely randomized design does not provide for the statistical control of environmental factors. Thus, if a completely randomized design is carried out and environmental variability is present that cannot be controlled experimentally, the measurements in the sample taken from the ith population will deviate from each other due to chance as well as due to the influence of the environmental effect. The estimate of σ^2 in the completely randomized design (i.e., error mean square) will consequently contain this environmental effect.

It is instructive to compare the degrees of freedom and sums of squares for the completely randomized and randomized-block designs. If an experiment were designed as a randomized-block design and the blocks ignored, the data could be analyzed as if the experiment were carried out as a completely randomized design. Technically, this is not proper because by the use of blocks, complete randomization, as specified by the completely randomized design, is not present. However, if this were done, the degrees of freedom and sums of squares for the two designs would be as in Table 9.4.

Table 9.4 illustrates that for both analyses the total and treatments sums of squares would be identical. Therefore, error sum of squares of the completely randomized design would be equal to the sum of blocks and error sum of squares of the randomized-block design. The same would be true for the degrees of freedom. Now if the environmental factors, and other factors, were constant from block to block [i.e., $\Sigma_1^n(\mu_j - \mu)^2 = 0$], then error and blocks mean square would both estimate σ^2 as shown by the above expectations. Combining error and blocks sums of squares and degrees of freedom would give a pooled estimate of σ^2 based on more degrees of freedom. This estimate would be equal to the error mean square of the completely randomized design.

Table 9.4

Completely Randomized Design		
Source	Degrees of Freedom	Sum of Squares
Total	$nk - 1$	$\sum_{1}^{nk} (X_{ij} - \bar{x})^2$
Treatments	$k - 1$	$n \sum_{1}^{k} (\bar{x}_i - \bar{x})^2$
Error	$k(n - 1)$	$\sum_{1}^{k} \left[\sum_{1}^{n} (X_{ij} - \bar{x}_i)^2 \right]$

Randomized Block Design		
Source	Degrees of Freedom	Sum of Squares
Total	$nk - 1$	$\sum_{1}^{nk} (X_{ij} - \bar{x})^2$
Treatments	$k - 1$	$n \sum_{1}^{k} (\bar{x}_i - \bar{x})^2$
Blocks	$n - 1$	$k \sum_{1}^{n} (\bar{x}_j - \bar{x})^2$
Error	$(n - 1)(k - 1)$	$\sum_{1}^{nk} (X_{ij} - \bar{x}_i - \bar{x}_j + \bar{x})^2$

However, if $\Sigma_1^n (\mu_j - \mu)^2$ does not equal zero, then error mean square of the randomized-block design would still be an estimate of σ^2, but blocks mean square would estimate $\sigma^2 + \dfrac{k}{n - 1} \sum_{1}^{n} (\mu_j - \mu)^2$, and consequently, the pooled estimate, which would still be equal to error mean square of the completely randomized design, would *overestimate* σ^2. This illustrates that if $\Sigma_1^n(\mu_j - \mu)^2$ does not equal zero, error mean square of the randomized-block design will be smaller than error mean square of the completely randomized design.

This can be expressed mathematically by considering the degrees of freedom and mean-square estimates for the various sources of variation in the two designs.

Table 9.5

Completely Randomized Design		
Source of Variation	Degrees of Freedom	Mean Square Estimates
Treatments	$k - 1$	$\sigma_1^{\,2} + \dfrac{n}{k - 1} \displaystyle\sum_1^k (\mu_i - \mu)^2$
Error	$k(n - 1)$	$\sigma_1^{\,2}$

Randomized Block Design		
Source of Variation	Degrees of Freedom	Mean Square Estimates
Treatments	$k - 1$	$\sigma_2^{\,2} + \dfrac{n}{k - 1} \displaystyle\sum_1^k (\mu_i - \mu)^2$
Blocks	$n - 1$	$\sigma_2^{\,2} + \dfrac{k}{n - 1} \displaystyle\sum_1^n (\mu_j - \mu)^2$
Error	$(k - 1)(n - 1)$	$\sigma_2^{\,2}$

Let error mean square of the completely randomized design be an estimate of σ_1^2, and error mean square of the randomized-block design an estimate of σ_2^2. Since a mean square is equal to sum of squares divided by degrees of freedom, an estimate of the sum of squares for each source of variation can be obtained by multiplying the mean-square estimates by the appropriate degrees of freedom. Since for both designs the total sums of squares are equal, the following relationship is true.

Total Sum of Squares for the
Completely Randomized Design

$$\left[(k-1)\left[\sigma_1{}^2 + \frac{n}{k-1}\sum_1^k (\mu_i - \mu)^2 \right] \\ + k(n-1)(\sigma_1{}^2) \right]$$

Total Sum of Squares for the
Randomized-Block Design

$$= \left[(k-1)\left[\sigma_2{}^2 + \frac{n}{k-1}\sum_1^k (\mu_i - \mu)^2 \right] \\ + (n-1)\left[\sigma_2{}^2 + \frac{k}{(n-1)}\sum_1^n (\mu_j - \mu)^2 \right] \\ + (n-1)(k-1)(\sigma_2{}^2) \right]$$

Simplifying and solving for $\sigma_2{}^2$ gives

$$\sigma_2{}^2 = \sigma_1{}^2 - \frac{k}{nk-1}\sum_1^n (\mu_j - \mu)^2$$

This shows that when $\Sigma_1^n(\mu_j - \mu)^2$ is equal to zero, $\sigma_2{}^2$ is equal to $\sigma_1{}^2$ and both error mean squares estimate the same value. When $\Sigma_1^n(\mu_j - \mu)^2$ does not equal zero, $\sigma_2{}^2$ is less than $\sigma_1{}^2$, and consequently error mean square of the randomized-block design is an estimate of a smaller value than error mean square of the completely randomized design. In the latter situation, F in the randomized-block design will be larger than F in the completely randomized design, since F is inversely related to the value of error mean square:

$$F = \frac{\text{Treatments Mean Square}}{\text{Error Mean Square}}$$

Thus, the efficiency of the two designs is largely dependent on the relative values of the two error mean squares. However, as will be shown below, efficiency also depends on the number of degrees of freedom associated with the estimate of σ^2.

After a randomized-block design has been carried out, it is logical to consider whether efficiency was gained or lost by using blocks. One method for doing this is to estimate what the value of error mean square would have been, for the same values of n and k, if complete randomization, instead of blocks, had been used. This estimated error mean square for the completely randomized design is symbolized by E_1. Error mean square for the randomized-block design is symbolized by E_2.

The formula for the estimated value of error mean square can be obtained algebraically from the equation derived above.

$$\sigma_2{}^2 = \sigma_1{}^2 - \frac{k}{nk-1}\sum_1^n (\mu_j - \mu)^2$$

Solving for σ_1^2 gives:

$$\sigma_1^2 = \sigma_2^2 + \frac{k}{nk-1} \sum_1^n (\mu_j - \mu)^2 = \sigma_2^2 + \frac{k(n-1)}{nk-1} \cdot \frac{\sum_1^n (\mu_j - \mu)^2}{n-1}$$

If E_b and E_2 are the mean squares for blocks and error in the randomized-block design, then

E_2 is an estimate of σ_2^2,

E_b is an estimate of $\sigma_2^2 + \dfrac{k}{n-1} \displaystyle\sum_1^n (\mu_j - \mu)^2$

and it can be shown that

$\dfrac{E_b - E_2}{k}$ is an estimate of $\dfrac{\sigma_2^2 + \dfrac{k}{n-1} \displaystyle\sum_1^n (\mu_j - \mu)^2 - \sigma_2^2}{k} = \dfrac{\displaystyle\sum_1^n (\mu_j - \mu)^2}{n-1}$

Substituting these estimates into the equation:

$$\sigma_1^2 = \sigma_2^2 + \frac{k(n-1)}{nk-1} \cdot \frac{\sum_1^n (\mu_j - \mu)^2}{n-1}$$

gives

$$E_1 = E_2 + \frac{k(n-1)}{nk-1} \cdot \frac{E_b - E_2}{k}$$

$$E_1 = \frac{n(k-1)E_2 + E_b(n-1)}{nk-1}$$

The ratio E_1/E_2 can be used as an efficiency test; however, a correction should be added for degrees of freedom. This is necessary because when $\Sigma_1^n(\mu_j - \mu)^2$ equals zero, both error mean squares estimate the same value. However, error mean square of the randomized-block design is associated with a smaller number of degrees of freedom. The use of blocks reduces the number of degrees of freedom available for the estimate of σ^2. When $\Sigma_1^n(\mu_j - \mu)^2$ equals zero, it is logical that the randomized-block design will be less efficient than the completely randomized design. Due to the smaller number of degrees of freedom available for the estimation of σ^2, it is necessary to determine the significance of the computed F value from a less-sensitive (upper) part of the F table.

It is therefore obvious that when relative efficiency is discussed, degrees of freedom should be considered in addition to the estimates of σ^2 from the two designs. R. A. Fisher (1947) has presented a formula for relative efficiency taking into consideration degrees of freedom.

$$\text{R.E.} = \frac{(\text{DF}_2 + 1)(\text{DF}_1 + 3)}{(\text{DF}_1 + 1)(\text{DF}_2 + 3)} \cdot \frac{E_1}{E_2}$$

DF_2 is the number of degrees of freedom associated with the estimate of σ^2 in the randomized-block design, and DF_1 is the number of degrees of freedom that would have been associated with this estimate if a completely randomized design had been carried out using the same values of n and k. Applying these formulae to the data obtained from the example of a randomized-block design gives:

$$E_1 = \frac{n(k-1)E_2 + E_b(n-1)}{nk-1} + \frac{(10)(3)(0.00121) + (0.02245)(9)}{39}$$
$$= 0.00611$$

and therefore

$$\text{R.E.} = \frac{(27+1)(36+3)}{(36+1)(27+3)} \cdot \frac{0.00611}{0.00121} = (0.98378)(5.0496) = 4.97$$

This means that the randomized-block design is 4.97 times more efficient than a completely randomized design would have been under similar conditions. Whenever R.E. is greater than 1.00, evidence is available that the reduction in the estimate of σ^2 was great enough to compensate for the reduction in the number of degrees of freedom associated with this estimate. This justifies the use of the randomized-block design.

9.4   Two-Way Classification

In a randomized-block design, both rows and columns may refer to treatments that are fixed or selected at random. In this type of problem blocks are not used to control environmental variability, but are set up in a specific way so that a null hypothesis may be tested. Such a randomized-block design is commonly referred to as analysis of variance with two-way classification.

Three different models may be encountered. When columns and rows are fixed, Model I (Analysis-of-Variance Model) is assumed. Model II (Components-of-Variance Model) is assumed if rows and columns refer to random effects. If columns are fixed and rows are random, or columns are random and rows are fixed, Model III (Mixed Model) is assumed. The expectations of the mean squares for these models are given in Table 9.6.

An example of a two-way classification experiment will be given. Assume that an investigator was interested in the effect of two drugs on blood pressure of cows. Twenty cows were randomly selected for testing. Each cow was measured three times: after drug A, after drug B, and after no drug (control). The three treatments were randomly applied to each cow. One week elapsed between treatments. The investigator knew that the effect of a given treatment would not carry over from one week to the next, and that time (at least over a three-week period) had no influence. He was interested in deter-

Table 9.6

Source of Variation	Degrees of Freedom	Model I — Columns fixed, Rows fixed	Model II — Columns random, Rows random
Columns	$k - 1$	$\sigma^2 + \dfrac{n}{k-1}\sum_1^k (\mu_i - \mu)^2$	$\sigma^2 + n\sigma_{\mu_i}^{\,2}$
Rows	$n - 1$	$\sigma^2 + \dfrac{k}{n-1}\sum_1^n (\mu_j - \mu)^2$	$\sigma^2 + k\sigma_{\mu_j}^{\,2}$
Error	$(k - 1)(n - 1)$	σ^2	σ^2

Source of Variation	Degrees of Freedom	Model III — Columns fixed, Rows random	Model III — Columns random, Rows fixed
Columns	$k - 1$	$\sigma^2 + \dfrac{n}{k-1}\sum_1^k (\mu_i - \mu)^2$	$\sigma^2 + n\sigma_{\mu_i}^{\,2}$
Rows	$n - 1$	$\sigma^2 + k\sigma_{\mu_j}^{\,2}$	$\sigma^2 + \dfrac{k}{n-1}\sum_1^n (\mu_j - \mu)^2$
Error	$(k - 1)(n - 1)$	σ^2	σ^2

mining the effects of the treatments and also if variability existed among the cows in response to the treatments. The treatments (drugs) were fixed but the cows were selected at random. There are two hypotheses: (1) No difference exists among treatments, i.e., $\mu_1 = \mu_2 = \mu_3$. (2) No variability exists among the cows in response to the treatments, i.e., $\sigma_{\mu_j}^2 = 0$. If the first null hypothesis is rejected, he will run a multiple-range test or partition treatments sum of squares and degrees of freedom to determine if any difference exists between the two drugs, and if the drugs as a group differ from the control. If the second null hypothesis is rejected, he will estimate the value of $\sigma_{\mu_j}^2$.

Model III is assumed. The sources of variation, degrees of freedom, and expectations of the mean squares are given in Table 9.7.

Table 9.7

Source of Variation	Degrees of Freedom	Mean Square Estimates
Total	59	
Treatments	2	$\sigma^2 + \dfrac{n}{k-1} \sum_{1}^{k} (\mu_i - \mu)^2$
Cows	19	$\sigma^2 + k\sigma_{\mu_j}^2$
Error	38	σ^2

The first null hypothesis would be tested by dividing treatments mean square by error mean square. The second null hypothesis would be tested by dividing cows mean square by error mean square. If justified, a multiple-range test, partitioning, and the estimation of $\sigma_{\mu_j}^2$ would be carried out in the standard manner.

9.5 Missing Data in the Randomized-Block Design

Accidents often occur in experimental research. Animals and plants die and errors are made in recording data. Missing data are of no serious consequence in the completely randomized design, since it is not necessary that $n_1 = n_2 = n_3 = \cdots = n_k$. This is not true for the randomized-block design.

Each block must have the same number of treatments. When a measurement is missing, one or the other of two procedures may be followed. The first is to discard the entire block. When there is a large number of blocks, this can be done without a great loss of efficiency, but when there is a small number of blocks, this procedure is not satisfactory. The second procedure is to estimate the value of the missing measurement. The estimate is obtained with the use of the following formula:

$$X_{ij} = \frac{kT + nB - S}{(k - 1)(n - 1)}$$

where X_{ij} = missing measurement, k = number of treatments, T = sum of all the measurements with the same treatment as the missing measurement, n = number of blocks, B = sum of all the measurements in the same block as the missing measurement, and S = sum of all the observed measurements.

When X_{ij} is obtained, the analysis proceeds as usual with the exception that the total number of degrees of freedom and the error degrees of freedom are each decreased by one. This procedure introduces a slight bias favoring the significance of treatments mean square. Hence, it is proper to correct treatments *sum of squares* unless only an approximate F value is needed. Treatments sum of squares is reduced by the following amount:

$$\text{Correction Value} = \frac{[B - (k - 1)X_{ij}]^2}{k(k - 1)}$$

This will give a new treatments sum of squares and treatments mean square. Total sum of squares should be changed accordingly in the analysis-of-variance table.

When two or three measurements are missing, a modification of the above procedure is required, but will not be discussed here. When several measurements are missing, the best procedure may be to begin a new experiment.

Problems

1. Outline a practical procedure for randomizing 4 treatments in 6 blocks.
2. Assume that for such a randomized-block design, the measurements on page 144 were obtained.
(a) Fill out an analysis-of-variance table for the following sources of variation: Total, Blocks, Treatments, and Error. (b) Give the expected values for treatments and error mean squares. (c) Test the null hypothesis that no difference exists among the treatment means, i.e., $H_0: \Sigma_1^k(\mu_i - \mu)^2 = 0$. (d) If you reject the null hypothesis, carry out a multiple-range test. What are your conclusions? (3) Calculate a relative-efficiency value. What are your conclusions?
3. For illustrative purposes, assume that because of an accident, the measurement for treatment B in block 5 is missing. Estimate the missing value and test the null hypothesis that no difference exists among the treatment means. (Remember that when

Blocks	Treatments			
	A	B	C	D
1	10.2	16.2	15.8	6.3
2	10.7	16.6	16.9	6.6
3	11.5	17.5	17.6	7.6
4	11.8	17.6	17.8	8.1
5	12.4	18.5	18.3	8.9
6	12.6	18.7	18.9	9.4

a missing measurement is estimated, Total and Error degrees of freedom are reduced by one, and after total, blocks, treatments, and error sum of squares are calculated, an adjustment should be made in treatments sum of squares before calculating F = Treatments Mean Square/Error Mean Square. In presenting the analysis of variance table, total sum of squares should be obtained so that it is the sum of blocks, error, and adjusted treatments sums of squares). Compare the results of the two F tests.

4. A two-way classification experiment was carried out where the column effects were random and the row effects were fixed. The analysis-of-variance table was as follows:

Source of Variation	Degrees of Freedom	Sum of Squares	Mean Squares
Total	49	177	
Columns	4	24	6
Rows	9	81	9
Error	36	72	2

(a) Give the expected values for columns and rows mean squares. (b) Carry out the F tests specified in this experiment. (c) Estimate the following components of variance: σ^2 and $\sigma_{\mu_i}^2$.

5. A physician compared three different methods of determining α-amino nitrogen levels in urine.

Patient	Method 1	Method 2	Method 3
1	205	86	132
2	165	40	324
3	180	100	170
4	106	90	286
5	90	70	140
6	105	80	169
7	160	70	300
8	207	62	157
9	200	89	140
10	29	12	101

(a) Test the hypothesis that the methods give similar results. (b) If you reject the hypothesis, carry out a multiple-range test. What are your conclusions?

6. Tomato plants given fertilizer treatments were grown in a greenhouse. Eight positions were designated on the greenhouse benches. Five plants were placed at each position. Each plant was given one of five different treatments. The treatments were applied randomly to the plants at each position. The yield of each plant was expressed as kilograms of ripe fruit.

Position	Treatment 1	Treatment 2	Treatment 3	Treatment 4	Treatment 5
1	1.29	1.33	1.24	1.28	1.31
2	1.10	1.00	1.05	1.03	1.17
3	1.34	1.31	1.41	1.39	1.28
4	1.39	1.31	1.41	1.39	1.28
5	1.30	1.26	1.35	1.36	1.39
6	1.19	1.24	1.17	1.18	1.14
7	1.33	1.35	1.29	1.38	1.32
8	1.00	1.09	1.19	1.14	1.14

(a) Test the hypothesis that no difference exists among fertilizer treatments. (b) If you reject the hypothesis, analyze the sample means further by the multiple-range test. (c) Was efficiency lost or gained by using the randomized-block design as compared with the completely randomized design?

CHAPTER TEN

Latin-Square Design

The randomized-block design assumes that environmental conditions are uniform within blocks. In some situations this assumption may not be true. For example, if the blocks were laid out in a field as shown in the diagram below, soil variability in a north-south direction would be controlled, but if an environmental gradient were present in an east–west direction as well,

Block 1	B	D	A	C
Block 2	A	B	D	C
Block 3	A	C	D	B
Block 4	D	B	C	A
Block 5	C	A	B	D

N
↑
W ←—+—→ E
↓
S

conditions within each block would not be homogeneous. The east–west gradient would tend to increase the value of error mean square. In such a situation, increased control of the variability can be brought about by use of the Latin-square design. It is a modified randomized-block design, inasmuch as two series of blocks are used at right angles to each other. The blocks in a Latin-square design are referred to as rows and columns.

In the randomized-block design the treatments are allocated to the plots within each block at random with the restriction that each treatment is

146

represented once in each block. In the Latin-square design the same restriction applies, but since there are two series of blocks at right angles to each other, the restriction is actually two-fold. The treatments are allocated at random with the exception that a treatment can only occur once in each row and each column.

In a 3 × 3 Latin square there are 12 possible arrangements. One of the 12 is as follows:

B	C	A
A	B	C
C	A	B

In a 4 × 4 Latin square there are 576 possible arrangements, and in a 5 × 5 square there are 161,280 possible arrangements.

The advantage of the Latin-square design is that it controls the extraneous variability associated with both rows and columns. The rows and columns may be set up to control the effects of soil change in two directions at right angles or the rows may correspond to a soil or some other environmental change and the columns to a time trend. Animal-nutrition studies can often be designed so that rows correspond to initial weight and the columns to age. The Latin square is useful for many different types of experiments. The success of the design depends on the ability of the investigator to recognize the presence of the factors that can inflate the estimate σ^2 and to lay out the square accordingly. When the row and column effects are real, the Latin-square design will be an improvement over the randomized-block design in controlling the estimate of σ^2.

However, it has certain disadvantages. Controlling the variability in two directions further reduces the number of degrees of freedom available for the estimation of σ^2. The total degrees of freedom is partitioned into: treatments, rows, columns, and error. The numbers of degrees for each source of variation for various Latin-square designs are given in Table 10.1.

The data in Table 10.1 show that at least five or six treatments are necessary before error degrees of freedom becomes appreciable. For this reason the Latin-square design is seldom used when less than five treatments are to be tested. A 2 × 2 Latin square is not possible because of zero degrees of freedom for error. When there is a small number of treatments, the Latin-square design is usually unnecessary since the blocks can be made small enough that homogeneity within blocks is likely and the randomized-block design will be efficient.

Another disadvantage of the Latin-square design is that in field and green-

Table 10.1   Degrees of Freedom for Latin Square Designs .

	Source of Variation $n \times n$	Total $n^2 - 1$	Treatments $n - 1$	Rows $n - 1$	Columns $n - 1$	Error $(n - 1)(n - 2)$
Degrees of Freedom	2×2	3	1	1	1	0
	3×3	8	2	2	2	2
	4×4	15	3	3	3	6
	5×5	24	4	4	4	12
	6×6	35	5	5	5	20
	7×7	48	6	6	6	30
	8×8	63	7	7	7	42

house studies, the blocks must be adjacent to each other (i.e., the plots within the square must be contiguous). The blocks do not have to be adjacent in the randomized-block design. This restricts the flexibility of the Latin square. The size of the square is usually dependent on the number of treatments. Since field and greenhouse facilities usually curb the size of the square that is possible, this in turn may restrict the number of treatments that can be tested. Latin-square designs with more than twelve treatments are seldom used.

The shape of the Latin square can be square or rectangular; therefore the term "square" should not be taken literally.

10.1   Example of a Latin-Square Design

For ease of presentation the Latin-square design will be illustrated using a 3 × 3 square. However, it should be stressed that such a square is unrealistic because of the small number of error degrees of freedom.

A plant breeder compared the yields of three varieties of wheat. Since the soil and water conditions were presumed to be variable, a Latin-square design was used. The treatments were randomized to the rows and columns as follows:

B	A	C
A	C	B
C	B	A

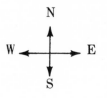

In the Latin square there are n replications so there are n columns and n rows. At the end of the growing season the number of bushels per plot was noted. The following calculations were made:

	Columns			$\sum\limits_{1}^{n} X_j$	$\sum\limits_{1}^{n} X_j^2$	$\bar{x}_j$
	B 15	A 16	C 22	53	965	17.7
Rows	A 17	C 26	B 19	62	1,326	20.7
	C 22	B 15	A 18	55	1,033	18.3
$\sum\limits_{1}^{n} X_i$	54	57	59	$\sum\limits_{1}^{n} X_{ij}^{} = 170$		
$\sum\limits_{1}^{n} X_i^2$	998	1,157	1,169		$\sum\limits_{1}^{n} X_{ij}^2 = 3324$	
$\bar{x}_i$	18.0	19.0	19.7			$\bar{x} = 18.9$

The sums of the measurements and means for the three varieties are obtained by rearranging the data.

	A	B	C
	17	15	22
	16	15	26
	18	19	22
$\sum\limits_{1}^{n} X_k$	51	49	70
$\bar{x}_k$	17.00	16.33	23.33

The formulae for sum of squares are derived in a similar manner as was shown for the randomized-block design. Since there are two series of blocks, the total sum of squares is divided into one extra component.

$$\text{Correction Factor} = \frac{\left(\sum_{1}^{n^2} X_{ij}\right)^2}{n^2} = \frac{(170)^2}{9} = 3211.11$$

$$\text{Total Sum of Squares} = \sum_{1}^{n^2} (X_{ij} - \bar{x})^2 = \sum_{1}^{n^2} X_{ij}^2 - \frac{\left(\sum_{1}^{n^2} X_{ij}\right)^2}{n^2}$$

$$= \sum_{1}^{n^2} X_{ij}^2 - \text{C.F.}$$

$$= 3{,}324 - 3{,}211.11 = 112.89$$

$$\text{Treatments (Varieties) Sum of Squares} = n \sum_{1}^{n} (\bar{x}_k - \bar{x})^2 = \sum_{1}^{n} \frac{\left(\sum_{1}^{n} X_k\right)^2}{n} - \text{C.F.}$$

$$= \frac{(51)^2}{3} + \frac{(49)^2}{3} + \frac{(70)^2}{3} - 3211.11$$

$$= \frac{(51)^2 + (49)^2 + (70)^2}{3} - 3211.11$$

$$= 89.56$$

$$\text{Rows Sum of Squares} = n \sum_{1}^{n} (\bar{x}_j - \bar{x})^2 = \sum_{1}^{n} \frac{\left(\sum_{1}^{n} X_j\right)^2}{n} - \text{C.F.}$$

$$= \frac{(53)^2}{3} + \frac{(62)^2}{3} + \frac{(55)^2}{3} - 3211.11$$

$$= \frac{(53)^2 + (62)^2 + (55)^2}{3} - 3211.11$$

$$= 14.89$$

$$\text{Columns Sum of Squares} = n \sum_{1}^{n} (\bar{x}_i - \bar{x})^2 = \sum_{1}^{n} \frac{\left(\sum_{1}^{n} X_i\right)^2}{n} - \text{C.F.}$$

$$= \frac{(54)^2}{3} + \frac{(57)^2}{3} + \frac{(59)^2}{3} - 3211.11$$

$$= \frac{(54)^2 + (57)^2 + (59)^2}{3} - 3211.11$$

$$= 4.22$$

Error Sum of Squares = Total Sum of Squares minus Treatments Sum of Squares minus Rows Sum of Squares minus Columns Sum of Squares = 112.89 − 89.56 − 14.89 − 4.22 = 4.22.

The mathematical model for the Latin-square design is as follows (Model I): If $X_{ij(k)}$ is a measurement occurring in the ith column and jth row which is associated with the kth treatment, then $X_{ij(k)} = \mu + C + R + T + e$ where μ is the general mean, $C = (\mu_i - \mu)$ is the column effect, $R = (\mu_j - \mu)$ is the row effect, $T = (\mu_k - \mu)$ is the treatment effect, and $e = (X_{ij(k)} - \mu_{ij(k)})$ is the error effect. The C, R, and T effects are fixed; therefore,

$$\sum_1^n (\mu_i - \mu) = \sum_1^n (\mu_j - \mu) = \sum_1^n (\mu_k - \mu) = 0$$

The random variables $(X_{ij(k)} - \mu_{ij(k)})$ are independently and normally distributed with a mean of zero and a common variance (σ^2). It is apparent that $\mu_{ij(k)}$ is a cell mean corresponding to the ith column, jth row, and kth treatment. Note that k is a function of i and j. For example, in the above example, the Latin square was laid out as follows:

B	A	C
A	C	B
C	B	A

When $i = 2$ and $j = 3$, the kth variety is B. Since k is not independent of i and j, a parenthesis is used in the symbols $X_{ij(k)}$ and $\mu_{ij(k)}$.

The expected values (expectations) of the mean squares in a Latin-square design, assuming Model I, are given as follows:

$$E\text{ [Varieties (Treatments) Mean Square]} = \sigma^2 + \frac{n}{n-1} \sum_1^n (\mu_k - \mu)^2$$

$$E\text{ [Rows Mean Square]} = \sigma^2 + \frac{n}{n-1} \sum_1^n (\mu_j - \mu)^2$$

$$E\text{ [Columns Mean Square]} = \sigma^2 + \frac{n}{n-1} \sum_1^n (\mu_i - \mu)^2$$

$$E\text{ [Error Mean Square]} = \sigma^2$$

The appropriate mean squares are given in Table 10.2

The null hypothesis that no difference exists among the variety means [i.e., $\Sigma_1^n(\mu_k - \mu)^2 = 0$] is tested as follows:

$$F = \frac{\text{Varieties Mean Square}}{\text{Error Mean Square}} = \frac{44.780}{2.110} = 21.2$$

Table 10.2 Analysis of Variance.

Source of Variation	Degrees of Freedom	Sum of Squares	Mean Square
Total	8	112.89	
Varieties	2	89.56	44.780
Rows	2	14.89	7.445
Columns	2	4.22	2.110
Error	2	4.22	2.110

Since $F\left[\begin{smallmatrix}2\\2\end{smallmatrix} 0.05\right] = 19.0$, the hypothesis can be rejected. The standard error used in the setting of confidence limits and a multiple-range test is as follows:

$$s_{\bar{x}} = \sqrt{\frac{s^2}{n}} = \sqrt{\frac{\text{Error Mean Square}}{n}} = \sqrt{\frac{2.110}{3}} = 0.839$$

10.2 Efficiency of a Latin-Square Design Relative to a Completely Randomized Design

Let E_3 signify the error mean square in a Latin-square design and E_1 the estimated error mean square of a completely randomized design. If E_r and E_c are the row and column mean squares, then it can be shown that

$$E_1 = \frac{E_r + E_c + (n-1)E_3}{n+1} \quad \text{and R.E.} = \frac{(\text{DF}_3 + 1)(\text{DF}_1 + 3)}{(\text{DF}_1 + 1)(\text{DF}_3 + 3)} \times \frac{E_1}{E_3}$$

where DF_1 and DF_3 are the numbers of degrees of freedom associated with the estimates of σ^2 in the completely randomized and Latin-square designs, respectively. For the above example these values become

$$E_1 = \frac{7.445 + 2.110 + (2)(2.110)}{4} = 3.444$$

$$\text{R.E.} = \frac{(2+1)(6+3)}{(6+1)(2+3)} \times \frac{3.444}{2.110} = 1.26$$

The Latin-square design is 1.26 times more efficient than the completely randomized design would have been under similar conditions.

10.3 Efficiency of a Latin-Square Design Relative to a Randomized-Block Design

In this case E_2 is the estimated value of error mean square in a randomized-block design, assuming that either the rows or columns were used as blocks.

Rows Used as Blocks   Columns Used as Blocks

$$E_2 = \frac{E_c + (n-1)E_3}{n} \qquad\qquad E_2 = \frac{E_r + (n-1)E_3}{n}$$

$$\text{R.E.} = \frac{(DF_3 + 1)(DF_2 + 3)}{(DF_2 + 1)(DF_3 + 3)}$$

In the above example, as shown by the mean squares, there appeared to be little or no environmental variability among the columns. Therefore, using the rows as blocks,

$$E_2 = \frac{2.110 + (2)(2.110)}{3} = 2.110$$

$$\text{R.E.} = \frac{(2+1)(4+3)}{(2+3)(4+1)} \times \frac{2.110}{2.110} = 0.84$$

The Latin-square design is less efficient than this randomized-block design would have been. When the columns are used as blocks, R.E. is equal to 1.55, which indicates that the Latin-square design is more efficient than this randomized-block design would have been under similar conditions.

10.4 Estimation of a Missing Measurement in a Latin Square

A missing measurement in a Latin-square design is estimated by using the equation given below. The total and error degrees of freedom are reduced by one.

$$X_{ij} = \frac{n(R + C + T) - 2S}{(n-1)(n-2)}$$

where X_{ij} = missing measurement, n = number of treatments, rows and columns, R = sum of all the measurements in the same row as the missing measurement, C = sum of all the measurements in the same column as the missing measurement, T = sum of all the measurements with the same treatment as the missing measurement, and S = sum of all the observed measurements.

The estimated value is then placed in the proper row and column, and total, treatments, rows, columns, and error sum of squares are calculated in the ordinary manner. As for the randomized-block design, using the estimated value introduces a bias. Therefore, a correction should be made in treatments sum of squares before the F test is carried out. Treatments sum of squares is *reduced* by the amount:

$$\text{Correction Value} = \frac{[S - R - C - (n - 1)T]^2}{(n - 1)^2(n - 2)^2}$$

In the analysis-of-variance table, total sum of squares then becomes the sum of error, rows, columns and adjusted treatments sums of squares.

10.5   Laboratory Example of a Latin-Square Design

Even though the Latin-square design is used most frequently in field experiments, it can be used to great advantage in laboratory experimental work.

Several investigators in a pharmacology laboratory were studying the relative toxicities of six different drugs (A, B, C, D, E, and F) on rabbits. The rabbits were of the same sex and came from the same inbred strain. A standard dilution was prepared of each of the drugs and injected into a femoral vein at a specified rate. Death was determined by means of a stethoscope. Previous experiments had shown that the toxic dose was related to body size (i.e., large rabbits are more tolerant of the drugs than small rabbits). Since the rabbits were not of similar size, the measurement taken was micrograms of drug required to cause death per gram of body weight.

Drugs B, C, D, and F were derived from the same genus of plant (Genus #1), while A and E came from a different genus (Genus #2). The investigators supposed that a similarity in toxicity might exist for drugs derived from the same genus. Therefore, they planned to partition accordingly, if treatments (drugs) mean square were significant.

Due to the nature of the experiment, it was suspected that extraneous factors could influence the results of the study: (1) Several days were required to complete the experiment. The drugs were prepared fresh each day. It was suspected that the techniques of preparing the drugs could vary slightly from day to day. (2) The injection of the drugs into the rabbits by the observers could become more routine after several days. (3) Six different observers were used in the experiment. It was suspected that the skill of administering the drug and determining when death occurred could vary from one observer to another.

In order to eliminate the effects of these potential sources of variability, the experiment was designed as a 6 × 6 Latin square. Once a day for six days, each observer injected a single rabbit with one of the drugs. An observer only tested a specific drug once, and thus each drug was only tested once a day.

The plan was to calculate sum of squares for the following sources of variation: (1) Total; (2) Drugs (Treatments); (3) Days (Columns); (4) Observers (Rows); (5) Error.

The experimental layout is given in Table 10.3.

Table 10.3

| Observer | Days | | | | | | $\sum_{1}^{n} X_j$ | $\sum_{1}^{n} X_j^2$ |
	Thurs. 11/3	Sat. 11/5	Mon. 11/7	Wed. 11/9	Fri. 11/11	Sat. 11/12		
1	F 26.6	B 39.7	E 25.5	A 20.1	C 33.1	D 30.1	175.1	5,339.53
2	E 18.4	A 22.2	D 35.0	B 35.6	F 38.5	C 40.1	189.8	6,414.02
3	D 29.0	E 24.1	A 20.3	C 29.8	B 38.5	F 36.3	178.0	5,521.88
4	C 28.1	D 35.5	B 34.1	F 30.1	A 24.2	E 18.1	170.1	5,031.93
5	B 30.4	C 38.7	F 33.1	D 39.7	E 24.3	A 22.2	188.4	6,176.88
6	A 17.1	F 38.5	C 34.9	E 18.2	D 32.1	B 35.6	176.4	5,621.68
$\sum_{1}^{n} X_i$	149.6	198.7	182.9	173.5	190.7	182.4	4,077.8	
$\sum_{1}^{n} X_i^2$	3,893.30	6,889.93	5,763.77	5,372.75	6,266.65	5,919.52		34,105.92

The data in Table 10.3 must now be rearranged to give information on the specific drugs. This is done in Table 10.4.

Correction Factor $= \dfrac{(1,077.8)^2}{36} = 32,268.13$

Total Sum of Squares $= 34,105.92 - 32,268.13 = 1,837.79$

Drugs Sum of Squares
$$= \frac{(126.1)^2 + (213.9)^2 + (204.7)^2 + (201.4)^2 + (128.6)^2 + (203.1)^2}{6}$$
$$- 32,268.13 = 1,382.88$$

Table 10.4

Drugs	A	B	C	D	E	F
	20.1	39.7	33.1	30.1	25.5	26.6
	22.2	35.6	40.1	35.0	18.4	38.5
	20.3	38.5	29.8	29.0	24.1	36.3
	24.2	35.1	28.1	35.5	18.1	30.1
	22.2	30.4	38.7	39.7	24.3	33.1
	17.1	35.6	34.9	32.1	18.2	38.5
$\sum_{1}^{n} X_k$	126.1	213.9	204.7	201.4	128.6	203.1
$\bar{x}_k$	21.02	35.65	34.12	33.57	21.43	33.85

Observers Sum of Squares

$$= \frac{(175.1)^2 + (189.8)^2 + (178.0)^2 + (170.1)^2 + (188.4)^2 + (176.4)^2}{6}$$

$$- 32,268.13 = 50.80$$

Days Sum of Squares

$$= \frac{(149.6)^2 + (198.7)^2 + (182.9)^2 + (173.5)^2 + (109.7)^2 + (182.4)^2}{6}$$

$$= 240.66$$

Error Sum of Squares $= 1,837.79 - 1,382.88 - 50.80 - 240.66 = 163.45$

Table 10.5 Analysis of Variance.

Source of Variation	Degrees of Freedom	Sum of Squares	Mean Square
Total	35	1,837.79	
Drugs	5	1,382.88	276.57
Observers	5	50.80	10.16
Days	5	240.66	48.13
Error	20	163.45	8.17

The null hypothesis that no difference exists among drug means [i.e., $\Sigma_1^n(\mu_k - \mu)^2 = 0$] is tested by:

$$F = \frac{\text{Drugs Mean Square}}{\text{Error Mean Square}} = \frac{267.57}{8.17} = 33.8$$

$$F\left[\begin{matrix} 5 \\ 20 \end{matrix} \ 0.05\right] = 2.7$$

The null hypothesis is rejected. This opens the way for partitioning. The samples for drugs B, C, D, and F are grouped, and likewise the samples for drugs A and E are grouped. This is done in Tables 10.6. and 10.7.

Table 10.6 Drugs from Genus #1.

Drugs	B	C	D	F
$\sum\limits_1^n X_k$	213.9	204.7	201.4	203.1
Sum of all Measurements	823.1			

Genus #1 Sum of Squares
$$= \frac{(213.9)^2 + (204.7)^2 + (201.4)^2 + (203.1)^2}{6} - \frac{(823.1)^2}{24} = 15.59$$

Table 10.7 Drugs from Genus #2.

Drugs	A	E
$\sum\limits_1^n X_k$	126.1	128.6
Sum of all Measurements	254.7	

$$\text{Genus #2 Sum of Squares} = \frac{(126.1)^2 + (128.6)^2}{6} - \frac{(254.7)^2}{12} = 0.52$$

A groups sum of squares is now calculated. This will lead to a mean square used to determine if any significant difference exists between the group means. The mean of group #1 is given by 823.1/24 = 34.30, while the mean of group #2 is 254.7/12 = 21.22.

$$\text{Groups Sum of Squares} = \frac{(823.1)^2}{24} + \frac{(254.7)^2}{12} - \frac{(1{,}077.8)^2}{36} = 1{,}366.77$$

Drugs sum of squares has now been partitioned into three components: Genus #1, Genus #2, and Groups. Note that the sum of the three components equals drugs sum of squares $(15.59 + 0.52 + 1,366.77 = 1,382.88)$. The completed analysis of variance is given in Table 10.8.

Table 10.8

Source of Variation	Degrees of Freedom	Sum of Squares	Mean Square
Genus #1 (BCDF)	3	15.59	5.19
Genus #2 (AE)	1	0.52	0.52
Groups (BCDF vs. AE)	1	1,366.77	1,366.77
Error	20	163.45	8.17

Genus #1, genus #2, and groups mean squares are then divided by error mean square. It is concluded that no difference exists among the drugs extracted from plants belonging to the same genus, but that drugs *(BCDF)* belonging to genus #1 are significantly less toxic than drugs *(AE)* belonging to Genus #2. The only significant mean square is groups mean square $(F = 1,366.77/8.17 = 167.3)$.

The identical conclusions would be reached by comparing the six drug sample means by a multiple-range test or by setting the 95% confidence limits for the six drug population means. The standard error in either procedure becomes:

$$s_{\bar{x}} = \sqrt{\frac{s^2}{n}} = \sqrt{\frac{\text{Error Mean Square}}{n}} = \sqrt{\frac{8.17}{6}} = 1.167$$

The q or t tables would be entered with 20 degrees of freedom.

The efficiency of this Latin-square design can now be compared with a completely randomized design and the two different types of randomized-block designs.

10.6 Comparison With a Completely Randomized Design

$$E_1 = \frac{E_r + E_c + (n - 1)E_r}{n + 1} = \frac{10.16 + 48.13 + (5)(8.17)}{7} = 14.16$$

$$\text{R.E.} = \frac{(20 + 1)(30 + 3)}{(30 + 1)(20 + 3)} \cdot \frac{14.16}{8.17} = 1.68$$

It is concluded that this Latin square design is 1.68 times more efficient than the completely randomized design would have been under similar conditions.

10.7 Comparison With a Randomized-Block Design Where Rows (Observers) Are Used as Blocks

$$E_2 = \frac{E_c + (n - 1)E_3}{n} = \frac{48.13 + (5)(8.17)}{6} = 14.83$$

$$\text{R.E.} = \frac{(20 + 1)(25 + 3)}{(25 + 1)(20 + 3)} \cdot \frac{14.83}{8.17} = 1.78$$

The Latin-square design is 1.78 times more efficient than this design would have been.

10.8 Comparison With a Randomized-Block Design Where Columns (Days) Are Used as Blocks

$$E_2 = \frac{E_r + (n - 1)E_3}{n} = \frac{10.16 + (5)(8.17)}{6} = 8.50$$

$$\text{R.E.} = \frac{(20 + 1)(25 + 3)}{(25 + 1)(20 + 3)} \cdot \frac{8.50}{8.17} = 1.02$$

The Latin-square design was only slightly more efficient than this randomized-block design.

It is concluded that little variability was introduced by utilizing different observers; however, conducting the experiments on different days did introduce significant variability.

Problems

1. An investigator studied the effects of diet on milk yield of dairy cows. Five specific diets (A, B, C, D, and E), were tested. He selected five cows (same age) at random. Each cow was placed on an experimental diet for a four-week period. After a week's recess, the cow was then placed on another experimental diet. This was repeated until each cow had been placed on all five diets. Previous experiments had shown there was no carry-over from one period to the next. In order to control individual variability (genetic and environmental) among cows, and any variability because of periods (change of milk flow with time, etc.), the investigator used a Latin-square design. The data are below. The entries are pounds of milk for each four-week period.

Cows

Periods		1	2	3	4	5
	I	A449	B444	C401	D299	E292
	II	B463	C375	D323	E264	A415
	III	C393	D353	E278	A404	B425
	IV	D371	E241	A441	B410	C392
	V	E258	A430	B450	C385	D347

(a) Complete the analysis-of-variance table. (b) Give the expectations for cows, periods, diets, and error mean squares. (c) On the basis of the F test and multiple-range test, what are your conclusions about the five diets? (d) Calculate the 95% confidence limits for the five diet means. (e) Determine whether efficiency was lost or gained by using the Latin-square design as compared with the completely randomized design and randomized-block design. Interpret the meaning of the R.E. values.

2. An agronomist tested 5 different fertilizer treatments on the yield of tomatoes in a large field. The five treatments were as follows:

A no manure
B 100 lbs. of manure per plot
C 200 lbs. of manure per plot
D 300 lbs. of manure per plot
E 400 lbs. of manure per plot

A 5 × 5 Latin-square design was selected. Twelve plants were grown in each plot. One of the five treatments was applied to each plot. The measurement was kilograms of ripe fruit per plot.

Columns

	A	E	D	C	B
	15.71	21.97	23.43	21.00	18.32
	D	B	A	E	C
	21.96	18.92	17.22	23.59	23.20
Rows	B	A	C	D	E
	18.61	17.90	23.60	25.46	24.56
	C	D	E	B	A
	23.81	24.41	27.65	19.79	17.91
	E	C	B	A	D
	25.92	25.20	18.91	19.12	28.27

(a) Test the hypothesis that no difference exists among the five treatments. Compare the sample means with the aid of the multiple-range test. What are your conclusions?
(b) Calculate the 95% confidence limits for the population means. (c) Determine whether efficiency was gained or lost by using the Latin-square design.

3. Corn seedlings were grown in a greenhouse. Because of limitation of space, only one long bench was available for the experiment. Four sections were established on the bench.

Section 1	Section 2	Section 3	Section 4

Each section was given a different fertilizer treatment. The amount of growth was measured after a specified period of time by harvesting the seedlings and determining their oven-dry weight. The experiment was then repeated. The total number of replications was four.

Assume that an error was made during the third replication: One treatment was assigned to two sections on the bench. Becuase of this error, the measurement for the plants in one section could not be used in the analysis.

Columns (Sections)

	1	2	3	4
	C 11.4	D 8.2	B 13.1	A 14.4
	B 14.2	A 15.4	C 12.5	D 9.2
Rows (Replications)	D 7.1	C 13.9	A —	B 15.8
	A 14.9	B 14.3	D 7.6	C 12.4

(a) Estimate the missing measurement. (b) Complete the analysis-of-variance table, making the necessary corrections. (c) Test the hypothesis that the treatments have the same effect.

CHAPTER ELEVEN

Analysis of Variance — Factorial Experiments

Very often in analysis-of-variance problems, it is informative to consider the treatments in various combinations. For example, a variety of sugar beets may be grown in the presence of fertilizer treatments involving combinations of different concentrations of nitrogen and phosphorus, or several varieties may each be grown in the presence of different types of fertilizers. In animal experiments, several types of drugs or rations may be tested in various concentrations and combinations, and in some cases it may be of interest to determine the response of males and females from different strains. Several factors may be considered in a single experiment. Factors are usually symbolized by lower-case letters as shown below:

$$a_1 = \text{Variety 1} \qquad\qquad b_1 = \text{Fertilizer 1}$$

$$a_2 = \text{Variety 2} \qquad\qquad b_2 = \text{Fertilizer 2}$$

The varieties correspond to one factor and the fertilizers to another. When the factors are considered in various combinations, the experiments are referred to as factorial experiments. If there are two factors, it is called a two-factor factorial experiment. A more exact description of the case of the two varieties and two fertilizers shown above is a completely randomized design, or randomized-block design, etc., with a 2×2 factorial arrangement of the treatments, using the term "treatments" again in the broad sense. In statistical terminology, there are two *levels* of the first factor and two *levels* of the second factor.

a_1		a_2	
b_1	b_2	b_1	b_2
X_1	X_1	X_1	X_1
X_2	X_2	X_2	X_2
X_3	X_3	X_3	X_3
.	.	.	.
.	.	.	.
.	.	.	.
X_n	X_n	X_n	X_n

Two levels of the first factor, three of the second, and two of the third, would be designated as a $2 \times 3 \times 2$ factorial arrangement of the treatments. It would also be known as a three-factor factorial experiment.

The computational procedures involved in factorial experiments are merely an extension of those already encountered; however, a new concept enters in, known as interaction. Consider the hypothetical means (parameters) shown in Table 11.1. Assume that they are the means that are estimated in three different experiments and that in each experiment different varieties and fertilizers are used.

Table 11.1

Varieties	a_1		a_2	
Fertilizers	b_1	b_2	b_1	b_2
Experiment #1	$\mu_1 = 50$	$\mu_2 = 70$	$\mu_3 = 40$	$\mu_4 = 60$
Experiment #2	$\mu_1 = 50$	$\mu_2 = 70$	$\mu_3 = 40$	$\mu_4 = 90$
Experiment #3	$\mu_1 = 50$	$\mu_2 = 70$	$\mu_3 = 40$	$\mu_4 = 30$

Let a_1 and a_2 correspond to varieties 1 and 2, and b_1 and b_2 to fertilizers 1 and 2. In the first experiment, the yields of both varieties were increased 20 units in the presence of fertilizer 2, as compared with fertilizer 1. This is an example of *no interaction*. In the second and third experiments a similarity in response was not observed. In the second experiment, variety 1 was increased 20 units in the presence of fertilizer 2, but variety 2 was increased 50 units. In the third experiment, variety 1 was increased 20 units, but variety 2 was decreased 10 units. For these two experiments a differential response occurred, and it is said that an *interaction* occurred between the two factors a and b.

In analysis-of-variance problems it is often just as important to test for interactions as it is to test for differences among treatments. The method is best illustrated with an example.

In a nutrition experiment, an investigator studied the effects of different rations and vitamins on the growth of young rats. Forty rats from the same inbred strain were used in the experiment. They were divided at random into four groups of ten. A different ration was fed to each group. In addition, half of each group was given a concentration of vitamins, while the other half was given none. After a specified length of time the increase in growth of each rat was measured in grams. The completely randomized design was employed. In other experiments the randomized-block design or Latin-square design would be more appropriate. The data are given in Table 11.2. In this experiment, $a = 4$ (number of ration treatments), $b = 2$ (number of vitamin treatments), $k = ab = 8$ (number of treatments or samples), and $n = 5$ (sample size).

$$\sum_{1}^{nk} X_{ij} = 481 \qquad \sum_{1}^{nk} X_{ij}^2 = 6475$$

The total, treatments, and error sums of squares are computed as follows:

Total Sum of Squares $= 6475 - \dfrac{(481)^2}{40} = 690.98$

Treatments Sum of Squares $= \dfrac{(50)^2 + (32)^2 + (72)^2 + \cdots + (100)^2}{5}$

$$- \frac{(481)^2}{40}$$

$$= 605.38$$

Error Sum of Squares $= 690.98 - 605.38 = 85.60$

The next step is to partition the treatment sum of squares into three compartments: rations, vitamins, and interaction. A convenient procedure is to rearrange the data in new tables.

Table 11.2

	Ration A Vitamins	Ration A No Vitamins	Ration B Vitamins	Ration B No Vitamins	Ration C Vitamins	Ration C No Vitamins	Ration D Vitamins	Ration D No Vitamins
	10	6	13	9	12	10	15	21
	8	6	15	10	16	12	13	18
	12	9	14	8	13	10	15	20
	11	5	13	10	11	9	10	19
	9	6	17	8	15	9	12	22
$\sum_1^n X_{ij}$	50	32	72	45	67	50	65	100
$\sum_1^n X_{ij}^2$	510	214	1,048	409	915	506	863	2,010

	Ration A	Ration B	Ration C	Ration D	Total
Sum of the Measurements	82	117	117	165	481
Number of Measurements	10	10	10	10	40

$$\text{Rations Sum of Squares} = \frac{(82)^2 + (117)^2 + (117)^2 + (165)^2}{10} - \frac{(481)^2}{40}$$

$$= 348.68$$

	Vitamins	No Vitamins	Total
Sum of the Measurements	254	227	481
Number of Measurements	20	20	40

$$\text{Vitamins Sum of Squares} = \frac{(254)^2 + (227)^2}{20} - \frac{(481)^2}{40} = 18.23$$

$$\text{Interaction Sum of Squares} = 605.38 - 348.68 - 18.23 = 238.47$$

The data can now be placed in an analysis-of-variance table.

Source of Variation	Degrees of Freedom	Sum of Squares	Mean Square
Total	39	690.98	
Treatments			
Rations	3	348.68	116.227
Vitamins	1	18.23	18.230
Rations × Vitamins	3	238.48	79.493
Error	32	85.60	2.675

There are 7 degrees of freedom for treatments, 3 for rations, and 1 for vitamins. This leaves $7 - 4 = 3$ for interaction. The numbers of degrees of freedom for total and error are obviously 39 and 32, respectively. In the analysis-of-variance table, interaction is written as rations $\times$ vitamins.

The F tests may now be carried out. In most cases the analysis-of-variance model (Model I) is the appropriate model. Only rarely in factorial experiments is the component-of-variance model (Model II) assumed. Occasionally the third type of model is encountered, known as the mixed model (Model III).

11.1   Model I — Analysis-of-Variance Model

The above example clearly assumes Model I, since both the rations and vitamins are fixed. The mathematical model summarizing the assumptions of this test is best presented, perhaps, by rearranging the layout from:

a_1		a_2		a_3		a_4	
b_1	b_2	b_1	b_2	b_1	b_2	b_1	b_2
X_1	X_1	X_1	X_1	X_1	X_1	X_1	X_1
X_2	X_2	X_2	X_2	X_2	X_2	X_2	X_2
.	.	.	.	.	.	.	.
.	.	.	.	.	.	.	.
.	.	.	.	.	.	.	.
X_n	X_n	X_n	X_n	X_n	X_n	X_n	X_n

to:

	a_1	a_2	a_3	a_4
b_1	X_1 X_2 . . . X_n	X_1 X_2 . . . X_n	X_1 X_2 . . . X_n	X_1 X_2 . . . X_n
b_2	X_1 X_2 . . . X_n	X_1 X_2 . . . X_n	X_1 X_2 . . . X_n	X_1 X_2 . . . X_n

This layout gives 8 cells. The measurements within each cell represent a random sample from a population of measurements. The kth measurement from the jth row and ith column is represented by X_{ijk}. The mathematical model is expressed as:

$$X_{ijk} = \mu + A + B + AB_{ij} + e = \mu + (\mu_i - \mu) + (\mu_j - \mu)$$
$$+ (\mu_i - \mu)(\mu_j - \mu)_{ij} + (X_{ijk} - \mu_{ij})$$

where μ is the grand mean, A is the column effect, B is the row effect, AB_{ij} is the effect that occurs in the ith column and jth row because of interaction between the A and B effects, and e is the error effect. In Model I all effects are fixed except $e = (X_{ijk} - \mu_{ij})$. These random variables are independently and normally distributed with a mean of zero and a common variance (σ^2).

Two different situations will now be presented. In the first, AB_{ij} is equal to zero, i.e., there is no interaction. The following table illustrates this situation. The entries are hypothetical cell means (μ_{ij}), row means (μ_j), column means (μ_i), and grand mean (μ).

	a_1	a_2	a_3	a_4	Row Means (μ_j)
b_1	cell mean 9	cell mean 10	cell mean 12	cell mean 13	11
b_2	cell mean 7	cell mean 8	cell mean 10	cell mean 11	9
Column Means (μ_i)	8	9	11	12	Grand Mean (μ) 10

The mean of the cell occurring in the ith column and jth row is given by:

$$\mu_{ij} = \mu + A + B = \mu + (\mu_i - \mu) + (\mu_j - \mu)$$

For the first row and first column this becomes:

$$\mu_{ij} = 10 + (-2) + (+1) = 9$$

The theoretical population of measurements that could occur in this cell has a mean of 9, and the kth measurement deviates from the mean by the error effect $(e = X_{ijk} - \mu_{ij})$. Thus,

$$X_{ijk} = \mu + A + B + e$$

It should be noticed that when there is no interaction, the cell means can be determined from the grand mean, row means, and column means.

Now assume that AB_{ij} does not equal zero. Interaction can be introduced into this model by merely reversing the cell means occurring in the third column (or by altering the cell means in some other way so there is differential response).

Differential response is present. The effect of the second level of the b factor is to reduce the measurements by two units for all levels of the a factor except a_3.

When interaction is present, the cell means cannot be specified on the basis of the grand mean, row means, and column means. This can be demonstrated by considering again the first row and first column:

$$\mu + A + B = (10) + (-2) + (+0.5) = 8.5$$

Row Means (μ_j)

	a_1	a_2	a_3	a_4	
b_1	cell mean 9	cell mean 10	cell mean 10	cell mean 13	10.5
b_2	cell mean 7	cell mean 8	cell mean 12	cell mean 11	9.5

Column   Grand Mean (μ)

Means (μ_i) 8   9   11   12   10

The difference between 8.5 and 9 is due to the $+0.5$ interaction effect occurring in this row and column.

$$\mu_{11} = \mu + A + B + AB_{ij} = \mu + (\mu_i - \mu) + (\mu_j - \mu) + (\mu_i - \mu)(\mu_j - \mu)_{ij}$$
$$= 10 + (-2) + (+0.5) + (+0.5) = 9$$

The expression AB_{ij} is read as the interaction between the A and B effects in the ith column, jth row, and is not read as the product of the A and B effects.

The interaction effects can be calculated as above for each row and column in the model. They are presented below.

Row Mean (μ_j)

	a_1	a_2	a_3	a_4	
b_1	interaction $+0.5$	interaction $+0.5$	interaction -1.5	interaction $+0.5$	10.5
b_2	interaction -0.5	interaction -0.5	interaction $+1.5$	interaction -0.5	9.5

Column   Grand Mean (μ)

Means (μ_i) 8   9   11   12   10

Note that the sum of the interaction terms in each row and column is zero.

The mean-square estimates for a two-factor factorial experiment (completely randomized design) are given in Table 11.3. Let A represent the rations, B the vitamins, and AB the interaction. The sources of variation and the formulae for degrees of freedom and mean-square estimates are given below:

Table 11.3 Completely Randomized Design (Model I).

Source of Variation	Degrees of Freedom	Mean Square Estimate
Total	$abn-1$	
Treatments A	$a-1$	$\sigma^2 + \dfrac{nb}{a-1} \sum_1^a (\mu_i - \mu)^2$
B	$b-1$	$\sigma^2 + \dfrac{na}{b-1} \sum_1^b (\mu_j - \mu)^2$
AB	$(a-1)(b-1)$	$\sigma^2 + \dfrac{n}{(a-1)(b-1)} \sum_1^a \sum_1^b [(\mu_i - \mu)(\mu_j - \mu)]_{ij}^2$
Error	$ab(n-1)$	σ^2

For the above data dealing with four different levels of rations and two different levels of vitamins, the F tests are as follows:

(1) Hypothesis: $\sum_1^a \sum_1^b [(\mu_i - \mu)(\mu_j - \mu)]_{ij}^2 = 0$

$$F = \frac{79.492}{2.675} = 29.717 \qquad F\left[\frac{3}{32}\ 0.05\right] = 2.9$$

(2) Hypothesis: $\sum_1^a (\mu_i - \mu)^2 = 0$

$$F = \frac{116.227}{2.675} = 43.449 \qquad F\left[\frac{3}{32}\ 0.05\right] = 2.9$$

(3) Hypothesis: $\sum_{1}^{b} (\mu_j - \mu)^2 = 0$

$$F = \frac{18.225}{2.675} = 6.813 \qquad F\left[\begin{array}{c} 1 \\ 32 \end{array} 0.05\right] = 4.2$$

The first F test shows that a significant interaction exists. It is informative to examine the data closely:

Sample Means ($n = 5$)

	Ration A	Ration B	Ration C	Ration D
Vitamins	10.0	14.4	13.4	13.0
No Vitamins	6.4	9.0	10.0	20.0

For Rations A, B, and C, the addition of vitamins increased the growth of the young rats. The reverse reaction occured when vitamins were added to Ration D. Taking into consideration all four rations, it is apparent that a differential response occurred. This differential response was significant, and not just due to chance, as shown by the significant interaction mean square.

A significant interaction may cause the investigator to lose interest in the results of the other F tests. A significant interaction, by itself, indicates that the A and B effects do not equal zero. Two effects cannot interact if one is zero.

How is the above interaction explained? It might be presumed that rations A, B, and C were deficient in vitamins; therefore, the addition of the vitamins was beneficial. Ration D was already highly rich in vitamins, and the addition of more resulted in an overabundance which either had an adverse physiological effect on the rats or else made the ration less palatable. The results show that the most effective diet is ration D without the vitamin concentration.

The results also show that even in the presence of a significant interaction, the ration and vitamin effects by themselves were significant.

Confidence limits for the true population means could be set by using the following standard errors:

Treatments: $\sqrt{\dfrac{2.675}{5}}$

Rations: $\sqrt{\dfrac{2.675}{10}}$

Vitamins: $\sqrt{\dfrac{2.675}{20}}$

These standard errors could also be used in a multiple-range test.

11.2   Model II — Components-of-Variance Model

This model assumes that the levels of both factors are random variables. The computational procedure would be similar to that shown for Model I. However, a major difference exists between the two models in respect to the F tests. This can be seen from the formulae for the mean-square estimates (Table 11.4).

Table 11.4   Analysis of Variance–Two-Factor Factorial. Completely Randomized Design (Model II).

Source of Variation	Degrees of Freedom	Mean Square Estimate
Total	$abn-1$	
Treatments A	$a-1$	$\sigma^2 + n\sigma_{ab}^2 + nb\sigma_a^2$
B	$b-1$	$\sigma^2 + n\sigma_{ab}^2 + na\sigma_b^2$
AB	$(a-1)(b-1)$	$\sigma^2 + n\sigma_{ab}^2$
Error	$ab(n-1)$	σ^2

Interaction is tested by:

Hypothesis $\sigma_{ab}^2 = 0$ $F = \dfrac{\text{Interaction mean square}}{\text{Error mean square}}$

Notice that the mean squares for the A and B effects contain an interaction component of variance (σ_{ab}^2). Therefore, the hypotheses $\sigma_a^2 = 0$ and $\sigma_b^2 = 0$ should be tested as follows:

Hypothesis: $\sigma_a^2 = 0$ $F = \dfrac{\text{Mean square for } A \text{ effect}}{\text{Interaction mean square}}$

Hypothesis: $\sigma_b^2 = 0$ $F = \dfrac{\text{Mean square for } B \text{ effect}}{\text{Interaction mean square}}$

If error mean square were used as the denominator in these F tests, errors of the first kind would tend to occur when interaction is present.

11.3 Model III — Mixed Model

Assume that the levels of the a factor are fixed, but the levels of the b factor are random variables. The mean-square estimates are as follows:

Table 11.5 Analysis of Variance–Two-Factor Factorial. Completely Randomized Design (Model III). Levels of a factor fixed. Levels of b factor random.

Source of Variation	Degrees of Freedom	Mean Square Estimate
Total	$abn-1$	
Treatments A (Fixed)	$a-1$	$\sigma^2 + n\sigma_{ab}^2 + \dfrac{nb}{a-1} \sum\limits_{1}^{a} (\mu_i - \mu)^2$
B (Random)	$b-1$	$\sigma^2 + na\sigma_b^2$
AB	$(a-1)(b-1)$	$\sigma^2 + n\sigma_{ab}^2$
Error	$ab(n-1)$	σ^2

The mean square for the fixed A effect contains an interaction component of variance, but the mean square for the random B effect does not contain this component. Consequently, the hypothesis $\Sigma_1^a(\mu_i - \mu)^2 = 0$ should be tested by using the interaction mean square as the denominator of the F test, but the other two hypotheses ($\sigma_b^2 = 0$ and $\sigma_{ab}^2 = 0$) should be tested with error mean square as the denominator of the F test.

When the levels of a are random and the levels of b are fixed, the mean-square estimates appear as given in Table 11.6.

Factorial experiments are easily extended to three and four factors. In the majority of cases when this is done, Model I is the assumed model, and all of the tests are carried out by using the error mean square in the denominator.

Factorial experiments have certain advantages and disadvantages. The main advantage is that they supply valuable information about interactions. Another advantage is the increased number of degrees of freedom involved due to the factorial arrangement. Also, they supply a great deal of information

Table 11.6　Analysis of Variance–Two-Factor Factorial. Completely Randomized Design (Model III). Levels of a factors random. Levels of b factors fixed.

Source of Variation	Degrees of Freedom	Mean Square Estimate
Total	$abn-1$	
Treatments A (Random)	$a-1$	$\sigma^2 + nb\sigma_a^2$
B (Fixed)	$b-1$	$\sigma^2 + n\sigma_{ab}^2 + \dfrac{na}{b-1} \sum_1^b (\mu_j - \mu)^2$
AB	$(a-1)(b-1)$	$\sigma^2 + n\sigma_{ab}^2$
Error	$ab(n-1)$	σ^2

because of the various combinations that are tested. However, the disadvantages are obvious. They can become so complex that the interpretation of the interactions is difficult, and missing data may be so costly that the whole experiment is jeopardized. Furthermore, some of the combinations may be of no interest to the investigator, and therefore the design may be too extravagant.

Problems

1. An investigator studied the concentration of plankton in two different (specific) areas in a large lake by two different methods. He was interested in comparing the results of both methods in estimating total number of organisms per milliliter of water for the two areas. Samples were made on weekends for a total of six weeks.
(a) Describe the nature of the design. Which model is being assumed? (b) Fill out the first two columns of the analysis-of-variance table under *Source of Variation* and *Degrees of Freedom*. (c) Give the mean-square estimates.
2. An agronomist was interested in comparing four different fertilizer treatments on two different varieties of wheat. Each variety was to be grown in a 15 foot × 15 foot plot in the presence of one of the fertilizers. Environmental conditions in the field were greatly variable, so he decided to use a Latin-square design.
(a) Discuss how the plots should be laid out in the field. (b) Describe the nature of the design. Which model is being assumed? (c) Fill in an analysis-of-variance table under the headings: *Source of Variation* and *Degrees of Freedom*.
3. A human geneticist selected at random fifteen families showing two males and two females with the sickle-cell trait. He measured the percent of abnormal hemoglobin possessed by each individual.
(a) Give the number of degrees of freedom for each source of variation.

Source of Variation	Mean Square
Total	
Families (F)	100.70
Sex (S)	13.72
$F \times S$	11.10
Error	12.52

(b) Give the nature of the design. What model is being assumed? Give the mean-square estimates. (c) Test the significance of the families, sex, and interaction mean squares. Show the numerator and denominator of each F test. What are your conclusions? (d) Estimate the values of the variance within families and between family means.

4. A venomologist selected at random 10 male rattlesnakes. The snakes were kept in the laboratory. During October and April, venom was taken from each snake on four successive weekends. The proteolytic activity was determined for each sample of venom *in vitro*.
(a) Fill in the first two columns of an analysis-of-variance table. (b) Which model is being assumed? Give the appropriate mean-square estimates.

5. For the following analysis-of-variance table:

Source of Variation	Mean Squares
Total	
A	80
B	40
AB	10
Error	2

(a) Show the appropriate F tests when levels of a and b are fixed. (b) Show the appropriate F tests when levels of a are random and levels of b are fixed. (c) Show the appropriate F test when levels of a are fixed and levels of b are random. (d) Show the appropriate F test when levels of a and b are random.

6. A plant physiologist investigated the salt-tolerance properties of three different plant species. Each species was grown in a 0.0% and 0.3% salt solution. Seeds were placed in suitable containers and after a given length of time the growth of each plant was determined. Measurements were made in grams (oven-dry weight). Due to the limitation of the number of available containers, it was necessary to extend the experiment over a period of many months. The experiment was designed as a randomized-block design with a 3 × 2 factorial arrangement of the treatments. A section of a greenhouse bench was selected showing uniform lighting and heating conditions. Six containers, each containing one species and treatment, were randomized on this section of the bench. Five replications of the experiment were carried out.

Blocks	Species A		Species B		Species C	
	0.0%	0.3%	0.0%	0.3%	0.0%	0.3%
1	1.28	1.19	1.27	1.20	1.32	1.33
2	1.37	1.27	1.38	1.26	1.40	1.39
3	1.31	1.21	1.30	1.23	1.34	1.38
4	1.32	1.24	1.33	1.24	1.37	1.38
5	1.29	1.23	1.32	1.21	1.35	1.36

(a) Compute degrees of freedom, sum of squares, and mean squares for the following sources of variation: Total, Blocks (Replications), Salt Concentrations, Species, Interaction (Salt Concentrations × Species), and Error. Place the data in a typical analysis-of-variance table. Carry out the appropriate F tests. (b) What are your conclusions? Discuss in detail, placing special emphasis on the meaning of the interaction mean square. (c) Compare the six sample means by the multiple-range test.

7. Assume that a measurement of taxonomic interest was made on adult males and females of two closely related species of Peromyscus.

Species A		Species B	
Males	Females	Males	Females
1.24	1.28	1.31	1.25
1.29	1.31	1.32	1.26
1.31	1.32	1.34	1.24
1.21	1.22	1.33	1.21
1.31	1.24	1.39	1.27
1.22	1.26	1.36	1.26
1.26	1.31	1.34	1.24
1.25	1.21	1.37	1.29
1.27	1.27	1.30	1.31
1.28	1.28	1.29	1.22
1.30	1.25	1.30	1.20

(a) Complete the analysis-of-variance table for the following sources of variation: Total, Species, Sex, Species $\times$ Sex, and Error. (b) Calculate F values, carry out the multiple-range test, and determine the 95% confidence limits for the four population means. Interpret the biological meaning of interaction mean square. What are your conclusions?

Repli-cation	Strain 1		Strain 2	
	Homo-karyotypes	Hetero-karyotypes	Homo-karyotypes	Hetero-karyotypes
1	540	601	120	640
2	500	620	90	610
3	549	605	132	674
4	562	680	141	610
5	510	632	167	600

8. Fecundity experiments (No. of eggs laid per period) were carried out with two different tumorous-head strains of *Drosophila melanogaster*.
(a) Complete the analysis-of-variance table for the following sources of variation: Total, Replications, Strain, Karyotype, Strain $\times$ Karyotype, and Error. (b) Calculate F values. What are your conclusions?

CHAPTER TWELVE

Regression Coefficient

Variables in biological research are usually, if not always, influenced by other variables. For example, the yield of barley is dependent on the amount of fertilizer applied to the soil. Yield is also dependent on the amount of rainfall, type of soil, and insect and fungus infestation. A relationship exists between yield and amount of fertilizer, between yield and amount of rainfall, and also between yield and extent of insect or fungus infestation. The subject of relationship between variables is an important one in statistical inference. An investigator is interested in (1) determining whether a relationship exists between variables, and if so, in (2) estimating the degree of relationship that exists between the variables.

Mention has already been made of one measurement that enables an investigator to determine if a relationship exists between two variables. This measurement is known as the covariance

$$w_{XY} = \frac{\sum_{1}^{n} (X_i - \bar{x})(Y_i - \bar{y})}{n - 1}$$

The covariance is seldom calculated. A more informative measurement is the regression coefficient.

12.1 Regression Coefficient

A scatter diagram is a pictorial method of representing the relationship between two variables. In the following diagram, yield of barley (bushels per plot) is plotted against the number of pounds of fertilizer applied to the plots.

The number of points in the diagram corresponds to the number of plots studied. The measurement "bushels per plot" is the dependent variable (Y_i), while the measurement "pounds of fertilizer" is the independent variable (X_i).

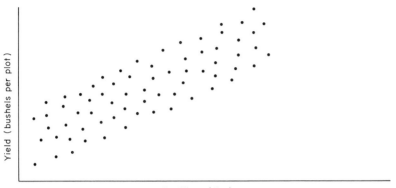

Fertilizer (lbs.)

A line that best fits the points of a scatter diagram is termed a regression line. If the line is horizontal, no correlation is present. A positive or negative slope is an indication that positive or negative correlation is present.

Positive Correlation   No Correlation   Negative Correlation

In many cases a curve best fits the points. However, this type of relationship will not be considered here. In the following sections only linear regression will be discussed.

A regression line can be drawn quite accurately by eye when all the points lie on or near the line. When this is done, the amount of increase in the dependent variable for a one unit increase in the independent variable can be fairly well established by noting the slope of the line. However, fitting a regression line by eye is a difficult task when extensive variability is present among the points. An objective method is needed. This is accomplished by the method of least squares: *The line which best fits a series of points is the line which passes through the points in such a way that the summation of the squared deviations between the points and the line is a minimum value.* The "summation of the squared deviations" is known as error sum of squares. The tangent of the angle this best-fitting line makes with the horizontal axis is termed the regression coefficient and is symbolized by b.

The discussion that follows is concerned with the derivation of the formulae for the regression coefficient.

Consider a regression line that passes through a series of points in such a way that the error sum of squares is a minimum value. One of these points (X,Y) is represented in the diagram below. For a given value of X, there is an estimated value of Y, symbolized by $\hat{Y}$, which lies on the regression line. The line intercepts the Y axis at point a (known as the Y intercept).

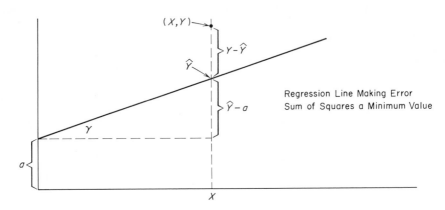

Regression Line Making Error Sum of Squares a Minimum Value

The tangent of the angle in the above diagram is given by

$$\tan \alpha = b = \frac{\hat{Y} - a}{X}$$

Solving for $\hat{Y}$ gives:

$$\hat{Y} = a + bX$$

which is the equation for a straight line, where a is the Y intercept, b is the regression coefficient (slope of the line), and X is a given point on the X axis. The deviation between the point shown in the diagram and the estimated value of Y is given by $Y - \hat{Y}$. Squaring this deviation gives $(Y - \hat{Y})^2$. Repeating the procedure for all points and then summing gives error sum of squares.

$$\text{Error Sum of Squares} = \sum_{1}^{n} (Y_i - \hat{Y})^2$$

Since $\hat{Y} = a + bX$, error sum of squares is also equal to

$$\sum_{1}^{n} (Y_i - a - bX_i)^2 = \sum_{1}^{n} Y_i^2 + na^2 + b^2 \sum_{1}^{n} X_i^2 - 2a \sum_{1}^{n} Y_i - 2b \sum_{1}^{n} X_i Y_i$$

$$+ 2ab \sum_{1}^{n} X_i$$

The procedure is to find the values of a and b which will make error sum of squares a minimum. This is done by partially differentiating with respect to a and b, equating the derivatives to zero, and then solving for a and b.

Differentiating with respect to a gives:

$$\frac{d\left[\sum_{1}^{n}(Y_i - \hat{Y})^2\right]}{da} = 2na - 2\sum_{1}^{n}Y_i + 2b\sum_{1}^{n}X_i$$

Differentiating with respect to b gives:

$$\frac{d\left[\sum_{1}^{n}(Y_i - \hat{Y})^2\right]}{db} = 2b\sum_{1}^{n}X_i^2 - 2\sum_{1}^{n}X_iY_i + 2a\sum_{1}^{n}X_i$$

Placing both expressions equal to zero gives two normal equations.

(1) $na - \sum_{1}^{n}Y_i + b\sum_{1}^{n}X_i = 0$

(2) $b\sum_{1}^{n}X_i^2 - \sum_{1}^{n}X_iY_i + a\sum_{1}^{n}X_i = 0$

Error sum of squares has now been minimized. (Students not acquainted with differential calculus should take the above operation for granted.)

Solving for a in the first normal equation gives:

$$a = \frac{\sum_{1}^{n}Y_i - b\sum_{1}^{n}X_i}{n} = \frac{\sum_{1}^{n}Y_i}{n} - \frac{b\sum_{1}^{n}X_i}{n}$$

$$a = \bar{y} - b\bar{x}$$

Solving for b in the second normal equation after substituting $\bar{y} - b\bar{x}$ in place of a gives:

$$b = \frac{\sum_{1}^{n}X_iY_i - \dfrac{\left(\sum_{1}^{n}X_i\right)\left(\sum_{1}^{n}Y_i\right)}{n}}{\sum_{1}^{n}X_i^2 - \dfrac{\left(\sum_{1}^{n}X_i\right)^2}{n}} = \frac{\sum_{1}^{n}(X_i - \bar{x})(Y_i - \bar{y})}{\sum_{1}^{n}(X_i - \bar{x})^2}$$

For simplicity, the deviations in the latter equation are abbreviated as follows:

$$X_i - \bar{x} = x$$

$$Y_i - \bar{y} = y$$

The formula for the regression coefficient (b) becomes:

$$b = \frac{\sum_{1}^{n} xy}{\sum_{1}^{n} x^2}$$

It is instructive to note the relationship that exists between the regression coefficient and the covariance. Dividing the numerator and denominator by $n - 1$ gives the following:

$$b = \frac{\dfrac{\sum_{1}^{n} xy}{n-1}}{\dfrac{\sum_{1}^{n} x^2}{n-1}} = \frac{\text{Covariance}}{\text{Variance of } X_i \text{ Measurements}} = \frac{w_{XY}}{s_X{}^2}$$

Thus the regression coefficient can be defined as the covariance divided by the variance of the independent variable.

Graphically, the regression coefficient is the tangent of the angle which the regression line makes with the horizontal axis.

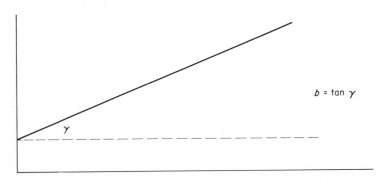

Statistically, the regression coefficient gives the amount of change that occurs in the dependent variable for a unit increase in the independent variable. Theoretically, the regression coefficient can vary from zero to plus or minus infinity. If the value is zero, this means that the regression line is horizontal and therefore that no relationship exists between the two variables. A positive value of the regression coefficient is an indication of positive correlation, and a negative value is an indication of negative correlation. In addition to the degree of relationship existing between the two variables, the slope of the regression line is also dependent on the units of measurement. Consequently, different regression coefficients can only be compared when the units of measurement are the same. This is one limitation of the regression coefficient.

12.2   Example of the Calculation of the Regression Coefficient

An ornithologist was interested in the possible relationship between latitude and length of wing of a given species of bird. Measurements (in millimeters) were made on male specimens taken at 25°N, 30°N, 35°N, 40°N, and 45°N. The specimens were taken in May and June. There are certain assumptions involved in this study. The first is that at each of the Latitudes studied there is a population of birds of this species with wing length distributed in a normal manner. The second assumption is that the variances of all these populations are equal. The data obtained are given in Table 12.1.

In a regression analysis three values should be calculated first. These are:

$$(1) \sum_{1}^{n} x^2 = \sum_{1}^{n} (X_i - \bar{x})^2 = \sum_{1}^{n} X_i^2 - \frac{\left(\sum_{1}^{n} X_i\right)^2}{n}$$

$$= 20{,}250 - \frac{(540)^2}{15} = 810.0$$

$$(2) \sum_{1}^{n} y^2 = \sum_{1}^{n} (Y_i - \bar{y})^2 = \sum_{1}^{n} Y_i^2 - \frac{\left(\sum_{1}^{n} Y_i\right)^2}{n}$$

$$= 318{,}156 - \frac{(2{,}180)^2}{15} = 1{,}329.33$$

$$(3) \sum_{1}^{n} xy = \sum_{1}^{n} (X_i - \bar{x})(Y_i - \bar{y}) = \sum_{1}^{n} X_i Y_i - \frac{\left(\sum_{1}^{n} X_i\right)\left(\sum_{1}^{n} Y_i\right)}{n}$$

$$= 79{,}495 - \frac{(540)(2{,}180)}{15} = 1{,}015.0$$

The regression coefficient becomes:

$$b = \frac{\sum_{1}^{n} xy}{\sum_{1}^{n} x^2} = \frac{1{,}015.0}{810} = 1.253$$

It is estimated that for a one-degree increase in latitude, the increase in wing length for this species of bird is 1.253 millimeters.

Since the value of b is known, the value of a can be determined.

$$a = \bar{y} - b\bar{x} = 145.333 - (1.253)(36.00) = 100.225$$

Table 12.1

Specimens	Latitude (X_i)	Wing Length in Millimeters (Y_i)	$X_i Y_i$
1	25° N	132	3,300
2	25° N	131	3,275
3	25° N	128	3,200
4	30° N	138	4,140
5	30° N	139	4,170
6	35° N	146	5,110
7	35° N	147	5,145
8	35° N	143	5,005
9	40° N	149	5,960
10	40° N	154	6,160
11	40° N	151	6,040
12	45° N	155	6,975
13	45° N	158	7,110
14	45° N	154	6,930
15	45° N	155	6,975
$n = 15$	$\sum_{1}^{n} X_i = 540$	$\sum_{1}^{n} Y_i = 2,180$	$\sum_{1}^{n} X_i Y_i = 79,495$
	$\sum_{1}^{n} X_i^2 = 20,250$	$\sum_{1}^{n} Y_i^2 = 318,156$	
	$\bar{x} = 36.0$	$\bar{y} = 145.33$	

The equation for the regression line becomes

$$\hat{Y} = a + bX$$

$$\hat{Y} = 100.225 + 1.253X$$

The equation is also commonly expressed as

$$\hat{Y} = a + bX$$
$$= \bar{y} - b\bar{x} + bX$$
$$= \bar{y} + bX - b\bar{x}$$
$$= \bar{y} + b(X - \bar{x})$$

For each value of X, an estimated value of Y can now be calculated. This is shown in the following table for the latitudes under study.

Table 12.2

Specimens	Latitude	Observed Value of Y (Y)	Estimated Value of Y ($\hat{Y}$)	$Y-\hat{Y}$	$(Y-\hat{Y})^2$
1	25° N	132	131.6	0.4	0.16
2	25° N	131	131.6	−0.6	0.36
3	25° N	128	131.6	−3.6	12.96
4	30° N	138	137.8	0.2	0.04
5	30° N	139	137.8	1.2	1.44
6	35° N	146	144.1	1.9	3.61
7	35° N	147	144.1	2.9	8.41
8	35° N	143	144.1	−1.1	1.21
9	40° N	149	150.3	−1.3	1.69
10	40° N	154	150.3	3.7	13.69
11	40° N	151	150.3	0.7	0.49
12	45° N	155	156.6	−1.6	2.56
13	45° N	158	156.6	1.4	1.96
14	45° N	154	156.6	−2.6	6.76
15	45° N	155	156.6	−1.6	2.56
		Sum 2,180.0	Sum 2,180.0	Sum 0.0	Sum 57.90

The regression line can now be accurately drawn. Even though the Y intercept has statistical meaning, it is unrealistic from a biological standpoint in this case. The species of bird under study does not normally occur near the equator. For this reason it is more appropriate to draw the regression line using $\bar{x}$ and $\bar{y}$ as the reference point.

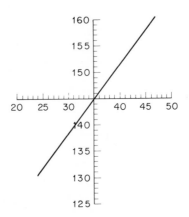

Several important features of the analysis may now be noted:

(1) The regression line passes through the point $\bar{x}$, $\bar{y}$. This can be shown directly from the equation $\hat{Y} = \bar{y} + b(X - \bar{x})$. If $X = \bar{x}$, the term $b(X - \bar{x}) = 0$, and $\hat{Y} = \bar{y}$.

(2) The values of X were chosen by the experimenter. Consequently, if the study were repeated an infinite number of times with the same number of specimens taken at the given latitudes, the value of $\bar{x}$ would remain the same. It can be regarded as a fixed constant.

(3) The sum of the deviations from regression [i.e., $\Sigma_1^n(Y - \hat{Y})$] is equal to zero. This can be seen from Table 12.2. The regression line passes through the points in such a manner that the sum of the positive deviations is equal to the sum of the negative deviations. Thus it is apparent that the regression line acts as a "running mean."

12.3   Estimates of Parameters in a Regression Analysis

In a regression analysis several parameters are estimated. These parameters and their estimators are given in the following table.

The sample regression coefficient (b) is an unbiased estimate of β. Likewise, a is an unbiased estimate of α.

$$E(b) = \beta$$

$$E(a) = \alpha$$

Parameter	Name	Estimator
β	True Regression Coefficient	$b = \dfrac{\displaystyle\sum_1^n xy}{\displaystyle\sum_1^n x^2}$
α	True Y intercept	$a = \bar{y} - b\bar{x}$
μ_{YX}	Mean of Y values for a given value of X	1) $\bar{y}_g$ 2) $\hat{Y} = a + bX$
σ^2_{YX}	Variance of Y values for a given value of X	$s^2_{YX} = \dfrac{\displaystyle\sum_1^n (Y - \hat{Y})^2}{n - 2}$

For a given value of X, the possible Y values are assumed to follow a normal distribution. The mean of all the Y values for a given value of X is symbolized by μ_{YX}. For a given value of X there are two estimates of μ_{YX}. The first is the mean of all observed Y values for a given value of X. This mean is termed group mean and is symbolized by $\bar{y}_g$. For example, at latitude 25°N, there are three Y values. The mean of these values is

$$\bar{y}_g = \frac{131 + 132 + 128}{3} = 130.3$$

Another estimate of μ_{YX} is $\hat{Y}$ computed from the formula $\hat{Y} = a + bX$. For 25°N, this estimate is 131.6. If *linear regression* is present, this latter estimate is the more reliable of the two estimates, since it is based on 15 measurements instead of 3. Each estimate is unbiased.

$$E[\bar{y}_g] = \mu_{YX}$$

$$E[\hat{Y}] = \mu_{YX}$$

If a relationship exists between the independent and dependent variables, the values of μ_{YX} change for each different value of X. Assuming linear regression, these parameters can be connected by a straight line. This line is called the true regression line. The tangent of the angle this line makes with the horizontal is β. It crosses the Y intercept at point α.

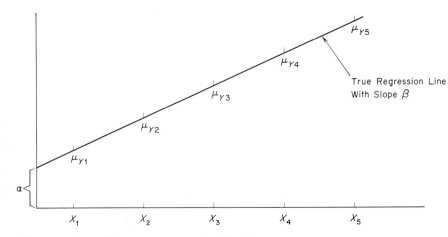

The equation of the true regression line is

$$\mu_{YX} = \alpha + \beta X$$

Variability exists about the true regression line. The variance of the Y measurements for each value of X is symbolized by σ_{YX}^2.

$$\sigma_{YX}^2 = E[Y_i - \mu_{YX}]^2$$

This measure of variability is the second moment about the mean. Therefore, all deviations $(Y_i - \mu_{YX})$ for a given value of X are squared, summed, and divided by the total number.

Even though the value of μ_{YX} changes for each different value of X, it is usually assumed in a regression analysis that σ_{YX}^2 remains constant for all values of X. Therefore, all squared deviations $(Y_i - \mu_{YX})^2$ can be pooled for all X values. For N points in the scatter diagram, the equation becomes:

$$\sigma_{YX}^2 = \frac{\sum_{1}^{N} (Y_i - \mu_{YX})^2}{N}$$

Since the means (μ_{YX}) lie on the true regression line, this variance is a measure of variability about the true regression line, and is known as variance from regression. This parameter is estimated by replacing μ_{YX} in the equation by the best estimator, and dividing by the appropriate number of degrees of freedom. The best estimator of μ_{YX} is $\hat{Y}$. This statistic is based on two other statistics: a and b. The rule holds that in obtaining an unbiased estimate of a variance, one degree of freedom is lost each time a parameter is replaced by a statistic. Two degrees of freedom are lost here because a and b are statistics, and each is used in calculating $\hat{Y}$. The estimate of σ_{YX}^2 becomes:

$$s_{YX}^2 = \frac{\sum_1^n (Y_i - \hat{Y})^2}{n - 2}$$

The equation for a sample regression line is also given as $\hat{Y} = \bar{y} + b(X - \bar{x})$. In this equation it may appear that there are three statistics: $\bar{y}$, b, and $\bar{x}$. However, the value of $\bar{x}$ is fixed; therefore, only $\bar{y}$ and b are subject to sampling error. Hence, only two degrees of freedom are lost.

The numerator of the above estimator is error sum of squares. This sum of squares has already been calculated (see Table 12.2).

$$s_{YX}^2 = \frac{\sum_1^n (Y - \hat{Y})^2}{n - 2} = \frac{\text{Error Sum of Squares}}{n - 2} = \frac{57.90}{13} = 4.45$$

The above statistic is usually calculated from a formula which is derived in the following manner:

$$s_{YX}^2 = \frac{\sum_1^n (Y_i - \hat{Y})^2}{n - 2}$$

$$= \frac{\sum_1^n (Y_i - \bar{y} - bx)^2}{n - 2} \qquad \text{since } \hat{Y} = \bar{y} + b(X - \bar{x}) = \bar{y} + bx$$

$$= \frac{\sum_1^n (y - bx)^2}{n - 2} \qquad \text{since } Y = \bar{y} = y$$

$$= \frac{\sum_1^n (y^2 - 2ybx + b^2x^2)}{n - 2}$$

$$= \frac{\sum_1^n y^2 - 2b \sum_1^n xy + b^2 \sum_1^n x^2}{n - 2}$$

$$= \frac{\sum_1^n y^2 - \dfrac{\left(\sum_1^n xy\right)^2}{\sum_1^n x^2}}{n - 2} \qquad \text{WORKING FORMULA}$$

The terms $\Sigma_1^n x^2$, $\Sigma_1^n y^2$, and $\Sigma_1^n xy$ have already been calculated. The sample variance from regression becomes:

$$s_{YX}^2 = \frac{1,329.333 - \dfrac{(1,015.00)^2}{810.0}}{13} = \frac{57.4506}{13} = 4.42$$

This value is slightly different from the one previously obtained. This latter calculation is more accurate, since the former was based on squared deviations from regression that were rounded off.

12.4   Linear Regression Models

For a given value of X, the ith dependent variable deviates from the true regression line by an error effect, symbolized by e. This is expressed as

$$Y_i = \mu_{YX} + e$$

Since $\mu_{YX} = \alpha + \beta X$, the full mathematical model becomes

$$Y_i = \alpha + \beta X + e$$

where α and β are fixed, and the deviations $e = Y_i - \mu_{YX}$ are random variables that are independently and normally distributed with a mean of zero and a variance of σ_{YX}^2.

In Model I, the X values are selected by the investigator; therefore they are fixed. In Model II, the X measurements as well as the Y measurements are random variables. Tests of significance are similar in both models. One distinguishing feature of Model II is that two different regression coefficients may be calculated. They are distinguished by subscripts. An example of each type will be given in Chapter 14.

Regression coefficient when Y is dependent on X

$$b_{YX} = \frac{\sum\limits_1^n xy}{\sum\limits_1^n x^2}$$

Regression coefficient when X is dependent on Y

$$b_{XY} = \frac{\sum\limits_1^n xy}{\sum\limits_1^n y^2}$$

12.5 Testing the Significance of a Regression Coefficient

A sample regression coefficient is subject to sampling error. It is an unbiased estimate of β, but of course it may deviate from this parameter due to chance alone. Thus, when $\beta = 0$, the estimate may have a positive or negative value. For a given set of data, it is usually important to determine if b deviates significantly from zero. The null hypothesis becomes: $\beta = 0$. This null hypothesis states that no relationship exists between the X and Y measurements.

The null hypothesis may be tested by (1) the techniques of analysis of variance or (2) the t-test method using a standard error.

The analysis-of-variance method will be introduced by returning to a diagram showing a regression line that best fits a set of data.

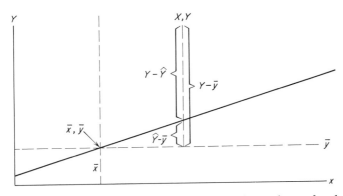

The deviation between the observed point and the estimated value of Y is given as $Y - \hat{Y}$. For brevity, call this deviation d, (i.e., $Y - \hat{Y} = d$). The deviation between the estimated value of Y and the mean of the Y measurements is $\hat{Y} - \bar{y} = \hat{y}$. Consequently, $y = \hat{y} + d$. Squaring the total deviation gives

$$y^2 = \hat{y}^2 + d^2 + 2\hat{y}d$$

Summing for all points gives the following sum of squares:

$$\sum_1^n y^2 = \sum_1^n \hat{y}^2 + \sum_1^n d^2 + 2\sum_1^n \hat{y}d$$

It can be shown that $2\Sigma_1^n \hat{y}d$ equals zero:

$$2\sum_1^n \hat{y}d = 2\sum_1^n (\hat{Y} - \bar{y})(Y - \hat{Y})$$

$$= 2\sum_1^n (\bar{y} + bx - \bar{y})(Y - \bar{y} - bx) \qquad \text{Since } \hat{Y} = \bar{y} + bx$$

$$= 2 \sum_{1}^{n} (bx)(y - bx)$$

$$= 2 \sum_{1}^{n} (bxy - b^2 x^2)$$

$$= 2b \sum_{1}^{n} xy - 2b^2 \sum_{1}^{n} x^2$$

$$= 2 \frac{\left(\sum_{1}^{n} xy \right)\left(\sum_{1}^{n} xy \right)}{\sum_{1}^{n} x^2} - 2 \frac{\left(\sum_{1}^{n} xy \right)^2 \left(\sum_{1}^{n} x^2 \right)}{\left(\sum_{1}^{n} x^2 \right)^2} = 0$$

Consequently, $\sum_{1}^{n} y^2 = \sum_{1}^{n} \hat{y}^2 + \sum_{1}^{n} d^2$

This shows that the total sum of squares can be divided into two components: one part due to regression and one part due to errors of random sampling.

$$\sum_{1}^{n} y^2 = \text{Total sum of squares}$$

$$\sum_{1}^{n} \hat{y}^2 = \text{Regression sum of squares}$$

$$\sum_{1}^{n} d^2 = \text{Error sum of squares}$$

Total and error sum of squares have already been calculated for the wing length and latitude data.

$$\text{Total sum of squares} = \sum_{1}^{n} y^2 = \sum_{1}^{n} (Y_i - \bar{y})^2 = \sum_{1}^{n} Y_i^2 - \frac{\left(\sum_{1}^{n} Y \right)^2}{n}$$
$$= 1{,}329.33$$

$$\text{Error sum of squares} = \sum_{1}^{n} d^2 = \sum_{1}^{n} (Y_i - \hat{Y})^2 = \sum_{1}^{n} y^2 - \frac{\left(\sum_{1}^{n} xy \right)^2}{\sum_{1}^{n} x^2}$$
$$= 57.45$$

Thus, regression sum of squares may be obtained by subtraction.

Regression sum of squares $= 1{,}329.33 - 57.45 = 1{,}271.88$

A clue as to the working equation for regression sum of squares comes from observing the working equation for error sum of squares: The first term is total sum of squares ($\sum_{1}^{n} y^2$). This is reduced by $(\sum_{1}^{n} xy)^2 / \sum_{1}^{n} x^2$ to give error sum of squares. Consequently, the second term must be regression sum of squares.

The working equation for regression sum of squares can be derived from the general equation as follows:

$$\sum_1^n \hat{y}^2 = \sum_1^n (\hat{Y} - \bar{y})^2 = \sum_1^n (\bar{y} + bx - \bar{y})^2 = \sum_1^n (bx)^2 = b^2 \sum_1^n x^2$$

$$= \frac{\left(\sum_1^n xy\right)^2 \left(\sum_1^n x^2\right)}{\left(\sum_1^n x^2\right)^2} = \frac{\left(\sum_1^n xy\right)^2}{\sum_1^n x^2} = \frac{(1,015.0)^2}{810.0} = 1,271.88$$

An analysis-of-variance table may now be filled out.

Table 12.3 Analysis of Variance Table for a Regression Analysis.

Source of Variation	Degrees of Freedom	Sum of Squares	Mean Square
Total	14	1,329.33	
Regression	1	1,271.88	1,271.88
Error	13	57.45	4.42

The number of degrees of freedom for total is $n - 1 = 14$. The number for error is $n - 2 = 13$, as previously explained. This leaves only 1 degree of freedom for regression: $(n - 1) - (n - 2) = n - 1 - n + 2 = 1$.

Degrees of Freedom

Total $= n - 1$

Regression $= 1$

Error $= n - 2$

Error mean square is variance from regression (s_{YX}^2). Therefore, the expectation of error mean square is σ_{YX}^2.

$$E[\text{Error Mean Square}] = \sigma_{YX}^2$$

The expectation of regression mean square is as follows:

$$E[\text{Regression Mean Square}] = \sigma_{YX}^2 + \beta^2 \sum_1^n x^2$$

The method of testing the null hypothesis of no relationship (i.e., $\beta = 0$) is now evident.

$$F = \frac{\text{Regression Mean Square}}{\text{Error Mean Square}} = \frac{1,271.88}{4.42} = 287.76$$

Since $F\begin{bmatrix} 1 \\ 13 \end{bmatrix} 0.05 = 4.7$, the hypothesis is rejected, and it is concluded that a relationship does exist between wing length and latitude for this species of bird.

Similar conclusions would be reached by the t-test method. The sample regression coefficient (b) is

$$b = \frac{\sum\limits_{1}^{n} xy}{\sum\limits_{1}^{n} x^2} = \frac{1,015.0}{810.0} = 1.253$$

The investigator *could* ask himself, "What values might this have been, using similar sampling techniques?" These possible values constitute the sampling distribution of regression coefficients. This sampling distribution is a normal distribution.

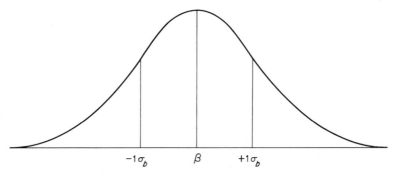

Figure 12.1 Sampling distribution of regression coefficients.

The mean of the sampling distribution is β because

$$E[b_i] = \beta$$

The variance (second moment) of the sampling distribution is expressed by

$$\sigma_b^2 = E[b_i - \beta]^2$$

It can be shown that

$$\sigma_b^2 = E[b_i - \beta]^2 = \frac{\sigma_{YX}^2}{\sum\limits_{1}^{n} x^2}$$

Thus, the standard deviation of the sampling distribution of regression coefficients has the formula:

$$\sigma_b = \sqrt{\frac{\sigma_{YX}^2}{\sum\limits_{1}^{n} x^2}}$$

This standard deviation is known as the true standard error of the regression coefficient.

If the true standard error were known, the null hypothesis ($\beta = 0$) would be tested as follows:

$$c = \frac{b - \beta}{\sqrt{\dfrac{\sigma_{YX}^2}{\sum\limits_1^n x^2}}} = \frac{b}{\sigma_b}$$

However, the variance (σ_{YX}^2) is unknown and must be estimated, therefore a c test is not appropriate. The t test becomes (Hypothesis: $\beta = 0$):

$$t = \frac{b - \beta}{\sqrt{\dfrac{s_{YX}^2}{\sum\limits_1^n x^2}}} = \frac{b}{s_b}$$

where s_b is the estimated standard error. Since the estimate of σ_{YX}^2 is based on $n - 2$ independent variables, the t table is entered with $n - 2$ degrees of freedom.

$$t = \frac{b}{\sqrt{\dfrac{s_{XY}^2}{\sum\limits_1^n x^2}}} = \frac{1.253}{\sqrt{\dfrac{4.42}{810.0}}} = \frac{1.253}{0.0738} = 16.96$$

For $n - 2 = 13$ degrees of freedom, $P < 0.01$.

Whenever there is one degree of freedom associated with the numerator of the F test, the following relationship holds: $F = t^2$. Since the number of degrees of freedom for regression is one, then F from analysis of variance should equal t^2 from the t test.

This can be demonstrated with the F and t values obtained in this analysis, realizing, of course, that slight errors were introduced by rounding off. This relationship leads to a simple method of deriving the equation for the estimated standard error:

$$F = t^2 = \frac{\text{Regression Mean Square}}{\text{Error Mean Square}}$$

Regression mean square has the formula

$$\frac{\left(\sum\limits_1^n xy\right)^2}{\sum\limits_1^n x^2}$$

Multiplying the numerator and denominator by $\Sigma_1^n x^2$ gives

$$\frac{\left(\sum_1^n xy\right)^2}{\sum_1^n x^2} \cdot \frac{\sum_1^n x^2}{\sum_1^n x^2} = \frac{\left(\sum_1^n xy\right)^2}{\left(\sum_1^n x^2\right)^2} \cdot \sum_1^n x^2 = b^2 \sum_1^n x^2$$

The $F = t^2$ equation can now be expressed as follows:

$$F = t^2 = \frac{\text{Regression Mean Square}}{\text{Error Mean Square}} = \frac{b^2 \sum_1^n x^2}{s_{YX}^2}$$

Dividing numerator and denominator by $\Sigma_1^n x^2$ gives

$$F = t^2 = \frac{b^2}{\dfrac{s_{YX}^2}{\sum_1^n x^2}}$$

Therefore

$$t = \frac{b}{\sqrt{\dfrac{s_{YX}^2}{\sum_1^n x^2}}} = \frac{b}{s_b}$$

which demonstrates that

$$s_b = \sqrt{\frac{s_{YX}^2}{\sum_1^n x^2}}$$
Estimated standard error of the regression coefficient.

12.6   Confidence Limits for the True Regression Coefficient (β)

It was concluded that $\beta \neq 0$; therefore, a relationship does exist between wing length and latitude for this species of bird. The next procedure is to set confidence limits for the true regression coefficient. The 95% confidence limits are represented by

$$\beta = b \pm t_{0.05} s_b \qquad \text{(Degrees of Freedom} = n - 2)$$

These become:

$$L_1 = 1.253 - 2.16(0.0738) = 1.094$$

$$L_2 = 1.253 + 2.16(0.0738) = 1.412$$

The investigator is 95% confident that the limits include β. Note that the range of the confidence limits is largely dependent on the value of s_{YX}^2 which appears in the numerator of the standard error. This shows that the reliability of the estimate of β increases as variability around the regression line decreases. If there were no variability (i.e., $s_{YX}^2 = 0$), the estimate would be the same as the parameter.

12.7 Confidence Limits for the Mean of the Y Values for a Given Value of X(μ_{YX})

A common procedure in a regression analysis is to set confidence limits for the mean of the Y values for a specific value of X. It has been stated that $\hat{Y}$ for a given value of X is the best estimate of μ_{YX}. A sampling distribution of $\hat{Y}$ can be constructed. This sampling distribution is normal in form, with a mean of μ_{YX} and a standard deviation symbolized by $\sigma_{\hat{Y}}$.

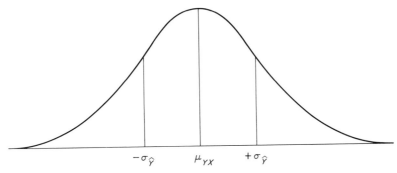

Figure 12.2 Sampling distribution of Y values for a given value of X.

The derivation of the formula for the standard deviation of this sampling distribution requires a knowledge of important concepts.

(1) The question may be asked, "What are the mean and variance of a distribution of measurements if each measurement is multiplied by a constant?"

$$\text{New Mean} = \frac{\sum\limits_{1}^{N} aX_i}{N} = \frac{a\sum\limits_{1}^{N} X_i}{N} = a\mu$$

$$\text{New Variance} = \frac{\sum\limits_{1}^{N} (aX_i - a\mu)^2}{N} = \frac{\sum\limits_{1}^{N} a^2(X_i - \mu)^2}{N} = \frac{a^2\sum\limits_{1}^{N} (X_i - \mu)^2}{N} = a^2\sigma^2$$

The rule may be stated: Multiplying each variable by a constant is the same as multiplying the mean by the constant and multiplying the variance by the square of the constant. A fundamental equation comes from this rule:

$$\sigma_{aX}^2 = a^2 \sigma_X^2$$

(2) In the discussion of the group comparison and pairing design tests, the following rule was demonstrated

$$\sigma_{X \pm Y}^2 = \sigma_X^2 + \sigma_Y^2 \qquad \text{(if } X \text{ and } Y \text{ are independent)}$$

(3) If Y values were selected without regard to the X values, the variance of the sampling distribution of sample means ($\bar{y}$) would have the equation

$$\sigma_{\bar{y}}^2 = \frac{\sigma_Y^2}{n}$$

where σ_Y^2 is the variance (second moment) of all Y values.

However, when Y values are selected for fixed X values (Model I) or random X values (Model II), the variance of the sampling distribution of sample means has the equation

$$\sigma_{\bar{y}}^2 = \frac{\sigma_{YX}^2}{n}$$

where σ_{YX}^2 is the variance from regression. The latter will be smaller in value than the former. This can be demonstrated by a special situation. Suppose that a complete relationship exists between the X and Y values (i.e., for a given value of X, the Y values are constant). All the Y values would lie exactly on the regression line and σ_{YX}^2 would equal zero. If one observation of Y were taken for a fixed set of X values, the mean ($\bar{y}$) would have a given value. If the study were repeated an infinitely large number of times, the value of $\bar{y}$ in each case would remain constant. It would not vary, and therefore the variance of the sampling distribution ($\sigma_{\bar{y}}^2 = \sigma_{YX}^2/n$) would equal zero.

However, variation would exist among the Y values, and therefore σ_Y^2 would have a value other than zero. Consequently, $\sigma_{\bar{y}}^2 = \sigma_Y^2/n$ would not equal zero. This is not sensible and demonstrates that $\sigma_{\bar{y}}^2$ is a function of σ_{YX}^2 and not σ_Y^2.

The above concepts can now be used to derive the standard error of $\hat{Y}$. The term $\sigma_{\bar{y}}^2$ is equivalent to $\sigma_{\bar{y}+b(X-\bar{x})}^2$ since $\hat{Y} = \bar{y} + b(X - \bar{x})$. Furthermore, $\sigma_{\bar{y}+b(X-\bar{x})}^2 = \sigma_{\bar{y}}^2 + \sigma_{b(X-\bar{x})}^2$ because the terms $\bar{y}$ and $b(X - \bar{x})$ are independent. Now $\sigma_{\bar{y}}^2$ has been shown to be equal to σ_{YX}^2/n and since $(X - \bar{x})$ is constant for any given value of X because of the fixed values of X, then

$$\sigma_{b(X-\bar{x})}^2 = (X - \bar{x})^2 \sigma_b^2$$

Consequently,

$$\sigma_{\hat{Y}}^2 = \sigma_{YX}^2/n + (X - \bar{x})^2 \sigma_b^2$$

The formula for $\sigma_{\hat{Y}}^2$ is more commonly expressed as:

$$\sigma_{\hat{Y}}^2 = \frac{\sigma_{YX}^2}{n} + (X - \bar{x})^2 \frac{\sigma_{YX}^2}{\sum\limits_{1}^{n} x^2} = \sigma_{YX}^2 \left(\frac{1}{n} + \frac{(X - \bar{x})^2}{\sum\limits_{1}^{n} x^2} \right)$$

and the true standard error of $\hat{Y}$ becomes

$$\sigma_{\hat{Y}} = \sqrt{ \sigma_{YX}^2 \left(\frac{1}{n} + \frac{(X - \bar{x})^2}{\sum\limits_{1}^{n} x^2} \right) }$$

Two degrees of freedom are lost in estimating σ_{YX}^2. The 95% confidence limits for μ_{YX} for each value of X are given as

$$L_1 = \hat{Y} - t_{0.05} \sqrt{ s_{YX}^2 \left(\frac{1}{n} + \frac{(X - \bar{x})^2}{\sum\limits_{1}^{n} x^2} \right) }$$

$$L_2 = \hat{Y} + t_{0.05} \sqrt{ s_{YX}^2 \left(\frac{1}{n} + \frac{(X - \bar{x})^2}{\sum\limits_{1}^{n} x^2} \right) }$$

Table 12.4   Estimates of Population Means (μ_{YX}).

Latitude	$\hat{Y}$	$L_1 = \hat{Y} - t_{0.05}(s_Y)$
25° N	131.6	$131.6 - 2.16(0.9772) = 129.49$
30° N	137.8	$137.8 - 2.16(0.7007) = 136.29$
35° N	144.1	$144.1 - 2.16(0.5440) = 142.92$
40° N	150.3	$150.3 - 2.16(0.6181) = 148.96$
45° N	156.6	$156.6 - 2.16(0.8579) = 154.75$
Latitude	$\hat{Y}$	$L_2 = \hat{Y} + t_{0.05}(s_Y)$
25° N	131.6	$131.6 + 2.16(0.9772) = 133.71$
30° N	137.8	$137.8 + 2.16(0.7007) = 139.31$
35° N	144.1	$144.1 + 2.16(0.5440) = 145.98$
40° N	150.3	$150.3 + 2.16(0.6181) = 151.64$
45° N	156.6	$156.6 + 2.16(0.8579) = 158.45$

For 25°N latitude these are

$$L_1 = 131.6 - 2.16\sqrt{4.42\left(\frac{1}{15} + \frac{(25-36)^2}{810}\right)} = 129.49$$

$$L_2 = 131.6 + 2.16\sqrt{4.42\left(\frac{1}{15} + \frac{(25-36)^2}{810}\right)} = 133.71$$

These limits for all the different latitudes sampled are summarized in Table 12.4. Limits could be obtained for any of the latitudes such as 38°N, 43°N, etc., in exactly the same manner.

Table 12.4 shows that as X moves away from $\bar{x}$, the value of the standard error is increased. The range of the confidence limits is at a minimum when $X = \bar{x}$. These confidence limits are unique because of their curvature.

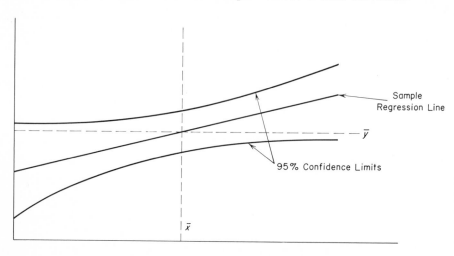

12.8   Confidence Limits for the True Y Intercept

The equation for a straight line is $\hat{Y} = a + bX$. When X is equal to zero, $\hat{Y} = a$. Consequently, $\sigma_a{}^2 = \sigma_{\hat{Y}}{}^2$ when X is set equal to zero.

A sampling distribution of Y intercept values is normal in form, with a mean of α and a standard deviation of σ_a.

The equation for the true standard error is

$$\sigma_a = \sqrt{\sigma_{YX}{}^2\left(\frac{1}{n} + \frac{\bar{x}^2}{\sum\limits_1^n x^2}\right)}$$

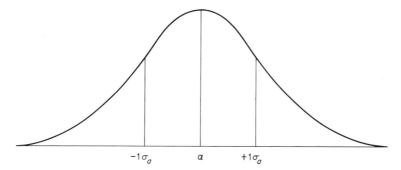

Figure 12.3 Sampling distribution of $_Y$ intercept values.

Substituting s_{YX}^2 in place of σ_{YX}^2 gives the estimated standard error.

$$s_a = \sqrt{s_{YX}^2\left(\frac{1}{n} + \frac{\bar{x}^2}{\sum\limits_1^n x^2}\right)} \qquad \text{Degrees of freedom} = n - 2$$

This standard error is useful in setting the 95% confidence limits for the true Y intercept,

$$\alpha = a \pm t_{0.05}s_a$$

or in testing the hypothesis that the true regression line passes through the origin (i.e., through the points with coordinates 0,0), or through some other point.

$$t = \frac{a}{s_a}$$

12.9   Testing the Hypothesis That $\beta_1 = \beta_2$

A relationship was demonstrated between wing length of a given species of bird and latitude. This species shall be designated species #1. Now assume that the investigator collected data on wing length and latitude for species #2, for the purpose of testing the hypothesis that $\beta_1 = \beta_2$. Pertinent data for both studies are given on page 204.

A sampling distribution may be constructed of all possible theoretical $b_1 - b_2$ values. The mean of this normal distribution is $E(b_1 - b_2) = E(b_1) - E(b_2) = \beta_1 - \beta_2$. The variance of this sampling distribution is

$$\sigma_{b_1-b_2}^2 = \sigma_{b_1}^2 + \sigma_{b_2}^2 = \frac{\sigma_{YX_1}^2}{\sum\limits_1^n x_1^2} + \frac{\sigma_{YX_2}^2}{\sum\limits_1^n x_2^2} \quad \text{(since } b_1 \text{ and } b_2 \text{ are independent)}$$

	Species #1	Species #2
n	15	10
$\sum_{1}^{n} x^2$	810.0	500.00
$\sum_{1}^{n} y^2$	1,329.33	3,624.90
$\sum_{1}^{n} xy$	1,015.00	1,335.00
$\sum_{1}^{n} d^2$	57.45	60.45
b	1.253	2.670

Assuming homogeneous variances from regression (i.e., $\sigma_{YX_1}^2 = \sigma_{YX_2}^2$), the expression is modified to:

$$\sigma_{b_1-b_2}^2 = \sigma_{YX}^2 \left(\frac{1}{\sum_{1}^{n} x_1^2} + \frac{1}{\sum_{1}^{n} x_2^2} \right)$$

The properties of this sampling distribution of differences between regression coefficients are now known.

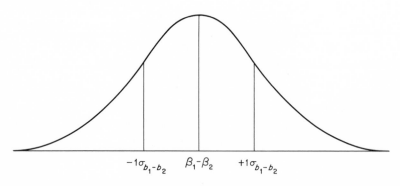

Figure 12.4 Sampling distribution of differences between regression coefficients.

If the variance from regression (σ_{YX}^2) were known, the null hypothesis $(\beta_1 = \beta_2)$ could be tested by calculating a c value.

$$c = \frac{(b_1 - b_2)}{\sqrt{\sigma_{YX}^2 \left(\dfrac{1}{\sum\limits_1^n x_1^2} + \dfrac{1}{\sum\limits_1^n x_2^2} \right)}}$$

However, the variance is not known and must be estimated. The best estimate is a pooled estimate.

$$s_{YX(pooled)}^2 = \frac{\sum\limits_1^n d_1^2 + \sum\limits_1^n d_2^2}{(n_1 - 2) + (n_2 - 2)}$$

$$= \frac{57.45 + 60.45}{13 + 8} = 5.61$$

Using this estimate instead of the parameter leads to a t test.

$$t = \frac{b_1 - b_2}{\sqrt{s_{YX(pooled)}^2 \left(\dfrac{1}{\sum\limits_1^n x_1^2} + \dfrac{1}{\sum\limits_1^n x_2^2} \right)}} = \frac{1.253 - 2.670}{\sqrt{5.61 \left(\dfrac{1}{810} + \dfrac{1}{500} \right)}} = 10.52$$

$$\text{D.F.} = (n_1 - 2) + (n_2 - 2) = 21$$

Since $P < 0.01$, the hypothesis is rejected.

The 95% confidence limits for the true difference between regression coefficients can be determined in the ordinary fashion from the formula:

$$\beta_1 - \beta_2 = (b_1 - b_2) \pm t_{0.05} s_{b_1 - b_2}$$

where $s_{b_1 - b_2}$ is the estimated standard error.

Problems

1. For specific values of X, an investigator obtained the following Y values:

X	Y
0.5	3.1
1.0	3.8
1.5	4.4
2.0	5.2
2.5	5.8
3.0	6.7

(a) Sketch by eye on graph paper the regression line best fitting the series of points. Does the relationship appear to be linear? (b) Determine the value of the regression coefficient. Interpret the meaning. (c) Determine the value of the Y intercept. (d) For each value of X, calculate $\hat{Y}$. Calculate the variance from regression using the general formula. (e) Calculate the variance from regression using the working formula. (f) Determine whether the regression coefficient deviates significantly from zero. For demonstrative purposes, determine the significance by the analysis-of-variance method as well as by a t test. Compare the F value with t^2. (g) Determine the 95% confidence limits for the true regression coefficient. Interpret the meaning.

2. An investigator carried out a regression analysis. The fixed X values gave a mean of 10.0. The mean of all the Y values was 10.0. The Y intercept had a value of 5.0. The 95% confidence limits (L_1 and L_2) for the mean of all the Y values for an X value of 10.0 were 8 and 12. The 95% confidence limits for the true Y intercept were 1 and 9. (a) Give the exact value of the regression coefficient. (b) Does a deviate significantly from zero? (c) Based on all the available data, sketch the regression line and the 95% confidence limits for the mean of all the Y values for all values of X from 0 to 20.

3. A Drosophila geneticist mated female heterokaryotypes with male homokaryotypes from a given strain. The expected frequency of homokaryotypes in the offspring was 50%. The parental flies were transferred to fresh bottles each day. Hence the offspring eclosing in each bottle were produced by parents of different ages. One thousand offspring from each bottle were classified as homokaryotypes or heterokaryotypes.

Age of Parents in Days	% Homokaryotype Offspring
1	47.3
2	52.9
3	51.1
4	44.8
5	42.7
6	44.4
7	38.2
8	38.5
9	40.8
10	34.7
11	39.8
12	39.0
13	41.9
14	35.8
15	34.5
16	33.4
17	27.2
18	27.6

(a) Determine the value of the regression coefficient and Y intercept. (b) Determine whether the regression coefficient deviates significantly from zero. Determine the 95% confidence limits for the true regression coefficient. (c) Determine the 95% confidence limits for the true Y intercept. (d) What conclusion can be drawn regarding parental age and eclosion of homokaryotype offspring.

4. An investigator studied the growth rate of an organism (strain 1) from day 1 through day 12.

Age in Days X	Dry Weight (milligrams) Y
1	3.8
2	6.4
3	8.7
4	13.7
5	19.3
6	27.7
7	43.9
8	75.2
9	115.2
10	119.4
11	283.5
12	510.2

(a) On graph paper, plot the Y values for each X value. Is there a linear or curvilinear relationship between X and Y?

Data of this kind may follow the exponential growth curve. The equation is

$$Y = AB^X$$

where A and B are constants. Such data must be transformed before a linear regression analysis is possible. Applying logarithms to the equation gives

$$\log Y = \log A + (\log B)X$$

Setting $Y = \log Y$, $a = \log A$, and $b = \log B$, gives the equation for a straight line, i.e.,

$$Y = a + bX$$

(b) On graph paper, plot log Y for each X value. Is the relationship linear? (c) Compute a regression coefficient on the transformed data (make the logs accurate to at least 2 decimals). Give the meaning in words. (d) Test the hypothesis that $\beta = 0$ by a t test. (e) Determine the 95% confidence limits for β. (f) Calculate the 95% confidence limits for the population means (in log milligrams) for each day. (g) Assume that the investigator repeated the study for strain 2. The regression coefficient was $b = 0.1646$. The variance from regression was $s_{YX}^2 = 0.00314$. Test the hypothesis that $\beta_1 = \beta_2$, i.e., the growth rates (during the same period of time) are similar.

5. A study was made of the effect of enzyme concentration on the rate of a reaction in the presence of excess substrate.

Yeast saccharase (ml.)	Rate of sucrose hydrolysis (mg./unit time)
1.0	110
1.5	201
2.0	240
2.5	305
3.0	390
3.5	445
4.0	495

(a) Calculate b. Interpret the meaning of this statistic. (b) Test the hypothesis that $\beta = 0$. (c) Set confidence limits for β.

Test for Linearity of Regression

Many relationships between independent and dependent variables are best described by a curve, and not a straight line. Therefore, it is apparent that the techniques described in Chapter 12 would not be appropriate for analyzing the data unless some transformation can be employed. Consequently, in many cases, it may be important to test for the linearity of regression. This can be done by combining a completely randomized design with a regression analysis, *if* there are two or more Y measurements for each X value.

Table 13.1

					$\sum_{1}^{n} Y_i$	$\sum_{1}^{n} Y_i^2$	$\bar{y}_g$
25° N	132	131	128		391	50,969	130.33
30° N	138	139			277	38,365	138.50
35° N	146	147	143		436	63,374	145.33
40° N	149	154	151		454	68,718	151.33
45° N	155	158	154	155	622	96,730	155.50
					$\sum_{1}^{k}\sum_{1}^{n} Y_i$ $= 2,180$	$\sum_{1}^{k}\sum_{1}^{n} Y_i^2$ $= 318,156$	$\bar{y} = 145.33$

The procedure can be demonstrated by using the data presented in the previous chapter on wing length and latitude. Samples of Y measurements were taken for five different latitudes, giving a total of five groups with a total of 15 different measurements. *Total* sum of squares and degrees of freedom are partitioned into *groups* and *within* groups.

$$\text{Total sum of squares} = 318{,}156 - \frac{(2{,}180)^2}{15} = 1{,}329.333$$

$$\text{Groups sum of squares} = \frac{(391)^2}{3} + \frac{(277)^2}{2} + \frac{(436)^2}{3} + \frac{(454)^2}{3} + \frac{(622)^2}{4}$$
$$- \frac{(2{,}180)^2}{15} = 1{,}289.833$$

Within-groups sum of squares $= 1{,}329.333 - 1{,}289.833 = 39.500$

The groups sum of squares can in turn be partitioned into two parts. These are termed *regression* sum of squares and *deviation from linearity* sum of squares. These parts can be visualized by referring to Figure 13.1. The *total*

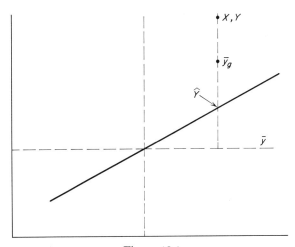

Figure 13.1

deviation is given by $(Y - \bar{y})$. The *within* deviation is given by $(Y - \bar{y}_g)$ and the *groups* deviation by $(\bar{y}_g - \bar{y})$. The groups deviation can be divided into $(\bar{y}_g - \hat{Y})$, called the non-linearity deviation, and $(\hat{Y} - \bar{y})$, which is the regression deviation. Consequently

Total Sum of Squares = Deviation from linearity Sum of Squares + Regression Sum of Squares + Within-Groups Sum of Squares

It has been shown previously that regression sum of squares is equal to

$$\frac{\left(\sum_{1}^{n} xy\right)^2}{\sum_{1}^{n} x^2}$$

Subtracting this value from groups sum of squares gives deviation from linearity sum of squares. From the above study this becomes:

$$\text{Regression Sum of Squares} = \frac{\left(\sum_{1}^{n} xy\right)^2}{\sum_{1}^{n} x^2} = \frac{(1{,}015)^2}{810} = 1{,}271.883$$

$$\begin{aligned}\text{Deviation from Linearity Sum of Squares} &= 1{,}289.833 - 1{,}271.883 \\ &= 17.950\end{aligned}$$

There are $k - 1$ degrees of freedom associated with groups, and one degree of freedom for regression. This leaves $k - 2$ degrees of freedom for deviation from linearity. The degrees of freedom for total and within groups are the same as for the completely randomized design.

Table 13.2

Source of Variation	Degrees of Freedom	Sum of Squares	Mean Square
Total	14	1,329.333	
Regression	1	1,271.883	
Deviation from Linearity	3	17.950	5.983
Within Groups	10	39.500	3.950

If linear regression is present, $\bar{y}_g$ and $\hat{Y}$ for each value of X are both unbiased estimates of μ_{YX}. Any variation between them is ascribed to chance. Under this situation deviation from linearity mean square and within-groups mean square both estimate σ_{YX}^2.

If curvilinear regression is present, the mean-square estimates are as follows:

E(Deviation from linearity mean square) $= \sigma_{YX}^2 +$ component due to nonlinearity

E(Within-groups mean square) $= \sigma_{YX}^2$

The hypothesis of linearity is tested as follows:

$$F = \frac{\text{Deviation from Linearity Mean Square}}{\text{Within-Groups Mean Square}}$$

$$F = \frac{5.983}{3.950} = 1.5 \qquad\qquad F\begin{bmatrix} 3 \\ 10 \end{bmatrix} 0.05 = 3.7$$

On the basis of the calculated F value, the hypothesis should be accepted that a linear relationship exists between wing length and latitude (from 25°N to 45°N.)

From the above discussion it follows that if a linear relationship is not present, $\bar{y}_g$ and $\hat{Y}$ will not be estimates of the same parameter for all values of X, and therefore the deviation from linearity mean square will tend to be significantly larger than the within-groups mean square. The following diagram illustrates such a situation.

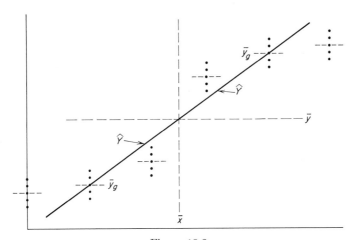

Figure 13.2

It is clear from the diagram that for some values of X a large variability exists between $\bar{y}_g$ and $\hat{Y}$; however, this variability is not as pronounced in the vicinity of $\bar{x}$.

In testing for the linearity of regression, the within-groups mean square is used as an estimate of σ_{YX}^2 (i.e., the variance of the Y measurements for the different values of X). This mean square is determined by measuring the variability existing within each group (i.e., $Y - \bar{y}_g$). Previously, the variance from regression (error mean square) was given as an estimate of σ_{YX}^2. When linear regression is present, error mean square and within-groups mean square both estimate this variance. However, if a linear relationship is not present, the variance from regression will be a biased estimate of σ_{YX}^2. It will tend to overestimate the true value of the population variance, since many of the Y measurements will deviate greatly from the regression line. For this reason, the within-groups mean square is used as the denominator in the F test.

Problems

1. An investigator wishes to test the hypothesis that a linear relationship exists between X and Y measurements. For each value of X, four Y measurements are obtained.

X	Y
0.5	3.0, 3.6, 2.8, 3.2
1.0	3.8, 4.6, 4.1, 4.2
1.5	4.5, 4.9, 4.1, 4.6
2.0	5.2, 5.6, 5.0, 5.1
2.5	5.4, 5.8, 5.9, 6.2
3.0	6.6, 6.8, 6.4, 7.2

(a) Sketch by eye on graph paper the regression line best fitting the series of points. (b) Test the hypothesis that linearity exists between the X and Y measurements by calculating F. What are your conclusions? (c) Calculate the value of the regression coefficient.

2. A study was made of the relationship between oxygen tension and respiratory rate of bacteria. Three Y measurements were obtained for each value of X.

Oxygen tension in mm. Hg (X)	Respiratory rate (Y)		
1	9	11	8
2	37	40	37
3	58	57	64
4	70	68	72
5	76	76	78
6	80	79	81
7	82	84	82
8	83	84	84
9	88	86	90
10	91	90	89
11	91	89	91
12	91	93	91
13	93	92	92
14	94	96	94
15	95	96	95

(a) Test the hypothesis that linearity exists between the X and Y measurements. What are your conclusions? (b) Plot the measurements on graph paper. What does the graph indicate about the linearity of the measurements?

CHAPTER FOURTEEN

Correlation Coefficient

A regression coefficient (b) may be appropriately used to describe the relationship between X and Y variables when either Model I (Fixed X, random Y) or Model II (random X, random Y) is assumed. Another coefficient, known as the *correlation coefficient*, may also be used when Model II is assumed. The correlation coefficient has one major advantage over the regression coefficient which accounts for its wide usage. It is divorced from units and therefore valuable in comparative studies. Two or more regression coefficients can only be compared when each is based on the same X and Y units.

Both the regression coefficient and correlation coefficient will indicate whether a relationship exists between two variables. They simply go about it in different ways. It is instructive to consider the following scatter diagrams and regression lines.

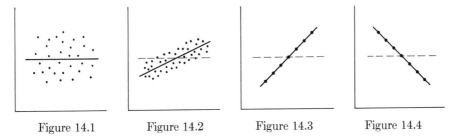

Figure 14.1   Figure 14.2   Figure 14.3   Figure 14.4

If no relationship exists between X and Y, the scatter of the points about the regression line is widespread as shown in Figure 14.1. The regression line is parallel and is similar to the line giving the position of $\bar{y}$. Any given point

213

in the scatter diagram, for any value of X, deviates from $\bar{y}$ due to chance alone. In Figure 14.2 the regression line has rotated slightly. A positive relationship now exists between the two variables but variability still exists about the regression line. A given point can vary from $\bar{y}$ due to the influence of two factors. One is chance and the other is attributable to regression. For example, a large value of Y may vary from $\bar{y}$ because of the errors of random sampling and also because it is associated with a large value of X. In Figures 14.3 and 14.4, complete relationship exists between the two variables. For a given value of X or Y the other measurement can be accurately specified. All the points lie on the regression line (i.e., $s_{YX}^2 = 0$). In this situation any given point deviates from $\bar{y}$ entirely due to the influence of regression or the association between the variables. In Figure 14.3 the correlation is positive, while in Figure 14.4 it is negative.

The above observations can be expressed objectively with the use of the sum of squares derived in Chapter 12.

$$\sum_1^n y^2 \quad = \quad \sum_1^n \hat{y}^2 \quad + \quad \sum_1^n d^2$$

Total Sum of Squares	Regression Sum of Squares	Error Sum of Squares

If X and Y are independent, the regression line is horizontal. The regression sum of squares is equal to zero and the equation $\Sigma_1^n y^2 = \Sigma_1^n \hat{y}^2 + \Sigma_1^n d^2$ becomes $\Sigma_1^n y^2 = \Sigma_1^n d^2$. The total sum of squares is equal to error sum of squares; thus, the total variability of the Y items about $\bar{y}$ is due to chance alone.

When complete correlation is present, the error sum of squares is equal to zero and the equation $\Sigma_1^n y^2 = \Sigma_1^n \hat{y}^2 + \Sigma_1^n d^2$ becomes $\Sigma_1^n y^2 = \Sigma_1^n \hat{y}^2$. The total sum of squares is equal to regression sum of squares. The association between X and Y accounts entirely for the variability of the Y items about $\bar{y}$. The ratio

$$\frac{\sum_1^n \hat{y}^2}{\sum_1^n y^2}$$

expresses the proportion of the total sum of squares which is due to the association between X and Y, or due to linear regression. This ratio is known as the *coefficient of determination* and is symbolized by r^2.

$$\text{Coefficient of Determination} = r^2 = \frac{\text{Regression Sum of Squares}}{\text{Total Sum of Squares}} = \frac{\sum_1^n \hat{y}^2}{\sum_1^n y^2}$$

The working formula for r^2 is derived as follows:

$$r^2 = \frac{\text{Regression Sum of Squares}}{\text{Total Sum of Squares}} = \frac{\dfrac{\left(\sum\limits_{1}^{n} xy\right)^2}{\sum\limits_{1}^{n} x^2}}{\sum\limits_{1}^{n} y^2} = \frac{\left(\sum\limits_{1}^{n} xy\right)^2}{\left(\sum\limits_{1}^{n} x^2\right)\left(\sum\limits_{1}^{n} y^2\right)}$$

When there is no relationship between variables (i.e., the regression line is horizontal), $r^2 = 0$. When there is complete relationship (i.e., all points are on the regression line), $r^2 = 1$. The coefficient of determination by itself does not indicate whether the relationship is positive or negative (unless the sign of $\sum_1^n xy$ in the numerator is noted before squaring). This slight inconvenience can be corrected by considering the square root of the coefficient of determination. The square root is known as the correlation coefficient (r).

$$r = \frac{\sum\limits_{1}^{n} xy}{\sqrt{\left(\sum\limits_{1}^{n} x^2\right)\left(\sum\limits_{1}^{n} y^2\right)}}$$

The value of r can vary from -1 to $+1$. When r is equal to 0, the two variables are independent. When complete correlation is present, r will equal $+1$ or -1, depending on whether the correlation is positive or negative. The degree of correlation depends on the value of the coefficient.

14.1 Example of the Calculation of the Correlation Coefficient

A mammalogist was interested in the possible correlation between the length of the skull and breadth of the mastoid bone in the Great Basin pocket mouse. Ten adult male specimens were collected. The measurements in millimeters were obtained and are given in Table 14.1.

The values for $\sum_1^n x^2$, $\sum_1^n y^2$, and $\sum_1^n xy$ are as follows:

$$\sum_{1}^{n} x^2 = \sum_{1}^{n} (X_i - \bar{x})^2 = \sum_{1}^{n} X_i^2 - \frac{\left(\sum\limits_{1}^{n} X_i\right)^2}{n} = 7{,}327.30 - \frac{(270.6)^2}{10} = 4.864$$

$$\sum_{1}^{n} y^2 = \sum_{1}^{n} (Y_i - \bar{y})^2 = \sum_{1}^{n} Y_i^2 - \frac{\left(\sum\limits_{1}^{n} Y_i\right)^2}{n} = 1{,}730.27 - \frac{(131.5)^2}{10} = 1.045$$

$$\sum_{1}^{n} xy = \sum_{1}^{n} (X_i - \bar{x})(Y_i - \bar{y}) = \sum_{1}^{n} X_iY_i - \frac{\left(\sum\limits_{1}^{n} X_i\right)\left(\sum\limits_{1}^{n} Y_i\right)}{n}$$

$$= 3{,}560.35 - \frac{(270.6)(131.5)}{10} = 1.96$$

Table 14.1

Specimen	Length of Skull X_i	Breadth of Mastoid Y_i	$X_i Y_i$
1	26.2	12.9	337.98
2	26.4	12.6	332.64
3	27.2	13.3	361.65
4	26.8	13.2	353.76
5	28.1	13.6	382.16
6	26.5	13.1	347.15
7	26.2	12.7	332.74
8	27.6	13.5	372.60
9	28.0	13.5	378.00
10	27.6	13.1	361.56
	$\sum_1^n X_i = 270.6$	$\sum_1^n Y_i = 131.5$	$\sum_1^n X_i Y_i = 3{,}560.35$
	$\sum_1^n X_i^2 = 7{,}327.30$	$\sum_1^n Y_i^2 = 1{,}730.27$	

The value of the correlation coefficient becomes:

$$r = \frac{\sum_1^n xy}{\sqrt{\left(\sum_1^n x^2\right)\left(\sum_1^n y^2\right)}} = \frac{1.96}{\sqrt{(4.864)(1.045)}} = 0.869$$

This shows that a high positive correlation exists between these two variables. When either X or Y is increased, the other is increased as well. The correlation coefficient is an index of correlation but it is not as expressive as the coefficient of determination.

$$r^2 = (0.869)^2 = 0.756$$

Approximately 75.6% of the variation in Y, as measured by the sum of squares, is due to the linear regression of Y (mastoid breadth) on X (length of skull).

If 75.6% of the variation in Y, as measured by the sum of squares, is due to the linear regression of Y on X, then 24.4% must be due to chance. This follows from the definition of the coefficient of non-determination (k^2).

$$\text{Coefficient of Non-Determination} = k^2 = \frac{\text{Error Sum of Squares}}{\text{Total Sum of Squares}} = \frac{\sum_{1}^{n} d^2}{\sum_{1}^{n} y^2}$$

The working equation is $k^2 = 1 - r^2$

14.2 Relationship Between the Correlation and Regression Coefficients

When Model II is assumed, two different regression coefficients may be calculated.

$$b_{YX} = \frac{\sum_{1}^{n} xy}{\sum_{1}^{n} x^2} \qquad\qquad \text{Regression of } Y \text{ on } X$$

$$b_{XY} = \frac{\sum_{1}^{n} xy}{\sum_{1}^{n} y^2} \qquad\qquad \text{Regression of } X \text{ on } Y$$

Substituting the data from the above study into the formulae gives:

$$b_{YX} = \frac{1.96}{4.864} = 0.403; \qquad\qquad b_{XY} = \frac{1.96}{1.045} 1.876$$

For a millimeter increase in the length of the skull, the mastoid breadth increases 0.403 millimeters. For a millimeter increase in the mastoid breadth, the length of the skull increases 1.876 millimeters.

One relationship between the correlation and regression coefficients can be shown as follows:

$$r^2 = \frac{\left(\sum_{1}^{n} xy\right)^2}{\left(\sum_{1}^{n} x^2\right)\left(\sum_{1}^{n} y^2\right)} = \frac{\left(\sum_{1}^{n} xy\right)\left(\sum_{1}^{n} xy\right)}{\left(\sum_{1}^{n} x^2\right)\left(\sum_{1}^{n} y^2\right)} = b_{YX} \cdot b_{XY}$$

$$r = \sqrt{b_{YX} \cdot b_{XY}}$$

The value of r is intermediate between the values of the two regression coefficients. Substituting the above data into this latter formula gives

$$r = \sqrt{(0.403)(1.876)} = 0.869$$

Dividing the numerator and denominator of the correlation coefficient by $n - 1$ shows another characteristic of r.

$$r = \frac{\sum\limits_{1}^{n} xy}{\sqrt{\left(\sum\limits_{1}^{n} x^2\right)\left(\sum\limits_{1}^{n} y^2\right)}} = \frac{\dfrac{\sum\limits_{1}^{n} xy}{n - 1}}{\sqrt{\dfrac{\sum\limits_{1}^{n} x^2}{n - 1} \dfrac{\sum\limits_{1}^{n} y^2}{n - 1}}} = \frac{\text{Covariance}}{\sqrt{(s_X^2)(s_Y^2)}}$$

14.3   Testing the Significance of the Correlation Coefficient

The true correlation coefficient (parameter) is symbolized by the Greek letter rho (ρ). In the above study, this parameter was estimated by $r = 0.869$. When samples are small, as in this case, positive and negative values occur due to chance alone even when ρ is zero. It is often necessary to test the significance of r, i.e., determine if r deviates significantly from zero. The null hypothesis is $\rho = 0$. It may be tested by the analysis-of-variance method or the standard-error method. The former is identical to that for testing the significance of a regression coefficient.

Table 14.2

Source of Variation	Degrees of Freedom	Sum of Squares	Mean Square
Total	$n - 1$	$\sum\limits_{1}^{n} y^2$	
Regression	1	$\sum\limits_{1}^{n} \hat{y}^2$	$\sum\limits_{1}^{n} \hat{y}^2$
Error	$n - 2$	$\sum\limits_{1}^{n} d^2$	$\dfrac{\sum\limits_{1}^{n} d^2}{n - 2}$

Regression mean square is equal to:

$$\frac{\left(\sum\limits_{1}^{n} xy\right)^2}{\sum\limits_{1}^{n} x^2} = \frac{\left(\sum\limits_{1}^{n} xy\right)^2}{\sum\limits_{1}^{n} x^2} \cdot \frac{\sum\limits_{1}^{n} x^2}{\sum\limits_{1}^{n} x^2} = b^2 \sum\limits_{1}^{n} x^2$$

Regression mean square is also equal to:

$$\frac{\left(\sum\limits_1^n xy\right)^2}{\sum\limits_1^n x^2} = \frac{\left(\sum\limits_1^n xy\right)^2}{\sum\limits_1^n x^2} \cdot \frac{\sum\limits_1^n y^2}{\sum\limits_1^n y^2} = r^2 \sum\limits_1^n y^2$$

This demonstrates that regression mean square can be expressed in terms of b^2 or r^2. Since $\rho = \sqrt{\beta_{YX} \cdot \beta_{XY}}$, ρ will equal zero if β_{YX} is zero. Therefore, the null hypothesis that $\rho = 0$ is tested by:

$$F = \frac{\text{Regression Mean Square}}{\text{Error Mean Square}}$$

The sums of squares are as follows:

$$\text{Total sum of squares} = \sum\limits_1^n y^2 = 1.045$$

$$\text{Regression sum of squares} = \sum\limits_1^n \hat{y}^2 = \frac{\left(\sum\limits_1^n xy\right)^2}{\sum\limits_1^n x^2} = \frac{(1.96)^2}{4.864} = 0.790$$

Error sum of squares $= 1.045 - 0.790 = 0.255$

Table 14.3 Analysis of Variance Table.

Source of Variation	Degrees of Freedom	Sum of Squares	Mean Square
Total	9	1.045	
Regression	1	0.790	0.790
Error	8	0.255	0.032

$$F = \frac{0.790}{0.032} = 24.7 \qquad F\left[\frac{1}{8}\ 0.05\right] = 5.3$$

Since the F value is clearly significant, it is accepted that a true relationship exists between the length of the skull and the mastoid breadth in this species of mouse.

Note that r^2 and k^2 can be obtained directly from the data in the analysis-of-variance table.

$$\text{Coefficient of Determination} = r^2 = \frac{\text{Regression Sum of Squares}}{\text{Total Sum of Squares}}$$

$$= \frac{0.790}{1.045} = 0.756$$

$$\text{Coefficient of Non-determination} = k^2 = \frac{\text{Error Sum of Squares}}{\text{Total Sum of Squares}}$$

$$= \frac{0.255}{1.045} = 0.244$$

14.4   Sampling Distribution of the Correlation Coefficient

The sampling distribution of the regression coefficient is normal in form. This is true if $\beta = 0$ or has some value other than zero. Unfortunately, this is not the case for the sampling distribution of the correlation coefficient. This becomes apparent when it is realized that r has a range from -1 to $+1$. When $\rho = 0$ and n is small (i.e., 10 or 15), the sampling distribution of r is essentially normal for practical purposes. As n increases in value, the sampling distribution becomes exactly normal. However, when $\rho \neq 0$ and n is small, the sampling distribution is skewed.

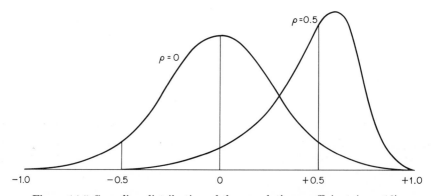

Figure 14.5 Sampling distribution of the correlation coefficient ($n = 10$).

If $\rho \neq 0$, the sampling distribution will approach normality only if n is a very large number. For sample sizes usually encountered in biological research, a test of significance for the correlation coefficient can only be carried out in the regular fashion when testing the hypothesis that $\rho = 0$. In all other cases a modification of the procedure is necessary. The F test carried out above was legitimate because the hypothesis being tested was that no relationship exists between the two variables.

When $\rho = 0$, the variance of the sampling distribution of correlation coefficients is given by

$$\sigma_r^2 = E[r - \rho]^2 = \frac{\sigma_{YX}^2}{\displaystyle\sum_1^n y^2}$$

The square root of this value is known as the true standard error of the correlation coefficient.

$$\sigma_r = \sqrt{\dfrac{\sigma_{YX}^2}{\sum\limits_1^n y^2}}$$

Substituting s_{YX}^2 in place of σ_{YX}^2 gives the estimated standard error.

$$s_r = \sqrt{\dfrac{s_{YX}^2}{\sum\limits_1^n y^2}}$$

The t test becomes $t = \dfrac{r - \rho}{s_r}$ where $\rho = 0$.

The estimated standard error can also be derived indirectly.

$$F = t^2 = \frac{\text{Regression Mean Square}}{\text{Error Mean Square}} = \frac{r^2 \sum\limits_1^n y^2}{s_{YX}^2}$$

Dividing the numerator and denominator by $\Sigma_1^n y^2$ gives

$$F = t^2 = \frac{\dfrac{r^2 \sum\limits_1^n y^2}{\sum\limits_1^n y^2}}{\dfrac{s_{YX}^2}{\sum\limits_1^n y^2}} = \frac{r^2}{\dfrac{s_{YX}^2}{\sum\limits_1^n y^2}}$$

or

$$t = \frac{r}{\sqrt{\dfrac{s_{YX}^2}{\sum\limits_1^n y^2}}}$$

Since the t test is $t = \dfrac{r}{s_r}$, it follows that $s_r = \sqrt{\dfrac{s_{YX}^2}{\sum\limits_1^n y^2}}$

The estimated standard error is usually expressed in a more convenient form.

$$s_r = \sqrt{\dfrac{s_{YX}^2}{\sum\limits_1^n y^2}} = \sqrt{\dfrac{\sum\limits_1^n d^2}{n - 2} \cdot \dfrac{1}{\sum\limits_1^n y^2}} = \sqrt{\dfrac{\sum\limits_1^n d^2}{\sum\limits_1^n y^2} \cdot \dfrac{1}{n - 2}} = \sqrt{\dfrac{k^2}{n - 2}} = \sqrt{\dfrac{1 - r^2}{n - 2}}$$

Using the data from the above study,

$$s_r = \sqrt{\frac{1 - 0.756}{8}} = 0.175$$

The hypothesis that $\rho = 0$ can now be tested.

$$t = \frac{0.869}{0.175} = 4.97 \qquad \qquad \text{Degrees of Freedom } n - 2 = 8$$

$$P < 0.01$$

Since the standard error of the correlation coefficient can only be used to test the hypothesis $\rho = 0$, and no other, it follows that this standard error cannot be used in setting confidence limits for an unknown value of ρ. Yet, when the null hypothesis is rejected, it is often of extreme importance to set confidence limits for the true correlation coefficient. This can be accomplished by first converting r into z with the aid of the equation

$$z = 1.15129 \log \frac{1 + r}{1 - r}$$

or by using a table (see Table VI).

The distribution of z is not strictly normal for small values of n, but near enough, and as n increases in value the distribution becomes normal in form. The variance of the sampling distribution of z values is

$$\sigma_z{}^2 = \frac{1}{n - 3}$$

Taking the square root gives a standard error that is unique because of its simplicity.

$$\sigma_z = \sqrt{\frac{1}{n - 3}}$$

Nothing is estimated; therefore, the properties of the sampling distribution are known.

The 95% confidence limits come from the expression: $z \pm c_{0.05}\sigma_z$. An r value of 0.869 corresponds to a z value of 1.33. The standard error is

$$\sigma_z = \sqrt{\frac{1}{(10 - 3)}} = \sqrt{\frac{1}{7}} = 0.378$$

The 95% confidence limits become:

$$L_1 = 1.33 - (1.96)(0.378) = 0.59$$

$$L_2 = 1.33 + (1.96)(0.378) = 2.07$$

Note that since the true standard error is known, these limits are obtained by using an infinite number of degrees of freedom (Table of c).

The above values of L_1 and L_2 are in terms of z. Transforming back/to r with the use of the table gives $L_1 = 0.530$ and $L_2 = 0.969$. The investigator can be 95% confident that ρ is equal to some value between 0.530 and 0.969. The upper limit varies much less from r than the lower limit. This is typical of the confidence limits for the correlation coefficient when r is a large value.

14.5 Testing the Hypothesis That $\rho_1 = \rho_2$

The z transformation can be used to test the null hypothesis; $\rho_1 = \rho_2$. Assume that in addition to the above study where $r = 0.869$, a study was also made of two other variables in 10 mice and an r value of 0.558 was obtained. The z transformations are 1.33 and 0.63, respectively. A sampling distribution of all $z_1 - z_2$ values can be constructed. The mean of this sampling distribution is zero by hypothesis:

$$E(z_1 - z_2) = E(z_1) - E(z_2) = 0$$

and the variance becomes:

$$\sigma_{z_1-z_2}{}^2 = \sigma_{z_1}{}^2 + \sigma_{z_2}{}^2$$

The c test (or t test with an infinite number of degrees of freedom) becomes:

$$t = c = \frac{z_1 - z_2}{\sqrt{\sigma_{z_1}{}^2 + \sigma_{z_2}{}^2}} = \frac{1.33 - 0.63}{\sqrt{\dfrac{1}{10 - 3} + \dfrac{1}{10 - 3}}} = 1.31$$

The difference between z_1 and z_2 is not significant $(0.20 > P > 0.10)$: therefore, the null hypothesis that $\rho_1 = \rho_2$ is accepted.

Because of the inconvenience of the z transformation, some investigators prefer to use the regression coefficient when studying the relationship between variables. There is also the opinion held by some investigators that two regression coefficients (b_{YX} and b_{XY}), taken together, are more informative than the correlation coefficient. There is also a theoretical reason why the correlation coefficient is losing favor. The sample regression coefficient (b) is an unbiased estimate of β when the X values are fixed (Model I) or selected at random (Model II). However, even though the sample correlation coefficient is an estimate of ρ, it can be demonstrated mathematically that it is slightly biased. If the X values are fixed (Model I), a further bias enters into the estimate. Nevertheless, the usefulness of the correlation coefficient cannot be denied for comparative studies. Also, expressing the correlation in terms of r^2 gives a unique description of the relationship between variables that the regression coefficient does not supply. This description is valid even though Model I is assumed.

Problems

1. An investigator selected at random 25 plants from a species living in a given geographic area. The largest basal leaf was selected from each plant and the following measurements were taken in millimeters:

Leaf	Length (X)	Breadth (Y)
1	81	32
2	149	40
3	85	32
4	119	49
5	86	14
6	57	15
7	82	21
8	126	21
9	122	25
10	97	24
11	45	17
12	84	23
13	104	34
14	106	30
15	123	35
16	88	29
17	91	27
18	136	41
19	67	16
20	144	52
21	129	33
22	134	28
23	112	22
24	132	25
25	62	16

(a) Calculate $\Sigma_1^n x^2$, $\Sigma_1^n y^2$, $\Sigma_1^n xy$. (b) Set up the analysis-of-variance table to test the hypothesis that $\rho = 0$. What is your conclusion? (c) From the data found in the analysis-of-variance table, calculate the coefficient of determination. Express the meaning in words. (d) Calculate the coefficient of non-determination. Express the meaning in words. (e) Calculate the correlation coefficient. (f) Test the hypothesis that $\rho = 0$ by a t test. Compare t^2 with the F value obtained above. (g) Determine the 95% confidence limits for ρ. (h) Calculate two different regression coefficients, where in one case X is set as the independent variable, and in the other case when Y is set as the independent variable. Interpret each one in words. (i) Give one advantage a correlation coefficient has over a regression coefficient.

2. Oxygen consumption (cubic millimeters) was measured for fish fry of different weights (grams).

Weight (X)	Oxygen Consumption (Y)
7.2	187.6
5.6	170.1
8.4	249.2
6.0	121.4
7.0	200.5
7.5	269.2
7.7	239.2
4.2	129.7
4.8	107.2
5.8	180.3
6.9	141.9
9.7	270.4
7.4	249.1
4.5	130.2
4.1	100.8

(a) Calculate b_{YX} and b_{XY}. Interpret the meaning of each statistic. From these values calculate r. Interpret the meaning of r and r^2. (b) Test the hypothesis that $\rho = 0$. (c) Set the 95% confidence limits for ρ.

3. In a study, $r_1 = 0.51$ and $r_2 = 0.58$. The number of paired measurements in each case was $n = 150$.

(a) Does each correlation coefficient deviate significantly from zero? (b) Test the null hypothesis $\rho_1 = \rho_2$.

4. The following paired measurements were obtained:

X	Y
29	6
16	17
11	13
9	4
23	16
21	14
8	7
32	8
13	7
39	7
9	15
39	13
12	17
15	12
21	10
22	7
31	14
33	18
28	11

Test the null hypothesis that $\rho = 0$.

CHAPTER FIFTEEN

Intraclass Correlation Coefficient

The correlation coefficient considered in the previous chapter is often referred to as the *interclass correlation coefficient* (r) in order to distinguish it from the *intraclass correlation coefficient* (r_i) to be discussed in the present chapter.

Distributions of X and Y variables are presented in Table 15.1.

Table 15.1

Variables	
X_1	Y_1
X_2	Y_2
X_3	Y_3
.	.
.	.
.	.
X_N	Y_N
Parameters	
μ_X	μ_Y
σ^2_X	σ^2_Y

If the X variables refer to length of skull and the Y variables to breadth of mastoid, then μ_X will not equal μ_Y, and σ_X^2 will not likely equal σ_Y^2. Differences in means will also prevail if the X variables refer to the stature of fathers and the Y variables to the stature of their daughters, since males, in general, are taller than females. If equality or inequality exists between these parameters, the interclass correlation coefficient may be used. However, one major assumption of the intraclass correlation coefficient is that both sets of variables have the same mean and variance. If equality exists between these parameters, the intraclass correlation coefficient is the preferred statistic. This can be discerned by noting the equation for the interclass correlation coefficient.

$$r = \frac{\sum_1^n xy}{\sqrt{\left(\sum_1^n x^2\right)\left(\sum_1^n y^2\right)}} = \frac{\sum_1^n (X - \bar{x})(Y - \bar{y})}{\sqrt{\sum_1^n (X - \bar{x})^2 \cdot \sum_1^n (Y - \bar{y})^2}} = \frac{\text{covariance}}{\sqrt{s_X^2 \cdot s_Y^2}}$$

There are four parameters to be estimated: μ_X, μ_Y, σ_X^2, and σ_Y^2. The estimates of the means are based on n variables, and $n - 1$ independent variables are available for estimating each variance. However, if the means are equal and the variances are equal, only two parameters need to be estimated, and the samples of X and Y measurements may be grouped to determine these estimates. By doing so, the estimate of the mean is based on $2n$ measurements, and $2n - 1$ independent variables are available for estimating the variance; thus, the intraclass correlation coefficient is more reliable.

The intraclass correlation coefficient also has appeal because it can be obtained through analysis of variance. In a completely randomized design (Model II), the mean expectation of treatments mean square is $\sigma^2 + n\sigma_{\mu_i}^2$, where σ^2 and $\sigma_{\mu_i}^2$ are components of variance. The true intraclass correlation coefficient, symbolized by ρ_i, is defined as:

$$\rho_i = \frac{\sigma_{\mu_i}^2}{\sigma_T^2} = \frac{\sigma_{\mu_i}^2}{\sigma^2 + \sigma_{\mu_i}^2}$$

This parameter is estimated in the following way.

$$r_i = \frac{s_{\mu_i}^2}{s_T^2} = \frac{s_{\mu_i}^2}{s^2 + s_{\mu_i}^2}$$

An example will now be given. An investigator collected at random 10 pairs of male monozygotic twins for the purpose of studying stature. In calculating an interclass correlation coefficient, the problem would arise as to which twin would be noted by X, and which by Y. No such problem exists for an intraclass correlation coefficient.

The measurements were taken in inches and rounded-off to the nearest half-inch. It is important to keep in mind the meaning of n. In an interclass correlation analysis, n refers to the number of paired measurements. When the intraclass correlation coefficient is obtained through analysis of variance, n refers to the number of measurements per sample, and k is the number of paired measurements. The stature measurements are given in Table 15.2.

Table 15.2

Pair	Monozygotic Twins		$\sum_1^n X_i$	$\sum_1^n X_i^2$
1	71.0	70.5	141.5	10,011.25
2	68.5	68.5	137.0	9,384.50
3	67.0	66.0	133.0	8,845.00
4	75.5	77.0	152.5	11,629.25
5	76.0	76.0	152.0	11,552.00
6	69.5	68.5	138.0	9,522.50
7	75.5	75.5	151.0	11,400.50
8	70.5	70.0	140.5	9,870.25
9	68.5	69.0	137.5	9,453.25
10	71.5	72.0	143.5	10,296.25

$$\sum_1^n X_i = 1{,}426.5 \qquad \sum_1^n X_i^2 = 101{,}964.75$$

Correction factor $= \dfrac{(1{,}426.5)^2}{20} = 101{,}745.11$

Total sum of squares $= 101{,}964.75 - 101{,}745.11 = 219.64$

MZ twin pairs sum of squares $= \dfrac{(141.5)^2 + (137.0)^2 + \cdots + (143.5)^2}{2}$
$$- 101{,}745.11 = 217.01$$

Error sum of squares $= 219.64 - 217.01 = 2.63$

A typical analysis-of-variance table may now be completed.

Table 15.3 Analysis of Variance Table.

Source of Variation	Degrees of Freedom	Sum of Squares	Mean Square
Total	19	219.64	
MZ Twins	9	217.01	24.112
Error	10	2.63	0.263

In some cases it may be of interest to test the hypothesis that $\rho_i = 0$. From the formula

$$\rho_i = \frac{\sigma_{\mu_i}^2}{\sigma^2 + \sigma_{\mu_i}^2}$$

it can be observed that ρ_i will equal zero if $\sigma_{\mu_i}^2$ equals zero. Therefore, the hypothesis that $\rho_i = 0$ is tested by merely testing the hypothesis that $\sigma_{\mu_i}^2 = 0$.

$$F = \frac{24.112}{0.263} = 91.7$$

It is apparent that the hypothesis should be rejected.

The components of variance can be estimated from the data in the analysis-of-variance table.

$$\text{Error mean square} = s^2 = 0.263$$

$$MZ \text{ twins mean square} = 24.112 = s^2 + ns_{\mu_i}^2$$

$$s_{\mu_i}^2 = \frac{24.112 - 0.263}{2} = 11.924$$

With these values, the intraclass correlation coefficient may be estimated.

$$r_i = \frac{s_{\mu_i}^2}{s^2 + s_{\mu_i}^2} = \frac{11.924}{0.263 + 11.924} = 0.9784$$

The intraclass correlation coefficient may be calculated in another way.

$$r_i = \frac{E_T - E_1}{E_T + (n - 1)E_1}$$

where E_T is twins (treatments) mean square and E_1 is error mean square.

$$r_i = \frac{24.112 - 0.263}{24.112 + (2 - 1)(0.263)} = 0.9784$$

The intraclass correlation coefficient is interpreted in the same manner as the interclass correlation coefficient. If the measurements in each sample are equal, error mean square will equal zero, and r_i will equal $+1$.

$$r_i = \frac{s_{\mu_i}^2}{s^2 + s_{\mu_i}^2} = \frac{s_{\mu_i}^2}{0 + s_{\mu_i}^2} = 1$$

If treatments (twins) mean square is less than error mean square, $s_{\mu_i}^2$ will have a negative value, and consequently r_i will be negative. However, r_i cannot equal -1 unless n equals 2. Assume that treatments mean square equals zero (i.e., the sample means are all equal); then

$$r_i = \frac{E_T - E_1}{E_T + (n - 1)E_1} = \frac{-E_1}{n - 1(E_1)} = -\frac{1}{n - 1}$$

This illustrates a property that distinguishes an intraclass correlation coefficient from an interclass correlation coefficient. The latter may range from -1 to $+1$, while the former has an upper limit of $+1$ and a lower limit of $-\dfrac{1}{n-1}$, or $-\dfrac{1}{n_0-1}$ when n is not constant.

As the equation for the lower limit of r_i implies, the sample sizes *do not* have to be equal in calculating the intraclass correlation coefficient. This is one important advantage the intraclass correlation coefficient has over the interclass correlation coefficient.

An intraclass correlation coefficient can be calculated in an analysis-of-variance study whenever Model II is assumed. This was alluded to in Chapter 8 where bird egg-length data were analyzed. The investigator was interested in determining if a within-nest correlation existed among the egg-length measurements. Eight nests were selected at random. The number of eggs per nest varied from 2 to 6. The following values were obtained:

$$s^2 = 1.80$$

$$s_{\mu_i}^2 = 1.81$$

$$n_0 = 3.95$$

Using these values, the true intraclass correlation coefficient can be estimated.

$$r_i = \frac{s_{\mu_i}^2}{s^2 + s_{\mu_i}^2} = \frac{1.81}{1.80 + 1.81} = 0.501$$

The estimate can also be obtained from the equation

$$r_i = \frac{E_T - E_1}{E_T + (n_o - 1)E_1} = \frac{8.95 - 1.80}{8.95 + (2.95)(1.80)} = 0.501$$

When families or litters are studied, the intraclass correlation coefficient is often referred to as the within-family or within-litter correlation coefficient.

Problems

1. Refer to the problems at the end of Chapter 8. Calculate r_i for Problems 1 and 5. What are your conclusions?

2. Under what conditions is it permissible to calculate an intraclass correlation coefficient? If these conditions are true, why is an intraclass correlation coefficient preferred over the interclass correlation coefficient?

3. Intraclass correlation coefficients calculated for monozygotic (MZ) and dizygotic (DZ) twins are often used to appraise the importance of nature and nurture for traits such as stature, performance on I.Q. tests, weight, etc. The equation for a heritability value is as follows:

$$H = \frac{\rho_{MZ} - \rho_{DZ}}{1 - \rho_{DZ}}$$

The value of H is bounded by 0 and 1. It measures the relative contribution of heredity (versus environment) to the variation observed, i.e., in the human populations how much of the variation in stature among individuals is due to heredity and how much is due to environment. In the above formula it is seen that as ρ_{MZ} tends toward 1, H tends toward 1. When H equals 1, the variation in the characteristic is due solely to heredity. As ρ_{MZ} tends toward ρ_{DZ}, H tends toward 0, and thus the variation in the characteristic becomes more environmentally determined.

This procedure of determining the relative roles of heredity and environment assumes that monozygotic twins have the same genotype and dizygotic twins have different genotypes. It also assumes that both members of a twin pair are exposed to the same environment before and after birth, which, of course, is a source of error.

The investigator who selected 10 pairs of monozygotic twins at random (see text) also selected 10 pairs of dizygotic (same sex) twins and measured stature. The intraclass correlation for the DZ twins was $r_i = 0.5733$.

(a) Estimate the heritability value (using h as an estimate of H). (b) What percent of the variability in stature in the population (from which the twins were selected) is due to heredity? What percent is due to the environment?

CHAPTER SIXTEEN

Chi-Square Analysis

A valuable and common procedure for testing certain types of hypotheses involves the calculation of a chi-square value. Examples of chi-square analyses will be given in the present and succeeding chapters.

An investigator tossed a coin 100 times. The null hypothesis is that the coin is honest, i.e., it is just as likely to land heads as tails. This hypothesis could be written formally as: $H_0 : q = \frac{1}{2}$, where q is the probability of a head occurring on a single toss (and $p = \frac{1}{2}$ is the probability of a tail). The alternative hypothesis is: $H_1 : q \neq \frac{1}{2}$. A significance level of 0.05 is assigned.

The sample size, symbolized by n, consists of 100 observations. This sample was taken from a hypothetical population, specified by the null hypothesis, consisting of an indefinitely large number of head and tail observations where $q = \frac{1}{2}$. Thirty seven of the 100 tosses were heads, and therefore 63 were tails. The investigator now asks himself, "If I were to repeat this experiment an indefinitely large number of times, what would be the expectation values according to the null hypothesis?" The answer is obviously 50 heads and 50 tails. If μ_1 is the expectation of heads, and μ_2 is the expectation of tails, then $\mu_1 = nq = 100 \times \frac{1}{2} = 50$, and $\mu_2 = np = 100 \times \frac{1}{2} = 50$.

Do the observed values ($X_1 = 37$ heads and $X_2 = 63$ tails) deviate significantly from the appropriate expected values? The deviation in each case has a value of 13. A conclusion can be reached by chi-square analysis or by use of the binomial theorem. The latter method will be discussed in Chapter 17.

The chi-square test is based on the chi-square (χ^2) distribution. A chi-square value is computed from the following formula:

$$\chi^2 = \sum \frac{(X_i - \mu_i)^2}{\mu_i}$$

where X_i is the observed value and μ_i the expectation for each class. The formula can be used for any number of classes. When there are only two classes, as in the coin problem, it becomes:

$$\chi^2 = \frac{(X_1 - \mu_1)^2}{\mu_1} + \frac{(X_2 - \mu_2)^2}{\mu_2}$$

In many types of problems the number of classes is more than two. This is certainly the case in genetic problems for the ratios $1:2:1$, $1:1:1:1$, $9:3:3:1$, and $27:9:9:9:3:3:3:1$.

For many problems, the chi-square value is obtained simply by placing the data in a table as in Table 16.1.

Table 16.1

Class	X_i	μ_i	$X_i - \mu_i$	$(X_i - \mu_i)^2$	$\dfrac{(X_i - \mu_i)^2}{\mu_i}$
Heads	37	50	-13	169	3.38
Tails	63	50	$+13$	169	3.38
Total	100	100			$\chi^2 = 6.76$

The chi-square value is equal to 6.76. A chi-square value can vary theoretically from zero to an infinitely large positive value. The size of the value depends on the number of classes involved and the discrepancy that exists between the observed and the expectation values. If the above study were repeated an indefinitely large number of times, a sampling distribution of chi-square values would result. A sampling distribution of chi square is independent of the sample size. Samples of 50, 100, 120, 1,000, or 10,000 give the same sampling distribution. This differs from the sampling distribution of sample means where a sampling distribution occurs for each different sample size. Furthermore, the sampling distribution of chi square is independent of the parameters. In the above study the value of q was $\frac{1}{2}$. The value of q can be $\frac{1}{4}$, $\frac{6}{16}$, $\frac{3}{16}$, $\frac{1}{16}$, or any other value, and the sampling distribution is the same. The sampling distribution is *only dependent upon the number of degrees of freedom that are available for the test.*

The number of degrees of freedom available for a test is reduced each time a piece of information is taken from the sample. The rule has been given in previous chapters that one degree of freedom is lost each time a statistic is substituted for a parameter. This generalization still holds for a chi-square test, but in addition, setting the total equal to a given value further reduces the number of degrees of freedom. In the above problem dealing with coins, there are two classes, and the parameters ($q = \frac{1}{2}$, $p = \frac{1}{2}$) of the population specified by the hypothesis are known. However, since the total number of observations is equal to 100, only one of the classes is independent. When the value of one class is known, the other is automatically fixed since the total of the two classes is given. Consequently, even though there are two classes, there is only one degree of freedom. The following rule may therefore be stated: "When the parameters are known, the number of degrees of freedom is equal to the number of classes that are independent."

A different chi-square sampling distribution occurs for each different number of degrees of freedom. In the following figure, chi-square sampling distributions are given for 1, 2, and 6 degrees of freedom. The three distributions are skewed. As the number of degrees of freedom is increased, the distribution becomes less skewed. For a large number of degrees of freedom (over about 30), the distribution is normal in form.

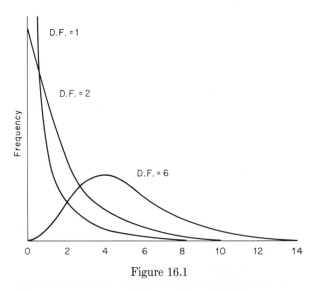

Figure 16.1

A table is available (Table VII) that gives the probability of obtaining the observed chi-square value or larger values for the appropriate number of degrees of freedom. Since all chi-square values are positive, the P value is obtained by determining the area under the curve to the right of any given chi-square value and dividing it by the total area.

$$P = \frac{\text{Area under the curve to the right of a given } \chi^2 \text{ value}}{\text{Total area}}$$

The total area under the curve is equal to one. In the above problem a chi-square value of 6.76 was obtained. For one degree of freedom (Table VII) the probability of obtaining this chi-square value, or greater chi-square value (according to the null hypothesis) is less than 0.01. The null hypothesis is rejected.

16.1 Limitations of the Chi-Square Test

A chi-square test is applicable to many different situations, but does have two limitations. (1) It is assumed that the possible observed values in any class form a normal distribution with the mean equal to the expected values (μ_1). When the expected values are small, the distribution of possible observed values cannot sufficiently approximate a normal distribution due to the limitation imposed by zero. The expected value in any class should not be less than 5 and preferably not less than 10. (2) Chi square should be calculated using actual numbers, *not* percentages or proportions.

16.2 Correction for Continuity

The chi-square distribution is a continuous distribution. It assumes that all possible chi-square values which "might have occurred," if a specific test were run over and over again, form a continuum. In the coin experiment, n was only 100. Deviations of $\pm$ 13 give a chi-square value of 6.76. Repeating the calculations for ± 12, and ± 14 deviations, gives chi-square values of 5.76 and 7.84, respectively. Calculating chi-square values for all possible deviations, and plotting the frequency of each, would yield a distribution of chi-square values that is discontinuous, not continuous. Such a sampling distribution can be represented by a frequency polygon (see Figure 16.2). Chi-square values (forming classes) are recorded on the X axis, with frequencies recorded on the Y axis. Classes are represented by rectangles with a line connecting the midpoint of each rectangle. The area of each rectangle is proportional to the frequency of each class (chi-square value). The total area under all rectangles is equal to one. In Figure 16.2, the portion of the frequency polygon is shown for classes 5.76 (± 12 deviations), 6.76 (± 13 deviations), and 7.84 (± 14 deviations).

The question is asked, "What is the probability of getting the observed chi-square value of 6.76, or greater chi-square value, as specified by the null hypothesis?" The exact probability value is

$$P = \frac{\text{Area in the rectangles right of (and including) class 6.76}}{\text{Total area in all rectangles}}$$

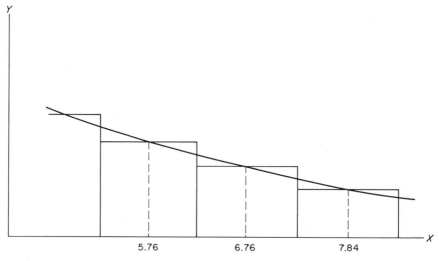

Figure 16.2 Chi-square distribution.

Since a continuum is assumed, the probability that is actually determined is:

$$P = \frac{\text{Area under the curve right of } 6.76}{\text{Total area under the curve}}$$

Using the point 6.76, however, leaves out half of the rectangle for class 6.76, from the left boundary of the rectangle to the midpoint.

In order to obtain the exact probability value, the area under the rectangle from the midpoint to the left boundary should be included. The position of the left boundary can be approximated by $\dfrac{6.76 + 5.76}{2} = 6.26$. Entering Table VII with this adjusted chi-square value gives a more exact probability value $(0.02 > P > 0.01)$ than before $(P < 0.01)$.

It is obvious that this procedure of obtaining adjusted chi-square values is laborious. A simpler method, known as Yates correction for continuity, consists of reducing each deviation by half a unit towards zero.

$$\chi^2 = \sum \frac{(|X_i - \mu_i| - 0.5)^2}{\mu_i}$$

The rationale for reducing the deviations by half a unit will be more obvious when the binomial distribution is discussed in Chapter 17.

Table 16.2 gives the adjusted chi-square value for the coin problem.

As n approaches infinity, the number of different chi-square values approaches infinity, and consequently, the area of each rectangle in the frequency polygon becomes infinitesimal. The line connecting the midpoints of each rectangle becomes continuous. When n is large, Yates correction is

Table 16.2

Class	X_i	μ_i	$\|X_i - \mu_i\| - 0.5$	$(\|X_i - \mu_i\| - 0.5)^2$	$\dfrac{(\|X_i - \mu_i\| - 0.5)^2}{\mu_i}$
Heads	37	50	12.5	156.25	3.125
Tails	63	50	12.5	156.25	3.125
Total	100	100			$\chi^2 = 6.25$

not necessary since it will have little influence on the final result. By custom, Yates correction is seldom used when n is larger than 200.

Yates correction should only be used when there is one degree of freedom. No simple correction for continuity is available when there is more than one degree of freedom.

Another example of a chi-square test using Yates correction will now be given. In sweet peas, the gene (R) for red flowers is dominant over the gene (r) for white flowers. An investigator crossed two F_1 red-flowered plants. Each was assumed to be heterozygous (Rr); therefore, a $3:1$ ratio was expected in the F_2 generation. The null hypothesis is: $H_0: q = \frac{1}{4}$. That is, the probability of white-flowered plants is $\frac{1}{4}$. The alternative hypothesis is: $H_1: q \neq \frac{1}{4}$.

Table 16.3

Phenotype	Red Flowers	White Flowers	Total
X_i	94	26	120
μ_i	90	30	120
$\|X_i - \mu_i\| - 0.5$	3.5	3.5	
$(\|X_i - \mu_i\| - 0.5)^2$	12.25	12.25	
$\dfrac{(\|X_i - \mu_i\| - 0.5)^2}{\mu_i}$	0.14	0.41	$\chi^2 = 0.55$

A total of 120 plants was grown. They constitute a sample from a hypothetical population consisting of three-fourths red-flowered and one-fourth white-flowered plants. In the sample, 94 plants had red flowers and 26 had white flowers. Can it be accepted, using the 0.05 level of significance, that the sample was taken from the population specified by the null hypothesis? The mean expectations are: $\mu_i = np = 120 \times \frac{3}{4} = 90$, $\mu_2 = nq = 120 \times \frac{1}{4} = 30$.

With one degree of freedom, the probability of obtaining the observed chi-square value of 0.55, or greater, chi-square values is between 0.50 and 0.30. The null hypothesis is accepted.

16.3   Chi-Square Test With Two Degrees of Freedom

In the F_2 generation of a cross with snapdragons, the following results were obtained: 20 red, 52 pink, and 24 white. Is this a good fit of a $1:2:1$ ratio? The population specified by the hypothesis consists of plants segregating in a ratio of $\frac{1}{4}$ red, $\frac{1}{2}$ pink, and $\frac{1}{4}$ white. These parameters are used to obtain expected values for each class.

Table 16.4

Phenotype	X_i	μ_i	$X_i - \mu_i$	$(X_i - \mu_i)^2$	$\dfrac{(X_i - \mu_i)^2}{\mu_i}$
Red	20	24	4	16	0.67
Pink	52	48	4	16	0.33
White	24	24	0	0	0.00
Total	96	96			$\chi^2 = 1.00$

There are three classes, but since the total number of plants is fixed, there are only two independent classes, and consequently there are only two degrees of freedom. The P value is between 0.50 and 0.70. It is accepted that the observed data are a good fit of a $1:2:1$ ratio. Yates correction is not used, since the number of degrees of freedom is more than one.

16.4   Chi-Square Test With Three Degrees of Freedom

In the F_2 generation of a cross with sweet peas, the following phenotypes were observed: 186 red–tall, 69 red–dwarf, 60 white–tall, and 25 white–dwarf.

Do the data fit the expected $9:3:3:1$ ratio? The expected values are obtained by using the parameters: $\frac{9}{16}$, $\frac{3}{16}$, $\frac{3}{16}$, and $\frac{1}{16}$.

Table 16.5

Phenotype	X_i	μ_i	$X_i - \mu_i$	$(X_i - \mu_i)^2$	$\dfrac{(X_i - \mu_i)^2}{\mu_i}$
Red-Tall	186	191.25	5.25	27.56	0.14
Red-Dwarf	69	63.75	5.25	27.56	0.43
White-Tall	60	63.75	3.75	14.06	0.22
White-Dwarf	25	21.25	3.75	14.06	0.66
Total	340	340.00			$\chi^2 = 1.45$

There are three independent classes. The chi-square value of 1.45 with three degrees of freedom gives a P value of about 0.70. The hypothesis is accepted that the data are segregating in a $9:3:3:1$ ratio.

16.5 Test for Homogeneity

One important attribute of chi square is that the sum of two or more independent chi-square values is itself a chi-square value with the number of degrees of freedom equal to the sum of the degrees of freedom of the component chi squares. This principle is used in a test of homogeneity.

Due to the nature of biological material, samples are often small and therefore of limited value for tests of significance and reliability. However, even though large samples may be difficult to obtain, it is often feasible to collect several small samples by replicating experiments and then to "pool" the small samples into one large sample. This procedure is legitimate if the small samples (subsamples) are homogeneous (i.e., come from the same population). Pooling implies homogeneity.

In mice there is a gene (A^Y) that is lethal in the homozygous condition but gives a yellow coat color when heterozygous. Progeny of two yellow mice segregate in a ratio of 2 yellow to 1 non-yellow. Ratios of $2:1$ are often mistaken for the more common $3:1$ ratio when the numbers are small. Assume that in the investigation of the genetics of this coat color, the results of several different experiments dealing with crosses between yellow mice were combined into one large sample. Further assume for illustrative purposes that the true mode of inheritance was unknown and the data were analyzed for a 3 : 1 ratio. The hypothesis to be tested is that the four subsamples were taken from a population that is segregating in a 3 : 1 ratio. Table 16.6 summarizes four different experiments with this trait.

Table 16.6

	Yellow	Non-Yellow	Total	χ^2	Degrees of Freedom	Probability
Experiment 1	21	11	32	1.50	1	0.20 − 0.30
Experiment 2	15	8	23	1.17	1	0.20 − 0.30
Experiment 3	20	9	29	0.56	1	0.30 − 0.50
Experiment 4	33	15	48	1.00	1	0.30 − 0.50
Sum of four chi squares 4.23					4	
Pooled	89	43	132	4.04	1	less than 0.05

A chi-square value may be calculated for each of the four subsamples separately as shown in the above table. It is observed that each of these values is non-significant. Consequently, on the basis of the subsamples there is no evidence against the hypothesis. However, pooling the four samples results in one large sample composed of 89 yellow and 43 non-yellow mice. The chi-square value (4.04) based on the pooled data is significant ($P < 0.05$). A different conclusion is reached on the basis of the large sample than by considering any of the subsamples by itself.

The next question that arises is whether it was justified to pool the subsamples. If not, then the pooled chi-square value is of questionable value. This is answered by determining whether the four subsamples were taken from the same population. Due to the additive nature of chi square, it is permissible to sum the chi-square values and the degrees of freedom for the four subsamples. This gives a total chi-square value of 4.23 with four degrees of freedom. The difference between the total chi-square value and the pooled chi-square value is distributed with degrees of freedom equal to the difference between those of the total and pooled degrees of freedom.

The homogeneity chi square is a measure of homogeneity (i.e., whether the subsamples were taken from the same population). In this case, due to the high P value, it can be concluded that homogeneity is present and consequently it

Table 16.7

Analysis of Chi Square for the Four Subsamples on the Basis of a 3:1 Ratio			
	Degrees of Freedom	Chi Square	Probability
Total	4	4.23	
Pooled	1	4.04	Less than 0.05
Homogeneity	3	0.19	0.90 − 0.95

was permissible to pool the subsamples. This in turn indicates that the pooled chi-square value has real meaning.

In some cases homogeneity chi square may be significant, as in the following hypothetical example, where the subsample and pooled data are compared with an expected 1:1 ratio.

Table 16.8

	A	B	Total	χ^2	Degrees of Freedom	Probability
Subsample 1	42	58	100	2.56	1	0.10 − 0.20
Subsample 2	59	41	100	3.24	1	0.05 − 0.10
Sum of Two Chi Square Values				5.80	2	
Pooled	101	99	200	0.02	1	0.80 − 0.90

The chi-square values based on the subsample totals are non-significant at the 0.05 level of significance, but the trend away from the expected values is different in each case. Subsample 1 has a deficiency of A individuals, while subsample 2 has an excess of these individuals. When the subsamples are pooled, an almost perfect fit of a 1 : 1 ratio is observed. This leads to the conclusion that the homogeneity chi-square value will be large.

The results shown in the above table indicate that the two subsamples were not taken from the same population and therefore the pooled chi-square value is meaningless.

Table 16.9

	Degrees of Freedom	Chi Square	Probability
Analysis of Chi Square for the two Subsamples on the Basis of a 1:1 Ratio			
Total	2	5.80	
Pooled	1	0.02	0.80 − 0.90
Homogeneity	1	5.78	Less than 0.05

In general, if subsamples are not homogeneous, the technique of the whole experiment is immediately questioned. Frequent causes of heterogeneity are: poor classification, material not uniform to begin with (i.e., some of the subsamples may have had a different genetic history), as well as different methods of collecting the data from one subsample to another. It is up to the investigator to find the reason for the lack of homogeneity.

16.6   Testing the Goodness of Fit of a Group of Data to a Normal Distribution

One method for gaining information as to whether a population is normal in form, as assumed in many tests of significance and reliability, is to calculate estimates of gamma-one and gamma-two and then with the aid of the appropriate standard errors, determine whether the estimates deviate significantly from zero. Formulae for these estimates (k statistics) and their standard errors can be found in various statistical textbooks, such as Snedecor (1956). Another method is to determine the "goodness of fit" of a large sample taken from that population to a normal distribution by a chi-square test. If the sample is normally distributed, then it is legitimate to accept the hypothesis that the population is normally distributed. But if the sample deviates markedly from normality, due to skewness or kurtosis, then the hypothesis should be rejected. The procedure is to calculate the sample mean ($\bar{x}$) and standard deviation (s) and then arrange the data in a frequency table. By the use of the table for the areas under the normal curve (Table I), an expected frequency of individuals can be determined for each class in the frequency table, assuming normality. A comparison can then be made with the observed frequencies. This will be illustrated with an example.

A stand of aspen trees was studied in order to ascertain the distribution of diameters of the tree trunks. A sample consisting of 280 trees was taken by the transect method. The measurements were made in inches. The mean of the sample was equal to 8.0 inches and the standard deviation was equal to 2.0 inches. The data are summarized in Table 16.10.

Table 16.10

Class Interval	Observed Frequency	Probability of an Individual Falling Within Class Interval	Expected Frequency	Deviation
1.0 − 2.0	0 ⎤	0.0013	0.4 ⎤	−0.4 ⎤
2.0 − 3.0	2 ⎬ 6	0.0049	1.4 ⎬ 6.4	+0.6 ⎬ −0.4
3.0 − 4.0	4 ⎦	0.0165	4.6 ⎦	−0.6 ⎦
4.0 − 5.0	12	0.0441	12.3	−0.3
5.0 − 6.0	24	0.0919	25.7	−1.7
6.0 − 7.0	42	0.1498	41.9	+0.1
7.0 − 8.0	55	0.1915	53.6	+1.4
8.0 − 9.0	51	0.1915	53.6	−2.6
9.0 − 10.0	42	0.1498	41.9	+0.1
10.0 − 11.0	26	0.0919	25.7	+0.3
11.0 − 12.0	14	0.0441	12.3	+1.7
12.0 − 13.0	6 ⎤	0.0165	4.6 ⎤	+1.4 ⎤
13.0 − 14.0	2 ⎬ 8	0.0049	1.4 ⎬ 6.4	+0.6 ⎬ +1.6
14.0 − 15.0	0 ⎦	0.0013	0.4 ⎦	−0.4 ⎦
Total	280	1.0000	280.0	

Substituting $\bar{x}$ and s for μ and σ in the formula for c gives

$$c = \frac{X - \bar{x}}{s}$$

Assuming normality, the probability that an individual will fall in the first class (1.0–2.0) is obtained by determining the proportionate area under the curve between 1.0 and 2.0 and dividing this area by the total area, or 1. The proportionate area left of 2.0 is obtained by entering Table I with the following value:

$$c = \frac{2.0 - 8.0}{2.0} = \frac{-6.0}{2.0} = -3.0$$

From the table this is given as 0.0013. The proportionate area left of 1.0, for practical purposes, is zero, so the probability that an individual will fall in the first class is $0.0013/1 = 0.0013$. The probability that an individual will fall in the second class (2.0 – 3.0) is obtained by determining the proportionate area left of 3.0 and subtracting from it the proportionate area left of 2.0.

$$c = \frac{3.0 - 8.0}{2.0} = \frac{-5.0}{2.0} = -2.5$$

The proportionate area left of 3.0 is given as 0.0062, so subtraction ($0.0062 - 0.0013 = 0.0049$) gives the proportionate area between 2.0 and 3.0.

This procedure is carried out for each class. Multiplying each probability value by the total number of measurements (280) gives the expected frequency for each class. For this first class this becomes $0.0013 \times 280 = 0.4$. For the second class this is $0.0049 \times 280 = 1.4$. The same procedure is carried out for each class. As soon as the expected frequencies are obtained, they can be compared with the observed frequencies and a chi-square value computed.

Note that in the above table there are fourteen classes. Since the expected frequency in any class should not be less than 5, the first three classes can be grouped to form a single class with an expected frequency of 6.4; the last three classes can be grouped to form a single class with an expected frequency of 6.4. Grouping in this manner results in a total of ten classes. The chi-square value becomes:

$$\chi^2 = \frac{(0.4)^2}{6.4} + \frac{(0.3)^2}{12.3} + \frac{(1.7)^2}{25.7} + \frac{(0.1)^2}{41.9} + \frac{(1.4)^2}{53.6} + \frac{(2.6)^2}{53.6} + \frac{(0.1)^2}{41.9}$$
$$+ \frac{(0.3)^2}{25.7} + \frac{(1.7)^2}{12.3} + \frac{(1.6)^2}{6.4} = 0.95$$

There are ten classes, but three degrees of freedom are lost for using the sample total of 280 and for substituting $\bar{x}$ and s in place of μ and σ. This leaves seven degrees of freedom. The probability of getting the observed chi-square value or greater value due to chance alone is over 0.90. Consequently, the hypothesis can be accepted that the population is distributed in a normal manner.

16.7   95% Confidence Limits for a Population Variance

Assume that a random sample of size n is taken from a normal population with a given variance (σ^2), and the variance of the sample ($s^2 = $ S.S./D.F.) is calculated. A sampling distribution of the variable s^2/σ^2 can then be generated. This sampling distribution is an F distribution with $n - 1$ degrees of freedom associated with the numerator and an infinite number associated with the denominator. If $n - 1$ equals 6, then

$$F\left[\begin{matrix} 6 \\ \infty \end{matrix}\ 0.05\right] = 2.1$$

which indicates that 5% of the values would be 2.1 or larger.

Now note that if the chi-square value at the 0.05 level for 6 degrees of freedom is divided by six degrees of freedom, the answer is also 2.1, i.e., $12.59/6 = 2.1$. This observation leads to the generalization that:

(1) Sampling distribution of s^2/σ^2 is equivalent to the sampling distribution of $\chi^2/D.F.$ Since $s^2 = S.S./D.F.$, the expression can be changed to read:

(2) Sampling distribution of

$$\frac{\dfrac{S.S.}{D.F.}}{\sigma^2}$$

is equivalent to the sampling distribution of $\chi^2/D.F.$ Rearranging the terms gives:

(3) Sampling distribution of $\chi^2\sigma^2$ is equivalent to the sampling distribution of

$$\frac{S.S.}{D.F.} \cdot D.F. = S.S.$$

Or,

(4) Sampling distribution of χ^2 is equivalent to the sampling distribution of $S.S./\sigma^2$.

Expressing chi square in this form leads to a method for setting the 95% confidence limits for a population variance. By referring to Table VII, for six degrees of freedom, it can be observed that 97.5% of all chi-square values will be as large, or larger, than 1.24, and 2.5% will be as large, or larger, than 14.45. Therefore, 2.5% of all chi-square values will have a value between zero and 1.24, 2.5% will have a value of 14.45 or greater, and 95% will have a value between 1.24 and 14.45.

The following probability statements can now be made:

(1) The probability is 0.95 that χ^2 will lie between 1.24 and 14.45 for 6 degrees of freedom.

For the general case, the probability is 0.95 that χ^2 will lie between $\chi^2_{0.975}$ and $\chi^2_{0.025}$. This probability statement is expressed as

(2) $P[\chi^2_{0.975} \leq \chi^2 \leq \chi^2_{0.025}] = 0.95$

Since the sampling distributions of χ^2 and $S.S./\sigma^2$ are equivalent, the expression can be changed to:

(3) $P[\chi^2_{0.975} \leq S.S./\sigma^2 \leq \chi^2_{0.025}] = 0.95$

(4) Dividing each term of this inequality *into* one, changes the direction of the inequality.

$$P\left[\frac{1}{\chi^2_{0.975}} \geq \sigma^2/\text{S.S.} \geq \frac{1}{\chi^2_{0.025}}\right] = 0.95$$

(5) Multiplying through by S.S. gives

$$P\left[\frac{\text{S.S.}}{\chi^2_{0.975}} \geq \sigma^2 \geq \frac{\text{S.S.}}{\chi^2_{0.025}}\right] = 0.95$$

The last expression gives a simple method for setting the 95% confidence limits for a population variance. Assume that $s^2 = \text{S.S.}/\text{D.F.} = 48/6 = 8.00$

$$L_1 = \frac{\text{S.S.}}{\chi^2_{0.025}} = \frac{48}{14.45} = 3.32$$

$$L_2 = \frac{\text{S.S.}}{\chi^2_{0.975}} = \frac{48}{1.24} = 38.71$$

The investigator can be 95% confident that σ^2 is equal to some value between 3.32 and 38.71, which can be expressed as:

(6) $P[38.71 \geq \sigma^2 \geq 3.32] = 0.95$

16.8   Bartlett's Test for Homogeneity of Variances

One of the basic assumptions of analysis of variance is that of homogeneous variances. If in doubt, the investigator should test the null hypothesis of homogeneity (i.e., $\sigma_1^2 = \sigma_2^2 = \sigma_3^2 = \cdots = \sigma_k^2$) by using Bartlett's test. Logarithms are employed in Bartlett's test. Since many statistical computations are facilitated with the use of common logarithms, as will be demonstrated in later chapters, a review of the use of logarithms is presented at the end of the present chapter.

Table 16.11   Test of Homogeneity of Variance.

Sample	D.F.	S.S.	s^2	$\log s^2$	$(\text{D.F.})(\log s^2)$	$\dfrac{1}{\text{D.F.}}$
1	50	100.0	2.00	0.3010	15.0500	0.0200
2	50	200.0	4.00	0.6021	30.1050	0.0200
3	50	400.0	8.00	0.9031	45.1550	0.0200
Total	150	700.0			90.3100	0.0600

$$s_p{}^2 = \text{pooled variance} = \frac{700}{150} = 4.667$$

$$B = (\log s_p{}^2)\left(\sum_1^k \text{D.F.}\right) = (0.6690)(150) = 100.3500$$

$$\chi^2 \text{ with } k-1 \text{ degrees of freedom} = \log_e 10\left\{B - \sum_1^k [(\text{D.F.})(\log s^2)]\right\}$$

$$= (2.3026)(100.3500 - 90.3100)$$

$$= 23.1181$$

> *Note:* $\log_e 10 = 2.3026$

Since chi square is significant, the null hypothesis is rejected. The three sample variances are not estimating the same parameter.

If a more exact chi-square value is needed, a correction is available. However, in most cases, the uncorrected value is satisfactory.

$$\text{Correction factor} = C = 1 + \frac{1}{3(k-1)}\left[\sum_1^k \frac{1}{\text{D.F.}} - \frac{1}{\sum_1^k \text{D.F.}}\right]$$

$$= 1 + \frac{1}{6}\left[0.0600 - \frac{1}{150}\right]$$

$$= 1.0089$$

$$\text{Corrected } \chi^2 \text{ with } k-1 \text{ degrees of freedom} = \frac{\text{Uncorrected } \chi^2}{C}$$

$$= \frac{23.1181}{1.0089} = 22.9142$$

Populations may have different variances because they have different means. Large individuals of a species are more variable for certain quantitative characters than small individuals. For example, males 12 years of age are more variable in stature than males 1 year of age. The biological world is replete with examples where the variance increases with the value of the mean. For these cases, the relative values of the variance or standard deviation may be of more interest than the absolute values of these measures of variation. Consider the means and standard deviations of the following populations:

Population A	Population B
$\mu_1 = 20.00$	$\mu_2 = 100.00$
$\sigma_1 = 5.00$	$\sigma_2 = 25.00$

The standard deviation of population B is five times larger than that of population A; however, a similar relationship exists for the means. Dividing the standard deviation by the mean illustrates that the two populations have the same relative variation : $\sigma/\mu = 5/20 = 25/100 = 0.25$.

The statistic used to estimate relative variation is known as the coefficient of variation (symbolized by C.V.). It may be expressed as a proportion or percentage:

$$C.V. = \frac{s}{\bar{x}} \quad \text{or} \quad \frac{100\ s}{\bar{x}}$$

Assume that an entomologist compared the length (in millimeters) of the thorax of two different species of insects:

Species 1	Species 2
$\bar{x}_1 = 26.00$	$\bar{x}_2 = 43.00$
$s_1 = 6.25$	$s_2 = 10.51$
$n_1 = 90$	$n_2 = 90$

The absolute values of the standard deviations suggest that species 2 is more variable for this trait than Species 1; however, there is little difference in the values of the coefficients of variation:

$$\text{Species 1: C.V.} = \frac{(100)(6.25)}{26.00} = 24.04\%$$

$$\text{Species 2: C.V.} = \frac{(100)(10.51)}{43.00} = 24.44\%$$

It is concluded that the difference in the standard deviations is attributable to the fact that a positive relationship exists between the means and standard deviations.

The coefficient of variation is commonly used in taxonomic work as a measure of variability. Excessive variability is sometimes present even though a correction has been made for the mean. For example, a large coefficient of variation would be expected for a sample taken from a region where two different subspecies are intergrading.

The coefficient of variation is also useful for comparing variability when the measurements are in different units. An investigator may be interested in determining whether weight measurements (grams) are more variable than length measurements (centimeters) for a given species. Since coefficients of variation are expressed as proportions or percentages, and therefore divorced from units, they can be compared directly. If the coefficient of variation of the sample of weight measurements was 31.50% while that of the sample of length measurements was 14.28%, it would be concluded that more variability exists for weight than length for this species.

A completely satisfactory method is not available for setting confidence limits for the true coefficient of variation, especially when the sample is small. The standard error usually employed is

$$s_{C.V.} = \frac{C.V.}{\sqrt{2n}}$$

In the derivation of this formula, it is assumed that n is large and for a given value of a sample mean, the sample standard deviation is a variable, i.e., s and $\bar{x}$ are independent. In practice, the coefficient of variation is reserved for those situations where a positive correlation exists between these two statistics. However, when a positive correlation is present, the above standard error can be used to determine approximate confidence limits. The 95% confidence limits are given by

$$L_1 = C.V. - 1.96 \frac{C.V.}{\sqrt{2n}}$$

$$L_2 = C.V. + 1.96 \frac{C.V.}{\sqrt{2n}}$$

The procedure will be illustrated with the thorax data given above for species 1.

$$L_1 = 24.04 - 1.96 \frac{24.04}{\sqrt{2(90)}} = 20.528$$

$$L_2 = 24.04 + 1.96 \frac{24.04}{\sqrt{2(90)}} = 27.552$$

When samples are large, these confidence limits, even though approximate, serve as a method for testing the hypothesis that two or more populations show the same relative variability. This is done in the regular manner by noting whether the limits overlap. When the samples are large, a test of significance concerning two of these values can be carried out by calculating a c value. The insect data will serve as an example.

$$c = \frac{C.V._{.1} - C.V._{.2}}{\sqrt{s_{C.V._{.1}}^2 + s_{C.V._{.2}}^2}}$$

$$= \frac{24.04 - 24.44}{\sqrt{\left[\frac{24.04}{\sqrt{2(90)}}\right]^2 + \left[\frac{24.44}{\sqrt{2(90)}}\right]^2}}$$

$$= -0.156$$

Since $0.90 > P > 0.80$, the null hypothesis is accepted.

16.9   Common Logarithms

As stated above, computations may be facilitated with the use of common logarithms. The common logarithm of a positive number N is equal to x in the equation:

$$N = 10^x.$$

For example, the common logarithm of 100 is 2, since $100 = 10^2$. By definition then, the common logarithm of a positive number (N) is the exponent (x) which must be applied to 10 to give N. It is expressed as $\log_{10} N = x$.

The system of common logarithms employs the base 10. Any positive number, other than 1, may serve as the base. The system of natural logarithms employs the base $e = 2.71828$. Both common and natural logarithms are encountered in statistical methods; however, common logarithms are more useful than any other type as a computational tool. For this reason, it is customary in statistical calculations to identify natural logarithms with the symbol $\log_e N$, and to interpret the expression $\log N$ as $\log_{10} N$, and the word logarithm as common logarithm.

The relationship between certain numbers and the logarithms of these numbers is given in Table 16.12.

Table 16.12

Number (N)	$10^x = N$	$\log N = x$
1	$10^0 = 1$	$\log 1 = 0$
10	$10^1 = 10$	$\log 10 = 1$
100	$10^2 = 100$	$\log 100 = 2$
1000	$10^3 = 1000$	$\log 1000 = 3$
0.1	$10^{-1} = 1/10^1 = 0.1$	$\log 0.1 = -1$
0.01	$10^{-2} = 1/10^2 = 0.01$	$\log 0.01 = -2$
0.001	$10^{-3} = 1/10^3 = 0.001$	$\log 0.001 = -3$
0.0001	$10^{-4} = 1/10^4 = 0.0001$	$\log 0.0001 = -4$

Since logarithms are exponents, it will be useful to review certain rules pertaining to exponents.

RULE 1: $(10^x)(10^y) = 10^{x+y}$

RULE 2: $(10^x)/(10^y) = 10^{x-y}$

RULE 3: $(10^x)^y = 10^{xy}$

RULE 4: $10^{x/y} = \sqrt[y]{10^x}$

16.10 Properties of Common Logarithms

Since $10^2 = 100$, and $10^3 = 1000$, it follows that $10^{2.5}$ is equal to some number between 100 and 1000, and 2.5 is the logarithm of that number. The number can be obtained as follows:

$$10^{2.5} = 10^1 \cdot 10^1 \cdot 10^{1/2}$$
$$= 10^1 \cdot 10^1 \cdot \sqrt[2]{10^1}$$
$$= 10 \cdot 10 \cdot \sqrt{10}$$
$$= (100)(3.162)$$
$$= 316.2$$

A logarithm consists of a *characteristic* (an integer which may be positive, zero, or negative) and a *mantissa* (which may be zero, greater than zero, but less than 1). As shown above, the logarithm of 316.2 is 2.5. The characteristic of this logarithm is 2, and the mantissa is .5000 (using four decimal places).

Negative characteristics are usually written as the difference between two positive numbers where the latter number is 10, or a multiple of 10. For example, the characteristic -1 is written as $9 - 10$; -2 as $8 - 10$; -6 as $4 - 10$; and -14 as $6 - 20$, etc.

The sign and numerical value of the characteristic of a logarithm is determined by the position of the decimal point in the number.

(a) If the number is 1.0 or greater, the characteristic of its logarithm is equal to *one less* than the number of digits left of the decimal point.

EXAMPLES:

Number	Characteristic
1462.91	3
571.35	2
89.40	1
1.52	0
1.00	0

(b) If the number is less than 1.0, the characteristic of its logarithm is obtained by noting the number of zeros between the decimal point and the first non-zero digit, and subtracting this number from 9 in the expression $9 - 10$.

EXAMPLES:

Number	Characteristic
0.3168	9 − 10 or −1
0.0321	8 − 10 or −2
0.0032	7 − 10 or −3
0.0003	6 − 10 or −4

Mantissas are obtained from tables of logarithms, also known as tables of mantissas (see Table X). Mantissas are read directly from these tables, or obtained by interpolation.

EXAMPLE 1. Determine the logarithm of 35.6.
(a) The characteristic is 1.
(b) Find the mantissa at the intersection of the row headed by the number 35 and the column headed by the number 6. The mantissa is .5514.
(c) log 35.6 = 1.5514. This expression states that $10^{1.5514} = 35.6$.

EXAMPLE 2. Determine the logarithm of 0.0356.
(a) The characteristic is 8 − 10, or −2.
(b) Beginning with the first non-zero digit in the number, find the mantissa (.5514) at the intersection of the row headed by 35 and the column headed by 6.
(c) log 0.0356 = 8.5514 − 10. Note that 8.5514 − 10 is equivalent to −2 + 0.5514 = −1.4486, which comes from

$$\begin{array}{r} -2.0000 \\ +0.5514 \\ \hline -1.4486 \end{array}$$

This states that $10^{8.5514-10} = 10^{-1.4486} = \dfrac{1}{10^{1.4486}} = 0.0356$. Mantissas cannot be negative. Therefore, in the logarithm −1.4486, which equals −1 + (−0.4486), the digits right of the decimal do not represent a mantissa because of the sign. To convert such a logarithm to one with a positive mantissa, add algebraically the logarithm to 10.0000−10, as follows

$$\begin{array}{r} 10.0000 - 10 \\ -1.4486 \\ \hline 8.5514 - 10 \end{array}$$

A property of common logarithms is that the mantissa is independent of the position of the decimal point in the number. This allows for simplified logarithm tables. The logarithms of the numbers 356.0, 3.56, 0.00356 all have the same mantissa (.5514); only the characteristics differ. A system of logarithms using a base other than 10 does not have this property. This accounts for the fact that common logarithms are more practical to use as a tool in calculations than any other type.

EXAMPLE 3. Find the logarithm of 1324.0.

(a) The characteristic is 3.

(b) Enter the row headed by 13 and the column headed by 2. The mantissa at this intersection is $m_1 = .1206$ (which is the mantissa of the logarithm of the number 1320.0). Interpolation is now necessary. The mantissa appearing in the next column of this row is $m_2 = .1239$ (which is the mantissa of the logarithm of the number 1330.0). When the number under consideration has four digits (and the last is not zero), as 1324, the mantissa is given by the equation

$$m = m_1 + f/10(m_2 - m_1)$$

where f is the value of the fourth digit. Substitution gives

$$m = 0.1206 + 4/10(0.1239 - 0.1206)$$
$$= 0.1219.$$

(c) log 1324.0 = 3.1219.

EXAMPLE 4. Find the logarithm of 0.0064032.

(a) The characteristic is $7 - 10$ or -3.

(b) The mantissa at the intersection of the row headed by 64 and the column headed by 0 is $m_1 = 0.8062$ (which is the mantissa of the logarithm of the number 64000). The mantissa in the next column of this row is $m_2 = 0.8069$ (which is the mantissa of the logarithm of the number 64100). When the number has five digits (and the last is not zero), as 64032, the mantissa is given by the equation

$$m = m_1 + f/100(m_2 - m_1)$$

where f represents the remaining two digits in the number under consideration.

$$m = 0.8062 + 32/100(0.8069 - 0.8062)$$
$$= 0.8064.$$

(c) log 0.0064032 = 7.8064 − 10. Likewise, log 64.032 = 1.8064; log 6403.2 = 3.8064; log 6.4032 = 0.8064; log 0.64032 = 9.8064 − 10; log 6403200.0 = 6.8064

16.11 Finding the Value of a Number When Its Logarithm Is Known

In the equation $N = 10^x$, x may be known and N is to be determined. In this case it is stated that the antilogarithm of x is N, which is expressed as antilog $x = N$. For example, the antilogarithm of 2 (or 2.0000) is 100.

EXAMPLE 1. The logarithm of N is 1.6571. Find N.

(a) The exact mantissa is found in the table. Join the figures which appear at the head of the row and column giving 454.

(b) The characteristic of 1 indicates that there are two digits to the left of the decimal point.

(c) $N = 45.4$. Likewise, antilog $9.6571 - 10 = 0.454$; antilog $4.6571 = 45400.0$; antilog $7.6571 - 10 = 0.00454$.

EXAMPLE 2. The logarithm of N is 1.2475. Find N.

(a) The exact mantissa is not found in the table. It is between $m_1 = 0.2455$ and $m_2 = 0.2480$. The difference between m_2 and m_1 is $0.2480 - 0.2455 = 0.0025$. The difference between m and m_1 is $0.2475 - 0.2455 = 0.0020$.

(b) Combining the figures at the heads of the row and columns corresponding to m_1 and m_2 gives the antilogarithm 17.60 and 17.70. The difference between these antilogarithms is $17.70 - 17.60 = 0.10$.

(c) Interpolation gives

$$N = 17.60 + 0.10\left(\frac{0.0020}{0.0025}\right)$$

$$= 17.60 + 0.08$$

$$= 17.68.$$

The fourth digit (f), equal to the nearest whole number, can be obtained from the equation

$$f = 10\,\frac{(m - m_1)}{(m_2 - m_1)}.$$

16.12   Computations Using Logarithms

Additional properties of logarithms will illustrate the value of logarithms in computational procedures.

Property 1. The logarithm of a product is the sum of the logarithms of the factors

$$\log MN = \log M + \log N$$

Proof: (1) Let $M = 10^x$; therefore $\log M = x$.

Let $N = 10^y$; therefore $\log N = y$

(2) $MN = (10^x)(10^y) = 10^{x+y}$; therefore by definition $\log MN = x + y = \log M + \log N$.

EXAMPLE: What is the product $(321.0)(0.0064)$, accurate to two decimal places?

$$\begin{aligned} \log 321.0 &= 2.5065 \\ \log 0.0064 &= \underline{7.8062 - 10} \text{ (add)} \\ & \overline{10.3127 - 10} \end{aligned}$$

antilog $0.3127 = 2.05$ (Ans.)

Property 2. The logarithm of a quotient is the logarithm of the numerator minus the logarithm of the denominator

$$\log M/N = \log M - \log N$$

Proof: (1) Let $\log M = 10^x$; therefore $\log M = x$

Let $\log N = 10^y$; therefore $\log N = y$

(2) $M/N = 10^x/10^y = 10^{x-y}$; therefore
$\log M/N = x - y = \log M - \log N$

EXAMPLE: What is the quotient $0.247/3.84$?

$$\begin{aligned} \log 0.2470 &= 9.3927 - 10 \\ \log 3.84 &= \underline{0.5843} \quad \text{(subtract)} \\ & \overline{8.8084 - 10} \end{aligned}$$

antilog $8.8084 - 10 = 0.0642$ (Ans.)

Property 3. The logarithm of a power of a number is equal to the exponent of the number times the logarithm of the number

$$\log N^y = y \log N$$

Proof: (1) Let $N = 10^x$; therefore $\log N = x$

(2) $N^y = (10^x)^y = 10^{yx}$; therefore
$\log N^y = yx = y \log N$

EXAMPLE: Find $(0.165)^5$.

$$\begin{aligned} \log 0.165 &= 9.2175 - 10 \\ & \underline{ 5} \text{ (multiply)} \\ & \overline{46.0875 - 50} \end{aligned}$$

antilog $6.0875 - 10 = 0.0001223$ (Ans.)

Property 4. The logarithm of a root of a number is equal to the logarithm of the number divided by the index of the root

$$\log \sqrt[y]{N} = \log N/y$$

Proof: (1) $\log \sqrt[y]{N} = \log N^{1/y}$

(2) $\log N^{1/y} = 1/y \log N = \log N/y$

EXAMPLE: Find $\sqrt[2]{0.00522} = \sqrt{0.00522}$.

$$\log 0.00522 = 7.7177 - 10$$

$$\frac{17.7177 - 20}{2 \text{ (divide)}}$$
$$8.85885 - 10$$

antilog $8.8588 - 10 = 0.07225$ (Ans.)

This example can be used to demonstrate why it is more convenient to express characteristics as $9 - 10$, $8 - 10$, $7 - 10$, etc., rather than -1, -2, -3, respectively. The logarithm of $0.00522 = 7.7177 - 10 = -3 + 0.7177$. While $7.7177 - 10$ can be divided by 2 to give $8.85885 - 10$, it is necessary to add algebraically -3.0000 and 0.7177 before the division can be carried out

$$-3.0000$$
$$\frac{0.7177}{-2.2823}$$
$$\frac{2 \text{ (divide)}}{-1.14115}$$

The logarithm $-1.14115 = -1 + (-0.14115)$ has a negative mantissa. This must be rectified before the antilogarithm can be determined from the table of logarithms.

$$10.00000 - 10$$
$$\frac{-1.14115}{8.85885 - 10}$$

As before, antilog $8.8588 - 10 = 0.07225$ (Ans.)

Problems

1. A Drosophila geneticist mated a white-eyed male with a red-eyed (wild type) female, which was heterozygous for the recessive gene giving white eyes. In the off-spring were 80 red-eyed and 72 white-eyed flies. Test the hypothesis that the observed data follow the expected Mendelian ratio of $1:1$. Use Yates correction for continuity.

2. Discuss why Yates correction should be used when the sample is small, but is not too necessary when the sample is large.

3. A geneticist studied some F_2 ratios in corn. When a $9:3:3:1$ ratio was expected, five different matings gave the following chi-squares values: 1.44, 4.02, 2.76, 3.01, and 3.75. The pooled chi-square value was 3.36. Fill out an analysis-of-chi-square table. What are your conclusions?

4. A plant breeder raised a sample of corn plants from seed. After a given length of time, the heights of the plants were measured in inches. If 990 plants were raised with a mean of 65.5 inches and a standard deviation of 10.0 inches, calculate the expected frequencies for the following classes, in order to test the hypothesis that the sample was taken from a normally distributed population.

Class Intervals
$$\begin{array}{c} \hline 30.5- \ 40.5 \\ 40.5- \ 50.5 \\ 50.5- \ 60.5 \\ 60.5- \ 70.5 \\ 70.5- \ 80.5 \\ 80.5- \ 90.5 \\ 90.5-100.5 \end{array}$$

5. An investigator was interested in comparing the variability of four populations. A random sample was taken from each population.

Samples

1	2	3	4
60	40	53	91
57	72	47	93
63	31	49	90
61	96	51	92
62	21	48	89
63		49	90
			87

(a) Test the hypothesis that the variances are homogeneous using Bartlett's method. What are your conclusions? (b) Determine the 95% confidence limits for each population variance.

6. Samples were taken of insect species. The thorax of one species varied in length from 11 to 42 mm,. with a mean ($\bar{x}$) of 26 mm. and a standard deviation (s) of 6.34 mm. For another species, the measurements varied from 22 to 60 mm., with a mean of 42 mm. and a standard deviation of 11.16 mm. The sample size in each case was $n = 200$.
(a) Calculate the coefficient of variation for each sample of measurements. (b) Test the hypothesis that the populations have the same relative variability.

CHAPTER SEVENTEEN

Binomial Distribution

A few principles of elementary probability were introduced in Chapter 3. Two important theorems of probability will now be presented.

17.1   Multiplication Theorem of Probability

If $P(A)$ is the probability of event A and $P(B)$ is the probability of event B, and if these two events are independent, the probability that both events will occur together is the product of the individual probabilities.

$$P(A + B) = P(A) \times P(B)$$

If two coins were tossed, the probability that heads would occur on both is given by:

$$P(A + B) = \tfrac{1}{2} \times \tfrac{1}{2} = \tfrac{1}{4}$$

If dice were thrown, the probability of getting two sixes is given as:

$$P(A + B) = \tfrac{1}{6} \times \tfrac{1}{6} = \tfrac{1}{36}$$

In general,

$$P(A + B + \cdots + N) = P(A) \times P(B) \times \cdots \times P(N)$$

17.2   Addition Theorem of Probability

If $P(A)$ is the probability of event A and $P(B)$ is the probability of event B, and if the events are mutually exclusive (i.e., the occurrence of one excludes the occurrence of the other), the probability that event A or event B will occur is the sum of the individual probabilities.

$$P(A,B) = P(A) + P(B)$$

In general,

$$P(A,B, \cdots N) = P(A) + P(B) + \cdots + P(N)$$

For example, if a coin is tossed, the probability that a head or a tail will occur is certain. This is expressed as:

$$P(A,B) = \tfrac{1}{2} + \tfrac{1}{2} = 1$$

If a die is thrown, the probability of getting a 6, 4, or a 2 is given by:

$$P(A,B,C) = \tfrac{1}{6} + \tfrac{1}{6} + \tfrac{1}{6} = \tfrac{1}{36}$$

17.3 Permutations

Each different arrangement which can be made from a given number of things by taking part or all of them at a time is called a permutation. The number of permutations of the letters a, b, and c is six. These are: *abc, acb, bac, bca, cab,* and *cba.* The symbol for permutations is nPr which reads, "The number of permutations of n things taken r at a time."

Permutations can best be understood by considering n things that are *going to fill r places, positions, or slots.* The first place can be filled by any one of the n things or in n different ways, the second place by any one of the $(n-1)$ things remaining after the first place has been filled, the third place by any one of the $(n-2)$ things remaining after the second place has been filled, and so on, until the rth place is filled by any one of the $n-(r-1)$ things remaining after the $(r-1)$th place has been filled. The number of permutations of n different things r at a time is the product of all the integers between n and $(n-r+1)$ inclusive. This can be stated by the general formula:

$$nPr = n(n-1)(n-2) \cdots n - (r-1)$$

or

$$nPr = n(n-1)(n-2) \cdots (n-r+1)$$

In the above example the number of permutations of the three letters taken three at a time is given as:

$$nPr = 3P3 = 3 \times 2 \times 1 = 6$$

The number of permutations of four letters (a, b, c, and d) taken two at a time is:

$$nPr = 4P2 = 4 \times 3 = 12$$

For any problem, the rth place can be determined by substitution into the term $(n - r + 1)$. When $nPr = 3P3$, then $(n - r + 1) = 1$. When $nPr = 4P2$, then $(n - r + 1) = 3$.

17.4   Combinations

Combinations are concerned with n things taken r at a time without regard to the order of arrangement. Combinations are symbolized by nCr which reads, "The number of combinations of n things taken r at a time." The formula is:

$$nCr = \frac{\cdot nPr}{r!}$$

where $r!$ (read r factorial) is the product of all integers from r down to 1.

There are six permutations of the letters a, b, and c, but there is only one combination.

$$nCr = \frac{3P3}{3!} = \frac{3 \times 2 \times 1}{3 \times 2 \times 1} = 1$$

The number of combinations of the letters a, b, c, and d, taken two at a time is given by

$$nCr = \frac{4P2}{2!} = \frac{4 \times 3}{2 \times 1} = 6$$

17.5   Binomial Theorem

Permutations and combinations have been considered here because of their relationship to the general term of the binomial theorem. By actual multiplication, the following terms can be obtained:

$(p + q)^1 = p + q$

$(p + q)^2 = p^2 + 2pq + q^2$

$(p + q)^3 = p^3 + 3p^2q + 3pq^2 + q^3$

$(p + q)^4 = p^4 + 4p^3q + 6p^2q^2 + 4pq^3 + q^4$

$(p + q)^5 = p^5 + 5p^4q + 10p^3q^2 + 10p^2q^3 + 5pq^4 + q^5$

$(p + q)^6 = p^6 + 6p^5q + 15p^4q^2 + 20p^3q^3 + 15p^2q^4 + 6pq^5 + q^6$

If n is equal to the exponent of $(p + q)$ for any expansion, then the following can be noted:

(1) The number of terms is equal to $(n + 1)$.

(2) The first term is p^n. The second term is $np^{n-1}q$.

(3) The exponents of p decrease by 1 from term to term. The exponents of q increase by 1.

(4) If the coefficient of a given term is multiplied by the exponent of p and this product is divided by the exponent of q increased by 1, the quotient is the coefficient of the following term.

The following is known as the binomial formula:

$$(p + q)^n = p^n + np^{n-1}q + \frac{n(n - 1)}{2!}p^{n-2}q^2 + \frac{n(n - 1)(n - 2)}{3!}p^{n-3}q^3$$

$$+ \cdots + q^n$$

The general term of the binomial can be expressed as follows:

$$\frac{n(n - 1)(n - 2)\cdots(n - r + 1)}{r!}p^{n-r}q^r$$

This can also be expressed as:

(1) $\dfrac{nPr}{r!}p^{n-r}q^r$

or

(2) $\dfrac{n!}{r!(n - r)!}p^{n-r}q^r$

Two useful definitions are:

(1) $0! = 1$ [Note: $n! = n(n - 1)!$ Let $n = 1$. Therefore $1! = 1(0)!$ and $0! = 1!/1 = 1$].

(2) $p^0 = q^0 = 1$ (Note: $1 = q^n/q^n = q^{n-n} = q^0$).

The coefficient of the general term is the formula for obtaining the number of combinations of n things taken r at a time. The general term is useful when it is necessary to obtain the value of the coefficient of any term without considering the other terms. For example, in the binomial $(p + q)^7$, determine the value of the coefficient when the exponent of q equals 5.

$$\frac{nPr}{r!}p^{n-r}q^r = \frac{7P5}{5!}p^2q^5 = \frac{7 \times 6 \times 5 \times 4 \times 3}{5 \times 4 \times 3 \times 2 \times 1}p^2q^5 = 21p^2q^5$$

17.6 Special Case of the Multiplication Theorem of Probability

The general term of the binomial is also very important because it forms a special case of the multiplication theorem of probability. If the probability that an event will occur on a single trial is q, and the probability that it will fail is p, or $(1 - q)$, the probability that it will occur exactly r times in n trials is given by:

$$\frac{nPr}{r!} p^{n-r} q^r$$

EXAMPLES:

(1) If a coin is tossed four times, what is the probability of getting 2 heads? Here $n = 4$, and $r = 2$ (r successes in n trials). The probability of success (q) on a single trial equals $\frac{1}{2}$, and the probability of failure (p) equals $\frac{1}{2}$. Substitution into the general term of the binomial gives:

$$\frac{nPr}{r!} p^{n-r} q^r = \frac{4P2}{2!} (\tfrac{1}{2})^2 (\tfrac{1}{2})^2 = \frac{4 \times 3}{2 \times 1} (\tfrac{1}{4})(\tfrac{1}{4}) = \tfrac{3}{8}$$

(2) If an F_1 plant from a monohybrid cross is self-fertilized, what is the probability of getting 1 recessive individual out of 4? In this problem $n = 4$, $r = 1$, $q = \frac{1}{4}$, and $p = \frac{3}{4}$.

$$\frac{4P1}{1!} (\tfrac{3}{4})^3 (\tfrac{1}{4})^1 = \frac{108}{256}$$

(3) If a coin is tossed four times, what is the probability of getting 1 head *or* 2 heads? This problem is a combination of the special case of the multiplication theorem and the addition theorem. The probability of getting 1 head out of 4 is given by:

$$\frac{4P1}{1!} (\tfrac{1}{2})^3 (\tfrac{1}{2})^1 = \tfrac{1}{4}$$

The probability of getting 2 heads out of 4 is given by:

$$\frac{4P2}{2!} (\tfrac{1}{2})^2 (\tfrac{1}{2})^2 = \tfrac{3}{8}$$

Since these events are mutually exclusive, the total probability is their sum:

$$\tfrac{1}{4} + \tfrac{3}{8} = \tfrac{5}{8}$$

(4) If a penny and a nickel are each tossed 4 times, what is the probability of getting 1 head out of 4 on the penny and 2 heads out of 4 on the nickel? In this case the two events are independent, so the total probability is the product of the individual probabilities.

$$\tfrac{1}{4} \times \tfrac{3}{8} = \tfrac{3}{32}$$

17.7   Test of Significance Using the Binomial Distribution

Assume that an investigator wishes to test the null hypothesis that a coin is honest ($H_0: q = \frac{1}{2}$, i.e., the probability of a head occurring on a single toss

$= q = \frac{1}{2}$). This hypothesis specifies a population and a sampling distribution. The population consists of an indefinitely large number of tosses that are segregating in a 1:1 ratio. From this population a sample is taken consisting of n observations. The number of heads appearing is recorded. If this procedure were repeated *ad infinitum*, the resultant would be a sampling distribution consisting of the number of heads in samples of n tosses.

For simplicity, assume that the investigator planned to toss the coin only 8 times. The number of heads could vary from 0 to 8. By use of the special case of the multiplication theorem:

$$\frac{n!}{r!(n-r)!}p^{n-r}q^r$$

where $n = 8$, $p = \frac{1}{2}$, $q = \frac{1}{2}$, and r varies from 0 through 8, or by expanding the binomial $(p + q)^n$, it is possible to construct the sampling distribution in detail. This is given in Table 17.1.

Table 17.1 Expansion of the Binomial $(\frac{1}{2} + \frac{1}{2})^8$.

No. of Heads	0	1	2	3	4	5	6	7	8
Probability	$\frac{1}{256}$	$\frac{8}{256}$	$\frac{28}{256}$	$\frac{56}{256}$	$\frac{70}{256}$	$\frac{56}{256}$	$\frac{28}{256}$	$\frac{8}{256}$	$\frac{1}{256}$

The sampling distribution can be illustrated with the aid of a histogram as in Figure 17.1.

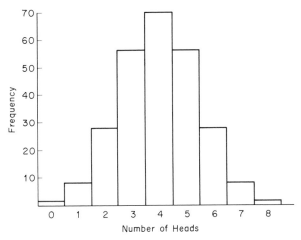

Figure 17.1 Sampling distribution of successes (heads) $(\frac{1}{2} + \frac{1}{2})^8$.

The mean number of heads in the sampling distribution is $\mu = nq = 8 \times \frac{1}{2} = 4$. This is the expectation.

Assume that upon tossing the coin 8 times, only 1 head was observed. On the basis of this observation, should the hypothesis be accepted or rejected? The procedure that is followed is determined by the alternative hypothesis. Assume that: $H_1: q \neq \frac{1}{2}$. A two-tailed test is specified. The deviation between the expectation and the number of heads actually obtained in the sample is $4 - 1 = 3$. The probability of getting a fit as bad or worse is obtained by determining the probability of getting the observed deviation from the expectation, *in either* direction, or larger deviations. This is the same as asking: "What is the probability of getting 0, 1, 7, or 8 heads?" Each of these events deviates from the expectation by 3 or more. Since these events are mutually exclusive, the probability value is obtained by adding the different values of:

$$\frac{nPr}{r!}p^{n-r}q^r$$

where r equals 0, 1, 7, and 8. The P value becomes:

$$\frac{1}{256} + \frac{8}{256} + \frac{8}{256} + \frac{1}{256} = \frac{18}{256} = 0.0703$$

Using the 0.05 level of significance, the null hypothesis is accepted.

The alternative hypothesis might have been: $H_1: q < \frac{1}{2}$. This situation would arise if the investigator had information that the coin is either honest or biased (loaded) in favor of tails. A one-tailed test is specified. The probability of getting a fit as bad or worse is obtained now by determining the probability of getting the observed deviation from the mean expectation, or larger deviation in the same direction. This is the probability of getting 0 or 1 head.

$$P = \frac{1}{256} + \frac{8}{256} = \frac{9}{256} = 0.03515$$

Using a 0.05 level of significance, the null hypothesis would be rejected in favor of the alternative hypothesis.

17.8   Test of Significance Using the Normal Substitution Method

It has been shown how the binomial can be used to carry out a test of significance. This will be referred to as the binomial method. An example was given where a coin was tossed 8 times. It is obvious that if an investigator were really interested in testing the hypothesis that a coin was honest, he would conduct a much more extensive experiment. Assume that another test was carried out and this time the same coin was tossed 100 times. Of this total number, 37 were heads. On the basis of this larger sample, should the hypothesis be accepted that the coin is honest?

As before, a theoretical sampling distribution should be constructed under the assumption that the coin is honest. This consists of an imaginary large number of sets of 100 tosses. The range of the distribution is from 0 heads to 100 heads. A probability value could be obtained using the binomial method assuming a one- or two-tailed test. However, this procedure would be laborious, and unnecessary since a probability value can be obtained in a simple manner.

The binomial distribution $(p + q)^n$ is clearly discontinuous for small values of n, but as n becomes large, a continuous distribution is approached *that is normal in form*. Consider the following histograms representing sampling distributions when $n = 2$, 4, and 8.

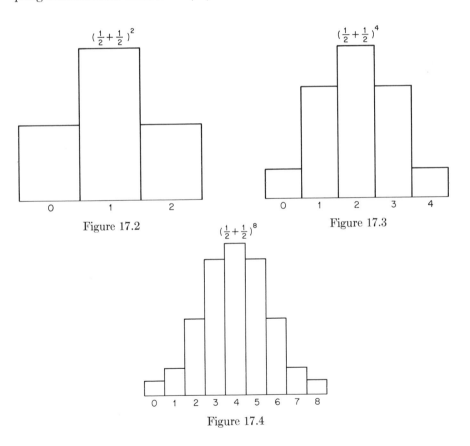

Figure 17.2

Figure 17.3

Figure 17.4

The total area in all rectangles in each histogram is equal to one square unit. As n becomes larger, the area in each rectangle becomes smaller in proportion to the total area. When n is a large number, the distribution is no longer discontinuous, since lines connecting the top midpoints of each rectangle become part of a smooth continuous curve.

The moments of the binomial are given as follows:

$$\text{Second moment} = V_2 = npq$$

$$\text{Third moment} = V_3 = npq(q - p)$$

$$\text{Fourth moment} = V_4 = npq + 3np^2q^2(k - 2)$$

These moments can be used to compute gamma-one and gamma-two.

$$\text{Gamma-one} = g_1 = \frac{V_3}{(V_2)^{3/2}} = \frac{q - p}{\sqrt{npq}}$$

$$\text{Gamma-two} = g_2 = \frac{V_4}{(V_2)^2} - 3 = \frac{1 - 6pq}{npq}$$

A consideration of the formulae for gamma-one and gamma-two will demonstrate that regardless of what degree of skewness or kurtosis may be present in the distribution, as n becomes infinitely large, both g_1 and g_2 approach zero. Therefore, under the condition that n is a large number, the binimial distribution approaches a normal distribution.

A method is now available for carrying out the test of significance, since the properties of the binomial distribution are known:

$$\mu = nq$$

$$\sigma^2 = npq$$

$$\sigma = \sqrt{npq}$$

For the coin problem:

$$\mu = nq = 100 \times \tfrac{1}{2} = 50$$

$$\sigma = \sqrt{npq} = \sqrt{100 \times \tfrac{1}{2} \times \tfrac{1}{2}} = 5$$

Since n is a relatively large number and the sampling distribution (binomial) is essentially normal, the P value can be obtained with the use of the table for the areas under the normal curve. Assuming a two-tailed test, the procedure is to obtain the proportion of times that samples would be expected to occur that deviate from the mean expectation by ± 13 or more units. This is given by the proportion of the total area under the normal curve that is left of 37 and right of 63.

$$P = \frac{\text{Area in both tails}}{\text{Total area}} = \frac{\text{Area in both tails}}{1}$$

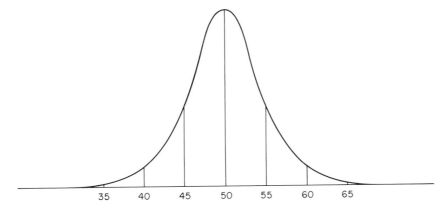

Figure 17.5 Sampling distribution of successes (heads).

The true standard deviation of the sampling distribution is known; therefore a c test is used.

$$c = \frac{\text{Observation} - \text{Mean}}{\text{Standard error}} = \frac{X - \mu}{\sigma} = \frac{37 - 50}{5} = -2.6$$

The observed c value is greater than 1.96, which is the value at the 0.05 level in Table II; therefore, the null hypothesis is rejected. (In a one-tailed test, the null hypothesis is rejected at the 0.05 level if the observed c value exceeds 1.64, which is the value in the table at the 0.10 level.)

An important relationship will now be demonstrated. In Chapter 16, a test of significance was carried out for the same coin data by calculating a chi-square value. This was:

$$\chi^2 = \frac{(37 - 50)^2}{50} + \frac{(63 - 50)^2}{50} = 6.76$$

Now note that $c^2 = \chi^2$, i.e., $(2.6)^2 = 6.76$

Thus a P value corresponding to any value of χ^2 for one degree of freedom may be obtained from the table of c, since the square root of the chi-square value is the c value by which the table is entered. Evidence that $c^2 = \chi^2$ can be shown algebraically:

$$\chi^2 = \frac{(X_1 - \mu_1)^2}{\mu_1} + \frac{(X_2 - \mu_2)^2}{\mu_2} = \frac{(X_1 - \mu_1)^2}{nq} + \frac{(X_2 - \mu_2)^2}{np}$$

In all cases of one degree of freedom, $(X_1 - \mu_1)^2 = (X_2 - \mu_2)^2$. Therefore:

$$\chi^2 = \frac{(X - \mu)^2}{nq} + \frac{(X - \mu)^2}{np} = \frac{p(X - \mu)^2}{npq} + \frac{q(X - \mu)^2}{npq}$$

$$= \frac{p + q(X - \mu)^2}{npq} = \frac{(X - \mu)^2}{npq} = \frac{(X - \mu)^2}{\sigma^2} = c^2,$$

since $c = \dfrac{(X - \mu)}{\sigma}$

Whenever data are distributed in the binomial manner and n is large, the normal substitution method is appropriate for a test of significance. This is a common procedure in genetics problems where $1:1, 3:1, 9:7, 13:3, 12:4$, $15:1$, etc., ratios are encountered. It should be stressed, however, that whenever $p \neq q$, the value of n has to be larger in order for the distribution to approximate normality than when $p = q$.

It should always be kept in mind that the binomial distribution only approaches the normal distribution when n is an infinitely large number. When n is as large as 200 or 250, the binomial distribution is still not completely continuous. However, when n is of this magnitude, the two distributions, for practical purposes, can be assumed to be similar. In fact, it is even permissible to compute P values by the normal substitution method when n is as low as 20 or 25. When n is this small, there is good agreement between P values computed by the exact binomial method and by use of the normal substitution method. For smaller values of n the agreement is less accurate and P values should only be obtained by the binomial method. When p and q are not equal, as is common in many genetic experiments (such as $p = \frac{3}{4}$ and $q = \frac{1}{4}$), the value of n has to be larger in order to have as good an agreement as when p and q are equal.

17.9   Yates Correction for Continuity

When the value of n is of such a magnitude that it is permissible to use the normal substitution method, but n is still not extremely large (not over 200), Yates' correction for continuity should be used. The following diagram shows an enlarged section of a frequency polygon illustrating the sampling distribution encountered in the coin study. The line connecting the midpoints almost forms a continuous curve, but nevertheless, discontinuity is still present. By using the normal substitution method of computing P values, it is assumed that the area of each rectangle is infinitesimal, but this assumption is only true when n is an extremely large value.

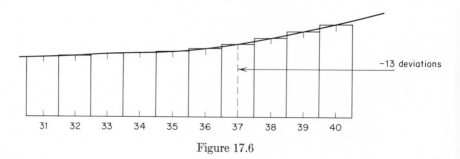

Figure 17.6

In the above example the P value was obtained by determining the area in both tails of the curve set off by ± 13 deviations from the mean expectation. It can be seen from the above diagram that this P value is slightly inaccurate because the area under the curve left of position 37 on the X axis only includes half of the area of the rectangle drawn in proportion to the frequency of class 37. All of the rectangle should be included with the area in the tail of the curve. The same is true for class 63, which is ± 13 deviations from the mean expectation.

This is the same problem that was encountered in the chi-square distribution. Correction for continuity (Yates correction) is made by decreasing the value of the deviation, towards zero, by 0.5 units. When the area of each rectangle is infinitesimal (i.e., when n is very large), it can be visualized that this correction is not necessary. Using Yates correction, the new c value becomes:

$$c = \frac{|37 - 50| - 0.5}{5} = \frac{-12.5}{5} = -2.5$$

Note that (adjusted c)^2 = adjusted χ^2. In Chapter 16, the adjusted χ^2 value for these data was 6.25.

17.10   Proportions

An investigator may wish to test the hypothesis that a coin is honest ($H_0: q = \frac{1}{2}$) by using proportions. Instead of recording the number of heads appearing in a sample of n tosses, the proportion is noted. This sample proportion ($\bar{q}$) is an unbiased estimate of the population proportion (q) which is a parameter. If 37 heads were observed among $n = 100$ tosses (as in the analysis previously presented), the sample proportion is $\bar{q} = 37/100 = 0.37$, where $\bar{p} + \bar{q} = 1$. The mean and standard deviation of the sampling distribution are

$$\mu = q = 0.50$$

$$\sigma = \sqrt{\frac{pq}{n}} = \sqrt{\frac{(0.5)(0.5)}{100}} = 0.05$$

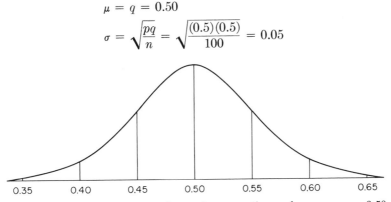

Figure 17.7 Sampling distribution of sample proportions where $\mu = q = 0.50$ and $\sigma = 0.05$.

For large samples, a c value can be calculated as follows:

$$c = \frac{\bar{q} - q}{\sqrt{\dfrac{pq}{n}}} = \frac{0.37 - 0.50}{\sqrt{\dfrac{(0.50)(0.50)}{100}}} = \frac{-0.13}{0.05} = -2.6$$

Using a proportion (0.37) or the actual number (37) obviously yields the same c value since $\mu = q$ and $\sigma = \sqrt{pq/n}$ are obtained by multiplying $\mu = nq$ and $\sigma = \sqrt{npq}$ by $1/n$. A two-tailed test is implied. From Table II, it is observed that $P < 0.01$.

Confidence Limits for a Population Proportion

Whenever n is large and np and nq are larger than about 5, the sampling distribution of sample proportions is approximately normally distributed, and therefore confidence limits can be established by using the mean and standard deviation of this sampling distribution. Since the true standard deviation ($\sqrt{pq/n}$) is unknown, it is estimated by inserting the sample proportion ($\bar{q}$) in place of the parameter (q). This gives an estimated standard deviation ($\sqrt{\bar{p}\bar{q}/n}$). Even if $\bar{q}$ deviates markedly from q, the estimated standard deviation will differ only slightly from the true standard deviation. This fact can be illustrated with the above data. If it is assumed that $q = 0.5$, the true standard deviation is $\sqrt{(0.5)(0.5)/100} = 0.05$, which is not too different from the estimated value of $\sqrt{(0.63)(0.37)/100} = 0.04828$. The difference between the true and estimated standard deviations is slight, even though $\bar{q}$ differs significantly from q. Approximate 95% confidence limits can be obtained as follows:

$$L_1 = \bar{q} - 1.96\sqrt{\frac{\bar{p}\bar{q}}{n}}$$

$$= 0.37 - 1.96\sqrt{\frac{(0.63)(0.37)}{100}}$$

$$= 0.37 - (1.96)(0.04828)$$

$$= 0.275$$

$$L_2 = \bar{q} + 1.96\sqrt{\frac{\bar{p}\bar{q}}{n}}$$

$$= 0.37 + 1.96\sqrt{\frac{(0.63)(0.37)}{100}}$$

$$= 0.37 + (1.96)(0.04828)$$

$$= 0.465$$

The investigator can be 95% confident that the true proportion (q) is between 0.275 and 0.465.

The usefulness of confidence limits can be appreciated by considering the following situations.

(1) In a large metropolitan area, a human geneticist examined 424 siblings of individuals with a given genetic defect. The parents were all normal. Sixty-four of the siblings had the same defect. Assuming random sampling, the question is asked, "What is the true frequency of the defect among siblings?" The observed proportion is $\bar{q} = 64/424 = 0.151$. Using this estimate, the 95% confidence limits are given by $\bar{q} \pm 1.96 \sqrt{\bar{p}\bar{q}/n}$

$$L_1 = 0.151 - 1.96\sqrt{\frac{(0.849)(0.151)}{424}} = 0.116$$

$$L_2 = 0.151 + 1.96\sqrt{\frac{(0.849)(0.151)}{424}} = 0.185$$

(2) Five-hundred individuals were polled a week before a municipal election to determine if they were going to vote for the incumbent mayor. The number of yes votes was 390. Based on this random sample of the voting population, can the outcome of the election be predicted? The estimate of q is $\bar{q} = 390/500 = 0.78$. The 99% confidence limits are given by $\bar{q} \pm 2.58\sqrt{\bar{p}\bar{q}/n}$

$$L_1 = 0.78 - 2.58\sqrt{\frac{(0.22)(0.78)}{500}} = 0.732$$

$$L_2 = 0.78 + 2.58\sqrt{\frac{(0.22)(0.78)}{500}} = 0.828$$

It is concluded with 99% confidence, that the percentage of votes the mayor will receive is between 73.2% and 82.8%. Since this is a large plurality, his re-election seems highly likely.

(3) A parasitologist examined 50 pigeons for an intestinal parasite. The proportion infected was $15/50 = 0.30$. He wished to determine the 95% confidence limits for the proportion infected in the entire population.

$$L_1 = 0.30 - 1.96\sqrt{\frac{(0.70)(0.30)}{50}} = 0.173$$

$$L_2 = 0.30 + 1.96\sqrt{\frac{(0.70)(0.30)}{50}} = 0.427$$

Assuming random sampling, the probability is 0.95% that the proportion infected in the population is between 0.173 and 0.427.

As stated above, this procedure for setting confidence limits assumes a normal sampling distribution of sample proportions. The distribution will be skewed when q deviates markedly from 0.50 in either direction, unless n is very large. If extreme skewness is present, confidence limits should not be determined with the use of the standard error $\sqrt{pq/n}$. Confidence belts (see Dixon and Massey, 1951) and tables (see Table IX) are available for determining confidence limits for various values of n and proportions. Table IX can be used to good advantage when n is 10, 15, 20, 30, 50, 100, 250, or 1000. Indeed, an experiment may be designed so that n is equal to one of these values. For a given sample proportion, from 0.00 to 1.00, the 95% or 99% confidence limits can be read from the table. For example, an investigator may select a sample size of $n = 15$. If the number of positive individuals was $f = 3$ (therefore $\bar{q} = 3/15 = 0.20$), the 95% confidence limits are read from the table as $L_1 = 0.04$ and $L_2 = 0.48$. Note that the sample proportion is not equidistant between L_1 and L_2, which is an indication of a skewed sampling distribution. Equidistant relationships appear in the table when n becomes large or $\bar{q}$ approaches 0.50.

Difference Between Two Sample Proportions

An investigator wished to compare two different pigeon populations for the proportion infected with an intestinal parasite. A random sample ($n = 100$) was taken from each population. Each pigeon was dissected and scored as infected or not infected. Fifty-eight percent were infected in sample 1 and 30% in sample 2.

The estimated standard deviation of the sampling distribution of differences between sample proportions will be nearly similar in value to the true standard deviation. Hence, the test of significance ($H_0 : q_1 = q_2$) may be carried out by calculating a c value *if* the samples are large and $n_1 p_1$, $n_1 q_1$, $n_2 p_2$, and $n_2 q_2$ are all larger than about 5.

$$c = \frac{(\bar{q}_1 - \bar{q}_2)}{\sqrt{\dfrac{\bar{p}_1 \bar{q}_1}{n_1} + \dfrac{\bar{p}_2 \bar{q}_2}{n_2}}} = \frac{0.58 - 0.30}{\sqrt{\dfrac{(0.42)(0.58)}{100} + \dfrac{(0.70)(0.30)}{100}}} = 4.16$$

Since $P < 0.01$, the null hypothesis is rejected. If the above assumptions are true, the 95% confidence limits for the difference between population proportions ($q_1 - q_2$) are given by

$$L_1 = (\bar{q}_1 - \bar{q}_2) - 1.96\sqrt{\bar{p}_1\bar{q}_1/n_1 + \bar{p}_2\bar{q}_2/n_2}$$

$$= 0.28 - 1.96\sqrt{(0.42)(0.58)/100 + (0.70)(0.30)/100}$$

$$= 0.148$$

$$L_2 = (\bar{q}_1 - \bar{q}_2) + 1.96\sqrt{\bar{p}_1\bar{q}_1/n_1 + \bar{p}_2\bar{q}_2/n_2}$$

$$= 0.28 + 1.96\sqrt{(0.42)(0.58)/100 + (0.70)(0.30)/100}$$

$$= 0.412$$

17.11 Testing the Goodness of Fit of a Group of Data to a Binomial Distribution

Four coins were tossed and the number of heads that appeared was recorded (i.e., either 0, 1, 2, 3, or 4). The procedure was than repeated 32 times. The hypothesis to be tested consists of two parts: (1) Each coin is honest (i.e., the probability of obtaining a head on a single coin is $\frac{1}{2}$). (2) The coins are independent (i.e., the occurrence of a head on one coin is independent of the occurrence of a head on any other coin). The following table summarizes the observed and expected frequencies of 0, 1, 2, 3, and 4 heads.

Table 17.2

Heads (Successes)	Observed Frequency	Expected Frequency
0	4	2
1	10	8
2	11	12
3	6	8
4	1	2
Total	32	32

The expected frequencies come from the expansion of the binomial $32(\frac{1}{2} + \frac{1}{2})^4$. The population specified by the hypothesis is made up of an infinite number of sets of tosses of five kinds in the following proportions:

Table 17.3

Heads	0	1	2	3	4
Proportion	1/16	4/16	6/16	4/16	1/16

The comparison of the observed and expected frequencies can be done by a chi-square test. However, grouping is necessary since the expected frequencies for the first and last classes are less than 5.

Table 17.4

Heads (Successes)	Observed Frequency	Expected Frequency
0	4 $\Big\}$ 14	2 $\Big\}$ 10
1	10	8
2	11	12
3	6 $\Big\}$ 7	8 $\Big\}$ 10
4	1	2
Total	32	32

The chi-square value becomes:

$$\chi^2 = \frac{(14 - 10)^2}{10} + \frac{(11 - 12)^2}{12} + \frac{(7 - 10)^2}{10} = 2.58$$

After grouping there are three classes, but since the total is set equal to 32, there are only two degrees of freedom. The P value is between 0.20 and 0.30, so the hypothesis is acceptable.

In the above example, the parameters are known (i.e., p and q both equal $\frac{1}{2}$). In other cases the parameters are unknown and must be estimated. For example, a plant pathologist was studying a fungal disease occurring in oranges. Infected oranges were detected following shippage by train from the packing company to the wholesale distributor. The question to be answered was whether the disease was spread in transit after the oranges were placed in the boxes because of faulty refrigeration, or whether each case of infection occurred before the oranges were placed in the boxes at the packing company.

Twelve oranges from each box were selected randomly from 50 boxes after shippage and examined for disease. One diseased orange was found in twelve boxes; two in four boxes; while in the remaining thirty-four boxes none was infected. The results are shown in Table 17.5.

Table 17.5

Number of Diseased Oranges	0	1	2	3 or more
Observed Frequency	34	12	4	0

The hypothesis to be tested is that the probability of infection is similar for each orange in all boxes, and the infection of one orange is independent of the infection of any other. If so, the above data should be distributed in a binomial manner. If the disease is transmitted in transit within the boxes, then the data should not follow the binomial distribution.

The hypothesis is tested by comparing the observed frequency values with the expected values calculated by expanding the binomial

$$50(\bar{p} + \bar{q})^{12}$$

where $\bar{p}$ and $\bar{q}$ are estimated values.

The value of $\bar{q}$ is equal to the observed number of diseased oranges divided by the total number observed.

$$\bar{q} = \frac{20}{600} = \frac{1}{30} = 0.0333$$

Table 17.6

Class	Symbol	Calculations	Expected Frequency
1	$50[\bar{p}^{12}]$	log 50(0.9667)^{12} = log 50 + 12(log 0.9667) = 1.6990 + 12(9.9853−10) = 121.5226−120 = 1.5226 antilog 1.5226 = 33.31	33.31
2	$50[12\bar{p}^{11}\bar{q}]$	log 50 [12(0.9667)^{11}(0.0333)^1] = log 50 + [log 12 + 11(log 0.9667) + log 0.0333] = 1.6990 + [1.0792 + 109.8483−110 + 8.5224−10] = 1.1389 antilog 1.1389 = 13.77	13.77
3	$50[66\bar{p}^{10}\bar{q}^2]$	log 50[66(0.9667)^{10}(0.0333)^2] = log 50 + [log 66 + 10(log 0.9667) + 2(log 0.0333)] = 1.6990 + [1.8195 + 10(9.9853−10) + 2(8.5224−10)] = 1.6990 + [1.8195 + 99.9530−100) + 17.0448−20)] = 0.4163 antilog 0.4163 = 2.61	2.61

Since $\bar{p} + \bar{q} = 1$, the value of $\bar{p} = 1 - \bar{q} = 1 - \dfrac{1}{30} = \dfrac{29}{30} = 0.9667$

The distribution is now completely specified.

$$50\left(\frac{29}{30} + \frac{1}{30}\right)^{12}$$

The expected frequencies for each class can be obtained from expansion of this binomial. When $\bar{p}$ and $\bar{q}$ are markedly different, as in this case, or n is very large, the use of logarithms often simplifies the calculations (see Table 17.6). The sum of the three expected values equals 49.69. The expected frequencies for all the remaining classes is given by $50 - 49.69 = 0.31$.

Table 17.7

Number	Observed Frequency	Expected Frequency
0	34	33.31
1	12	13.77
2	4	2.61
3 or more	0	0.31
Total	50	50.00

It is observed that there is good agreement between the observed and expected frequencies. If a chi-square test were to be carried out, it would be necessary to group the last three classes so that the expected frequency for each class is greater than 5.

Table 17.8

Number	Observed Frequency	Expected Frequency
0	34	33.31
1 or more	16	16.69
Total	50	50.00

Yet when this is done, it becomes obvious that a chi-square test cannot be carried out. There are only two classes. One degree of freedom is lost for setting the total equal to 50, and another is lost for estimating the value of q. This leaves zero degrees of freedom for the chi-square test.

Even though a chi-square test is not appropriate in this case, it is obvious from the data that a good fit was observed. It appears legitimate to accept the hypothesis.

The above examples illustrate that in fitting a group of data to a binomial distribution either *one* or *two* degrees of freedom will be lost. The rule states that in addition to losing one degree of freedom for setting the total equal to a given value, a degree of freedom will be lost for each independent parameter that is estimated. It is abvious that p and q are not independent, since $p + q = 1$. Thus, when a group of data is fitted to a binomial distribution, two degrees of freedom, and no more, may be lost.

Problems

1. Twenty students in a biometry laboratory are going to work in pairs using desk calculators. How many different combinations of students are possible?

2. Give the number of permutations of ten letters taken four at a time.

3. If an F_1 plant from a monohybrid cross is self-fertilized, what is the probability of getting two recessive offspring out of a total of six?

4. If a penny and nickel are each tossed 5 times, what is the probability of getting 1 head out of 5 on the penny and 3 heads out of 5 on the nickel?

5. An investigator tested the hypothesis that a coin was honest ($H_0: q = \frac{1}{2}$). He tossed the coin 10 times and observed 2 heads. The alternative hypothesis is $H_0: q \neq \frac{1}{2}$, calculate the probability value associated with the null hypothesis.

6. If the above investigator had tossed the same coin 100 times and observed 55 heads, calculate the probability value associated with the null hypothesis using the normal substitution method and Yates correction.

7. An epidemiologist determined the frequency of cancer among the members of 500 families of size 6. If the probability of cancer is 0.15 and this is a random event, predict the number of families with 0, 1, 2, 3, 4, 5, and 6 cases.

8. (a) What is the probability that in a family of two individuals, both are males? (b) What is the probability that the first is a male and the second is a female? (c) What is the probability that a boy-girl combination will occur?

9. In flipping a coin five times, what is the probability that (a) one head and four tails will occur? (b) What is the probability that two heads and three tails will occur? (c) What is the probability that one head and four tails, or two heads and three tails will occur?

10. Suppose a card is drawn at random from a pack of playing cards. What is the probability that it is either a heart *or* the queen of spades?

11. From a pack of playing cards, two cards are successively drawn at random, the first being replaced before the second is drawn. What is the probability that the first is a heart *and* the second not a king?

12. A coin is tossed three times. What is the probability of getting at least one head?

13. Six speakers are to be heard on a radio program. In how many ways can the order of their appearance be arranged?

14. An executive is to appoint first, second, and third assistants from a group of fourteen applicants. In how many ways can the assistants be appointed?

15. How many permutations are there of the letters a, b, c, d, and e, (a) taken two at a time? (b) taken three at a time?

16. A debate coach has eight students. How many different debating teams can he form, (a) when two students make up a single team? (b) when three students make up a single team?

17. A plant breeder has 45 different strains of tomato plants. How many different hybrids can be obtained?

18. What is the coefficient of the term in the binomial $(p + q)^8$ when the exponent of q is equal to 7? (*Note*: use $nCr\ p^{n-r}\ q^r$).

19. What is the coefficient of the term in the binomial $(p + q)^{24}$ when the exponent of q is equal to 3? (*Note*: use $nCr\ p^{n-r}\ q^r$).

20. Test the hypothesis discussed in Problem 6 by using proportions instead of actual numbers. Compare your answers.

21. A venomologist injected 100 rats with scorpion venom. He then injected each with Drug A. Sixty-three of the rats died. Determine the 95% confidence limits for the true proportion that would die under these experimental conditions.

22. Assume that in another experiment with 100 rats injected with venom, only 26 rats died when they were given Drug B. Test the hypothesis that no difference exists between the two proportion values. If the hypothesis is rejected, determine the 95% confidence limits for the true difference between proportion values.

CHAPTER EIGHTEEN

Poisson Distribution

The binomial distribution becomes normal in form when n increases to a very large number. If, however, n is very large and q is very small, so that nq is a small finite number, the resulting distribution is discontinuous and positively skewed. Such a distribution is known as a Poisson distribution. The normal distribution is often substituted for a binomial distribution to ease the analysis of the data. For a similar reason, a Poisson distribution may be substituted for a binomial distribution. Since many types of biological data follow the distribution generated by a very large n and very small q, the Poisson distribution is of value in biological research.

The general term for the Poisson distribution can be derived from the general term for the binomial distribution:

$$\frac{nPr}{r!}p^{n-r}q^r = \frac{n(n-1)(n-2)\cdots(n-r+1)}{r!}p^{n-r}q^r$$

Now when n becomes very large, the terms $n-r$, $n-1$, $n-2$, etc., for practical purposes, are equal to n. Consequently, the general term can be given as:

$$\frac{n^r}{r!}p^nq^r = \frac{n^rq^r}{r!}p^n = \frac{n^rq^r}{r!}(1-q)^n$$

Since $\mu = nq$ and $q = \mu/n$, the general term can be expressed as:

$$\frac{\mu^r}{r!}\left(1 - \frac{\mu}{n}\right)^n = \frac{\mu^r}{r!}\left(1 - \frac{\mu}{n}\right)^{\frac{n\mu}{\mu}} = \frac{\mu^r}{r!}\left[\left(1 - \frac{\mu}{n}\right)^{\frac{n}{\mu}}\right]^\mu$$

Let $n/\mu = t$ and $n = \mu t$. Now the expression becomes:

$$\frac{\mu^r}{r!}\left[\left(1 - \frac{\mu}{\mu t}\right)^t\right]^\mu = \frac{\mu^r}{r!}\left[\left(1 - \frac{1}{t}\right)^t\right]^\mu$$

Expanding the binomial within the brackets gives:

$$\frac{\mu^r}{r!}\left[1^t - t1^{t-1}\left(\frac{1}{t}\right)^1 + \frac{t(t-1)}{2!}1^{t-2}\left(\frac{1}{t}\right)^2 - \frac{t(t-1)(t-2)}{3!}1^{t-3}\left(\frac{1}{t}\right)^3 \right.$$
$$\left. + \frac{t(t-1)(t-2)(t-3)}{4!}1^{t-4}\left(\frac{1}{t}\right)^4 - \cdots\right]^\mu$$

Since $n = \mu t$, as n becomes a very large number, t also becomes a very large number, so that the terms $t - 1$, $t - 2$, $t - 3$, etc., for practical purposes are all equal to t. The expression now becomes:

$$\frac{\mu^r}{r!}\left[1 - 1 + \frac{1}{2} - \frac{1}{6} + \frac{1}{24} - \cdots\right]^\mu \text{ which equals } \frac{\mu^r}{r!}[0.3678796]^\mu$$

Note that $e^{-1} = \dfrac{1}{e} = \dfrac{1}{2.71828} = 0.3678796$. Thus the expression $\left(1 - \dfrac{1}{t}\right)^t$ has e^{-1} as the limit as t becomes very large. Incorporating this limit into the equation gives the general term for the Poisson distribution:

$$\frac{\mu^r}{r!}[e^{-1}]^\mu = \frac{\mu^r}{r!}e^{-\mu}$$

Since r can take the values $0, 1, 2, 3, \cdots$ etc., the various terms of the Poisson distribution are given by:

$$e^{-\mu}, \ \mu e^{-\mu}, \ \frac{\mu^2}{(2!)}e^{-\mu}, \ \frac{\mu^3}{(3!)}e^{-\mu}, \ \frac{\mu^4}{(4!)}e^{-\mu}, \cdots \text{ or}$$

$$\frac{1}{e^\mu}, \ \frac{\mu}{e^\mu}, \ \frac{\mu^2}{e^\mu(2!)}, \ \frac{\mu^3}{e^\mu(3!)}, \ \frac{\mu^4}{e^\mu(4!)}, \cdots$$

Of interest is the relationship that exists between the mean and variance of a Poisson distribution. The variance of a binomial distribution is:

$$\sigma^2 = npq$$

Since $\mu = nq$, the variance can be given as:

$$\sigma^2 = \mu p$$

Now in the Poisson distribution q is a very small number, and therefore p is nearly equal to 1, since $p + q = 1$. Consequently, in the Poisson distribution, the mean and variance are equal.

$$\sigma^2 = \mu$$

When fitting a group of data to a Poisson distribution, even though n is assumed to be a large number, it is usually unknown and does not enter into the calculations. In fact, in actual practice, the value of n may vary slightly from sample to sample without introducing an error. However, it should be confined within reasonably narrow limits. Since n is required for a binomial distribution, this is one major advantage of the Poisson distribution.

For small values of μ, the Poisson distribution is discontinuous and skewed, but for very large values of μ, the Poisson distribution is normal in form. It was shown in a previous section that the binomial distribution becomes normally distributed when n necomes large. Since $\mu = nq$, it follows that as n increases in value, μ will also increase; and if n is made large enough, the Poisson distribution will become normal in form. In fact, when μ is greater than about 25, a good approximation to the normal distribution occurs.

18.1   Example of the Poisson Distribution

A plant ecologist was studying the density and distribution of a given plant species (species A) in grassland associations. In an area 0.2% of an acre, he took 200 random samples with the aid of an eighteen-inch quadrat. Counts were made of the number of times individual plants of species A occurred in each sample (i.e., 0, 1, 2, 3, 4, etc.). Within the area marked off by the quadrat, there are n "positions" where the plant may occur; n is a large unspecified number. Since species A is not common, the probability (q) is small that a given position will be occupied by this species.

The ecologist wished to determine if species A is occurring at random in the area. If the plants are occurring at random, then it would be expected that the observed data would follow a Poisson distribution.

The following results were obtained:

Table 18.1

Number of plants (species A)	0	1	2	3	4	5 or more
Observed frequency	106	64	24	5	1	0

The first step is to estimate the value of μ. This is done with the aid of a frequency table (see Table 18.2).

$$\bar{x} = \frac{\sum fX}{\sum f} = \frac{131}{200} = 0.655 \text{ plants per sample}$$

Now that an estimate of μ is available, the expected frequency for each class can be obtained. For ease of computation, logarithms are usually employed

Table 18.2

Number of plants (species A) per sample X	Observed Frequency f	fX	fX^2
0	106	0	0
1	64	64	64
2	24	48	96
3	5	15	45
4	1	4	16
5	0	0	0
	$\sum f = 200$	$\sum fX = 131$	$\sum fX^2 = 221$

and the various terms are given as follows, where N is the number of quadrats.

$$\frac{N}{e^\mu}, \ \frac{N}{e^\mu}\left(\frac{\mu}{1}\right), \ \frac{N}{e^\mu}\left(\frac{\mu}{1}\right)\left(\frac{\mu}{2}\right), \ \frac{N}{e^\mu}\left(\frac{\mu}{1}\right)\left(\frac{\mu}{2}\right)\left(\frac{\mu}{3}\right), \cdots$$

The sixth class can be obtained by subtraction:

$$(200) - (103.9 + 68.0 + 22.3 + 4.9 + 0.8) = 0.1$$

The observed and expected frequencies can now be compared by a chi-square test (see Table 18.4).

Grouping the last three classes results in four classes.

$$\chi^2 = \frac{(106 - 103.9)^2}{103.9} + \frac{(64 - 68.0)^2}{68} + \frac{(24 - 22.3)^2}{22.3} + \frac{(6 - 5.8)^2}{5.8} = 0.41$$

One degree of freedom is lost for using 200 as the total, and another is lost for estimating μ. Since there are four classes, this leaves two degrees of freedom. The P value for two degrees of freedom is between 0.80 and 0.90. Thus the hypothesis is accepted that species A is occurring at random in the area.

When fitting data to a Poisson distribution, two degrees of freedom, and no more, may be lost.

Organisms may occur randomly in a given area or may be distributed in a *contagious* or *uniform* (infradispersed) manner. If the presence of one individual at a given position increases the probability that other individuals of the same species will occur close by, then the organism is distributed contagiously.

Table 18.3

Class	Symbol	Calculation		Expected Frequency
1	$\dfrac{N}{e^{\bar{x}}}$	log 200 (log e)($\bar{x}$)	2.3010 <u>−0.2845</u> 2.0165	103.9
2	$\dfrac{N}{e^{\bar{x}}}\ \dfrac{\bar{x}}{1}$	log $\bar{x}$	2.0165 <u>+9.8162 − 10</u> 11.8327 − 10	68.0
3	$\dfrac{N}{e^{\bar{x}}}\ \dfrac{\bar{x}}{1}\ \dfrac{\bar{x}}{2}$	log $\bar{x}$ log 2	1.8327 <u>+9.8162 − 10</u> 11.6489 − 10 <u>−0.3010</u> 1.3479	22.3
4	$\dfrac{N}{e^{\bar{x}}}\ \dfrac{\bar{x}}{1}\ \dfrac{\bar{x}}{2}\ \dfrac{\bar{x}}{3}$	log $\bar{x}$ log 3	1.3479 <u>+9.8162 − 10</u> 11.1641 − 10 <u>−0.4771</u> 0.6870	4.9
5	$\dfrac{N}{e^{\bar{x}}}\ \dfrac{\bar{x}}{1}\ \dfrac{\bar{x}}{2}\ \dfrac{\bar{x}}{3}\ \dfrac{\bar{x}}{4}$	log $\bar{x}$ log 4	0.6870 <u>+9.8162 − 10</u> 10.5032 − 10 <u>−0.6021</u> 9.9011 − 10	0.8

Gregarious animals and immobile organisms developing from eggs or seeds occurring in quantity at a given position are distributed in this manner. There are numerous biological explanations for contagious distributions. If the presence of one individual at a given position decreases the probability that another will occur close by, the distribution is said to be uniform. Animals exhibiting territoriality follow this type of distribution. The same is true of a plant species that will not grow in close proximity to another member of the same species for one or more reasons.

As outlined above, the test for randomness is a matter of determining whether the observed data follow the Poisson distribution. If the chi-square value is nonsignificant, the hypothesis of randomness is accepted. A significant

Table 18.4

Number of Plants per Sample	Observed Frequency	Expected Frequency
0	106	103.9
1	64	68.0
2	24	22.3
3	6 { 5	5.8 { 4.9
4	1	0.8
5 or more	0	0.1
Total	200	200.0

chi-square value indicates that a non-random distribution is present. Information as to whether the distribution is contagious or uniform may often be obtained by dividing the sample variance by the sample mean. The rationale for such a test is illustrated in Figures 18.1, 18.2, and 18.3.

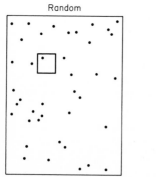

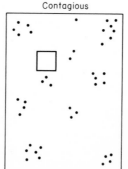

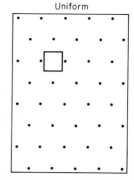

Figure 18.1 Random distribution ($\sigma^2/\mu = 1$).

Figure 18.2 Contagious distribution ($\sigma^2/\mu > 1$).

Figure 18.3 Uniform distribution ($\sigma^2/\mu < 1$).

A random distribution is illustrated by the dots in Figure 18.1. The small square within the figure represents a quadrat. If samples were taken by the quadrat method, the dots would follow the Poisson distribution. For such a distribution $\sigma^2/\mu = 1$. If a contagious distribution is present, as illustrated in Figure 18.2, there would be an excess of quadrats with zero and many organisms, as compared with expected values based on the Poisson distribution. This would result in a large variance; hence the ratio σ^2/μ would be greater than unity. Sampling from an area showing a uniform distribution of organisms (see Figure 18.3), would yield many quadrats with zero or one organism. There would be a deficiency of quadrats with many organisms, resulting, therefore, in a relatively small variance. The ratio σ^2/μ would be less than unity.

The procedure then is to calculate $s^2/\bar{x}$ if the chi-square value is significant. If the value is greater than one, a contagious distribution is present. A value less than one indicates that a uniform distribution is present. The calculations for this test can be illustrated with the data appearing in Table 18.2.

$$\bar{x} = \frac{\sum fX}{\sum f} = \frac{131}{200} = 0.655$$

$$s^2 = \frac{\sum fX^2 - \dfrac{(\sum fX)^2}{\sum f}}{\sum f - 1} = \frac{221 - \dfrac{(131)^2}{200}}{199} = 0.679$$

The ratio $s^2/\bar{x} = 0.679/0.655 = 1.04$ is close to unity as expected since the data follow the Poisson distribution.

Assume that an investigator was interested in the distribution of a given species of snail in a large tide pool. The snails burrow into the mud as the tide goes out. Samples were taken at random by the quadrat method. The quadrat was one square foot in size. The number of quadrats was 418. The observed and expected values are shown in Table 18.5.

Table 18.5

No. of Snails per quadrat X	Observed Frequency f	fX	fX^2	Expected Frequency (Poisson Distribution)
0	305	0	0	277.0
1	75	75	75	114.0
2	22 ⎫	44	88	23.5 ⎫
3	12 ⎪	36	108	3.2 ⎪
4	3 ⎬ 38	12	48	0.3 ⎬ 27.0
5	1 ⎪	5	25	0.0 ⎪
6	0 ⎭	0	0	0.0 ⎭
	$\sum f = 418$	$\sum fX = 172$	$\sum fX^2 = 344$	

$$\bar{x} = \frac{172}{418} = 0.4115 \qquad\qquad s^2 = \frac{344 - \dfrac{(172)^2}{418}}{417} = 0.6572$$

Grouping the terms so that each expected value is greater than five, gives a chi-square value based on three classes.

$$\chi^2 = \frac{(305 - 277.0)^2}{277.0} + \frac{(75 - 114.0)^2}{114.0} + \frac{(38 - 27.0)^2}{27.0} = 20.65$$

With one degree of freedom, the hypothesis that the snails are distributed randomly in the tide pool is rejected ($P < 0.01$). Since the ratio $s^2/\bar{x} = 0.6572/0.4115 = 1.60$, is greater than unity, it is concluded that the snails are distributed contagiously.

Problems

1. The distribution of worms (Eunicidae) was studied in a tide pool by the quadrat method. The quadrat was one square foot. Test the hypothesis that the worms are distributed randomly within the tide pool. What are your conclusions?

Observed number per quadrat	Frequency
0	362
1	370
2	185
3	61
4	15
5	3
6	1
7 or more	0

2. The distribution of bunch grass was studied in an area comprising about 3 acres. The area was divided into plots six feet square. Plots were randomly selected. Test the hypothesis that the individual plants are occurring randomly in the area. What are your conclusions? (See Table at top of page 287 for data.)

3. An inspector took one-pound random samples of wheat seeds from a railroad car. He counted the number of weed seeds per sample.

Observed Number of Plants per Plot	Frequency
0	201
1	204
2	18
3	0
4	0
5	0
6	0

Observed Number of Weed Seeds per Sample	Frequency
0	5
1	14
2	23
3	22
4	17
5	11
6	5
7	2
8	1
9 or more	0

(a) Test the hypothesis that the weed seeds occur randomly in the bulk lot of wheat seeds. (b) If the average number of weed seeds per pound sample is less than 2, the bulk lot will be classified as grade A. Will the bulk receive this grade? (c) Based on available data, what is the probability that a one-pound sample will contain 2 or more weed seeds per pound sample?

CHAPTER NINETEEN

Bioassay

An active field of biological research deals with the assay of drugs, vitamins, sera, and other stimuli. The objective in bioassay work is to estimate what level of stimulus is necessary to bring about a response in a given percentage of individuals in the population. The parameter usually estimated is LD_{50} (median lethal dose) or ED_{50} (median effective dose), or the level of stimulus which will bring about a response in 50 percent of the individuals in the population. This assumes that for genetic or other reasons, variation in response exists among individuals in the population. For any one individual in the population there is a level of stimulus below which response does not occur and above which response does occur.

Assume that an investigator is studying the toxicity of a certain drug, using mice as the test organism. He uses drug doses varying from 0.3 units to 2.4 units. Assume further that the distribution of tolerance doses is normal in form, as shown in Figure 19.1.

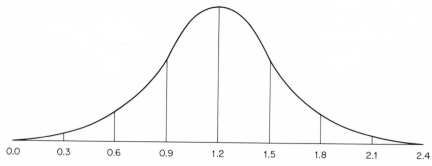

Figure 19.1 Normal distribution of tolerance doses when $LD_{50} = 1.2$ and $\sigma = 0.3$.

In this case the LD_{50} value is 1.2, which means that a dose of 1.2 will kill 50 percent of the mice in the population. The standard deviation of the distribution is 0.3. If dose is plotted against percent killed, the result is a sigmoid curve (see Figure 19.2). This curve can be drawn by referring to the table giving the areas under the normal curve (Table I). A dose of 0.3 units is three standard deviations left of the median; therefore, $c = -3$. For this dose 0.13 percent of the mice will be killed. For a dose of 0.6 units, 2.27 percent of the mice will die, etc.

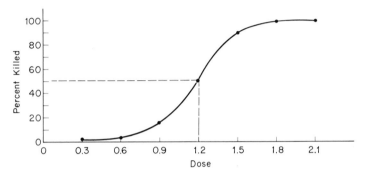

Figure 19.2 Relationship between dose and percent killed when the distribution of tolerance doses is normal ($LD_{50} = 1.2$ and $\sigma = 0.3$).

From such a sigmoid curve the LD_{50} value is read off by determining the value on the X axis for a value of 50% on the Y axis.

Since a curvilinear relationship is cumbersome to work with, a transformation can be made to another scale so that a linear relationship exists between dose and response. One transformation is to convert the percentage values (proportion values) to c values occurring in Table I. However, negative numbers can be a nuisance; therefore, a value of 5 is added to each c value. This is known as the *probit transformation*.

Dose	Percentage	c	Probit ($c + 5$)
0.3	0.13	-3	2
0.6	2.27	-2	3
0.9	15.87	-1	4
1.2	50.00	0	5
1.5	84.13	1	6
1.8	97.73	2	7
2.1	99.87	3	8

The linear relationship between doses and probit values is illustrated in Figure 19.3. The LD_{50} value on the X axis now corresponds to a probit value of 5.0 on the Y axis.

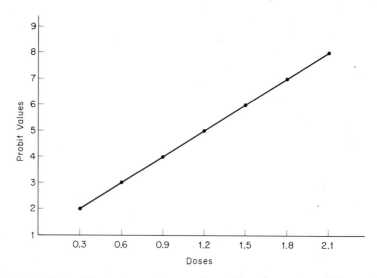

Figure 19.3 Relationship between doses and probit values when $LD_{50} = 1.2$ and $\sigma = 0.3$.

19.1   Estimation of LD_{50} Values

The probit transformation leads to a method of estimating LD_{50} values. A reliable estimate of this parameter would be available if an indefinitely large number of individuals were exposed to each dose of a given drug. The percent that died would be recorded for each dose. The observed percentage values would be transformed to probits and plotted against dose. These points would then be replaced by a regression line and the LD_{50} value read off the graph corresponding to a probit value of 5.0.

However, for practical reasons, the number of animals given each dose cannot be indefinitely large. If insects or other invertebrates are being used as the test organism, the number (n) of animals tested at each dose may be quite large, such as 100 or 50, but when vertebrates are used, such as mice, rats, guinea pigs, or monkeys, the samples are usually much smaller, and may go as low as four animals for each dose. Since the reliability of the estimate is dependent on n, a concerted effort should be made to use as large a number of test animals as feasible.

Reliability is also increased if the investigator is able to bracket the estimate well between the highest and lowest dose, and at the same time use a small interval between doses. The ability to do this usually requires that the investigator has previous knowledge of drug toxicity, or that he employs many doses covering a wide range. Since the latter may not be practical, the investigator may consider carrying out a small pilot study in order to gain information on drug toxicity. This study could then be followed up with a well-designed large study, with the estimate bracketed equidistant between the extreme doses.

A basic assumption in this type of analysis is that the tolerance doses are distributed normally. However, this assumption is not always justified. For example, the tolerance doses may be skewed. If so, the logarithms of the doses will be more normally distributed than the doses. The question as to whether the log transformation is necessary can often be answered by observing the scatter of the points around the regression line, using both doses and log doses. If there is less scatter with the latter, then the transformation is appropriate. In most bioassay work, it is usually routine to use the logarithmic transformation. It should be emphasized, however, that for some drugs and organisms, another type of transformation is more appropriate, but this fact can only be discovered by trial and error.

An example will now be given. The toxicity of a drug was studied using rats as the test organism. Ten rats were exposed to each of the following doses: 1.0, 1.5, 2.0, 2.5, 3.0, 3.5, 4.0, and 4.5 units. Using the logarithmic transformation, the results are given in Table 19.1.

Table 19.1

Dose (Log Scale)	n	Number Alive	Number Dead	Proportion Dead	Probit Value
0.0000	10	10	0	0.00	—
0.1761	10	9	1	0.10	3.72
0.3010	10	8	2	0.20	4.16
0.3979	10	6	4	0.40	4.75
0.4771	10	4	6	0.60	5.25
0.5441	10	3	7	0.70	5.52
0.6021	10	3	7	0.70	5.52
0.6532	10	1	9	0.90	6.28

The probit values can be read from Table IX of Fisher and Yates (1948) or Table I of Finney (1951). There are no probit values for 0 and 100%. The scatter diagram and regression line drawn by eye are shown in Figure 19.4.

Caution must be taken in drawing the regression line. Points for doses near the estimate of the LD_{50} value should be weighted more heavily than those points for low and high doses. When a relationship is represented by a sigmoid curve and the number of organisms exposed to each dose is small,

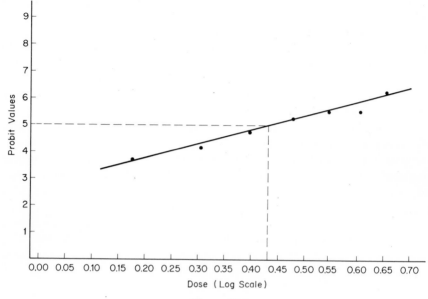

Figure 19.4

a unit increase in dose near the LD_{50} value is more informative, in terms of response, than a unit increase near the LD_{10} or LD_{90} value. This principle is illustrated in Figure 19.5. An increase in dose from 0.3 to 0.6 units or 1.8 to

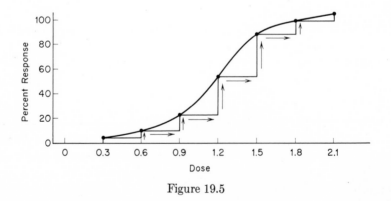

Figure 19.5

2.1 units has little effect on the percent response. However, this is not the case when the dose is increased from 0.9 to 1.2 units or from 1.2 to 1.5 units. Hence, when percentages are converted to probits, greater emphasis should be placed on the responses for middle doses in determining the slope of the regression line, than the responses for the low and high doses. In actual practice the regression line is drawn using mainly the center points in the scatter diagram as a guide. The end points are ignored or else allowed to influence the slope only slightly.

After the regression line is drawn by eye, an estimate of the LD_{50} value can be made graphically. However, this is only an approximate estimate, since the drawing of the regression line is done by eye giving more weight to the center points than the end points. A regression line drawn through the points by one individual may be different than one drawn by another individual; therefore, the estimates would be different. For the graph shown in Figure 19.4, the dose (log scale) corresponding to a probit value of 5.0 is about 0.435. It is a statistic and symbolized by $\overline{LD}_{50}$. This is the estimate of the LD_{50} value.

A regression analysis, as discussed in Chapter 12, assumes, among other things, that each point in the scatter diagram has the same weight and that the variance of the Y values is the same for each value of X. When Y values are in percentage, the variance of the Y values is at a maximum when the mean of the Y values is at 50 percent, and it decreases as the mean tends away from this value because of the limits imposed by 0 and 100%. Obviously, the variance is at a minimum for those X values giving Y values of 0 and 100%. The probit transformation does not make the variances more homogeneous. This fact plus the weighting problem make it apparent that the properties of the regression line encountered in probit analysis cannot be studied using simple linear-regression techniques. Consequently, in order to determine a reliable slope of the probit regression line as well as the standard error of the LD_{50} value, additional steps are necessary. Finney (1951) has given an excellent discussion of the procedures involved in probit analysis. However, since the calculations are extremely time consuming, other investigators have derived simpler methods of obtaining estimates of LD_{50}. The one to be presented here is commonly known as the Reed-Muench method. It is one of the simplest methods for computing an estimate of the LD_{50} value, and for this reason it has appeal. Even though it has been widely used, its originators gave no method for computing a standard error. This was a major defect, since confidence limits could not be calculated. However, this was rectified by Pizzi (1950). Pizzi compared $\overline{LD}_{50}$ values obtained by the Reed-Muench and probit-analysis method for 50 different sets of data and observed that no significant difference occurred among any of the paired $\overline{LD}_{50}$ values. An excellent agreement also occurred for the standard errors obtained by both methods. He concluded that for small samples there is no way to know which is the more efficient, but the Reed-Muench method has the advantage of its extreme simplicity.

19.2 Reed–Muench Method of Estimating LD_{50}

The Reed-Muench method employs, for a given set of data, a procedure of artificially increasing the number of organisms exposed to a given level of a stimulus. It is assumed that any individual responding to a given dose of a drug, would respond to all higher doses. Likewise, it is assumed that any individual not responding to a given dose would not respond to lower doses. This principle is illustrated with the data from Table 19.1. The analysis by the Reed-Muench method is given in Table 19.2. The number dead in the

Table 19.2

(1) Dose (Log Scale)	(2) n	(3) No. Dead	(4) No. Alive	Accumulated		(7) Total	(8) Cumulative % Mortality
				(5) No. Dead	(6) No. Alive		
0.0000	10	0	10	0	44	44	0.00
0.1761	10	1	9	1	34	35	2.86
0.3010	10	2	8	3	25	28	10.71
0.3979	10	4	6	7	17	24	29.17
0.4771	10	6	4	13	11	24	54.17
0.5441	10	7	3	20	7	27	74.07
0.6021	10	7	3	27	4	31	87.10
0.6532	10	9	1	36	1	37	97.30

third column are accumulated (going down) and the results are placed in column 5. The number alive in the fourth column are accumulated (going up); the results are placed in the sixth column. The values in the eighth column are cumulative percent mortality values. They are obtained by dividing the values in column 5 by the total values in column 7 and multiplying by 100.

A comparison of the percentage values in column 8 with the doses (log scale) in column 1 shows that the estimate of LD_{50} lies between 0.3979 and 0.4771. The exact estimate is obtained *by interpolation:*

$$\overline{LD}_{50} = 0.3979 + \frac{20.83}{25.00}(0.0792)$$

$$= 0.4639$$

where 25.00 is the difference between 54.17% and 29.17%, 20.83 is the difference between 50.00% and 29.17%, and 0.0792 is the difference between the doses 0.4771 and 0.3979.

The formula for the standard error of the median response value ($\overline{LD}_{50}$), derived by Pizzi, is

$$S.E. = \sqrt{\frac{0.79\,h\,R}{n}}$$

where 0.79 is a constant, h is the interval between doses, R is the interquartile range, and n is the number of organisms given each dose. When h and n are not constant, the means of these values should be used. The interquartile range is estimated by $\overline{LD}_{75} - \overline{LD}_{25}$. If either point is not bracketed, R can be estimated by $2(\overline{LD}_{50} - \overline{LD}_{25})$ or $2(\overline{LD}_{75} - \overline{LD}_{50})$.

In the above example,

$$\overline{LD}_{75} = 0.5441 + \frac{0.93}{13.03}(0.0580) = 0.5482$$

$$\overline{LD}_{25} = 0.3010 + \frac{14.29}{18.46}(0.0969) = 0.3760$$

$$\bar{R} = 0.5482 - 0.3760 = 0.1722$$

$$n = 10$$

$$h = \frac{0.1761 + 0.1249 + 0.0969 + 0.0792 + 0.0670 + 0.0580 + 0.0511}{7}$$

$$= 0.09331$$

or more simply, $h = $ (highest dose $-$ lowest dose)/No. of intervals $= (0.6532 - 0.0000)/7 = 0.09331$

$$\overline{\text{S.E.}} = \sqrt{\frac{0.79\, h\, \bar{R}}{n}} = \sqrt{\frac{(0.79)(0.09331)(0.1722)}{10}} = 0.035628$$

Assuming a large-sample method, the 95% confidence limits are given by the equation: $LD_{50} = \overline{LD}_{50} \pm 1.96\, \overline{\text{S.E.}}$ These limits become:

$$L_1 = 0.4639 - (1.96)(0.035628) = 0.3941$$

$$L_2 = 0.4639 + (1.96)(0.035628) = 0.5337$$

With the usual limitation, the 95% confidence limits may be used to determine the significance of two or more $\overline{LD}_{50}$ values. If two $\overline{LD}_{50}$ values are to be compared, an approximate test is

$$c = \frac{\overline{LD}_{50_1} - \overline{LD}_{50_2}}{\sqrt{(\text{S.E.}_1)^2 + (\text{S.E.}_2)^2}}$$

This test is only approximate, since it assumes that the samples are large and therefore the standard errors are close to the true values.

The Reed-Muench method is useful in bioassay work because the calculations are minimal when compared with probit analysis, and it does not require the extensive tables or aids of other abbreviated methods. However, when it is used, every effort should be made to bracket the estimate of the median dose value well between the extreme doses. It is also desirable to use a constant number of organisms per dose level and to have an equal interval between doses. The intervals on the log scale can be made equal, if the experiment is designed so the original doses are on the geometric scale, such as 1 unit, 2 units, 4 units, 8 units, 16 units, etc. The logs of these numbers have a constant interval of 0.3010. As outlined above, all the calculations and tests of significance are carried out using the log scale. However, if desired, the presentation of the results could be made on the original scale by taking the antilog of $\overline{LD}_{50}$, L_1, and L_2.

Problems

1. An investigator wished to compare the toxicity of venom from two different species of scorpions. Rats of the same sex, age, and weight were used as the test organism. The rats, which were from an inbred line, were randomly assigned to the two experiments.

Species A			Species B		
Dose (Units of Venom)	n	No. Dead	Dose (Units of Venom)	n	No. Dead
1.0	8	0	1.0	8	0
2.0	8	2	2.0	8	0
4.0	8	5	4.0	8	2
8.0	8	6	8.0	8	3
16.0	8	8	16.0	8	5
32.0	8	8	32.0	8	6
64.0	8	8	64.0	8	7

(a) Convert the doses to log doses and calculate both $\overline{LD}_{50}$ values as well as the 95% confidence limits. Do the limits overlap? (b) Test the hypothesis that no difference exists in the toxicity of the two venoms. What are your conclusions?

2. Different concentrations of an insecticide were applied to batches of *Drosophila melanogaster*.

Dose	n	No. Dead
0.2	100	0
0.4	100	15
0.6	100	35
0.8	100	57
1.0	100	82
1.2	100	91
1.4	100	100
1.6	100	100

Estimate LD_{50} and set the 95% confidence limits.

3. Different concentrations of a different insecticide were applied to batches of *Drosophila melanogaster*.

Dose	n	No. Dead
0.2	100	40
0.4	100	62
0.6	100	85
0.8	100	100
1.0	100	100
1.2	100	100
1.4	100	100
1.6	100	100

(a) Estimate LD_{50} and set the 95% confidence limits. (b) What procedure should be followed if the insecticide were tested again?

4. A drug was tested which caused convulsions in mice.

Dose	n	No. Responding
1.0	10	0
2.0	10	2
4.0	10	4
8.0	10	5
16.0	8	6
32.0	8	7
64.0	8	8

Convert the doses to log doses and estimate the ED_{50} (effective dose). Determine the 95% confidence limits for this parameter.

CHAPTER TWENTY

Non-Parametric Statistics

Assumptions are inherent in tests of significance. For example, among other things, analysis of variance assumes that the measurements are taken from normally distributed populations with homogeneous variances. What procedure should be followed if the investigator knows that a specific assumption is not true, doubts that it is true, or, as is frequently the case, does not know if it is true? Two procedures may be followed. He may transform the original measurements to a different scale so that the assumption in question is more nearly justified, or he may employ a test of significance that does not require the assumption.

An investigator may wish to compare the means of samples of measurements taken from populations distributed in a Poisson manner. Such measurements might consist of small whole numbers with a range perhaps from 0 to 9 or 10. The variance of a Poisson distribution is equal to the mean. Hence, if the sample means are reliable estimates of their respective parameters and a difference exists among these means, then a difference will also exist among the variances. The investigator is therefore dealing with skewed distributions with different variances. An appropriate procedure is to take the square root of each measurement. This transformation will make the means more independent of the variances. When zeros are present, each measurement should be increased by a small constant, such as $\frac{1}{2}$, before the square root is taken. The transformed measurements ($\sqrt{X_i + \frac{1}{2}}$) are then analyzed in a routine manner.

Data that follow the binomial distributions are also frequently encountered in biological research. Examples are proportions and percentages. The mean and variance of a binomial distribution are $\mu = nq$, and $\sigma^2 = npq = \mu p$, respectively. It is apparent from the equation $\sigma^2 = \mu p$ that the variance is a function of the mean. Furthermore, the distributions are skewed when μ is near 0% or 100%. The hypothesis that the means of the populations are equal may be tested by transforming the proportions or percentages to angles. This is known as the arc sine transformation. It is given as follows: angle = arc sin $\sqrt{\text{percentage}}$. Tables are available in several textbooks for this transformation (Snedecor, 1956).

Some data follow neither the Poisson or binomial distribution, but the variance is still a function of the mean. When the standard deviation is proportional to the mean, as shown by the coefficient of variation, a logarithmic transformation makes the variances more homogeneous.

Because an investigator may question the legitimacy of a transformation for his data, he may seek another method of testing the hypothesis that the samples are taken from the same population. He may choose a non-parametric test. Even though an accurate definition is not available, a non-parametric test might be defined as a method of testing a hypothesis with a procedure that may not require the scale of measurement or many of the assumptions of a parametric test.

Parametric tests (group comparison test, pairing design test, analysis of variance) which involve the calculation of t, F, and q are more efficient than non-parametric tests, i.e., parametric tests give a lower probability of making a Type II error. However, as implied above, non-parametric tests have an advantage in some cases, for one or more reasons. (1) Parametric tests have quite rigid assumptions. Whenever an investigator publishes the results of a parametric test, he implies that the assumptions of the test have been fulfilled. However, no test is usually run to determine if they really are true, and it should be remembered that a presumption that the assumptions are true does not make them true. A variety of different types of non-parametric tests exists and each has its own assumptions. Yet, in each case, the assumptions are less stringent than for a corresponding parametric test. For example, an investigator may contemplate using a randomized-block design, but he is suspicious that the random variables are not distributed normally. A corresponding non-parametric test is the Friedman χ_r^2 test. This test does not assume that the populations are normally distributed. (2) Many non-parametric tests are simpler from a computational point of view, especially when the samples are relatively small. (3) A parametric test assumes that the measurements have the "strength" of at least the interval scale. Non-parametric tests are available for measurements that have the strength of less than the interval scale. An appreciation of this last advantage of non-parametric tests requires a discussion on the subject of scales. Assume that an investigator has some plants that he wishes to measure. He may use either a nominal, ordinal, interval, or ratio scale. The strengths of the scales may be ranked in ascending order as follows: nominal < ordinal < interval < ratio. Strength is determined by the communicative properties of the scale and whether the measurements lend themselves to arithmetic manipulation. Examples will now be given.

1. Nominal Scale.

A plant may be measured simply by the words tall or short, using some arbitrary point as the dividing line. When an object or individual is classified by such terms as tall or short, blue eyes or brown eyes, rough or smooth, dead or alive, normal or abnormal, etc., the investigator is using the nominal or classificatory scale. The series of measurements might appear as follows: X_1 = tall, X_2 = short, X_3 = short $\cdots X_n$ = tall. Even though a measurement with the strength of the nominal scale is the only measurement possible in some cases, and therefore most informative, it is nevertheless a "weak" measurement for some situations. The measurement *short* is not as communicative, for example, as the measurement 21.2 inches. Furthermore, the word *short* cannot be used in arithmetic manipulation. There is no meaning to the term *short* divided by two.

2. Ordinal Scale.

More informative measurements for plant height are the terms short, submedium, medium, supramedium, tall, very tall. A plant that is submedium is $>$ short and $<$ medium. By using symbols such as $>$ and $<$, the plants are being ranked, and therefore the investigator is using the ordinal or ranking scale. A series of measurements might appear as X_1 = short, X_2 = very tall, X_3 = submedium $\cdots X_n$ = tall. Although stronger than the nominal scale because it is more communicative, the ordinal scale still exhibits a weakness since a ranking measurement should not be used in arithmetic manipulation.

The ordinal scale is being used whenever the investigator implies greater than, less than, or uses any ranking system, such as 0, 1, 2, 3, 4, 5, 6 and 7, etc. For example, serum dilutions are given as $\frac{1}{2}$, $\frac{1}{4}$, $\frac{1}{8}$, $\frac{1}{16}$, $\frac{1}{32}$, $\frac{1}{64}$, etc. It is clear that for these dilutions a ranking system is being employed. *Parametric tests should not be used for measurements with the strength of only the ordinal scale.*

3. Interval Scale.

If the exact interval between any two measurements is known, then the measurement is stronger than one on the ordinal scale. The plants may be measured using some arbitrary units, such as delta units (ficticious units): X_1 = 34.2, X_2 = 36.4, X_3 = 35.0 $\cdots X_n$ = 32.7. The interval scale is stronger than the ordinal and nominal scales, because the measurements are more communicative and they lend themselves to arithmetic manipulation. For example, the difference between 35.0 units and 70.0 units is more meaningful than the difference between short and tall. The measurements 35.0 units and 70.0 units impart more understanding than the terms short and tall. Furthermore, the term "half of 36.8 delta units" is meaningful, especially when the zero point is known. An interval scale has an arbitrary zero point, just as 32°F is the freezing point when temperature is measured using the Fahrenheit scale.

Many biological measurements are presented as if they have the strength of the interval scale, when in fact they are really no stronger than the ordinal scale.

4. Ratio Scale.

A ratio scale is an interval scale with a true zero point. A scale with a true zero point is a stronger scale than one with an arbitrary zero point because it is more communicative. For example, zero inches may correspond to 10 delta units. Measurements made in inches would be more informative because there is a true zero. A reader can visualize the size of a plant 21 inches tall, but he would have difficulty visualizing the size of a plant 34.6 delta units tall unless he knew that 10 is the arbitrary zero point. Half of 22 inches is more communicative than half of 22 delta units, unless one is thoroughly accustomed to the latter units. Measurements have the strength of the ratio scale when the units are inches, centimeters, pounds, or grams, etc.

If measurements have the strength of at least the interval scale (i.e., interval or ratio) and all the assumptions of the parametric test are true, then the investigator should calculate a t, F, or q value when he wishes to compare sample means. However, if the measurements have the strength of at least the interval scale, but the investigator questions a certain assumption, such as normal distributions or homogeneous variances, then the investigator should test the hypothesis concerning means by making some suitable transformation or using a non-parametric test that does not require that assumption. If the measurements are weaker than interval scaling, a non-parametric test should be used.

Non-parametric statistics are contrasted with parametric statistics, because by definition the interest is not in the estimation of parameters and tests of significance are carried out independently of them. The term non-parametric statistics is often used synonymously with *distribution-free statistics*, which implies that if the test does not assume a specific distribution, then it makes no assumptions about parameters. Many different tests are grouped under the classification of non-parametric or distribution-free; however, in some cases both terms might not be appropriate for a given test. Some tests are designed to determine if distributions differ in any manner, even though not specifying what this manner might be; while others are designed to test for differences in central tendency. The latter may make some assumption about the distribution, such as they are symmetrical or identical (which implies homogeneous variances); hence these tests are not always distribution-free or completely free of assumptions concerning parameters.

Examples of non-parametric tests will be given for measurements on the nominal, ordinal, and interval (or ratio) scale, when the samples are independent and related.

20.1   Contingency Tables (Independent Samples)

A non-parametric test of hypothesis for data on the nominal scale can be carried out with the aid of contingency tables. This type of table is composed of r rows and c columns. The simplest case is a 2×2 contingency table. Individuals are classified and placed in a particular row and column. The hypothesis tested by this method is that rows and columns are independent (i.e., the probability that an individual will fall in any particular row is unaffected by the particular column to which he belongs).

Assume that 25 individuals with blue eyes and 25 with brown eyes were classified as to hair color (light or dark). The hypothesis is that eye color is independent of hair color (i.e., a person with blue eyes is just as likely to have light hair as dark hair). The following 2×2 contingency table summarizes the data.

Table 20.1

	Light Hair	Dark Hair	Total
Blue Eyes	20	5	25
Brown Eyes	7	18	25
Total	27	23	50

The data in the table suggest there is a tendency for blue-eyed individuals to have light hair and for brown-eyed individuals to have dark hair. To test the hypothesis it is necessary to find expected frequencies (symbolized by E_{ij}) for the four cells or classes on the assumption that independence is present. These expected frequencies in the cells are proportional to both sets of marginal totals. *They are not based on parameters.* For example, the expected value in the first row and first column is obtained by:

$$E_{11} = \frac{25 \times 27}{50} = 13.5$$

which comes from the expression:

$$\frac{E_{11}}{27} = \frac{25}{50}$$

The expected frequencies for the other three cells can be obtained in a similar way. However, since the marginal totals are given, it is only necessary to calculate the expected frequency for one cell in a 2×2 table; the others can be obtained by subtraction. In the following table the expected frequencies are given in parentheses:

Table 20.2

	Light Hair	Dark Hair	Total
Blue Eyes	20 (13.5)	5 (11.5)	25
Brown Eyes	7 (13.5)	18 (11.5)	25
Total	27	23	50

The hypothesis is tested by calculating chi square:

$$\chi^2 = \sum \frac{(X_{ij} - E_{ij})^2}{E_{ij}}$$

$$\chi^2 = \frac{(20 - 13.5)^2}{13.5} + \frac{(5 - 11.5)^2}{11.5} + \frac{(7 - 13.5)^2}{13.5} + \frac{(18 - 11.5)^2}{11.5} = 13.61$$

Even though these are four classes in a 2×2 table, there is only one degree of freedom. Since the marginal totals are given, only one class is independent. In any contingency table with r rows and c columns, the number of degrees of freedom available for the test is given by:

$$\text{D.F.} = (r - 1)(c - 1)$$

For one degree of freedom, the P value is less than 0.01; therefore, the hypothesis is rejected. Since there is only one degree of freedom, some authors recommend the use of Yates correction for continuity for small samples. Each deviation is reduced (towards zero) by 0.5, before it is squared.

20.2   Further Examples of the Use of Contingency Tables

A plant physiologist carried out germination experiments on three different species of desert shrubs in the presence of 0.2% salt solution. One-hundred seeds of each type were tested. The hypothesis is that the frequency of germination is similar in all three species (see Table 20.3).

$$\chi^2 = \frac{(3)^2}{84} + \frac{(3)^2}{16} + \frac{(1)^2}{84} + \frac{(1)^2}{16} + \frac{(2)^2}{84} + \frac{(2)^2}{16} = 1.04$$

There are six cells, but only two can be filled-in arbitrarily, so there are only two degrees of freedom.

$$\text{D.F.} = (3 - 1)(2 - 1) = 2$$

The P value is between 0.50 and 0.70, so the hypothesis is accepted.

Table 20.3

Species	Number Germinated	Number Not Germinated	Total
A	87 (84)	13 (16)	100
B	83 (84)	17 (16)	100
C	82 (84)	18 (16)	100
Total	252	48	300

A radiologist was studying the effect of radiation on transplanted tumors in mice. A highly malignant neuroblastoma was transplanted to the eyes of 100 mice belonging to strain *DBA*. Fifty of the mice were given radiation treatment beginning three weeks after the transplantation had been made. The other 50 mice were not given radiation treatment. After 70 days the number of mice were counted in each group that were still alive. The hypothesis to be tested is that the radiation is ineffective.

Table 20.4

	Alive	Dead	Total
X-Ray Treatment	41 (23.5)	9 (26.5)	50
No X-Ray Treatment	6 (23.5)	44 (26.5)	50
Total	47	53	100

$$\chi^2 = \frac{(17.5)^2}{23.5} + \frac{(17.5)^2}{26.5} + \frac{(17.5)^2}{23.5} + \frac{(17.5)^2}{26.5} = 49.18$$

For one degree of freedom, it is clear that the hypothesis should be rejected $(P < 0.01)$.

A test of independence involving a 2×2 contingency table may be carried out by using the general formula:

$$\chi^2 = \sum \frac{(X_{ij} - E_{ij})^2}{E_{ij}}$$

or by a working formula which makes the computations somewhat easier, especially if a calculator is available. A 2×2 table consists of 4 cells:

Totals

a	b	$a + b$
c	d	$c + d$

Totals $a + c$ $b + d$ n

The working formula is:

$$\chi^2 = \frac{n(ad - bc)^2}{(a + b)(c + d)(a + c)(b + d)}$$

A test of homogeneity is also appropriate when an investigator wishes to pool the results of a series of $r \times c$ contingency tests. For example, an investigator studied the effects of cortisone treatment in conjunction with X-ray treatment on transplanted tumors in mice. A highly malignant tumor was transplanted to each of a group of mice from the same inbred strain. Half the mice (picked at random) were given injections of 1.0 mg. of cortisone (following adrenalectomy) and were treated with X-rays. The other half, used as controls, were given X-ray treatment only. After 70 days, each mouse was scored as dead or alive. The hypothesis was that cortisone treatment is ineffective (i.e., the rapidity with which death occurs is independent of cortisone treatment). Since the number of mice available at one time was limited, it was necessary for the investigator to replicate the experiment at three different times in order to increase the number of animals tested. He wished to pool the results of the three different experiments if they showed consistent (homogeneous) results. This would give a chi-square value based on an increased number of mice.

Experiment 1

Alive Dead Total

	Alive	Dead	Total
Treatment	15	10	25
Control	8	16	24
Total	23	26	49

$$\chi^2 = \frac{49[(15)(16) - (10)(8)]^2}{(25)(24)(23)(26)} = 3.51$$

Experiment 2

	Alive	Dead	Total
Treatment	15	8	23
Control	12	13	25
Total	27	21	48

$$\chi^2 = \frac{48[(15)(13) - (8)(12)]^2}{(23)(25)(27)(21)} = 1.44$$

Experiment 3

	Alive	Dead	Total
Treatment	17	8	25
Control	12	13	25
Total	29	21	50

$$\chi^2 = \frac{50[(17)(13) - (8)(12)]^2}{(25)(25)(29)(21)} = 2.05$$

Pooled

	Alive	Dead	Total
Treatment	47	26	73
Control	32	42	74
Total	79	68	147

$$\chi^2 = \frac{147[(47)(42) - (26)(32)]^2}{(73)(74)(79)(68)} = 6.66$$

The data may now be summarized as in Table 20.5.

Pooling is permissible, as shown by the homogeneity chi-square value. On the basis of the pooled data, the hypothesis is rejected. It is concluded that cortisone treatment is effective in prolonging the life of the mice.

The contingency-table method of testing hypotheses may be used for measurements with the strength of the nominal or ordinal scale. It assumes that the observed values in any cell are normally distributed. Therefore, if an expected value is close to zero, the distribution is skewed and this assumption is violated. An expected value should not be less than 5, and preferably, not

Table 20.5

	Treatment Group Alive Dead	Control Group Alive Dead	χ^2	D.F.	P.
Experiment 1	15 10	8 16	3.51	1	0.10 − 0.05
Experiment 2	15 8	12 13	1.44	1	0.30 − 0.20
Experiment 3	17 8	12 13	2.05	1	0.20 − 0.10
	Sum of three chi square values		7.00	3	
Pooled	47 26	32 42	6.66	1	0.01 − 0.0001
	Homogeneity		0.34	2	0.90 − 0.80

less than 10. Fisher (see Siegel, 1956) has given the procedure for carrying out a test of significance when expected values of less than 5 occur in a 2 × 2 contingency table.

20.3 Kruskal-Wallis *H* Test

Both the group comparison test and completely randomized design assume that the random variables are distributed normally and have homogeneous variances. The Kruskal–Wallis *H* test is a non-parametric counterpart of these parametric tests and may be used in place of them when the investigator does not want to make certain assumptions inherent in the parametric tests, or the measurements have the strength of only the ordinal scale. The hypothesis states that the *k* samples are taken from *identical continuous populations*. In theory, the hypothesis may be rejected if the populations differ in any form, but since the test is insensitive to differences in variability, it may be used to test the hypothesis the populations have the same central tendency (such as medians) without assuming homogeneous variances. The Kruskal–Wallis *H* test does not assume that the populations are normally distributed. For these reasons it is a valuable tool in biological research for comparing central tendencies. Two numerical examples will be given.

A geneticist compared the productivity, as measured by the number of offspring produced, of Drosophila females from two different laboratory strains. Twenty-four females from strain *A* and 22 females from strain *B* were placed singly in vials with 5 males. They were allowed to lay eggs for seven days. The measurement recorded was the number of offspring produced.

The investigator did not know if the measurements were distributed normally or if the variances were homogeneous. For these reasons the investigator chose the non-parametric Kruskal–Wallis H test.

The original measurements appear in columns 1 and 3 of Table 20.6. These measurements are ranked in magnitude array for easy manipulation.

Table 20.6

Strain A	Rank	Strain B	Rank
70	17.5	36	1
72	20	37	2
74	21	38	3
79	25	40	4.5
83	27	40	4.5
84	28	44	6
87	29.5	46	7
87	29.5	51	8
91	31	53	9
92	32	54	10
93	33	59	11
94	34	61	12
96	35	62	14
98	36	62	14
99	37	62	14
102	38	69	16
105	39	70	17.5
108	40	71	19
112	41	75	22
114	42	76	23
116	43	79	25
120	44	79	25
121	45		
130	46		
Median = 95	n_1 = 24 R_1 = 813.5	Median = 60	n_2 = 22 R_2 = 267.5

The measurements in both samples are transformed to ranks (columns 2 and 4 in Table 20.6). If all 46 measurements had different values, each measurement would be transformed to an integer from 1 to 46. The smallest measurement in either sample would be given the rank of 1 and the largest the rank of 46. The smallest measurement occurs in sample B; it is ranked 1. The second and third measurements are also in sample B, and are given the ranks of 2 and 3. Measurements 4 and 5 in sample B have the same value of 40. When the same measurement occurs in one or both samples, the procedure is to transform each to the mean of the ranks, which in this case is 4.5. Similarly, the 13th, 14th, and 15th measurements in sample B have the same value of 62. Each is assigned the rank of 14, or the mean of 13, 14, and 15. Special care must be taken when the same measurement occurs in both samples, as the measurement 70 in this example. This measurement would appear in the 17th and 18th positions if the measurements from both samples were placed in magnitude array; therefore, it is transformed to 17.5 in each sample.

After ranking is completed, R_1 and R_2 are obtained, where R_1 is the sum of the n_1 ranks and R_2 is the sum of the n_2 ranks.

The general formula for H is

$$H = \frac{12}{T(T+1)} \sum_1^k \frac{R_i^2}{n_i} - 3(T+1)$$

where k = number of samples, T = total number of measurements in all k samples, n_i = number of measurements in the ith sample, and R_i = sum of the ranks for the ith sample.

Substituting the values from Table 20.6 into the equation gives:

$$H = \frac{(12)}{(46)(47)}\left[\frac{(813.5)^2}{24} + \frac{(267.5)^2}{22}\right] - 3(47)$$
$$= 30.1$$

The sampling distribution of H values is approximately equal to a chi-square distribution with $k - 1$ degrees of freedom. From Table VII for one degree of freedom, it is observed that $P < 0.01$. The hypothesis is rejected that the two populations have the same central tendency.

A correction may be made in the H value when measurements occur with the same value. This is known as the correction for ties. In this example there were:

2 measurements of 40

3 measurements of 62

2 measurements of 70

3 measurements of 79

2 measurements of 87

If m is the number of measurements with the same value, then the m values become 2, 3, 2, 3, and 2. The procedure is to calculate $m^3 - m$ for each value of m. These terms are then summed.

$$S = \sum (m_i^3 - m_i) = (2^3 - 2) + (3^3 - 3) + (2^3 - 2) + (3^3 - 3) + (2^3 - 2)$$
$$= 66$$

The correction factor (C.F.) is

$$\text{C.F.} = 1 - \frac{S}{T^3 - T} = 1 - \frac{66}{97290} = 0.9993$$

Dividing H by this correction factor gives a corrected H value.

$$\text{Corrected } H = \frac{H}{\text{C.F.}} = \frac{30.1}{0.9993} = 30.12$$

When the number of ties is small, as in this case, there is little difference between the H value and corrected H value. Furthermore, the corrected H value will always be larger than the H value. Therefore, in actual practice, the corrected H value is not calculated if the hypothesis is rejected with the H value.

The sampling distribution of H only approximates a chi-square sampling distribution when each sample is larger than about 5. If n_i is less than 5 in each case, special tables can be used to obtain the probability value (Kruskal and Wallis, 1952).

The second example will now be given. Assume that an immunologist studied antibody levels in rabbits immunized by three different methods. Even though the number of antibody molecules varies from individual to individual in a continuous manner, the method of measuring antibody level is by the dilution method. Hence, the observed measurements fall into discrete categories even though there is an underlying continuity. Dilution measurements have the strength of only the ordinal scale. For this reason the immunologist tested the hypothesis that the dilution samples are taken from the same population with the aid of the Kruskal–Wallis H test.

Eighteen rabbits were available for the study. They were divided randomly in three groups. The rabbits in each group were immunized by a different method. The dilution measurements and ranks appear in Table 20.7.

$$H = \frac{12}{T(T + 1)} \sum_{1}^{k} \frac{R_i^2}{n_i} - 3(T + 1)$$

where k = number of samples = 3; T = total number of measurements in all k samples = 18; n = number of measurements in each sample = 6; and

Table 20.7

Method 1		Method 2		Method 3	
Dilutions	Rank	Dilutions	Rank	Dilutions	Rank
$\frac{1}{4}$	2.5	$\frac{1}{16}$	7	$\frac{1}{32}$	11.5
$\frac{1}{4}$	2.5	$\frac{1}{32}$	11.5	$\frac{1}{32}$	11.5
$\frac{1}{16}$	7	$\frac{1}{16}$	7	$\frac{1}{64}$	15
$\frac{1}{2}$	1	$\frac{1}{64}$	15	$\frac{1}{128}$	17
$\frac{1}{8}$	4	$\frac{1}{32}$	11.5	$\frac{1}{256}$	18
$\frac{1}{16}$	7	$\frac{1}{16}$	7	$\frac{1}{64}$	15
$R_1 = 24$		$R_2 = 59$		$R_3 = 88$	

R_i = sum of the ranks in the ith sample = $R_1 = 24$, $R_2 = 59$, and $R_3 = 88$
Substituting these values into the equation gives

$$H = \frac{12}{(18)(19)}\left[\frac{(24)^2}{6} + \frac{(59)^2}{6} + \frac{(88)^2}{6}\right] - 3(19)$$

$$= 12.01$$

Degrees of freedom = $k - 1 = 2$; $P < 0.01$. The null hypothesis is rejected. Since the hypothesis is rejected, there is no need to correct the H value for ties.

20.4   Chi-Square Test for Related Samples

The contingency-table method of analyzing independent samples was outlined in a previous section when the measurements have the strength of only the nominal scale. Measurements placed in a 2×2 table require a different method of analysis if the samples are not independent, i.e., the design of the experiment is a before-and-after type, an individual serves as his own control, or two treatments are given to one individual.

Assume that arthritic patients were given experimental drugs 1 and 2. The hypothesis states that no difference exists between these drugs in regard to the relief of the symptoms of the disorder. A patient is given drug 1. Several months later the same patient is given drug 2. If the symptoms are relieved by either drug, a plus score is recorded. If no relief occurs, a minus score is recorded. Several months elapsed between treatments. It was known that no carry-over effect is present, i.e., response to drug 1 has no effect on response to drug 2. The results are summarized in the following 2 × 2 table:

Drug 2

		−	+
Drug 1	+	Cell A 22	Cell B 10
	−	Cell C 9	Cell D 48

Twenty-two patients responded to drug 1 but not to drug 2; nine responded to neither drug, etc. Only the cells A and D contribute information leading to the acceptance or rejection of the hypothesis. If a patient responds to both drugs, or neither, no decision can be made as to which drug is more effective. Cells B and C are ignored for this test.

The expected values in cells A and D come from $(A + D)/2 = (22 + 48/2 = 35$. A chi-square value is then calculated as follows:

$$\chi^2 = \frac{(22 - 35)^2}{35} + \frac{(48 - 35)^2}{35} = \frac{(13)^2}{35} + \frac{(13)^2}{35} = 9.66$$

There are two classes and one degree of freedom. From Table VII it is observed that $P < 0.01$. The hypothesis is rejected. It is concluded that drug 2 helps more patients than drug 1. Yates correction for continuity can be used, since there is only one degree of freedom. Each deviation is reduced towards zero by 0.5 units.

Note that for this test a parameter of $\frac{1}{2}$ is implied. The population consists of an indefinitely large number of individuals who respond to drug 1 or drug 2. The null hypothesis states that $p = \frac{1}{2}$, i.e., half respond to drug 1. Since a parameter is implied, this test may technically be removed from among the list of non-parametric tests. However, it is presented in this chapter because of its relationship with the 2 × 2 contingency test for independent samples.

20.5 Wilcoxon Signed Rank Test

The parametric pairing design test assumes that the measurements have the strength of at least the interval scale, and the sample of differences is taken from a normally distributed population. One non-parametric counterpart of this test is the Wilcoxon signed rank test. This test may be used when the measurements have an underlying continuity and the strength of only the ordinal scale. It makes no assumption about the normality of the population differences.

The Wilcoxon signed rank test will be illustrated with data for two different strains of wheat grown at eleven different experimental stations. Covariance exists between the paired measurements. The measurement recorded was bushels of wheat per plot (see Table 20.8).

Table 20.8

Station	Strain 1	Strain 2	d_i	Rank of d_i	Rank with less frequent sign
1	21.4	20.2	+1.2	4.0	
2	13.4	12.1	+1.3	5.0	
3	19.8	16.2	+3.6	7.0	
4	36.4	31.5	+4.9	8.5	
5	22.1	22.4	−0.3	−1.5	1.5
6	14.9	14.9	0.0	—	
7	40.9	37.7	+3.2	6.0	
8	10.2	11.0	−0.8	−3.0	3.0
9	26.1	21.2	+4.9	8.5	
10	41.5	35.5	+6.0	10.0	
11	14.3	14.0	+0.3	1.5	
					$T = 4.5$

As in the pairing design test, differences (d_i) are obtained between the paired measurements. The differences are than ranked *ignoring* the sign of the differences. Only the absolute value is considered. A difference of zero will occur only if the paired measurements have the same value. Such paired measurements are dropped from the analysis. In this example there was one difference of zero (station 6). Therefore, even though the study was carried out at 11 experimental stations, the number of differences becomes $n = 10$. After the differences are ranked, the sign of the difference is then assigned to the rank. It is then noted which sign appears less frequently. The ranks with this sign are then summed. This sum is symbolized by T. In Table 20.8, $T = 4.5$.

When n is between 5 and 25, a special table is available that allows the investigator to reject or accept the hypothesis by observation (see Table VIII). For these data ($n = 10$), P is slightly less than 0.02 for a two-tailed test. When n is over 25, the sampling distribution of T is approximately normal in form with the following mean and variance.

$$\mu_T = \frac{n(n + 1)}{4}$$

$$\sigma_T^2 = \frac{n(n + 1)(2n + 1)}{24}$$

A c value may be calculated with the equation:

$$c = \frac{T - \dfrac{n(n + 1)}{4}}{\sqrt{\dfrac{n(n + 1)(2n + 1)}{24}}}$$

Substituting the data from Table 20.8 into this equation gives:

$$c = \frac{4.5 - \dfrac{(10)(11)}{4}}{\sqrt{\dfrac{(10)(11)(21)}{24}}} = 2.34$$

From Table II, it is observed that P is, again, slightly less than 0.02, which shows how well the sampling distribution of T approximates a normal distribution for even a relatively small value of n.

20.6   Friedman χ_r^2 Test

The parametric randomized-block design assumes that each measurement (X_{ij}) in a cell is a random variable selected from a normally distributed population. It assumes further that the measurements have the strength of the interval scale. A non-parametric counterpart of this test is the Friedman χ_r^2 test. It only requires ordinal scaling and makes no assumption about normality. The null hypothesis tested is that measurements in each block (row) are from the same population. Even though this implies that the underlying populations for each block have the same form, no such assumption is necessary for the populations underlying the different blocks.

When compared with the randomized-block design, the calculations for the Friedman χ_r^2 test are exceedingly simple. The procedure is to rank the measurements in the blocks, sum the ranks in each column, and then calculate

$$\chi_r^2 = \frac{12}{nk(k + 1)} \sum_1^k (R_i)^2 - 3n(k + 1)$$

where k = number of treatments (columns), n = number of blocks (rows), and R_i = sum of the ranks in the ith column.

When the number of blocks (rows) is reasonably large, the sampling distribution of χ_r^2 follows a chi-square distribution with $k - 1$ degrees of freedom. When $k = 2$, and n is not too large, the Wilcoxon signed rank test is preferred over the Friedman χ_r^2 test because it is more efficient. However, when $k > 2$, the Friedman χ_r^2 is an appropriate test. Tables have been published (see Siegel, 1956) for obtaining probability values when k equals 3 and 4 and n is as small as 2.

The Friedman χ_r^2 test will be illustrated with the data from Table 9.1 (Chapter 9). The measurements plus the ranks are given in Table 20.9.

Table 20.9

Block	Subspecies A (Rank)	Subspecies B (Rank)	Subspecies C (Rank)	Subspecies D (Rank)
1	1.28 (1)	1.41 (3)	1.40 (2)	1.43 (4)
2	1.43 (1)	1.62 (3)	1.56 (2)	1.69 (4)
3	1.29 (1)	1.49 (4)	1.43 (3)	1.42 (2)
4	1.43 (1)	1.68 (4)	1.59 (2)	1.62 (3)
5	1.26 (1)	1.40 (2)	1.46 (3)	1.47 (4)
6	1.39 (1)	1.56 (2.5)	1.58 (4)	1.56 (2.5)
7	1.31 (1)	1.55 (4)	1.47 (2.5)	1.47 (2.5)
8	1.37 (1)	1.60 (4)	1.51 (2.5)	1.51 (2.5)
9	1.38 (1)	1.54 (3)	1.44 (2)	1.58 (4)
10	1.27 (1)	1.44 (3.5)	1.42 (2)	1.44 (3.5)
	$R_1 = 10$	$R_2 = 33$	$R_3 = 25$	$R_4 = 32$

χ_r^2 is now calculated as follows:

$$\chi_r^2 = \frac{12}{(10)(4)(5)}[(10)^2 + (33)^2 + (25)^2 + (32)^2] - 3(10)(5)$$

$$= 20.28$$

For $k - 1 = 3$ degrees of freedom, it is observed from Table VII that $P < 0.01$.

20.7   The Spearman Rank-Correlation Coefficient

The interclass-correlation coefficient assumes at least interval scaling for the measurements and that the measurements are from a bivariate normal population, i.e., for a given value of X, the Y measurements are normally distributed, and for a given value of Y, the X measurements are normally distributed. If either assumption is not valid, then the non-parametric Spearman rank-correlation coefficient, symbolized by r_s, is a useful statistic for measuring the degree of relationship between paired variables.

The calculations are minimal for obtaining this statistic. The paired measurements are ranked columnwise, and then the differences are obtained between the ranks appearing in each row. The deviations are squared, and the sum of the squared deviations is then obtained. An example is given in Table 20.10, for $n = 11$ paired measurements.

Table 20.10

Pairs	X_i (Rank)	Y_i (Rank)	d_i	d_i^2
1	21 (6)	20 (6.5)	−0.5	0.25
2	14 (3)	12 (2.5)	+0.5	0.25
3	19 (5)	16 (5)	0	0
4	36 (9)	31 (9)	0	0
5	26 (7.5)	22 (8)	−0.5	0.25
6	14 (3)	14 (4)	−1	1
7	40 (10.5)	37 (11)	−0.5	0.25
8	10 (1)	11 (1)	0	0
9	26 (7.5)	20 (6.5)	+1	1
10	40 (10.5)	35 (10)	+0.5	0.25
11	14 (3)	12 (2.5)	+0.5	0.25
				$\sum d_i^2 = 3.5$

When there are no ties, or the proportion of ties is small, r_s is calculated from the equation:

$$r_s = 1 - \frac{6 \sum d_i^2}{n^3 - n}$$

$$= 1 - \frac{6(3.5)}{(11)^3 - 11}$$

$$= 0.9841$$

The correction factor for ties is

$$T = \frac{m^3 - m}{12}$$

where m is the number of measurements with the same value. For the X variables, there are

3 measurements of 14

2 measurements of 26

2 measurements of 40

The correction for ties among the X variables is

$$\sum T_X = \frac{3^3 - 3}{12} + \frac{2^3 - 2}{12} + \frac{2^3 - 2}{12} = 3$$

For the Y variables, there are

2 measurements of 12

2 measurements of 20

Therefore

$$\sum T_Y = \frac{2^3 - 2}{12} + \frac{2^3 - 2}{12} = 1.0$$

The following terms are now obtained:

(1) $\sum x^2 = \dfrac{n^3 - n}{12} - \sum T_X$

$$= \frac{(11)^3 - 11}{12} - 3 = 107$$

(2) $\sum y^2 = \dfrac{n^3 - n}{12} - \sum T_Y$

$$= \frac{(11)^3 - 11}{12} - 1.0 = 109$$

The Spearman rank-correlation coefficient may be calculated from the equation:

$$r_s = \frac{\sum x^2 + \sum y^2 - \sum d^2}{2\sqrt{(\sum x^2)(\sum y^2)}}$$

$$= \frac{107 + 109 - 3.5}{2\sqrt{(107)(109)}}$$

$$= 0.9838$$

The correction for ties decreased the value of the coefficient only slightly in this case. When the proportion of ties is large in either the X or Y variables, the correction should be employed.

When n is about 10 or larger, the significance of the Spearman rank-correlation coefficient is determined from the equation:

$$t = r_s \frac{n - 2}{\sqrt{1 - r_s^2}}$$

$$= 0.9838 \frac{11 - 2}{\sqrt{1 - (0.9838)^2}}$$

$$= 49.45$$

For $n - 2 = 9$ degrees of freedom, $P < 0.01$. Therefore, r_s deviates significantly from zero. The probability value can be obtained from a table when $n < 10$ (see Siegel, 1956).

20.8   Other Non-Parametric Tests

Non-parametric tests are important tools for the research biologist. The terminology associated with these tests will constitute an even greater part of the biologist's vocabulary in future years as more biologists become aware of the appropriateness of these tests for much of the data they obtain.

In this chapter, only a small sample of the available non-parametric tests has been presented. Biologists engaged in the collection of quantitative data should become aware of the usefulness of other non-parametric tests such as Kolmogorov–Smirnov one-sample and two-sample tests, the sign test, the one-sample-run test, the Mann–Whitney U test, and the Kendall rank-correlation coefficient (see Siegel, 1956).

Problems

1. Several investigators in three different hospitals wished to compare the effects of two different drugs on patients with arthritis. The null hypothesis is that there is no difference in the treatments. Each patient was given drug 1, and at a later date, drug 2. It was known there was no carry-over effect of the drugs, i.e., response or no response to drug 1 had no influence on response or no response to drug 2. The data from each hospital are given in the table at the top of page 319. Response (relief from pain) is given by +. No response is given by −.
(a) Compute a χ^2 value for each subsample. What are your conclusions on the basis of each subsample? (b) Fill out an analysis-of-chi-square table with the following

Hospital 1

Treatment 2

	−	+
+	22	10
−	9	48

Treatment 1

Hospital 2

Treatment 2

	−	+
+	26	7
−	10	59

Treatment 1

Hospital 3

Treatment 2

	−	+
+	14	3
−	3	30

Treatment 1

sources of variation: Total, Pooled, and Homogeneity. Was it permissible to pool subsamples? (c) What are your final conclusions concerning the hypothesis?

2. A geneticist compared the frequency of aspermia in two different strains of Drosophila. One-hundred males from each strain were dissected. The testes were squashed and an examination was made for motile sperm. Test the hypothesis that the samples were taken from the same population.

	Sperm Present	Aspermic
Strain 1	72	28
Strain 2	99	1

3. Refer to the data in Table 7.6 (Chapter 6). Test the hypothesis that the samples were taken from the same population using the Kruskal–Wallis H test.

4. The following paired measurements were obtained (see chapter 6). Positive covariance is present. Test the hypothesis that the samples came from the same population using the Wilcoxon signed rank test and the Friedman χ_r^2 test. Compare the results obtained by the two non-parametric tests and the pairing design test.

Sample 1	Sample 2
21.4	17.6
20.9	15.0
23.2	21.7
19.8	18.1
23.1	21.5
18.9	13.6
25.6	24.7
28.7	27.9
26.2	25.2
22.7	19.1
37.0	33.9
31.5	25.3

5. Refer to the measurements occurring in Table 14.1 (Chapter 14). Test the hypothesis that no relationship exists between the paired measurements by using the Spearman rank-correlation coefficient. Compare your results with those obtained by using the interclass-correlation coefficient.

6. By using a paper-chromotography technique, a geneticist studied the concentration of sepiapteridines in the eyes of two different strains of *Drosophila melanogaster*. Heads of males were removed and squashed on paper. The concentration was determined quantitatively by a fluorometric method.

(a) Is the investigator dealing with a nominal, ordinal, interval, or ratio scale? (b) Since the investigator did not known if the population measurements were normally distributed or if the population variances were equal, he decided to use the Kruskal–Wallis H test. State and discuss the assumptions of this test. The data are as follows:

Strain A		Strain B	
40.1	46.8	55.8	59.1
48.4	39.6	64.2	61.9
44.5	46.4	60.4	63.2
41.0	40.0	57.8	59.1
41.2	46.2	60.0	64.3

Calculate H. Determine P. What are your conclusions?

7. An investigator immunized 10 rabbits to a given species of bacteria. He then obtained the antibody titre for each rabbit by the usual dilution method. The spleen of each rabbit was removed. Another determination was then made. Test the hypothesis that splenectomy has no influence on antibody titre.

| | Splenectomy | |
Rabbit	Before	After
1	1/1024	1/256
2	1/256	1/128
3	1/2048	1/1024
4	1/2048	1/512
5	1/512	1/256
6	1/2048	1/1024
7	1/256	1/64
8	1/1024	1/512
9	1/4096	1/2048
10	1/64	1/16

(a) What test should be used? What are your conclusions?

8. Members of species A of the Desert Pup fish are characterized by a complete ventral lateral stripe (belly stripe). Members of species B lack this stripe. Variation exists in "hybridizing" populations. The population consists of individuals with no stripes, various degrees of broken stripes, and complete stripes. Assume that an investigator studied populations in two different geographical areas. An arbitrary scoring procedure was devised, ranging from 0 (no stripe) to 6 (complete stripe). The score a fish received depended on the completeness of the stripe. Each fish collected was compared with "type" fish which were representative of the 7 possible scores. (Note: In many cases, the "score" was only approximate). The scores, ranked in magnitude array, are below.

Sample 1 (Belly-Stripe Score)	Sample 2 (Belly-Stripe Score)
0	2
0	3
0	3
1	3
1	3
1	4
1	4
1	4
2	4
2	4
2	4
2	5
2	5
2	5
2	5
2	5
3	6
3	6
3	6
3	6
3	
3	
4	
4	
5	

(a) Do the measurements have the strength of the nominal, ordinal, interval, or ratio scale? (b) Test the hypothesis that the samples came from populations with the same central tendency (correct for ties). What is your conclusion?

9. The fish from another population were scored as above. The relative length of the caudal fin was also determined.

Specimen	Belly-Stripe Score	Length of Caudal Fin (% of body length)
1	6	32.0
2	3	28.2
3	5	30.5
4	0	27.3
5	4	29.8
6	3	28.1
7	4	29.2
8	2	27.9
9	3	29.0
10	4	28.9
11	3	28.2
12	1	27.3
13	2	28.4
14	4	29.2

The investigator wishes to test the hypothesis that no relationship exists between these "sets of measurements."

(a) Is he entitled to calculate an interclass-correlation coefficient? Why? (b) Calculate the appropriate correlation coefficient (correct for ties) and test the hypothesis that it does not deviate significantly from zero. What is your conclusion?

10. An investigator tested two different scorpion traps. He wished to determine which was the better trap. They were placed side-by-side in 16 different areas. The measurement recorded was the number of scorpions falling into each trap over a 10-hour (night) period.

Area	Trap 1	Trap 2
1	6	4
2	0	1
3	9	3
4	5	1
5	7	4
6	10	2
7	2	0
8	6	6
9	0	0
10	1	0
11	5	4
12	2	0
13	6	1
14	5	2
15	3	5
16	4	0

(a) Are the "differences" taken from a normally distributed population? (b) Test the hypothesis of "no difference" between traps by using the Wilcoxon non-parametric test. What is your conclusion?

11. A clinician was interested in the effect of two different treatments on serum urate level (mg./100) ml. in gout patients. The following determinations were made for ten adult males with the gout: before treatment, following treatment A, and following treatment B. Enough time elapsed between treatments so there was no carry-over effect. Assume that some gout patients show more variation in urate levels from day-to-day than others because of different diets. Therefore, even though the within-cell variances within a block may be homogeneous, they are not likely to be homogeneous from block to block. The data are as follows:

Patient	No Treatment	Treatment A	Treatment B
1	12.0	9.4	8.3
2	6.2	8.9	7.4
3	11.1	11.9	6.2
4	7.9	8.5	8.1
5	9.4	9.3	9.6
6	10.4	10.1	10.4
7	8.1	10.2	9.4
8	12.2	12.2	11.9
9	6.9	7.1	6.9
10	10.1	6.1	12.4

Test the hypothesis that the treatments have no influence on urate level. What is your conclusion? Defend your choice of the statistical test used to analyze these data.

References

General Textbooks, Articles, and Citations Made in This Text

Dixon, W. J., and F. J. Massey (1957), *Introduction to Statistical Analysis*, McGraw-Hill Book Company, New York.

Dunn, J. D. (1964), *Basic Statistics: A Primer for the Biomedical Sciences*, John Wiley & Sons, Inc., New York.

Finney, D. J. (1951), *Probit Analysis*, Cambridge University Press, Cambridge.

Fisher, R. A. (1947), *The Design of Experiments*, Oliver and Boyd, Edinburgh and London.

Fisher, R. A. (1948), *Statistical Methods for Research Workers*, Oliver and Boyd, Edinburgh and London.

Fisher, R. A., and F. Yates (1948), *Statistical Tables for Biological, Agricultural and Medical Research*, Oliver and Boyd, Edinburgh and London.

Friedman, M. (1937), "The use of ranks to avoid the assumption of normality implicit in the analysis of variance, " *J. Amer. Statist. Assoc.* 32:675–701.

Kruskal, W. H., and W. A. Wallis (1952), "Use of ranks in one-criterion variance analysis," *J. Amer. Statist. Assoc.* 47:583–621.

Li, Jerome C. R. (1957), *Introduction to Statistical Analysis*, McGraw-Hill Book Company, New York.

Mather, K. (1949), *Statistics in Research*, The Iowa State Univeristy Press, Ames, Iowa.

Pearce, S. C. (1965), *Biological Statistics: An Introduction*, McGraw-Hill Book Company, New York.

Pizzi, M. (1950), "Sampling variation of the 50% end point, determined by the Reed-Muench (Behrens) method," *Human Biology* 22:151–180.

Scheffé, H. A. (1959), *The Analysis of Variance*, John Wiley & Sons, Inc., New York.

Siegel, S. (1956), *Nonparametric Statistics for the Behavioral Sciences*, McGraw-Hill Book Company, New York.

Snedecor, G. W. (1956), *Statistical Methods*, The Iowa State University Press, Ames, Iowa.

Steel, R. G. D., and J. H. Torrie (1960), *Principles and Procedures of Statistics*, McGraw-Hill Book Company, New York.

Wilcoxon, F. (1945), "Individual comparisons for ranking methods," *Biometrics Bulletin* 1:80–83.

Winer, B. J. (1962), *Statistical Principles in Experimental Design*, McGraw-Hill Book Company, New York.

Appendix

Table I Areas of the Normal Curve.

c	Area	c	Area
−3.0	0.0013	0.1	0.5398
−2.9	0.0019	0.2	0.5793
−2.8	0.0026	0.3	0.6179
−2.7	0.0035	0.4	0.6554
−2.6	0.0047	0.5	0.6915
−2.5	0.0062	0.6	0.7258
−2.4	0.0082	0.7	0.7580
−2.3	0.0107	0.8	0.7881
−2.2	0.0139	0.9	0.8159
−2.1	0.0179	1.0	0.8413
−2.0	0.0227	1.1	0.8643
−1.9	0.0287	1.2	0.8849
−1.8	0.0359	1.3	0.9032
−1.7	0.0446	1.4	0.9192
−1.6	0.0548	1.5	0.9332
−1.5	0.0668	1.6	0.9452
−1.4	0.0808	1.7	0.9554
−1.3	0.0968	1.8	0.9641
−1.2	0.1151	1.9	0.9713
−1.1	0.1357	2.0	0.9773
−1.0	0.1587	2.1	0.9821
−0.9	0.1841	2.2	0.9861
−0.8	0.2119	2.3	0.9893
−0.7	0.2420	2.4	0.9918
−0.6	0.2742	2.5	0.9938
−0.5	0.3085	2.6	0.9953
−0.4	0.3446	2.7	0.9965
−0.3	0.3821	2.8	0.9974
−0.2	0.4207	2.9	0.9981
−0.1	0.4602	3.0	0.9987
0.0	0.5000		

Table II   Table of c.

Probability ...	0.95	0.90	0.80	0.70	0.60	0.50	0.40
c	0.063	0.13	0.25	0.39	0.52	0.67	0.84
Probability ...	0.30	0.20	0.10	0.05	0.02	0.01	0.001
c	1.04	1.28	1.64	1.96	2.33	2.58	3.29

Table II is abridged from Table III of Fisher & Yates: *Statistical Tables for Biological, Agricultural, and Medical Research,* published by Oliver & Boyd Ltd., Edinburgh, and by permission of the authors and publishers.

Table III   Table of t.

DF	Probability									
	0.90	0.80	0.70	0.50	0.30	0.20	0.10	0.05	0.02	0.01
1	0.16	0.33	0.51	1.00	1.96	3.08	6.31	12.71	31.82	63.66
2	0.14	0.29	0.45	0.82	1.39	1.89	2.92	4.30	6.97	9.93
3	0.14	0.28	0.42	0.77	1.25	1.64	2.35	3.18	4.54	5.84
4	0.13	0.27	0.41	0.74	1.19	1.53	2.13	2.78	3.75	4.60
5	0.13	0.27	0.41	0.73	1.16	1.48	2.02	2.57	3.37	4.03
6	0.13	0.27	0.40	0.72	1.13	1.44	1.94	2.45	3.14	3.71
7	0.13	0.26	0.40	0.71	1.12	1.42	1.90	2.37	3.00	3.50
8	0.13	0.26	0.40	0.71	1.11	1.40	1.86	2.31	2.90	3.36
9	0.13	0.26	0.40	0.70	1.10	1.38	1.83	2.26	2.82	3.25
10	0.13	0.26	0.40	0.70	1.09	1.37	1.81	2.23	2.76	3.17
11	0.13	0.26	0.40	0.70	1.09	1.36	1.80	2.20	2.72	3.11
12	0.13	0.26	0.40	0.70	1.08	1.36	1.78	2.18	2.68	3.06
13	0.13	0.26	0.39	0.69	1.08	1.35	1.77	2.16	2.65	3.01
14	0.13	0.26	0.39	0.69	1.08	1.35	1.76	2.15	2.62	2.98
15	0.13	0.26	0.39	0.69	1.07	1.34	1.75	2.13	2.60	2.95
16	0.13	0.26	0.39	0.69	1.07	1.34	1.75	2.12	2.58	2.92
17	0.13	0.26	0.39	0.69	1.07	1.33	1.74	2.11	2.57	2.90
18	0.13	0.26	0.39	0.69	1.07	1.33	1.73	2.10	2.55	2.88
19	0.13	0.26	0.39	0.69	1.07	1.33	1.73	2.09	2.54	2.86
20	0.13	0.26	0.39	0.69	1.06	1.33	1.73	2.09	2.53	2.85
22	0.13	0.26	0.39	0.69	1.06	1.32	1.72	2.07	2.51	2.82
24	0.13	0.26	0.39	0.69	1.06	1.32	1.71	2.06	2.49	2.80
26	0.13	0.26	0.39	0.68	1.06	1.32	1.71	2.06	2.48	2.78
28	0.13	0.26	0.39	0.68	1.06	1.31	1.70	2.05	2.47	2.76
30	0.13	0.26	0.39	0.68	1.06	1.31	1.70	2.04	2.46	2.75
40	0.13	0.26	0.39	0.68	1.05	1.30	1.68	2.02	2.42	2.70
60	0.13	0.25	0.39	0.68	1.05	1.30	1.67	2.00	2.39	2.66
120	0.13	0.25	0.39	0.68	1.04	1.29	1.66	1.98	2.36	2.62
∞	0.13	0.25	0.39	0.67	1.04	1.28	1.64	1.96	2.33	2.58

Table IVa   Table of F (0.05 Probability Point).

DF_2 \ DF_1	1	2	3	4	5	6	12	24	∞
1	161.4	199.5	215.7	224.6	230.2	234.0	243.9	249.0	254.3
2	18.5	19.0	19.2	19.3	19.3	19.3	19.4	19.5	19.5
3	10.1	9.6	9.3	9.1	9.0	8.9	8.7	8.6	8.5
4	7.7	6.9	6.6	6.4	6.3	6.2	5.9	5.8	5.6
5	6.6	5.8	5.4	5.2	5.1	5.0	4.7	4.5	4.4
6	6.0	5.1	4.8	4.5	4.4	4.3	4.0	3.8	3.7
7	5.6	4.7	4.4	4.1	4.0	3.9	3.6	3.4	3.2
8	5.3	4.5	4.1	3.8	3.7	3.6	3.3	3.1	2.9
9	5.1	4.3	3.9	3.6	3.5	3.4	3.1	2.9	2.7
10	5.0	4.1	3.7	3.5	3.3	3.2	2.9	2.7	2.5
11	4.8	4.0	3.6	3.4	3.2	3.1	2.8	2.6	2.4
12	4.8	3.9	3.5	3.3	3.1	3.0	2.7	2.5	2.3
13	4.7	3.8	3.4	3.2	3.0	2.9	2.6	2.4	2.2
14	4.6	3.7	3.3	3.1	3.0	2.9	2.5	2.3	2.1
15	4.5	3.7	3.3	3.1	2.9	2.8	2.5	2.3	2.1
16	4.5	3.6	3.2	3.0	2.9	2.7	2.4	2.2	2.0
17	4.5	3.6	3.2	3.0	2.8	2.7	2.4	2.2	2.0
18	4.4	3.6	3.2	2.9	2.8	2.7	2.3	2.1	1.9
19	4.4	3.5	3.1	2.9	2.7	2.6	2.3	2.1	1.9
20	4.4	3.5	3.1	2.9	2.7	2.6	2.3	2.1	1.8
22	4.3	3.4	3.1	2.8	2.7	2.6	2.2	2.0	1.8
24	4.3	3.4	3.0	2.8	2.6	2.5	2.2	2.0	1.7
26	4.2	3.4	3.0	2.7	2.6	2.5	2.2	2.0	1.7
28	4.2	3.3	3.0	2.7	2.6	2.4	2.1	1.9	1.6
30	4.2	3.3	2.9	2.7	2.5	2.4	2.1	1.9	1.6
40	4.1	3.2	2.8	2.6	2.5	2.3	2.0	1.8	1.5
60	4.0	3.2	2.8	2.5	2.4	2.3	1.9	1.7	1.4
120	3.9	3.1	2.7	2.5	2.3	2.2	1.8	1.6	1.3
∞	3.8	3.0	2.6	2.4	2.2	2.1	1.8	1.5	1.0

Table IVa is abridged from Table V of Fisher & Yates: *Statistical Tables for Biological, Agricultural, and Medical Research,* published by Oliver & Boyd Ltd., Edinburgh, and by permission of the authors and publishers.

Table IVb Table of F (0.01 Probability Point).

DF$_2$ \ DF$_1$	1	2	3	4	5	6	12	24	∞
1	4,052	4,999	5,403	5,625	5,764	5,859	6,106	6,234	6,366
2	98.5	99.0	99.2	99.3	99.3	99.3	99.4	99.5	99.5
3	34.1	30.8	29.5	28.7	28.2	27.9	27.1	26.6	26.1
4	21.2	18.0	16.7	16.0	15.5	15.2	14.4	13.9	13.5
5	16.3	13.3	12.1	11.4	11.0	10.7	9.9	9.5	9.0
6	13.7	10.9	9.8	9.2	8.8	8.5	7.7	7.3	6.9
7	12.3	9.6	8.5	7.9	7.5	7.2	6.5	6.1	5.7
8	11.3	8.7	7.6	7.0	6.6	6.4	5.7	5.3	4.9
9	10.6	8.0	7.0	6.4	6.1	5.8	5.1	4.7	4.3
10	10.0	7.6	6.6	6.0	5.6	5.4	4.7	4.3	3.9
11	9.7	7.2	6.2	5.7	5.3	5.1	4.4	4.0	3.6
12	9.3	6.9	6.0	5.4	5.1	4.8	4.2	3.8	3.4
13	9.1	6.7	5.7	5.2	4.9	4.6	4.0	3.6	3.2
14	8.9	6.5	5.6	5.0	4.7	4.5	3.8	3.4	3.0
15	8.7	6.4	5.4	4.9	4.6	4.3	3.7	3.3	2.9
16	8.5	6.2	5.3	4.8	4.4	4.2	3.6	3.2	2.8
17	8.4	6.1	5.2	4.7	4.3	4.1	3.5	3.1	2.7
18	8.3	6.0	5.1	4.6	4.3	4.0	3.4	3.0	2.6
19	8.2	5.9	5.0	4.5	4.2	3.9	3.3	2.9	2.5
20	8.1	5.9	4.9	4.4	4.1	3.9	3.2	2.9	2.4
22	7.9	5.7	4.8	4.3	4.0	3.8	3.1	2.8	2.3
24	7.8	5.6	4.7	4.2	3.9	3.7	3.0	2.7	2.2
26	7.7	5.5	4.6	4.1	3.8	3.6	3.0	2.7	2.1
28	7.6	5.5	4.6	4.1	3.8	3.5	2.9	2.5	2.1
30	7.6	5.4	4.5	4.0	3.7	3.5	2.8	2.5	2.0
40	7.3	5.2	4.3	3.8	3.5	3.3	2.7	2.3	1.8
60	7.1	5.0	4.1	3.7	3.3	3.1	2.5	2.1	1.6
120	6.9	4.8	4.0	3.5	3.2	3.0	2.3	2.0	1.4
∞	6.6	4.6	3.8	3.3	3.0	2.8	2.2	1.8	1.0

Table IVb is abridged from Table V of Fisher & Yates: *Statistical Tables for Biological, Agricultural, and Medical Research,* published by Oliver & Boyd Ltd., Edinburgh, and by permission of the authors and publishers.

Table Va   Table of q (0.05 Probability Point).

DF \ k	2	3	4	5	6	7	8	9	10	11
5	3.64	4.60	5.22	5.67	6.03	6.33	6.58	6.80	6.99	7.17
6	3.46	4.34	4.90	5.30	5.63	5.90	6.12	6.32	6.49	6.65
7	3.34	4.16	4.68	5.06	5.36	5.61	5.82	6.00	6.16	6.30
8	3.26	4.04	4.53	4.89	5.17	5.40	5.60	5.77	5.92	6.05
9	3.20	3.95	4.41	4.76	5.02	5.24	5.43	5.59	5.74	5.87
10	3.15	3.88	4.33	4.65	4.91	5.12	5.30	5.46	5.60	5.72
11	3.11	3.82	4.26	4.57	4.82	5.03	5.20	5.35	5.49	5.61
12	3.08	3.77	4.20	4.51	4.75	4.95	5.12	5.27	5.39	5.51
13	3.06	3.73	4.15	4.45	4.69	4.88	5.05	5.19	5.32	5.43
14	3.03	3.70	4.11	4.41	4.64	4.83	4.99	5.13	5.25	5.36
15	3.01	3.67	4.08	4.37	4.59	4.78	4.94	5.08	5.20	5.31
16	3.00	3.65	4.05	4.33	4.56	4.74	4.90	5.03	5.15	5.26
17	2.98	3.63	4.02	4.30	4.52	4.71	4.86	4.99	5.11	5.21
18	2.97	3.61	4.00	4.28	4.49	4.67	4.82	4.96	5.07	5.17
19	2.96	3.59	3.98	4.25	4.47	4.65	4.79	4.92	5.04	5.14
20	2.95	3.58	3.96	4.23	4.45	4.62	4.77	4.90	5.01	5.11
24	2.92	3.53	3.90	4.17	4.37	4.54	4.68	4.81	4.92	5.01
30	2.89	3.49	3.85	4.10	4.30	4.46	4.60	4.72	4.82	4.92
40	2.86	3.44	3.79	4.04	4.23	4.39	4.52	4.63	4.73	4.82
60	2.83	3.40	3.74	3.98	4.16	4.31	4.44	4.55	4.65	4.73
120	2.80	3.36	3.68	3.92	4.10	4.24	4.36	4.47	4.56	4.64
∞	2.77	3.31	3.63	3.86	4.03	4.17	4.29	4.39	4.47	4.55

Table Va is abridged from Table 29 of *Biometrika Tables for Statisticians,* Vol. I, Cambridge University Press, with the kind permission of Professor E.S. Pearson, Managing Editor, on behalf of the Biometrika Trustees. Corrections in the table are those of J. Pachares published in *Biometrika,* Vol. 46 (1959), pp. 464–466.

Table Vb Table of q (0.01 Probability Point).

DF \ k	2	3	4	5	6	7	8	9	10	11
5	5.70	6.98	7.80	8.42	8.91	9.32	9.67	9.97	10.24	10.48
6	5.24	6.33	7.03	7.56	7.97	8.32	8.61	8.87	9.10	9.30
7	4.95	5.92	6.54	7.01	7.37	7.68	7.94	8.17	8.37	8.55
8	4.75	5.64	6.20	6.62	6.96	7.24	7.47	7.68	7.86	8.03
9	4.60	5.43	5.96	6.35	6.66	6.91	7.13	7.33	7.49	7.65
10	4.48	5.27	5.77	6.14	6.43	6.67	6.87	7.05	7.21	7.36
11	4.39	5.15	5.62	5.97	6.25	6.48	6.67	6.84	6.99	7.13
12	4.32	5.05	5.50	5.84	6.10	6.32	6.51	6.67	6.81	6.94
13	4.26	4.96	5.40	5.73	5.98	6.19	6.37	6.53	6.67	6.79
14	4.21	4.89	5.32	5.63	5.88	6.08	6.26	6.41	6.54	6.66
15	4.17	4.84	5.25	5.56	5.80	5.99	6.16	6.31	6.44	6.55
16	4.13	4.79	5.19	5.49	5.72	5.92	6.08	6.22	6.35	6.46
17	4.10	4.74	5.14	5.43	5.66	5.85	6.01	6.15	6.27	6.38
18	4.07	4.70	5.09	5.38	5.60	5.79	5.94	6.08	6.20	6.31
19	4.05	4.67	5.05	5.33	5.55	5.73	5.89	6.02	6.14	6.25
20	4.02	4.64	5.02	5.29	5.51	5.69	5.84	5.97	6.09	6.19
24	3.96	4.55	4.91	5.17	5.37	5.54	5.69	5.81	5.92	6.02
30	3.89	4.45	4.80	5.05	5.24	5.40	5.54	5.65	5.76	5.85
40	3.82	4.37	4.70	4.93	5.11	5.26	5.39	5.50	5.60	5.69
60	3.76	4.28	4.59	4.82	4.99	5.13	5.25	5.36	5.45	5.53
120	3.70	4.20	4.50	4.71	4.87	5.01	5.12	5.21	5.30	5.38
∞	3.64	4.12	4.40	4.60	4.76	4.88	4.99	5.08	5.16	5.23

Table Vb is abridged from Table 29 of *Biometrika Tables for Statisticians,* Vol. 1, Cambridge University Press, with the kind permission of Professor E.S. Pearson, Managing Editor, on behalf of the Biometrika Trustees. Corrections in the table are those of J. Pachares published in *Biometrika,* Vol. 46 (1959), pp. 464–466.

Table VI   Table of z for values of r from 0.00 to 1.00.

r from zero to 0.89 by hundredths

r	0.00	0.01	0.02	0.03	0.04	0.05	0.06	0.07	0.08	0.09
0.0	0.0000	0.0100	0.0200	0.0300	0.0400	0.0500	0.0601	0.0701	0.0802	0.0902
0.1	0.1003	0.1104	0.1206	0.1307	0.1409	0.1511	0.1614	0.1717	0.1820	0.1923
0.2	0.2027	0.2132	0.2237	0.2342	0.2448	0.2554	0.2661	0.2769	0.2877	0.2986
0.3	0.3095	0.3205	0.3316	0.3428	0.3541	0.3654	0.3769	0.3884	0.4001	0.4118
0.4	0.4236	0.4356	0.4477	0.4599	0.4722	0.4847	0.4973	0.5101	0.5230	0.5361
0.5	0.5493	0.5627	0.5763	0.5901	0.6042	0.6184	0.6328	0.6475	0.6625	0.6777
0.6	0.6931	0.7089	0.7250	0.7414	0.7582	0.7753	0.7928	0.8107	0.8291	0.8480
0.7	0.8673	0.8872	0.9076	0.9287	0.9505	0.9730	0.9962	1.0203	1.0454	1.0714
0.8	1.0986	1.1270	1.1568	1.1881	1.2212	1.2562	1.2933	1.3331	1.3758	1.4219

r from 0.900 to 0.999 by thousandths

r	0.000	0.001	0.002	0.003	0.004	0.005	0.006	0.007	0.008	0.009
0.90	1.4722	1.4775	1.4828	1.4882	1.4937	1.4992	1.5047	1.5103	1.5160	1.5217
0.91	1.5275	1.5334	1.5393	1.5453	1.5513	1.5574	1.5636	1.5698	1.5762	1.5826
0.92	1.5890	1.5956	1.6022	1.6089	1.6157	1.6226	1.6296	1.6366	1.6438	1.6510
0.93	1.6584	1.6658	1.6734	1.6811	1.6888	1.6967	1.7047	1.7129	1.7211	1.7295
0.94	1.7380	1.7467	1.7555	1.7645	1.7736	1.7828	1.7923	1.8019	1.8117	1.8216
0.95	1.8318	1.8421	1.8527	1.8635	1.8745	1.8857	1.8972	1.9090	1.9210	1.9333
0.96	1.9459	1.9588	1.9721	1.9857	1.9996	2.0139	2.0287	2.0439	2.0595	2.0756
0.97	2.0923	2.1095	2.1273	2.1457	2.1649	2.1847	2.2054	2.2269	2.2494	2.2729
0.98	2.2976	2.3235	2.3507	2.3796	2.4101	2.4427	2.4774	2.5147	2.5550	2.5987
0.99	2.6467	2.6996	2.7587	2.8257	2.9031	2.9945	3.1063	3.2504	3.4534	3.8002

Table VI is reproduced from *Elements of Statistical Reasoning,* 1939, by A.E. Treloar, with the kind permission of the author and publisher, John Wiley & Sons, New York.

Table VII Table of χ^2.

DF	0.975	0.90	0.80	0.70	0.50	0.30	0.20	0.10	0.05	0.025	0.01
					Probability						
1	0.00098	0.016	0.064	0.15	0.46	1.07	1.64	2.71	3.84	5.02	6.64
2	0.0506	0.21	0.45	0.71	1.39	2.41	3.22	4.61	5.99	7.38	9.21
3	0.216	0.58	1.01	1.42	2.37	3.67	4.64	6.25	7.82	9.35	11.34
4	0.484	1.06	1.65	2.20	3.36	4.88	5.99	7.78	9.49	11.14	13.28
5	0.831	1.61	2.34	3.00	4.35	6.06	7.29	9.24	11.07	12.83	15.09
6	1.24	2.20	3.07	3.83	5.35	7.23	8.56	10.65	12.59	14.45	16.81
7	1.69	2.83	3.82	4.67	6.35	8.38	9.80	12.02	14.07	16.01	18.48
8	2.18	3.49	4.59	5.53	7.34	9.52	11.03	13.36	15.51	17.53	20.09
9	2.70	4.17	5.38	6.39	8.34	10.66	12.24	14.68	16.92	19.02	21.67
10	3.25	4.87	6.18	7.27	9.34	11.78	13.44	15.99	18.31	20.48	23.21
11	3.82	5.58	6.99	8.15	10.34	12.90	14.63	17.28	19.68	21.92	24.73
12	4.40	6.30	7.81	9.03	11.34	14.01	15.81	18.55	21.03	23.34	26.22
13	5.01	7.04	8.63	9.93	12.34	15.12	16.99	19.81	22.36	24.74	27.69
14	5.63	7.79	9.47	10.82	13.34	16.22	18.15	21.06	23.69	26.12	29.14
15	6.26	8.55	10.31	11.72	14.34	17.32	19.31	22.31	25.00	27.49	30.58
16	6.91									28.85	
18	8.23									31.53	
20	9.59									34.17	
24	12.40									39.36	
30	16.79									46.98	
40	24.43									59.34	
60	40.48									83.30	
120	91.58									152.21	

Table VII is abridged in part from Table IV of Fisher & Yates: *Statistical Tables for Biological, Agricultural, and Medical Research,* published by Oliver & Boyd Ltd., Edinburgh, and by permission of the authors and publishers.

Table VIII   Critical Values for the Wilcoxon Signed Rank Test.

n	One-Tailed Test			
	0.05	– –	0.01	– –
	Two-Tailed Test			
	– –	0.05	– –	0.01
5	1	0	–	–
6	2	1	–	–
7	4	2	0	–
8	6	4	2	0
9	8	6	3	2
10	11	8	5	3
11	14	11	7	5
12	17	14	10	7
13	21	17	13	10
14	26	21	16	13
15	30	25	20	16
16	36	30	24	19
17	41	35	28	23
18	47	40	33	28
19	54	46	38	32
20	60	52	43	37
21	68	59	49	43
22	75	66	56	49
23	83	73	62	55
24	92	81	69	61
25	101	90	77	68

Adapted from Table 2 of Wilcoxon and Wilcox: *Some Rapid Approximate Statistical Prodecures* (1964), Pearl River, New York: Lederle Laboratories (a division of American Cyanamid Co.), p. 28, with the kind permission of Miss R.A. Wilcox and publisher.

Table IXa 95% Confidence Interval (Percent) for Binomial Distribution.

Number Observed f	Size of Sample, n												Fraction Observed f/n	Size of Sample			
	10		15		20		30		50		100			250		1000	
0	0	31	0	22	0	17	0	12	0	07	0	4	0.00	0	1	0	0
1	0	45	0	32	0	25	0	17	0	11	0	5	0.01	0	4	0	2
2	3	56	2	40	1	31	1	22	0	14	0	7	0.02	1	5	1	3
3	7	65	4	48	3	38	2	27	1	17	1	8	0.03	1	6	2	4
4	12	74	8	55	6	44	4	31	2	19	1	10	0.04	2	7	3	5
5	19	81	12	62	9	49	6	35	3	22	2	11	0.05	3	9	4	7
6	26	88	16	68	12	54	8	39	5	24	2	12	0.06	3	10	5	8
7	35	93	21	73	15	59	10	43	6	27	3	14	0.07	4	11	6	9
8	44	97	27	79	19	64	12	46	7	29	4	15	0.08	5	12	6	10
9	55	100	32	84	23	68	15	50	9	31	4	16	0.09	6	13	7	11
10	69	100	38	88	27	73	17	53	10	34	5	18	0.10	7	14	8	12
11			45	92	32	77	20	56	12	36	5	19	0.11	7	16	9	13
12			52	96	36	81	23	60	13	38	6	20	0.12	8	17	10	14
13			60	98	41	85	25	63	15	41	7	21	0.13	9	18	11	15
14			68	100	46	88	28	66	16	43	8	22	0.14	10	19	12	16
15			78	100	51	91	31	69	18	44	9	24	0.15	10	20	13	17
16					56	94	34	72	20	46	9	25	0.16	11	21	14	18
17					62	97	37	75	21	48	10	26	0.17	12	22	15	19
18					69	99	40	77	23	50	11	27	0.18	13	23	16	21
19					75	100	44	80	25	53	12	28	0.19	14	24	17	22
20					83	100	47	83	27	55	13	29	0.20	15	26	18	23
21							50	85	28	57	14	30	0.21	16	27	19	24
22							54	88	30	59	14	31	0.22	17	28	19	25
23							57	90	32	61	15	32	0.23	18	29	20	26
24							61	92	34	63	16	33	0.24	19	30	21	27
25							65	94	36	64	17	35	0.25	20	31	22	28
26							69	96	37	66	18	36	0.26	20	32	23	29
27							73	98	39	68	19	37	0.27	21	33	24	30
28							78	99	41	70	19	38	0.28	22	34	25	31
29							83	100	43	72	20	39	0.29	23	35	26	32
30							88	100	45	73	21	40	0.30	24	36	27	33
31									47	75	22	41	0.31	25	37	28	34
32									50	77	23	42	0.32	26	38	29	35
33									52	79	24	43	0.33	27	39	30	36
34									54	80	25	44	0.34	28	40	31	37
35									56	82	26	45	0.35	29	41	32	38
36									57	84	27	46	0.36	30	42	33	39
37									59	85	28	47	0.37	31	43	34	40
38									62	87	28	48	0.38	32	44	35	41
39									64	88	29	49	0.39	33	45	36	42
40									66	90	30	50	0.40	34	46	37	43
41									69	91	31	51	0.41	35	47	38	44
42									71	93	32	52	0.42	36	48	39	45
43									73	94	33	53	0.43	37	49	40	46
44									76	95	34	54	0.44	38	50	41	47
45									78	97	35	55	0.45	39	51	42	48
46									81	98	36	56	0.46	40	52	43	49
47									83	99	37	57	0.47	41	53	44	50
48									86	100	38	58	0.48	42	54	45	51
49									89	100	39	59	0.49	43	55	46	52
50									93	100	40	60	0.50	44	56	47	53
												*		†		†	

* If f exceeds 50, read 100 − f = number observed and subtract each confidence limit from 100.
†If f/n exceeds 0.50, read 1.00 − f/n = fraction observed and subtract each confidence limit from 100.

Table IXb   99% Confidence Interval (Percent) for Binomial Distribution.

Number Observed f	Size of Sample, n												Fraction Observed f/n	Size of Sample			
	10		15		20		30		50		100			250		1000	
0	0	41	0	30	0	23	0	16	0	10	0	5	0.00	0	2	0	1
1	0	54	0	40	0	32	0	22	0	14	0	7	0.01	0	5	0	2
2	1	65	1	49	1	39	0	28	0	17	0	9	0.02	1	6	1	3
3	4	74	2	56	2	45	1	32	1	20	0	10	0.03	1	7	2	4
4	8	81	5	63	4	51	3	36	1	23	1	12	0.04	2	9	3	6
5	13	87	8	69	6	56	4	40	2	26	1	13	0.05	2	10	3	7
6	19	92	12	74	8	61	6	44	3	29	2	14	0.06	3	11	4	8
7	26	96	16	79	11	66	8	48	4	31	2	16	0.07	3	13	5	9
8	35	99	21	84	15	70	10	52	6	33	3	17	0.08	4	14	6	10
9	46	100	26	88	18	74	12	55	7	36	3	18	0.09	5	15	7	12
10	59	100	31	92	22	78	14	58	8	38	4	19	0.10	6	16	8	13
11			37	95	26	82	16	62	10	40	4	20	0.11	6	17	9	14
12			44	98	30	85	18	65	11	43	5	21	0.12	7	18	9	15
13			51	99	34	89	21	68	12	45	6	23	0.13	8	19	10	16
14			60	100	39	92	24	71	14	47	6	24	0.14	9	20	11	17
15			70	100	44	94	26	74	15	49	7	26	0.15	9	22	12	18
16					49	96	29	76	17	51	8	27	0.16	10	23	13	19
17					55	98	32	79	18	53	9	29	0.17	11	24	14	20
18					61	99	35	82	20	55	9	30	0.18	12	25	15	21
19					68	100	38	84	21	57	10	31	0.19	13	26	16	22
20					77	100	42	86	23	59	11	32	0.20	14	27	17	23
21							45	88	24	61	12	33	0.21	15	28	18	24
22							48	90	26	63	12	34	0.22	16	30	19	26
23							52	92	28	65	13	35	0.23	17	31	20	27
24							55	94	29	67	14	36	0.24	18	32	21	28
25							60	96	31	69	15	38	0.25	18	33	22	29
26							64	97	33	71	16	39	0.26	19	34	22	30
27							68	99	35	72	16	40	0.27	20	35	23	31
28							72	100	37	74	17	41	0.28	21	36	24	32
29							78	100	39	76	18	42	0.29	22	37	25	33
30							84	100	41	77	19	43	0.30	23	38	26	34
31									43	79	20	44	0.31	24	39	27	35
32									45	80	21	45	0.32	25	40	28	36
33									47	82	21	46	0.33	26	41	29	37
34									49	83	22	47	0.34	26	42	30	38
35									51	85	23	48	0.35	27	43	31	39
36									53	86	24	49	0.36	28	44	32	40
37									55	88	25	50	0.37	29	45	33	41
38									57	89	26	51	0.38	30	46	34	42
39									60	90	27	52	0.39	31	47	35	43
40									62	92	28	53	0.40	32	48	36	44
41									64	93	29	54	0.41	33	50	37	45
42									67	94	29	55	0.42	34	51	38	46
43									69	96	30	56	0.43	35	52	39	47
44									71	97	31	57	0.44	36	53	40	48
45									74	98	32	58	0.45	37	54	41	49
46									77	99	33	59	0.46	38	55	42	50
47									80	99	34	60	0.47	39	55	43	51
48									83	100	35	61	0.48	40	56	44	52
49									86	100	36	62	0.49	41	57	45	53
50									90	100	37	63	0.50	42	58	46	54
											*			†		†	

*If f exceeds 50, read $100 - f$ = number observed and subtract each confidence limit from 100.
†If f/n exceeds 0.50, read $1.00 - f/n$ = fraction observed and subtract each confidence limit from 100.

Reproduced by permission from *Statistical Methods*, 5th Ed., by George W. Snedecor, ©1956 by the Iowa State University Press.

Table X   A Four-Place Table of Common Logarithms

N	0	1	2	3	4	5	6	7	8	9
10	0000	0043	0086	0128	0170	0212	0253	0294	0334	0374
11	0414	0453	0492	0531	0569	0607	0645	0682	0719	0755
12	0792	0828	0864	0899	0934	0969	1004	1038	1072	1106
13	1139	1173	1206	1239	1271	1303	1335	1367	1399	1430
14	1461	1492	1523	1553	1584	1614	1644	1673	1703	1732
15	1761	1790	1818	1847	1875	1903	1931	1959	1987	2014
16	2041	2068	2095	2122	2148	2175	2201	2227	2253	2279
17	2304	2330	2355	2380	2405	2430	2455	2480	2504	2529
18	2553	2577	2601	2625	2648	2672	2695	2718	2742	2765
19	2788	2810	2833	2856	2878	2900	2923	2945	2967	2989
20	3010	3032	3054	3075	3096	3118	3139	3160	3181	3201
21	3222	3243	3263	3284	3304	3324	3345	3365	3385	3404
22	3424	3444	3463	3483	3502	3522	3541	3560	3579	3598
23	3617	3636	3655	3674	3692	3711	3729	3747	3766	3784
24	3802	3820	3838	3856	3874	3892	3909	3927	3945	3962
25	3979	3997	4014	4031	4048	4065	4082	4099	4116	4133
26	4150	4166	4183	4200	4216	4232	4249	4265	4281	4298
27	4314	4330	4346	4362	4378	4393	4409	4425	4440	4456
28	4472	4487	4502	4518	4533	4548	4564	4579	4594	4609
29	4624	4639	4654	4669	4683	4698	4713	4728	4742	4757
30	4771	4786	4800	4814	4829	4843	4857	4871	4886	4900
31	4914	4928	4942	4955	4969	4983	4997	5011	5024	5038
32	5051	5065	5079	5092	5105	5119	5132	5145	5159	5172
33	5185	5198	5211	5224	5237	5250	5263	5276	5289	5302
34	5315	5328	5340	5353	5366	5378	5391	5403	5416	5428
35	5441	5453	5465	5478	5490	5502	5514	5527	5539	5551
36	5563	5575	5587	5599	5611	5623	5635	5647	5658	5670
37	5682	5694	5705	5717	5729	5740	5752	5763	5775	5786
38	5798	5809	5821	5832	5843	5855	5866	5877	5888	5899
39	5911	5922	5933	5944	5955	5966	5977	5988	5999	6010
40	6021	6031	6042	6053	6064	6075	6085	6096	6107	6117
41	6128	6138	6149	6160	6170	6180	6191	6201	6212	6222
42	6232	6243	6253	6263	6274	6284	6294	6304	6314	6325
43	6335	6345	6355	6365	6375	6385	6395	6405	6415	6425
44	6435	6444	6454	6464	6474	6484	6493	6503	6513	6522
45	6532	6542	6551	6561	6571	6580	6590	6599	6609	6618
46	6628	6637	6646	6656	6665	6675	6684	6693	6702	6712
47	6721	6730	6739	6749	6758	6767	6776	6785	6794	6803
48	6812	6821	6830	6839	6848	6857	6866	6875	6884	6893
49	6902	6911	6920	6928	6937	6946	6955	6964	6972	6981
50	6990	6998	7007	7016	7024	7033	7042	7050	7059	7067
51	7076	7084	7093	7101	7110	7118	7126	7135	7143	7152
52	7160	7168	7177	7185	7193	7202	7210	7218	7226	7235
53	7243	7251	7259	7267	7275	7284	7292	7300	7308	7316
54	7324	7332	7340	7348	7356	7364	7372	7380	7388	7396
N	0	1	2	3	4	5	6	7	8	9

Table X   A Four-Place Table of Common Logarithms (Continued).

N	0	1	2	3	4	5	6	7	8	9
55	7404	7412	7419	7427	7435	7443	7451	7459	7466	7474
56	7482	7490	7497	7505	7513	7520	7528	7536	7543	7551
57	7559	7566	7574	7582	7589	7597	7604	7612	7619	7627
58	7634	7642	7649	7657	7664	7672	7679	7686	7694	7701
59	7709	7716	7723	7731	7738	7745	7752	7760	7767	7774
60	7782	7789	7796	7803	7810	7818	7825	7832	7839	7846
61	7853	7860	7868	7875	7882	7889	7896	7903	7910	7917
62	7924	7931	7938	7945	7952	7959	7966	7973	7980	7987
63	7993	8000	8007	8014	8021	8028	8035	8041	8048	8055
64	8062	8069	8075	8082	8089	8096	8102	8109	8116	8122
65	8129	8136	8142	8149	8156	8162	8169	8176	8182	8189
66	8195	8202	8209	8215	8222	8228	8235	8241	8248	8254
67	8261	8267	8274	8280	8287	8293	8299	8306	8312	8319
68	8325	8331	8338	8344	8351	8357	8363	8370	8376	8382
69	8388	8395	8401	8407	8414	8420	8426	8432	8439	8445
70	8451	8457	8463	8470	8476	8482	8488	8494	8500	8506
71	8513	8519	8525	8531	8537	8543	8549	8555	8561	8567
72	8573	8579	8585	8591	8597	8603	8609	8615	8621	8627
73	8633	8639	8645	8651	8657	8663	8669	8675	8681	8686
74	8692	8698	8704	8710	8716	8722	8727	8733	8739	8745
75	8751	8756	8762	8768	8774	8779	8785	8791	8797	8802
76	8808	8814	8820	8825	8831	8837	8842	8848	8854	8859
77	8865	8871	8876	8882	8887	8893	8899	8904	8910	8915
78	8921	8927	8932	8938	8943	8949	8954	8960	8965	8971
79	8976	8982	8987	8993	8998	9004	9009	9015	9020	9025
80	9031	9036	9042	9047	9053	9058	9063	9069	9074	9079
81	9085	9090	9096	9101	9106	9112	9117	9122	9128	9133
82	9138	9143	9149	9154	9159	9165	9170	9175	9180	9186
83	9191	9196	9201	9206	9212	9217	9222	9227	9232	9238
84	9243	9248	9253	9258	9263	9269	9274	9279	9284	9289
85	9294	9299	9304	9309	9315	9320	9325	9330	9335	9340
86	9345	9350	9355	9360	9365	9370	9375	9380	9385	9390
87	9395	9400	9405	9410	9415	9420	9425	9430	9435	9440
88	9445	9450	9455	9460	9465	9469	9474	9479	9484	9489
89	9494	9499	9504	9509	9513	9518	9523	9528	9533	9538
90	9542	9547	9552	9557	9562	9566	9571	9576	9581	9586
91	9590	9595	9600	9605	9609	9614	9619	9624	9628	9633
92	9638	9643	9647	9652	9657	9661	9666	9671	9675	9680
93	9685	9689	9694	9699	9703	9708	9713	9717	9722	9727
94	9731	9736	9741	9745	9750	9754	9759	9763	9768	9773
95	9777	9782	9786	9791	9795	9800	9805	9809	9814	9818
96	9823	9827	9832	9836	9841	9845	9850	9854	9859	9863
97	9868	9872	9877	9881	9886	9890	9894	9899	9903	9908
98	9912	9917	9921	9926	9930	9934	9939	9943	9948	9952
99	9956	9961	9965	9969	9974	9978	9983	9987	9991	9996
N	0	1	2	3	4	5	6	7	8	9

Answers to Problems

Chapter 2

1. $\sum_1^n X_i = 2{,}022.3$ $\quad$ $\sum_1^n X_i^2 = 164{,}639.25$
   (d) $\bar{x} = 80.89$
   (e) $s^2 = 43.81$
   (f) $s = 6.62$
   (g) There is no mode. Sample median $= 80.2$

5. $\sum_1^n X_i = 260.7$ $\quad$ $\sum_1^n X_i^2 = 4{,}569.99$
   (a) $\bar{x} = 17.38$
   (b) $s^2 = 2.79$
   (c) $s^2 = 2.79$
   (d) $s = 1.67$

7. $\sum_1^n X_i = 350.08$ $\quad$ $\sum_1^n X_i^2 = 10{,}462.014$
   (a) $\bar{x} = 29.173$ $\quad$ $s = 4.758$

8. $\sum_1^n X_i = 1{,}280.00$ $\quad$ $\sum_1^n X_i^2 = 109{,}274.02$
   (a) $\bar{x} = 85.33$ $\quad$ $s = 1.84$

Chapter 3

1. (a) mean $= 150$ $\quad$ Standard deviation $= 10$
   (b) mean $= 150$ $\quad$ Standard deviation $= 2.0$
2. $P = 0.2742$

3. $P = 0.6170$
4. (a) mean $= 172.5$ Standard deviation $= 4.0$
   (c) $168.5 - 176.5$
5. (a) mean $= 180$ Standard deviation $= 4.0$
   (c) 0.3830
   (d) 0.8664
   (e) $P = 0.6826$
   (f) $P = 0.6826$ The probability that the limits will not include the value is 0.2174.
6. $129{,}640 \times 0.4773 = 61{,}877$
8. (a) $P = 0.0454$
   (b) $P = 0.6826$
   (c) $P = 0.6826$
9. (a) 0.1587
   (b) 0.0227
   (c) 0.1587
   (d) 0.0062
10. (a) 0.1587
    (b) 0.0227

Chapter 4

1. (c) mean $= 50$ Standard deviation $= 1.5$
   (d) $c = -6.0$
   (e) $L_1 = 38.06$ $L_2 = 43.94$
3. $\sum_{1}^{n} X_i = 77.00$ $\sum_{1}^{n} X_i^2 = 835.00$
   (c) $\bar{x} = 8.55$ $s^2 = 22.0278$
   (d) $t = 5.469$
   (f) $L_1 = 4.94$ $L_2 = 12.17$
4. Problem 1: $L_1 = 78.16$ $L_2 = 83.62$
   Problem 5: $L_1 = 16.45$ $L_2 = 18.31$
   Problem 7: $L_1 = 26.152$ $L_2 = 32.195$
   Problem 8: $L_1 = 84.31$ $L_2 = 86.35$
9. $\sum_{1}^{n} X_i = 1{,}563.00$ $\sum_{1}^{n} X_i^2 = 122{,}461.00$ $\bar{x} = 78.15$
   (a) $t = 86.17$
   (b) $L_1 = 76.25$ $L_2 = 80.05$
10. $\sum_{1}^{n} X_i = 427.00$ $\sum_{1}^{n} X_i^2 = 15{,}685.00$ $\bar{x} = 35.58$
    (a) $t = 18.45$
    (b) $L_1 = 31.34$ $L_2 = 39.83$

Chapter 5

3. $\bar{x}_1 = 43.42$ $\bar{x}_2 = 60.58$ $s_p^2 = 9.6095$
   (a) $t = 12.38$
   (b) $\mu_1 - \mu_2$: $L_1 = -20.07$ $L_2 = -14.25$
   (c) μ_1: $L_1 = 41.36$ $L_2 = 45.48$
   μ_2: $L_1 = 58.52$ $L_2 = 62.64$
4. $\bar{x}_1 = 86.91$ $\bar{x}_2 = 81.36$ $s_p^2 = 12.4408$
   $H_0: \mu_1 = \mu_2$ $H_1: \mu_1 \neq \mu_2$
   $t = 3.32$
5. $\bar{x}_1 = 8.85$ $\bar{x}_2 = 4.53$ $s_p^2 = 2.2537$
   (a) $t = 6.43$
   (b) μ_1: $L_1 = 7.85$ $L_2 = 9.85$
   μ_2: $L_1 = 3.53$ $L_2 = 5.53$
   $\mu_1 - \mu_2$: $L_1 = 2.91$ $L_2 = 5.73$
6. $\bar{x}_1 = 5.26$ $\bar{x}_2 = 12.54$ $s_p^2 = 2.543$
   (a) $t = 7.22$
   (b) μ_1: $L_1 = 2.86$ $L_2 = 7.66$
   μ_2: $L_1 = 10.14$ $L_2 = 14.94$
   $\mu_1 - \mu_2$: $L_1 = -10.67$ $L_2 = -3.89$
7. $\bar{x}_1 = 5.36$ $\bar{x}_2 = 5.29$ $s_p^2 = 0.5085$ $t = 0.2195$
8. (a) $\bar{x}_1 = 31.14$ $\bar{x}_2 = 31.43$ $s_p^2 = 26.2143$
   $t = 0.104$
   (b) μ_1: $L_1 = 26.92$ $L_2 = 35.36$
   μ_2: $L_1 = 27.21$ $L_2 = 35.65$

Chapter 6

1. (a) $\bar{x}_d = 4.30$ $s_d^2 = 17.5667$ $t = 3.24$
   (b) $\bar{x}_1 = 16.0$ $\bar{x}_2 = 11.7$ $s_p^2 = 54.2278$ $t = 1.31$
3. (b) $\bar{x}_d = 0.030$ $s_d^2 = 0.2423$ $t = 0.193$
4. (b) $\bar{x}_d = 0.158$ $s_p^2 = 0.01771$ $t = 4.12$
   (c) μ_d: $L_1 = 0.0738$ $L_2 = 0.2428$
5. $\bar{x}_d = 1.80$ $s_d^2 = 55.733$ $t = 0.762$

Chapter 7

1. (d) Total sum of squares $= 157.275$
   Treatment sum of squares $= 97.033$
   Error sum of squares $= 60.242$
   $F = 21.74$

(e) 16.51 $\overline{20.34}$ $\overline{20.31}$

(f) μ_1: $L_1 = 15.54$ $L_2 = 17.48$
     μ_2: $L_1 = 19.37$ $L_2 = 21.31$
     μ_3: $L_1 = 19.34$ $L_2 = 21.28$

(g) Exp. groups sum of squares $= 0.0045$ $F = 0.00202$
     Exp. groups vs controls sum of squares $= 97.028$ $F = 43.49$

2. (a) Total sum of squares $= 339.568$
        Area sum of squares $= 161.926$
        Individuals sum of squares $= 177.642$
        $F = 15.496$
        $\bar{x}_1 = 18.36$ $\bar{x}_2 = 22.57$ $\bar{x}_3 = 18.17$

   (b) μ_1: $L_1 = 16.96$ $L_2 = 19.77$
        μ_2: $L_1 = 21.33$ $L_2 = 23.82$
        μ_3: $L_1 = 16.82$ $L_2 = 19.51$

   (c) $\mu_1 = \mu_3 \neq \mu_2$

3. (a) Total sum of squares $= 0.076582$
        Area sum of squares $= 0.00599$
        Individuals sum of squares $= 0.070592$
        $F = 1.24$
        $\bar{x}_1 = 0.763$ $\bar{x}_2 = 0.738$ $\bar{x}_3 = 0.747$ $\bar{x}_4 = 0.734$

   (b) μ_1: $L_1 = 0.740$ $L_2 = 0.787$
        μ_2: $L_1 = 0.715$ $L_2 = 0.762$
        μ_3: $L_1 = 0.723$ $L_2 = 0.770$
        μ_4: $L_1 = 0.711$ $L_2 = 0.758$

4. (a) Total sum of squares $= 134.3650$
        Variety sum of squares $= 114.6175$
        Error sum of squares $= 19.7475$
        $F = 60.94$
        $\bar{x}_1 = 6.86$ $\bar{x}_2 = 5.41$ $\bar{x}_2 = 10.60$

   (c) μ_1: $L_1 = 6.15$ $L_2 = 7.58$
        μ_2: $L_1 = 4.70$ $L_2 = 6.12$
        μ_3: $L_1 = 9.89$ $L_2 = 11.31$

5. (a) Total sum of squares $= 3{,}611.23$
        Strain sum of squares $= 3{,}479.40$
        Error sum of squares $= 131.83$
        $F = 131.97$
        $\bar{x}_1 = 62.52$ $\bar{x}_2 = 62.30$ $\bar{x}_3 = 83.46$ $\bar{x}_4 = 62.98$ $\bar{x}_5 = 89.30$

   (b) $\overline{62.30}$ $\overline{62.52}$ $\overline{62.98}$ $\overline{83.46}$ $\overline{89.30}$

   (c) μ_1: $L_1 = 60.12$ $L_2 = 64.92$
        μ_2: $L_1 = 59.90$ $L_2 = 64.70$
        μ_3: $L_1 = 81.06$ $L_2 = 85.86$
        μ_4: $L_1 = 60.58$ $L_2 = 65.38$
        μ_5: $L_1 = 86.90$ $L_2 = 91.70$

Chapter 8

1. (d) Total sum of squares = 114.4296
    Plants sum of squares = 111.8216
    Leaves sum of squares = 2.6080
    $F = 214.38$
   (e) $s^2 = 0.1304$ $s_{\mu_i}^2 = 5.5650$ $s_T^2 = 5.6954$
3. (c) Total sum of squares = 0.061085
    Hosts sum of squares = 0.005735
    Individuals sum of squares = 0.055350
    $F = 1.12$
4. (a) Total sum of squares = 10,692.74
    Plants sum of squares = 145.90
    Leaves sum of squares = 10,546.84
    $F = 0.190$

Chapter 9

2. (c) Total sum of squares = 434.8696
    Blocks sum of squares = 22.3371
    Treatments sum of squares = 411.9646
    Error sum of squares = 0.5679
    $F = 3,627.09$
    $\bar{x}_1 = 11.53$ $\bar{x}_2 = 17.52$ $\bar{x}_3 = 17.55$ $\bar{x}_4 = 7.82$
   (d) 7.82   11.53   <u>17.52   17.55</u>
3. Estimate of missing measurement = 18.40
    Total sum of squares = 413.6200
    Blocks sum of squares = 22.1550
    Treatment sum of squares = 390.9033
    Error sum of squares = 0.5617
    $F = 3,479.64$
5. (a) Total sum of squares = 171,405.50
    Blocks sum of squares = 41,022.83
    Treatment sum of squares = 75,689.60
    Error sum of squares = 54,693.07
    $F = 12.46$
    $\bar{x}_1 = 144.7$ $\bar{x}_2 = 69.90$ $\bar{x}_3 = 191.9$
   (b) 69.9   <u>144.7   191.9</u>
6. (a) Total sum of squares = 0.54624
    Blocks sum of squares = 0.45780
    Treatments sum of squares = 0.00604
    Error sum of squares = 0.08240
    $F = 0.51$
   (c) R.E. = 4.75

Chapter 10

1. (a) Total sum of squares = 108,362.7
   Diets sum of squares = 100,215.5
   Rows sum of squares = 239.5
   Columns sum of squares = 3,315.5
   Error sum of squares = 4,592.2
   $F = 65.47$
   (c) 266.6   338.6   389.2   <u>427.8   438.4</u>
   (d) μ_1: $L_1 = 408.73$ $L_2 = 446.87$
       μ_2: $L_1 = 419.32$ $L_2 = 457.47$
       μ_3: $L_1 = 370.13$ $L_2 = 408.27$
       μ_4: $L_1 = 319.53$ $L_2 = 357.67$
       μ_5: $L_1 = 247.53$ $L_2 = 285.67$
   (e) Completely randomized design: R.E. = 1.00
       Randomized block design, rows as blocks: R.E. = 1.19
       Randomized block design, columns as blocks: R.E. = 0.81
2. (a) Total sum of squares = 286.2330
   Treatments sum of squares = 227.8700
   Rows sum of squares = 36.8900
   Columns sum of squares = 4.5480
   Error sum of squares = 16.9250
   $F = 40.39$
   17.590   18.910   <u>23.362   24.706   24.738</u>
   (b) μ_1: $L_1 = 16.4327$ $L_2 = 18.7473$
       μ_2: $L_1 = 17.7527$ $L_2 = 20.0673$
       μ_3: $L_1 = 22.2047$ $L_2 = 24.5193$
       μ_4: $L_1 = 23.5487$ $L_2 = 25.8633$
       μ_5: $L_1 = 23.5807$ $L_2 = 25.8953$
   (c) Completely randomized design: R.E. = 1.79
       Randomized block design, rows as blocks: R.E. = 0.931
       Randomized block design, columns as blocks: R.E. = 2.04
3. (a) Estimate of missing measurement = 15.0
   (b) Total sum of squares = 116.3372
       Treatment sum of squares = 106.5222
       Rows sum of squares = 3.8475
       Columns sum of squares = 3.4725
       Error sum of squares = 2.4950
   (c) $F = 71.16$

Chapter 11

6. (a) Total sum of squares = 0.113147
   species sum of squares = 0.049927

Concentrations sum of squares = 0.024653
Interaction sum of squares = 0.015087
Blocks sum of squares = 0.021380
Error sum of squares = 0.002100

(c) 1.228   1.228   1.314   1.320   1.356   1.362

7. (a) Total sum of squares = 0.089280
Species sum of squares = 0.0059110
Sex sum of squares = 0.018002
Interaction sum of squares = 0.018821
Error sum of squares = 0.046546

(b) 1.250   1.267   1.268   1.332

8. (a) Total sum of squares = 856,470.60
Strains sum of squares = 203,011.30
Karyotypes sum of squares = 438,376.10
Interaction sum of squares = 201,402.40
Replications sum of squares = 4,338.30
Error sum of squares = 9,342.50

Chapter 12

1. (b) $b = 1.417$ $\sum_{1}^{n} x^2 = 4.375$ $\sum_{1}^{n} y^2 = 8.813$ $\sum_{1}^{n} xy = 6.200$

(c) $a = 2.353$

(d)

X	$\hat{Y}$
0.5	3.062
1.0	3.770
1.5	4.479
2.0	5.188
2.5	5.896
3.0	6.605

(e) 0.006762

(f) Total sum of squares = 8.81333
Regression sum of squares = 8.78629
Error sum of squares = 0.02705
$F = 1299.38$
$t = 36.0469$

(g) β: $L_1 = 1.30824$ $L_2 = 1.52604$

3. (a) $b = -1.1781$ $\sum_{1}^{n} x^2 = 484.5$ $\sum_{1}^{n} y^2 = 838.9$ $\sum_{1}^{n} xy = -570.8$

$a = 50.8922$

(b) Total sum of squares = 838.9000
Regression sum of squares = 672.4719
Error sum of squares = 166.4281
$F = 64.6498$

$t = 8.04051$
$\beta: L_1 = -1.48875 \qquad L_2 = -0.86749$
(c) $\alpha: L_1 = 49.9574 \qquad L_2 = 51.8269$

4. (c) $b = 0.1845 \qquad \sum_1^n x^2 = 143.00000 \qquad \sum_1^n y^2 = 4.91329$

$\sum_1^n xy = 26.38500$

(d) $t = 32.90$
(e) $\beta: L_1 = 0.17234 \qquad L_2 = 0.19668$
(f) $\mu_{Y1}: L_1 = 0.4903 \qquad L_2 = 0.6484$
     $\mu_{Y2}: L_1 = 0.6848 \qquad L_2 = 0.8229$
     $\mu_{Y3}: L_1 = 0.8785 \qquad L_2 = 0.9982$
     $\mu_{Y4}: L_1 = 1.0710 \qquad L_2 = 1.1748$
     $\mu_{Y5}: L_1 = 1.2616 \qquad L_2 = 1.3532$
     $\mu_{Y6}: L_1 = 1.4494 \qquad L_2 = 1.5344$
     $\mu_{Y7}: L_1 = 1.6340 \qquad L_2 = 1.7189$
     $\mu_{Y8}: L_1 = 1.8151 \qquad L_2 = 1.9067$
     $\mu_{Y9}: L_1 = 1.9936 \qquad L_2 = 2.0973$
     $\mu_{Y10}: L_1 = 2.1701 \qquad L_2 = 2.2898$
     $\mu_{Y11}: L_1 = 2.3454 \qquad L_2 = 2.2483$
     $\mu_{Y12}: L_1 = 2.5199 \qquad L_2 = 2.6780$
(g) $t = 2.72$

5. (a) $b = 128.0714 \qquad \sum_1^n x^2 = 7.000 \qquad \sum_1^n y^2 = 115{,}619.428$

$\sum_1^n xy = 896.500$

(b) Total sum of squares $= 115{,}619.428$
Regression sum of squares $= 114{,}816.035$
Error sum of squares $= 803.393$
$F = 714.5697$
$t = 26.7314$
(c) $\beta: L_1 = 116.7646 \qquad L_2 = 139.3783$ (95% confidence limits)

Chapter 13

1. (b) Total sum of squares $= 34.2983$
Regression sum of squares $= 31.9613$
Deviation from linearity sum of squares $= 0.4470$
Within groups sum of squares $= 1.8900$
$F = 1.06$

(c) $b = 1.3514 \qquad \sum_1^n x^2 = 17.5000 \qquad \sum_1^n y^2 = 34.2983$

$\sum_1^n xy = 23.6500$

2. (a) Total sum of squares $= 24{,}345.9111$
Regression sum of squares $= 16{,}965.0297$
Deviation from linearity sum of squares $= 7{,}306.2147$
Within groups sum of squares $= 74.6667$
$F = 225.81$

Chapter 14

1. (a) $\sum_1^n x^2 = 19{,}754.16$ $\qquad \sum_1^n y^2 = 2{,}444.96$ $\qquad \sum_1^n xy = 4{,}725.56$
(b) Total sum of squares $= 2{,}444.9600$
Regression sum of squares $= 1{,}130.4412$
Error sum of squares $= 1{,}314.5188$
$F = 19.78$
(c) $r^2 = 0.46236$
(d) $k^2 = 0.53764$
(e) $r = 0.67997$
(f) $t = 4.4474$
(g) $\rho: L_1 = 0.39$ $\qquad L_2 = 0.85$
(h) $b_{YX} = 0.2392$ $\qquad b_{XY} = 1.9328$
2. (a) $b_{YX} = 32.3791$ $\qquad b_{XY} = 0.0237$ $\qquad r = 0.8767$
(b) Total sum of squares $= 51{,}095.164$
Regression sum of squares $= 39{,}270.449$
Error sum of squares $= 11{,}824.715$
$F = 43.1736$
$t = 6.5707$
(c) $\rho: L_1 = 0.66$ $\qquad L_2 = 0.96$
3. (b) $t = 0.86$
4. (a) Total sum of squares $= 334.4210$
Regression sum of squares $= 0.1457$
Error sum of squares $= 334.2753$
$F = 0.0074$
$t = 0.0861$

Chapter 15

1. Problem 1: $r_i = 0.977$
Problem 5: $r_i = 0.035$

Chapter 16

1. $\chi^2 = 0.32$

3.

Source	D.F.	χ^2
Total	15	14.98
Pooled	3	3.36
Hom.	12	11.62

4. $\bar{x} = 65.5$ $s = 10.0$ $n = 990$

Class Intervals	Probability	Expected Frequency
30.5–40.5	0.0062	6.138
40.5–50.5	0.0606	59.994
50.5–60.5	0.2417	239.283
60.5–70.5	0.3830	379.170
70.5–80.5	0.2417	239.283
80.5–90.5	0.0606	59.994
90.5–100.5	0.0062	6.138

5. (a) $\chi^2 = 49.83$
   (b) σ_1^2: $L_1 = 2.03$ $L_2 = 31.29$
   σ_2^2: $L_1 = 348.47$ $L_2 = 8{,}020.66$
   σ_3^2: $L_1 = 1.83$ $L_2 = 28.28$
   σ_4^2: $L_1 = 1.62$ $L_2 = 18.87$

6. (a) Sample 1   C.V. = 0.2438
   Sample 2   C.V. = 0.2657
   (b) $c = 1.2$

Chapter 17

1. 190
2. 5040
3. 1215/4096
4. $5/32 \times 10/32 = 50/1024$
5. $P = 112/1024 = 0.1094$
6. $c = 0.90$
7. 0 cases: 188.6
   1 case: 199.7
   2 cases: 88.1
   3 cases: 20.7
   4 cases: 2.7
   5 cases: 0.2
   6 cases: 0.0
8. (a) $\frac{1}{4}$
   (b) $\frac{1}{4}$
   (c) $\frac{1}{2}$
9. (a) $\frac{5}{32}$
   (b) $\frac{10}{32}$
   (c) $\frac{15}{32}$
10. $\frac{14}{52}$
11. $\frac{3}{13}$

12. $\frac{7}{8}$
13. 720
14. 2,184
15. (a) 20
    (b) 60
16. (a) 28
    (b) 56
17. 990
18. 8
19. 2,024
21. q: $L_1 = 0.535$ $L_2 = 0.725$
22. $c = 5.67$
    $q_1 - q_2$: $L_1 = 0.242$ $L_2 = 0.498$

Chapter 18

1.

Observed No.	Expected Frequency
0	364.21
1	366.77
2	184.67
3	61.99
4	15.61
5	3.14
6	0.53
7	0.08

2.

Observed No.	Expected Frequency
0	239.85
1	136.08
2	38.61
3	7.30
4	1.04
5	0.12
6	0.01

3.

Observed No.	Expected Frequency
0	4.93
1	14.84
2	22.33
3	22.40
4	16.86
5	10.15
6	5.09
7	2.19
8	0.82
9	0.28

Chapter 19

1. (a) Species A

$$\overline{LD_{50}} = 0.54365 \qquad \bar{R} = 0.41072$$
$$\overline{LD_{25}} = 0.36842 \qquad h = 0.30103$$
$$\overline{LD_{75}} = 0.77914 \qquad \text{S.E.} = 0.110495$$
$$L_1 = 0.32708 \qquad L_2 = 0.76022$$

Species B

$$\overline{LD_{50}} = 1.08371 \qquad \bar{R} = 0.56514$$
$$\overline{LD_{25}} = 0.81230 \qquad h = 0.30103$$
$$\overline{LD_{75}} = 1.37744 \qquad \text{S.E.} = 0.129614$$
$$L_1 = 0.82967 \qquad L_2 = 1.33775$$

(b) $c = 3.17$

2. $\overline{LD_{50}} = 0.73746 \qquad \bar{R} = 0.32721$
$\overline{LD_{25}} = 0.58036 \qquad h = 0.2$
$\overline{LD_{75}} = 0.90757 \qquad \text{S.E.} = 0.022737$

3. $\overline{LD_{50}} = 0.32029 \qquad \bar{R} = 0.29679$
$\overline{LD_{25}} = \text{none} \qquad h = 0.2$
$\overline{LD_{75}} = 0.46869 \qquad \text{S.E.} = 0.021655$

4. $\overline{LD_{50}} = 0.81789 \qquad \bar{R} = 0.56047$
$\overline{LD_{25}} = 0.53259 \qquad h = 0.30103$
$\overline{LD_{75}} = 1.09306 \qquad \text{S.E.} = 0.120741$

Chapter 20

1. Sample 1 $\qquad \chi^2 = 9.66$
   Sample 2 $\qquad \chi^2 = 12.81$
   Sample 3 $\qquad \chi^2 = 5.82$
   Pooled $\qquad \chi^2 = 28.27$
2. $\chi^2 = 29.40$
3. $H_{\text{uncorrected}} = 24.77$
   $H_{\text{corrected}} = 24.89$
4. Wilcoxon signed rank test: $c = 3.06$
   Friedman χ_r^2 test: $\chi^2 = 12.00$
   Pairing design test: $t = 5.1$
5. $r_s = 0.7521$
6. $H_{\text{uncorrected}} = 14.29$
   $H_{\text{corrected}} = 14.30$
7. Wilcoxon signed rank test. A suitable transformation for analysis by this test is the rank of the titres, where the rank is n in the equation $\dfrac{1}{2^n}$.

Titre	Rank
1	0
$\frac{1}{2}$	1
$\frac{1}{4}$	2
$\frac{1}{8}$	3
$\frac{1}{16}$	4
$\frac{1}{32}$	5
$\frac{1}{64}$	6
.	.
.	.
.	.
$\frac{1}{4096}$	12

$T = 0.0$

8. $H_{\text{uncorrected}} = 21.24$
   $H_{\text{corrected}} = 21.89$
9. $r_s = 0.9189$
   $t = 27.96$
10. $T = 7.5$
11. $\chi_r^2 = 0.95$

Index

355